OSAP Prevention Monograph–5

COMMUNICATING ABOUT ALCOHOL AND OTHER DRUGS: STRATEGIES FOR REACHING POPULATIONS AT RISK

Editors:
Elaine Bratic Arkin
Judith E. Funkhouser

D0139868

U.S. DEPARTMENT OF HEALTH AND HUMAN SERVICES
Public Health Service
Alcohol, Drug Abuse, and Mental Health Administration

Office for Substance Abuse Prevention
5600 Fishers Lane
Rockville, Maryland 20857

OSAP Prevention Monographs are prepared by the divisions of the Office for Substance Abuse Prevention (OSAP) and published by its Division of Communication Programs. The primary objective of this series is to facilitate the transfer of prevention and intervention technology between and among researchers, administrators, policymakers, educators, and providers in the public and private sectors. The content of state-of-the-art conferences, reviews of innovative or exemplary programming models, and reviews of evaluative studies are important elements of OSAP's information dissemination mission.

This monograph is based on the findings of task forces that included researchers, policymakers, and prevention/intervention specialists at the national, State, and local levels.

The authors of the chapters include "High-Risk Families and Youth," Patricia Kassebaum; "Black Youth," J. Terry Edmonds; "Hispanics/Latinos," William A. Bogan; "Parents," Carolyn Burns and Marsha Margarella; "Primary Care Providers," Michele Hodak; and "Intermediary Organizations," Joseph Motter and Caroline McNeil.

The presentations herein are those of the authors and may not necessarily reflect the opinions, official policy, or position of OSAP; the Alcohol, Drug Abuse, and Mental Health Administration; the Public Health Service; or the U.S. Department of Health and Human Services.

Library of Congress Catalog Card Number: 89-063214
DHHS Publication No. (ADM)90-1665
Printed 1990
OSAP Production Officer: Linda Franklin

Project Officers:
Judith E. Funkhouser, Division of Communication Programs
Office for Substance Abuse Prevention

OSAP Prevention Monograph Series
Elaine M. Johnson, Ph.D.
Director, OSAP

Robert W. Denniston
Director, Division of Communication Programs, OSAP

Foreword

We know that some American children are at higher risk than others of developing alcohol and other drug problems. And we know that preventing these problems requires early, persistent communication programs that use diverse channels and target a variety of audiences.

The purpose of this monograph is to provide a foundation for such programs. It defines specific audiences; it summarizes what we have learned to date about the characteristics, knowledge, attitudes, and practices of these audiences; it discusses channels, sources, materials, and messages; and finally it offers ideas for reaching these groups.

Written for program planners at the national, State, and local level, this monograph offers guidelines, not answers. There is still much to be learned. It is hoped that the information and ideas presented here, as well as the needs identified, will provide leads for new research, demonstration, and evaluation agendas for the 1990s.

Research reports, the suggestions of experts, and ideas gleaned from some members of the target audiences form the basis for this report. The experts are listed at the end of each chapter. Their insights and suggestions, including the recommendations that conclude each chapter, are an important component of the monograph; more about the process that brought these experts together to share their ideas will be found in the Introduction.

The monograph addresses five specific audiences:

- Chapter 1 provides a comprehensive look at the priority target audience, *youth from high-risk environments and their families*. It serves as background for the chapters that follow.

- Chapter 2 addresses one group of high-risk youth, *Black children*.

- Chapter 3 discusses another important subgroup, *Hispanic/Latino youth*.

- Chapter 4 discusses a secondary audience, *parents*, who are important influences on youth at risk.

- Chapter 5 addresses another important secondary audience, *primary care physicians*.

A final chapter discusses one strategy of special importance to communications programs: working with *intermediary groups* to reach a target audience.

How To Use This Monograph

To help program planners use the research and expert opinions presented here, each chapter is divided into four sections:

- Understanding the Audience

- Knowledge, Attitudes, and Practices

- Planning Considerations

- Recommendations.

Each section begins with a summary page. Use the summary pages for both introduction to and review of the concepts that follow. They also may be reproduced for use in notebooks, meetings, and workshops. Throughout the monograph are tables summarizing statistics, risk factors, and communication strategies. These too may be reproduced and used in developing programs.

Appendices include materials that can be put to use as well: a guide to the planning process; guidelines for the review of prevention messages and materials, including evaluation forms; a guide to terminology; a guide to the Regional Alcohol and Drug Awareness Resource (RADAR) Network; and names and addresses of potential intermediary organizations.

The Office for Substance Abuse Prevention (OSAP) hopes that this report will stimulate the many participants in the prevention field to act on the recommended strategies, adapting them to their own communities and constituencies. I strongly encourage you to reproduce, reformat, repackage, disseminate, and otherwise use this monograph to help your prevention efforts. OSAP believes that the sustained and combined efforts of diverse communications programs over a long period are necessary to rid our society of alcohol and other drug abuse. We sincerely look forward to working together toward this goal. Nosotros esperamos tener la oportunidad de trabajar con ustedes para alcanzar esta meta.

Elaine M. Johnson, Ph.D., Director
Office for Substance Abuse Prevention

Contents

List of Tables

Chapter 1

Chapter 2

Chapter 3

Chapter 4

Chapter 5

Chapter 6

Agenda: OSAP Southeastern Regional Communications Seminar

Wednesday, September 14—Friday, September 16, 1988

TUESDAY, SEPTEMBER 13, 1988

8:00–8:30 PM   Informal Meeting of State Team Leaders

WEDNESDAY, SEPTEMBER 14, 1988

8:00–9:30 AM
Ballroom Foyer

Seminar Registration

9:30–10:30 AM
Continental
South Ballroom

Opening General Session
Welcome to Georgia
Ms. Patricia Redmond, Director, Georgia Alcohol and Drug Services Section

Introduction to the Office for Substance Abuse Prevention (OSAP)
Ms. Vivian L. Smith, M.S.W, Deputy Director, Office for Substance Abuse Prevention, Rockville, MD

The Role of Communications in the War on Drugs
Mr. Robert W. Denniston, Director, Division of Communication Programs, OSAP, Rockville, MD

10:30–10:45 AM   Health Break

10:45–11:30 AM
Continental
South Ballroom

Keynote Address
Dr. Omowale Amuleru-Marshall, "Reaching the Hard-to-Reach: 'Are We For Real?'"
The Cork Institute, Atlanta, GA

11:30–12:00 PM
Open Rooms

First State Team Meetings

12:00–1:30 PM	LUNCHEON
Continental	Speaker: **Charles Atkins, Ph.D.,** "Counteracting the
North Ballroom	Harmful Effects of Television on Youth"
	Michigan State University

WEDNESDAY, SEPTEMBER 14, 1988
CLEARINGHOUSE/DATA BASE Track
(Concurrent with Media/Communications Track)

2:00–3:00 PM	*Module I: Alcohol & Drug Information Resources*
Continental	Lead Presentation: *Alcohol and Other*
South Ballroom	*Drug Information Resources*
	Lisa Swanberg, National Clearinghouse
	for Alcohol and Drug Information
	NCADI, Rockville, MD

Concurrent
Workshops:
3:15–4:30 PM

Room C-416   Workshop A: *Getting Substance Abuse Information to Policymakers*
Judy Arendsee, National Federation of Parents for Drug-Free Youth, Rancho Santa Fe, CA
Sue Rusche, Families in Action, Atlanta, GA
Robert Halford, Metropolitan Atlanta Council on Alcohol and Drugs, Atlanta, GA
This workshop will discuss the methods employed by various special-interest groups as they develop and disseminate pertinent information to policymakers. A special focus will be on issues surrounding legalization.

Room C-412   Workshop B: *Alcohol & Drug Abuse Message & Materials Review Process*
Joseph Motter, Media and Materials Development Project, OSAP
Mr. Motter will review the progress of the OSAP Media and Materials Development Project (MMDP) in collecting and reviewing a wide variety of print and electronic media prevention materials. Effective media approaches identified through the OSAP screening procedures and criteria will be identified and workshop participants will have an opportunity to practice reviewing materials using these criteria.

Room C-420	Workshop C: *Developing Materials for Low-Literacy Populations* **Nelia Nadal,** National Clearinghouse for Alcohol and Drug Information, Rockville, MD *Ms. Nadal will explain and demonstrate the appropriate techniques for developing materials for low-literacy target populations.*
4:30–5:00 PM Open Rooms	State Team Meetings
5:30–6:30 PM	Reception—All seminar participants are invited.

WEDNESDAY, SEPTEMBER 14, 1988
MEDIA/COMMUNICATIONS Track
(Concurrent with Clearinghouse Track)

2:00–3:00 PM Room C-417	*Module I: Introduction to Social Marketing Principles* Lead Presentation: *What is Social Marketing Anyway?* **Elaine Bratic Arkin,** Communications Consultant, Arlington, VA
3:15–4:30 PM Concurrent Workshops	
Salon A	Workshop A: *Using Media in Prevention* **Jocelyn Dorsey,** WSB-TV, Atlanta, GA *Ms. Dorsey will provide an overview of how the television industry works. She will provide valuable insider tips on who to call, how to access the correct person, what you need to know before calling, and what a TV station looks for in a PSA.*
Salon B	Workshop B: *You've Gotta Be Kiddin': Getting Through to High-Risk Kids* **Nancy Saylor,** Consultant, Jupiter, FL *Participants will learn some specific strategies and approaches for talking to adolescents about alcohol and other drug use.*

Salon E   Workshop C: *Community Health Information and Education*
R. Keith Sikes, M.P.H., Division of Public Health, Georgia Department of Human Resources, Atlanta, GA
Dr. Sikes will present data from Georgia regarding acute and chronic alcohol drinking habits. He will provide descriptive and analytical data regarding risk factors of age, race, sex, income, and education as related to drinking habits of adult Georgians during 1986 and 1987 based upon CDC–BRFSS data.
Leandris Liburd, M.P.H., Division of Health Education, Centers for Disease Control, Atlanta, GA
The Planned Approach to Community Health (PATCH) is a model for planning community health promotion programs with a particular emphasis on community organization. Through the process of community involvement and education, priority health problems are identified and appropriate interventions are implemented. A close review of the PATCH process will provide useful strategies for the development of effective community-based substance abuse prevention programs.

4:30–5:00 PM   State Team Meetings
Open Rooms

5:30–6:30 PM   Reception—All seminar participants are invited.

THURSDAY, SEPTEMBER 15, 1988
CLEARINGHOUSE/DATA BASE Track
(Concurrent with Communications Track)

8:15–9:00 AM   Special Interest Group Networking
Continental
South Ballroom

9:00–11:30 AM   ***Module II: Session 1—Planning and Selecting PCs***
Room C-417   ***in the Alcohol/Drug Clearinghouse Environment***
Who should attend: Anyone considering purchasing or supplementing personal computers for their office. Session will attempt to address both beginners and more advanced participants.
Session 1 will address: What to consider before purchasing a system; use of data bases in the clearinghouse environment; what to ask for when you are ready to

xiii

	buy; how to select a supplier; management issues including cost and time. *Hardware & data base selection.*
10:00–10:15 AM	Health Break
10:15–11:30 AM Room C-417	**Session 2—Choosing Software for the Clearing-house Environment** *Who should attend: Anyone who is responsible for the purchase of software or is planning to make decisions and software selections. This session is biased toward DOS-based IBM or compatible systems software.* *Session 2 will address: What to consider before purchasing software; training; and the following software types will be discussed—word processing, desktop publishing and graphics, electronic spreadsheets, e-mail/communications and more data base discussion if possible.* *Software selection.*
11:30 AM– 12:00 PM Open Rooms	State Team Meetings
12:00–1:30 PM Continental North Ballroom	LUNCHEON Speaker: **William Hale, Ed.D.,** Prism Associates, Athens, GA "Don't Classify Me"

THURSDAY, SEPTEMBER 15, 1988
MEDIA/COMMUNICATIONS Track
(Concurrent with Clearinghouse Track)

8:15–9:00 AM Continental South Ballroom	Special Interest Group Networking
9:00–10:00 AM	**Module II: Using the Media to Reach High-Risk Youth** Lead Presentation: *Successful Prevention Programs to Reach High-Risk Populations* **Ellen Morehouse,** Student Assistance Service, White Plains, NY

10:00–10:15 AM   Health Break

10:15–11:30 AM
Concurrent
Workshops

Salon A   Workshop A: *Preventing Messages for Sight and Hearing Impaired*
Martine Roy, Spartenburg Commission on Alcohol and Drugs, Spartenburg, SC
Programming for sensory-impaired students lags far behind the increased need for substance abuse primary prevention. This presentation will describe how a unique project was designed to fill the gaps in services through the development of a curriculum for ages 12-21 sensory-impaired students. The presentation will include a discussion of project design and development of field-testing of pilot groups, evaluation, and networking in the community and with other professionals.

Salon B   Workshop B: *Signs / Symptoms of Possible Physical and / or Sexual Abuse*
Marlene Convey, Glenbeigh Hospital, West Palm Beach, FL
From this workshop, participants will have an understanding of dynamics within abusing families and some suggestions for treatment.

Salon E   Workshop C: *Collaborating to Respond to the Need for Prevention of Smokeless Tobacco*
Ruthellen Phillips, USDA Extension, University of West Virginia, Morgantown, WV
This session will examine ways to utilize diverse existing resources of different agencies to develop and systematically disseminate a substance abuse prevention program in the community

Room C-416   Workshop D: *City Lights—The Workplace*
Adrienne Goode, City Lights, Washington, DC
Ms. Goode will provide an overview of City Lights: The Workplace. She will examine each program component and highlight successful methods and materials used with multiproblem youth in an alternative educational setting in Washington, DC

11:30 AM −12:00 PM Open Rooms	State Team Meetings
12:00–1:30 PM Continental North Ballroom	LUNCHEON Speaker: **William Hale, Ed.D.,** Prism Associates, Athens, GA "Don't Classify Me"

THURSDAY, SEPTEMBER 15, 1988
CLEARINGHOUSE/DATA BASE Track
(Concurrent with Communications Track)

2:00–3:00 PM Continental South Ballroom	***Module III: Clearinghouse Operations*** Lead Presentation: *Overview of What A&D Clearing-houses Can Do* **Dr. Bettina Scott,** National Clearinghouse for Alcohol and Drug Information, Rockville, MD
3:00–3:15 PM	Health Break
3:15–4:30 PM Concurrent Workshops	
Room C-412	Workshop A: *Retrieving and Disseminating Information* **Deborah Hotchkiss,** South Carolina State Library, Columbia, SC *Ms. Hotchkiss will describe how libraries can help you access current, up-to-date information.* **Rebecca Adams,** PRIDE, Atlanta, GA *PRIDE's nationwide toll-free drug information line receives thousands of calls a year. How the line operates and the services it provides are offered in this workshop.*
Room C-416	Workshop B: *State and Other Clearinghouses* **Jim Neal,** South Carolina Commission on Alcohol and Drug Abuse, Columbia, SC *The Drugstore, South Carolina's clearinghouse for alcohol and other drug information, will be described within the context of a comprehensive plan for prevention.*

Steve Ranslow, Department of Health, St. Croix, Virgin Islands
Mr. Ranslow will describe a small, comprehensive clearinghouse that serves a population of 100,000 and integrates mental health, AIDS, and substance abuse prevention information.
Paula Kemp, National Drug Information Center, Families in Action, Atlanta, GA
Ms. Kemp will provide an introduction to the National Drug Information Center of the Families in Action and describe how it serves students, teachers, parents, and communities.

4:30–5:00 PM Open Rooms	State Team Meetings

THURSDAY, SEPTEMBER 15, 1988
MEDIA/COMMUNICATIONS Track
(Concurrent with Clearinghouse Track)

2:00–3:00 PM C-417	*Module III: Successful Strategies and Channels for Reaching At-Risk Populations* Lead Presentation: *Public Education Programs Directed at Children of Alcoholic Parents* **Robert V. Shear,** Chapel Hill, NC
3:00–3:15 PM	Health Break
3:15–4:30 PM Concurrent Workshops	
Continental South Ballroom	Workshop A: *Creative Use of the Media* **Roney Cates,** Executive Director, Durham Council on Alcoholism, Durham, NC *This workshop will demonstrate a number of unique methods to get your prevention messages to your target audience. Discussion will include ways to involve other agencies in your work and a "hands-on" experience will produce a 30-foot long exhibit.*

Salon A   Workshop B: *Reaching High-Risk Cherokee Youth*
Gil Jackson, Cherokee Boys Club, Cherokee, NC
Mr. Jackson will describe the Cherokee Challenge—a program designed to raise the self-esteem of American Indian youth. Its aim, successes, some problems that were encountered, and future plans will be covered.

Salon B   Workshop C: *Reaching Black Youth at High Risk*
Sharon Shaw, Division of Alcohol and Drug Abuse Services, Department of Mental Health and Mental Retardation, Nashville, TN
Participants in this workshop will consider alternative program strategies for reaching high-risk populations, including ethnic minority communities. Group discussion and exercises will involve participants in developing plans for their own communities.

Salon E   Workshop D: *Be Smart! Stay Smart!*
Terrie Ainsworth, D.R.E.A.M., Mississippi
Key elements and strategies will be outlined for implementing a statewide prevention project based on D.R.E.A.M.'s experience with "Be Smart! Don't Start!—Just Say No!"

4:30–5:00 PM
Open Rooms   State Team Meetings

FRIDAY, SEPTEMBER 15, 1988

9:00–9:45 AM
Continental
South Ballroom   Speech Presentation "Reaching High-Risk Takers Through the Mass Media"
Lewis Donohew, Ph.D., University of Kentucky

9:45–10:15 AM
Continental
South Ballroom   Final State Team Planning Meetings

10:15–10:30 AM   Health Break

10:30–11:30 AM
Continental
South Ballroom   State Team Presentations
Five-minute presentations from each State Team summarizing key points learned and plans to utilize new information.

11:30 AM
–12:00 PM
Continental
South Ballroom

Seminar Evaluation and Wrap-up
Robert Denniston, DCP/OSAP, Rockville, MD
"Summary of Knowledge Shared and Gained"

Introduction

The term "high-risk youth" is short for a more accurate term: "youth from high-risk environments." The environment may be high risk because it is a family in which adults are abusing alcohol or other drugs. It may be high risk because there are deficits in earning potential; it may be high risk because of the existence of pro-drug messages aimed at opening new markets. In no way is "high-risk youth," as used in this monograph, meant to imply a stereotyped image—youth who are "going to end up using drugs no matter what." What we have learned is that it may be best to use the term "youth from high-risk environments" to avoid stereotyping or projecting an image that could lead some youth to behave in a manner that becomes a self-fulfilling prophecy.

In the late 1980s, the Federal Government began to place a high priority on help to youth at high risk for alcohol and other drug problems and to their parents. The Anti-Drug Abuse Act of 1986 established the Office for Substance Abuse Prevention (OSAP) and charged it with initiating programs that would provide prevention and early intervention services for young people, especially high-risk youth. This monograph on communications is one outcome of OSAP efforts.

Youth from high-risk environments are also the focus of P.L. 100-690, the Anti-Drug Abuse Act of 1988. This law is particularly important for those planning communications, because it calls for a broad array of programs to serve high-risk populations. This new legislation provides

- Added assistance to communities in developing comprehensive, long-term strategies for the prevention of substance abuse (OSAP)

- Model drug abuse education projects for pregnant and postpartum women and infants (Special Supplemental Food Program for Women, Infants, and Children)

- Block grants to States for community youth activity programs, including such activities as counseling families, community education, assistance to rural youth, information and training for caregivers, and improved coordination of services pertaining to education, law enforcement, recreation departments, business organizations, community-based organizations and action agencies, and local/State community health departments (Department of Health and Human Services)

- School programs for children of alcoholics (CoAs) and training programs for educators on CoA issues, especially in grades 5 to 8 (Department of Education)

1

- Community-based volunteer demonstration projects for drug abuse education and prevention for high-risk youth and parents, particularly during the summer months (Domestic Volunteer Service Act)

- Development of early childhood education curricula on drug abuse prevention for preschools, such as the Head Start Program (Drug-Free Schools and Communities Act)

- A new program relating to youth gangs, involving grants and contracts with public/private agencies, organizations, institutions, and individuals to establish drug abuse education, prevention, and treatment for these high-risk youth (Administration on Children, Youth, and Families)

- A new program for runaway and homeless youth, involving counseling, prevention, and treatment for youth and for their families (Administration on Children, Youth, and Families).

High-risk youth initiatives also will strongly support the Youth 2000 Objectives, a collaborative public-private sector effort that focuses on the needs of youth. Cosponsored by the Department of Labor and the Public Health Service, the Youth 2000 Objectives stress the strengthening of today's young people to prepare them for expanded opportunities in the year 2000. The program emphasizes many factors important for youth at risk of alcohol and other drug abuse, such as their health, education, and family life.

Because the 5-year-olds of today will be 16 in the year 2000, communication strategies focused on primary prevention with young children will promote achievement of the two principal Public Health Service objectives for the Youth 2000 program:

- Reduce substance abuse among young people aged 12 to 17 by 50 percent by the year 2000

- Reduce the mortality rate from intentional and unintentional injury among 15- to 19-year-olds from 62.0 per 100,000 (1983) to 30.0 per 100,000 by the year 2000.

One analysis of significant national demographic trends based on current first graders shows that, by the year 2000, the education system will be faced with increased numbers of youth at risk (Hodgkinson 1985). According to this analysis, children in the year 2000 will be poorer, will be more ethnically and linguistically diverse, and will have more learning disorders than present school populations.

The Role of Communications in Prevention

Planners need to look at communication in its broadest sense. As Sheila Blume, M.D., an author and scientist in the alcohol field, states, "If we ever develop a rational prevention policy, it will have hundreds of items in it—they will all have to be done" (Blume 1984, p. 56). OSAP believes that for maximum effectiveness, prevention strategies need to address parental and peer influences, teachers, and community leaders; social norms about alcohol and other drug use; the marketing and availability of alcoholic beverages; and laws, regulations, and policies (OSAP 1987). OSAP recommends a systems approach to prevention, viewing the community and the environment as interconnected parts, each affected by the others (Johnson et al. 1988). The goal of prevention for any community is to make the parts work together.

Communication plays an important role in all these goals. The mass media—television, radio, magazines, and newspapers—are particularly effective at changing community norms. Communication efforts can raise the public's awareness about problems among people in high-risk environments and what the public can do to help; can stimulate a community to improve its services for those who are most vulnerable; and can mobilize people—businesses, organizations, and individuals—to give their time, money, and creative thinking to the effort.

A comprehensive approach is recommended to communities that are developing health campaigns. The ultimate objective is to provide information, skill-building, and support for a wide range of community-based prevention and intervention efforts. At this early stage, a dazzling assortment of communication ideas exists.

Experts recommend that media campaigns for social objectives go through three stages in order to be effective—cognition, motivation, and action (Flay 1986). The suggested strategies also follow the principle of supplementation, which has been a key ingredient in most successful health promotion campaigns. Supplementation refers to supplementing media programming with activities such as school programs, small group discussions, community organization, face-to-face intervention, and changes in laws or their enforcement. A mix is important in increasing the effectiveness of program efforts.

Combining activities

- Increases the likelihood of program dissemination

- Increases the speed of agenda setting and diffusion, thus exerting pressure on gatekeepers

- Increases interpersonal communication, making the issue more compelling to more people in different ways

- Decreases selectivity (ignoring of messages) by either increasing access to captive audiences or increasing interpersonal communication and thus breaking down selection barriers (Flay 1983).

Since the early 1960s, some innovative research has been focused on the issue of how to communicate health issues most effectively. How, through media and messages, can positive health behavior be encouraged and negative behaviors be prevented or even stopped? Major communication theories and models are summarized in appendix A. Some of the most important principles, which were used in developing this monograph, are as follows:

- Mass media should be used to support and reinforce community efforts.

- Knowledge, attitudes, intentions to use, and practices of the target group are key factors to consider in developing messages. (This report discusses these factors indepth for each special target audience.)

- Messages need to be specifically targeted to the needs and perceptions of the particular group being addressed, and not the "general public," which consists of many subgroups with differing needs, outlooks, and cultural perceptions.

- Messages must be appropriate for the developmental, cognitive, and social age of the recipient.

- Messages and materials must be culturally sensitive and appropriate.

- Major elements to consider in the communications process will be a credible source for the message, obstacles to hearing the message, understanding and appeal, the message itself, channels of communication, and settings for delivery.

- Messages should focus on the availability of solutions rather than on the seriousness of the problem and should suggest positive incentives and encouragement to change.

- For youth, the harm resulting from the use of alcohol or other drugs should be posed in light of the short-term (as opposed to long-range) effects. Appeals may need to address social harm (e.g., not fitting in with highly regarded group) as opposed to harm to health.

Media and Materials Development Program

OSAP's Media and Materials Development Program (MMDP) was conducted by Macro Systems, Inc., and the National Coalition of Hispanic Health and Human Services Organizations (COSSMHO) in 1988-89 in conjunction with a wide range of intermediary organizations interested in or experienced with reaching at-risk populations with prevention messages and materials. The goals of the project were to strengthen the visibility and credibility of prevention issues before the public; to improve the frequency of use and quality of media messages; to provide educational materials that move beyond information dissemination to encouraging behavior change; and to use these media and materials efforts to foster well-reasoned and coordinated communications programs nationwide. This monograph is one outcome of the MMDP.

The MMDP centered on six groups, where the need and potential effect of communications efforts were greatest:

- Families and youth from high-risk environments
- Blacks
- Hispanics/Latinos
- Parents
- Primary care physicians
- Intermediaries, such as professional and voluntary organizations

Reaching *youth at risk* involves early intervention, and families often are primary gatekeepers for communications. Further, a primary factor for many youth at high risk of alcohol or drug use is whether other family members are experiencing alcohol or other drug problems. Therefore, OSAP determined that the primary target audience should include both *youth and their families*. Families must be defined broadly as an isolated nuclear family; a very extended family that includes godparents, cousins, neighbors, or even the local pharmacist; single-parent families; foster care parent families; or institutional families for children in orphanages or reform schools.

Although all sectors of society are at risk, many people of low socioeconomic status, a disproportionate share of whom belong to minority groups, are particularly vulnerable to alcohol and other drug problems and their consequences. On the other hand, many from minority groups possess attitudes and values that are protective and instructive to the rest of society. This program limited its focus to *Blacks* and *Hispanics/Latinos*, not because other groups do not warrant special attention, but because these two minority groups are the largest. Some findings and strategies discussed in this monograph are relevant to all minority populations; some are very specific to either Blacks or Hispanics/Latinos.

Beginning in the late 1970s, *parents* began organizing to overcome alcohol and other drug use among youth in America. Several groups became major forces in prevention efforts. The MMDP focused attention on how to reach new parents who had never been involved in prevention. Research suggests that periods of transition, such as family moves and changes in schools, are important times to reach parents. These transitions are times of increased stress, when people naturally examine and evaluate their lives. Experts tapped by the MMDP hypothesized that families in transition periods would be particularly receptive to messages about the use of alcohol and other drugs.

Another MMDP target audience was *primary care physicians*. OSAP regards alcohol and other drug abuse as a health issue and prevention of alcohol and other drug abuse as a field in which health care professionals can play a major role. These professionals are trusted and credible authorities in our society. Although all health care professionals can play a role in prevention, OSAP focused its attention on four primary care physician groups—pediatricians, obstetrician/gynecologists, family practice specialists, and internists—because they are the major physician stakeholders for youth-oriented efforts. The American Medical Association has taken a major role in addressing alcohol and other drug abuse and has worked closely with OSAP, sharing data and helping define appropriate strategies.

The MMDP included *intermediary organizations* because of the powerful role they can play in reaching and influencing their constituents. National organizations, particularly those with affiliates in communities, can help implement "push/pull" strategies that use multiple forces to influence both attitudes and behavior. The mass media are also a powerful intermediary that must be enlisted in the effort to conquer alcohol and other drug abuse. Examples of strategies involving intermediaries will be found throughout the monograph, and a list of potential intermediaries is included in appendix E.

To address these target audiences, the MMDP created task forces composed of communications experts and representatives of intermediary groups. Task force participants are listed at the end of each chapter, along with other experts who contributed to these reports. The task forces met to define issues and recommend resources for research. Staff conducted library research and prepared reports on knowledge, attitudes, and practices for each audience.

Simultaneously, materials were collected from all over the Nation. Each task force reviewed materials relevant to its target audience to learn both what was available and what gaps existed and to identify communications models and strategies for the future.

Some of the materials identified through the review process are cited in this monograph. Such materials are mentioned as examples, and their inclusion should not be construed as an endorsement by OSAP. More information on the materials collected by each task force is available from the National Clearinghouse for Alcohol and Drug Information, P.O. Box 2345, Rockville, MD 20852.

Other Initiatives

The OSAP demonstration grant program for high-risk youth is another major initiative. The 131 OSAP grants initiated in 1987 deal with prevention, intervention, and treatment services for high-risk children of all ages, from birth to age 21. Many of these innovative programs serve minority populations. A series of monographs describing these grants and the grant program findings is being published.

OSAP has set up a Learning Community of program experts and researchers serving high-risk groups, which communicates through national conferences, a regular printed update, and other means. The high-risk grant programs, currently being evaluated, are producing a wide variety of materials—from videos to curricula—that are specifically targeted to high-risk groups and caregivers. It is expected that many of these products will soon be available to the field.

In addition, State and local initiatives are under way throughout the Nation. State agencies, schools, churches, youth groups, voluntary associations, and others have developed programs to prevent alcohol and other drug use among children.

The U.S. Social Climate

The next decade offers an extraordinary opportunity for changing the lives of children who are at risk for alcohol and other drug problems. New legislation, the President's agenda, and media reports all reflect a new, supportive public awareness. The following national concerns have special implications for communications programs:

- *The problems of disadvantaged children.* A recent CBS Poll (February 1989) concluded that after 8 years of low attention, the American public feels it is time to devote more national energy to problems of the poor, about half of whom are children. President Bush has made it clear that this issue is of concern to his Administration, and the recently expanded funding for the Women, Infants, and Children (WIC) program reflects this renewed priority for disadvantaged children.

  Prenatal and infant programs offer an ideal communications channel for identifying and reaching families who are at high risk because of the mother's chemical use or other problems; these programs also offer the opportunity to teach teenage or impaired mothers about positive parenting practices and family management.

- *Community devastation caused by drugs.* It is becoming increasingly clear that entire U.S. neighborhoods are being ravaged by the traffic in illegal drugs, with the homicide level due to drug-related violence rising at catastrophic levels in such urban areas as Washington, D.C. In a recent article in the *Washington Post* (February 5, 1989), a psychologist described children in Washington's drug-infested neighborhoods as having emotional and psychological problems similar to those of children living in violence-prone Northern Ireland. Drug-related violence is reported daily on television and in the newspapers.

It is a tremendous advantage that drugs are a "hot" media issue; the interest and involvement of the mass media are one important element of a communications program.

*   *The plight of children from alcoholic homes.* Although it came to national notice only during the 1980s, this issue touches thousands of people. Hundreds of local CoA groups now meet. Such television programs as ABC News "Nightline" have devoted major time segments to the issue, and both *Newsweek* and *Time* magazines ran feature articles on the topic during 1987/1988. CoAs have been identified by Congress as specific program recipients in major legislation of the Office for Substance Abuse Prevention, the Office of Juvenile Justice and Delinquency Prevention, the National Center on Child Abuse and Neglect, and the U.S. Department of Education.

School-based help for children of alcoholics is extremely important. Because the majority of CoAs live in homes where alcoholism or other drug abuse is untreated, many of these children can only be reached directly rather than through their families.

*   *Commitment to drug issues by people and institutions.* In a Louis Harris and Associates survey of 1,100 community leaders and grantmakers, more than 9 out of 10 respondents viewed use of illicit drugs as "compelling problems of youth today, ahead of cigarette smoking, teenage pregnancy, teenage unemployment, youth crime, school dropouts, and teenage suicide." This survey found that many grantmakers would fund alcohol/drug prevention programs, provided the programs were based on models that worked (Harris and Associates 1988).

The findings of such surveys are important for developing communications strategies, because they suggest a reservoir of concerned people and funding sources that could become involved.

The Division of Communication Programs, OSAP, as always, welcomes your feedback, comments, and suggestions.

Judith E. Funkhouser
Deputy Director
Division of Communication Programs

Bibliography

Flay, B.R. *The Role of Mass Media in Community Intervention for Drug Abuse Prevention: Research Recommendations.* Report prepared for NIDA/NIAAA Technical Review of Community Prevention Research. Washington, D.C.: June 1983.

Flay, B.R. Mass media linkages with school-based programs for drug abuse prevention. *Journal of School Health* 56(9):402–406, 1986.

Hodgkinson, H.L. *All One System: Demographics of Education—Kindergarten Through Graduate School.* Washington, D.C.: Institute for Educational Leadership, Inc., 1985.

Johnson, E.M.; Amatetti, S.; Funkhouser, J.E.; and Johnson, S. Theories and models supporting prevention approaches to alcohol problems among youth. *Public Health Reports* 103(6):578–586, 1988.

Louis Harris and Associates. *A Catalyst for Action: A National Survey To Mobilize Leadership and Resources for the Prevention of Alcohol and Other Drug Problems Among American Youth.* Survey conducted for the Boys Clubs of America. New York: Louis Harris and Associates, 1988.

Louis Harris and Associates. *Children's Needs and Public Responsibilities: A Survey of American Attitudes About the Problems and Prospects of American Children.* Survey conducted for Group W—Westinghouse Broadcasting Co., Study No. 863009, September 1986.

National Association of State Alcohol and Drug Abuse Directors. *NASADAD Annual Report. State Resources and Services Related to Alcohol and Drug Abuse Problems, Fiscal Year 1987: An Analysis of State Alcohol and Drug Abuse Profile Data.* Washington, D.C.: NASADAD, 1988.

Office for Substance Abuse Prevention (OSAP). *Literature Review on Alcohol and Youth.* Washington, D.C.: Public Health Service, Alcohol, Drug Abuse, and Mental Health Administration, November 1987.

Toward the Prevention of Alcohol Problems: Government, Business, and Community Action. Gerstein, D.R., ed. Washington, D.C.: National Academy Press, 1984.

CHAPTER 1

Reaching Families and Youth From High-Risk Environments

Understanding the Audience

High-risk youth

- May have conduct disorders
- May be children of alcoholics or other drug abusers
- Can come from diverse backgrounds—socioeconomic, cultural, and educational
- Are often disadvantaged, growing up in low-income, urban, crime-ridden environments
- May be experiencing multiple problems, such as school failure, unwanted pregnancy, or delinquency
- May come from high-risk families.

High-risk families

- May be dysfunctional, i.e., exhibit physical or sexual abuse of children, emotional neglect, mental disturbance
- May include parents who abuse alcohol or other drugs
- May be single-parent families
- May have a child with special needs
- May experience family risk factors: marital conflict; lack of contact between parent and child; parental alcohol or other drug abuse.

Narrowing the audience: youth with conduct disorders

- May be rebellious toward authority
- May exhibit antisocial behaviors in childhood
- May have chronic, serious delinquency problems
- May have a great need for independence

- May have difficulty bonding to family and peers
- May begin early use of alcohol and other drugs
- May tend to seek sensation, excitement, and risks.

Narrowing the audience: children of alcoholics and other drug abusers

- May have conduct disorders
- May be high achievers and "over-responsible"
- May have a sense of isolation and abandonment.

Which children should be the priority targets of communications efforts? Can those children most in jeopardy be identified early? What factors put these children at special risk and what can be done to help them? These sorts of questions need to be answered before we can develop communications strategies and messages.

In reality, any child or youth who starts to drink or use drugs is at risk. It is important, therefore, to have widespread communications programs aimed at preventing alcohol and drug use in all children and youth. Researchers stress, however, that youth at moderate risk should be segmented for communications purposes from high-risk youth. This chapter, therefore, explores the characteristics of youth and families in high-risk environments and discusses strategies for reaching them; a later chapter addresses communications with parents of children from moderate-risk environments.

This audience can be divided into two major groups: youth from high-risk environments and families from high-risk environments.

Youth From High-Risk Environments

Public Law 99-750, the Anti-Drug Abuse Act of 1986, as amended by P.L. 100-690 in 1988, defines a high-risk youth as

> An individual who has not attained the age of 21 years, who is at high risk of becoming, or who has become, a drug user or an alcohol abuser, and who—
>
> (1) Is identified as a child of a substance abuser;
>
> (2) Is a victim of physical, sexual, or psychological abuse;
>
> (3) Has dropped out of school;
>
> (4) Has become pregnant;

(5) Is economically disadvantaged;

(6) Has committed a violent or delinquent act;

(7) Has experienced mental health problems;

(8) Has attempted suicide;

(9) Has experienced long-term physical pain due to injury;

(10) Has experienced chronic failure in school.

In addition, Congress specified that the priority high-risk target groups should be

Children of substance abusers, latchkey children, children at risk of abuse or neglect, preschool children eligible for services under the Head Start Act, children at risk for dropping out of school, children at risk of becoming adolescent parents, and children who do not attend school and who are at risk of being unemployed.

Children may be considered high risk either because they are disadvantaged in a socioeconomic sense or because of other factors associated with the family. Both are discussed below.

Disadvantaged youth

The term "high-risk youth" often is used to refer to the truly disadvantaged children in our society—those who are growing up in urban, crime-ridden environments under conditions of poverty, with parents ill-equipped to nurture them, and with little hope of breaking out of a vicious cycle of school failure, delinquency, drug use, teenage pregnancy, and chronic unemployment.

Census data can be used to locate entire districts of children who live in extreme poverty and who are likely to suffer disproportionately high levels of prenatal damage, bad health during infancy and childhood, malnutrition, and emotional and physical abuse and neglect. The mothers of these children are often isolated or impaired, they have no decent place to live, and they often do not have access to either supportive schools or social services adequate for protecting their children from the effects of difficult life conditions.

Many children who grow up under this unfavorable scenario develop an interrelated pattern of problems in adolescence—doing poorly in school, dropping out, becoming teenage parents, becoming delinquent, and using alcohol and other drugs as part of a cycle of misery and hopelessness. The sheer volume of risk factors these youngsters endure puts them at high risk for alcohol and other drug problems. Such problems do occur more frequently at lower and blue collar socioeconomic levels (Parker and Harford 1987), but this may partly reflect the fact that parents are drinking or drugging themselves into poverty as the disease progresses. Low income can therefore be a consequence, as well as an antecedent, of drug and alcohol problems.

The problems—and potential solutions—for this entire underclass of children are delineated in two excellent recent books: *Within Our Reach: Breaking the Cycle of Disadvantage*, by L.B. Schorr and D. Schorr, and *The Truly Disadvantaged: The Inner City, the Underclass, and Public Policy*, by W.J. Wilson.

Other youth at high risk

The problem, however, is not restricted to lower socioeconomic levels; children from families of middle or middle-to-high income levels also show high problem rates. A prospective random sample of adolescents in a large Minnesota health maintenance organization, where 64 percent of fathers and 46 percent of mothers had a college education, found that 6 percent of families had at least one child in alcohol or drug treatment by age 14 to 17. Adolescents in an additional 5 percent of families were using at least as much alcohol or other drugs as those youth who were in treatment (Needle et al. 1988).

Children may live in environments considered high risk because of family disruption or dysfunction. Parental alcoholism and drug abuse, for example, are risk factors for youthful alcohol and drug use. Single-parent families are sometimes at risk (Steinberg 1986, 1987). Children with conduct disorders and runaway youth also are at high risk for alcohol and other drug abuse, regardless of socioeconomic background (Dryfoos 1987; Hawkins et al. 1986).

How many youth are at high risk?

Although we don't know how many children are at high risk for problems, we do know about how many are already in trouble. Based on an extensive summary of the epidemiologic and etiologic research literature, it is estimated that more than 1 in 10 of our Nation's 28 million adolescents already have serious difficulties (Dryfoos 1987). The report, *Youth at Risk: One in Four in Jeopardy,* estimates that 3 million boys and girls aged 10 to 17 in the United States are already in serious trouble and experiencing multiple problems resulting from alcohol and other drug use, unwanted pregnancy, school failure, and delinquency. Dryfoos estimates an additional 4 million boys and girls are engaged in problem behaviors and are at high risk of serious health and social consequences. The Fact Sheets at the end of this chapter summarize data on numbers of American children in selected categories of risk.

Families in High-Risk Environments

Parents of high-risk children generally are young themselves. Many are single teenagers. Today many families contain two working parents, some holding two jobs. This is a generation with many overworked, exhausted parents who have little unscheduled time. Other stresses may include financial problems; young families generally have less money than those in middle age, and alcohol and drug abuse can exacerbate the problem.

Parents in high-risk environments may have an unrealistic view of family life because of several factors:

- *Depression.* Many of these parents see life through a depressive filter. They do not know what "normal" is, so many think they are worse parents than in fact they are. In addition, they often have unrealistic developmental expectations for their children, so the children do not get positive reinforcement.

- *Romanticization of normal family life.* Many high-risk parents tend to believe the glamorized view of family life portrayed on television. They need to learn how imperfect and hard life is for all families.

- *Lack of structure.* Besides lacking good parenting skills, many high-risk parents do not know how to structure family activities and leisure time. Both the adults and the children need information and programs that provide structural and organizational skills.

The parental drug of choice seems to depend on what is available and accessible in the environment and to cluster with socioeconomic status. Use of inexpensive, illegal drugs may characterize the low-income family in a housing project; middle-income parents are primarily alcohol or cocaine abusers; and upper-class parents are likely to be abusing alcohol or prescription opiates. Dual and poly addictions have become commonplace. However, much overlap occurs in these classifications.

Types of families

Experts recommend that communications efforts specifically target dysfunctional families and families with a special-needs child. What must be kept in mind, however, is that dysfunctional families should not be "labeled." Stereotyping that can occur from such labeling may lead to self-fulfilling prophecies. Appropriate methods for reaching out to these families must be developed, so that the parents become positively motivated rather than feeling stigmatized. In targeting and helping families, care should be taken not to blame the victims, while still holding them accountable for their actions.

According to experts consulted for this chapter, the following types of families need special attention:

- Dysfunctional families of all types, including those manifesting parental alcohol and other drug use, physical or sexual abuse of their children, emotional neglect, or mental disturbance
- Alcohol-abusing families (both active and recovering)
- Other drug-abusing families (both active and recovering)
- Single parents facing multiple socioeconomic hardships, such as lack of family support, poverty, and low educational levels
- Functional families with a "special-needs" child.

The dysfunctional family. Families may be dysfunctional for a variety of reasons, including emotional illness of the parents or patterns of physical/sexual/emotional abuse by parents to children. Certain types of dysfunction, such as alcohol abuse and family violence, tend to pass from one generation to the next (Flanzer 1984; Sanchez-Dirks 1979). Ackerman (1970) calls relationships in such families an "interlocking pathology" made up of unstable behavior by individuals; conflicts and discord in the marriage; and arbitrary, inconsistent parenting practices. One study in Berkeley, California, followed the transmission of disadvantage across four generations, linking problem behavior (highstrung, irritable, explosive personalities) with unstable family relations (Elder et al. 1985).

The transmission of problem behavior across generations is not inevitable; in this study, the pattern was broken in some families. More needs to be known about the protective factors in these successful families, such as the presence of a nurturant mother or a child's physical attractiveness (Elder et al. 1985).

Children who are abused by their parents are at risk for many problem behaviors. Recent studies suggest, for example, that a high percent of runaway youth have both alcohol and other drug problems themselves and a family history of being abused from childhood. How much of this abuse by parents is the result of parental alcohol or other drug abuse is not clear. As an example, one study of 300 families who had been reported for child abuse/neglect found that 186 cases (two-thirds of the families) had severe and chronic drinking as a primary family problem (Young 1964). The overall picture was one of poverty, poor housing, unemployment, and large families. In cases of battered children in France, between 82 and 90 percent were attributed to parental alcoholism (Mainard et al. 1971). Steele and Pollock (1968), on the other hand, found alcohol intoxication rather than true alcoholism to be a precipitating factor in child abuse.

The alcoholic family. Families with an active alcohol abuser, whether a parent or a child, face an ongoing crisis. A large body of clinical and retrospective reports testify to the chaos and misery in such families. The alcoholic is involved with his or her addiction, the codependent spouse is desperately immersed in trying to control the alcoholic, and little energy or nurturing is left for children in the household.

As our understanding of the reasons for alcohol and other drug abuse improves, we will be better able to develop appropriate prevention messages. To date, three types of family alcoholism have been tentatively identified (Cloninger et al. 1986):

- *Antisocial behavior disorder with alcohol abuse,* inherited by males and characterized by criminality with repeated violence and untreated alcohol abuse; in daughters there is no excess of alcohol abuse but there is a high frequency of disability from abdominal, back, and psychiatric disorders.

- *Male-limited alcoholism,* probably the most severe form of alcoholism, inherited by males and characterized by recurrent alcoholism, teenage onset, alcohol treatment, and crime due to abuse; in daughters there is no excess of alcohol abuse but there is an excess of diversely distributed somatic complaints, such as headache, backache, and vague abdominal complaints.

- *Milieu-limited alcoholism,* inherited by both men and women and characterized for both by a generally mild form of the disease, onset in adulthood, and no criminality.

Research studies underscore the extent of problems experienced by members of the alcoholic's family. In one controlled study of wives of alcoholics matched against wives of nonalcoholics, 32 percent of the alcoholics' wives were judged to be "worn out" or emotionally disturbed versus 10 percent of the controls (Nylander 1960). In the alcoholic homes, there was more severe family disorganization, with 28 percent of the homes of alcoholics being broken versus 4 percent for controls. Among the children of these alcoholics, 29 percent showed emotional disturbance and 48 percent had been assessed as more likely to be "problem children" by their teachers; rates for these problems among children from nonalcoholic families were 5 percent and 10 percent, respectively. The children from alcoholic homes also had more hospitalization and outpatient visits for somatic complaints.

As the literature makes clear, many of these family problems lessen once the alcoholic begins the recovery process. The adjustment of the entire family to recovery, however, takes a number of years. It is a difficult process of refocusing family roles and living patterns and of facing deferred problems. But once parents control their alcohol problem, the children's stress related to alcoholism diminishes (Moos and Billings 1982). A more positive climate for reducing children's risks is thus established. Moos and Billings found significantly increased emotional and other problems among children from relapsed alcoholic families, compared with children from recovered alcoholic families and with matched community controls.

Many people lack basic knowledge about the process of the disease. The time lapse before family members seek help is often as much as 10 years. This kind of delay causes damage to both the family members and the alcoholic. One goal of communications to high-risk groups should be the message that alcoholics can and should be helped long before they reach "bottom." For educated, middle-income families, a good deal of material is available to help the alcoholic's codependent person. The techniques to intervene in alcoholism are available. However, even if intervention is not successful, the alcoholic's family members need and deserve help for themselves; that help, too, is increasingly available.

The drug-abusing family.   Much less is known about children growing up with drug-abusing parents. There are not even up-to-date estimates in the literature of the number of children living in such families. It is known that the number of women entering drug use treatment is rising, so the number of children with mothers in treatment probably is increasing also. Women in treatment for drug use are, on average, younger than those being treated for alcoholism, suggesting that their children also are younger and, perhaps, more vulnerable.

Clinicians state that families of drug abusers seem to be even more dysfunctional than those of alcoholics. Only about 58 percent of heroin-addicted women still have some or all of their children living with them at the time they enter treatment (Colton 1980). Their other children are living with relatives, adopted, or in foster care. One study found that about 13 percent of heroin-abusing mothers with 3- to 7-year-olds and 30 percent of those with 8- to 17-year-olds have children in surrogate care (Sowder et al. 1981).

The conditions surrounding drug use—illegality, criminality, often severe poverty—make for devastation in family life. Like the alcoholic family, the child living with a drug-using parent will be subjected to inconsistency, chaos, emotional neglect, and a paucity of the experiences that lead to trust and family attachment (Kumpfer 1987b).

The single-parent family.   Many children—60 percent, according to some surveys (Krauthammer 1988)—live with only one parent by the time they are 18. Although single-parent families are not necessarily dysfunctional, they may need special help to deal with alcohol and child-rearing issues. The concern is that there is only one parent to provide a role model and supervision of the child. Steinberg (1986, 1987) suggests that, although adolescents living in single-parent households are more likely to engage in deviant activity, the presence of an additional person in the household (grandmother, aunt, friend) significantly diminishes youngsters' rates of deviance. The presence of stepfathers did not diminish rates of deviance.

Children in single-parent families often must be home alone. Research is beginning to be conducted on risks and protective factors for the latchkey child. The Steinberg studies suggest child-rearing practices that may reduce risks for adolescents:

- Latchkey adolescents whose parents know their whereabouts after school, and who have been raised authoritatively, are less susceptible to negative peer influences.

- Adolescents who are home alone are less susceptible to peer pressure than those who are at a friend's house after school; "hanging out" is the highest risk situation.

Functional families with a special-needs child.   Functional families can successfully rear their other children, but face problems in dealing with a special-needs child. Such children may be born with a difficult temperament or with some neurological abnormality, such as attention-span deficit or hyperactivity. Adoptive and foster parents may have a child with the syndrome known as fetal alcohol or drug effects, or a child with an inherited vulnerability to alcohol and other drug abuse. Abstaining parents who were raised in alcoholic families may not realize that their children can be at increased risk of chemical problems; they also may be perpetuating dysfunctional family patterns learned in their original alcoholic homes. One study found grandchildren of alcoholics to be three times more likely than others to become alcoholic themselves (Kaij and Dock 1975).

Although these families can function well with their special child, researchers and clinicians report they need access to the following kinds of information:

- Knowledge about the nature of children's vulnerability to alcohol and other drug use

- Knowledge about the most efficacious approaches for setting family rules, limits, and values pertaining to both adolescent and adult alcohol use

- Training in child-rearing techniques and parenting styles that work most successfully with the high-risk child (e.g., flexibility is very important and may require modification of the parenting styles that worked well for other children in the family)

- Support from others who are dealing with difficult children and help with the marital conflict that can be engendered by this stress.

Family Risk Factors

According to Kandel (1974), three parental factors help to predict a child's initiation into drug use: parental drug-using behaviors, parental attitudes about drugs, and parent-child interactions characterized by lack of closeness.

Parental drug use

Kandel (1974) reports that when parents drink, their children also are more likely to use alcohol. In the case of marijuana, the parents' use in a rewarding family structure only slightly promotes extensive marijuana use by the children; when the family structure is unrewarding, there is a clear association between drug use by parents and drug use by children. For illicit drugs other than marijuana, the quality of the family relationship is inversely related to adolescent use—the poorer the relationship with the family, the more likely the adolescent is to use drugs (Kandel 1974).

Parental attitudes

Parental attitudes toward drugs may be as influential as the parents' actual use. McDermott (1984) found that a child's perception that his or her parents have permissive attitudes toward drug use may be as important as, or more important than, the parents' actual use.

Parent-child interactions

The relationship between parent and child appears to influence not only youthful use of drugs but also the development of problem drinking in adulthood. Zucker and Lisansky Gomberg, in a 1986 integrative review of all existing longitudinal literature, summarized key findings that were convergent across studies. The six available studies all originated in childhood or adolescence (ages 9 to 15), followed respondents into adulthood, and established an adult diagnosis of either alcoholism or problem drinking. The findings on the family environment in which problem drinkers grew up follow:

- Heightened marital conflict was reported with consistently greater frequency in the pre-alcoholic homes, which is hypothesized (1) to lead to the child's greater estrangement from the family and quicker movement into a heavier drinking peer culture or into antisocial behavior; and (2) to lead, through modeling of the parents' marital conflict, to the adult alcoholics' heightened level of marital discord and divorce.

- Parent-child interaction in the families of those who became alcoholics was characterized by inadequate parenting and by the child's lack of contact with the parents, including inadequate or lax supervision, absence of parental demands, parental disinterest, or lack of affection for the child.

- Parents of pre-alcoholics were also more often inadequate role models for later normalcy, since these parents were more likely to be alcoholic (consistently found across studies) and antisocial or sexually deviant (linkages consistently found when assessed).

Kumpfer (1987b), in an extensive review and discussion of longitudinal and cross-sectional studies of children of alcoholics, concludes that a poor early family environment is an important factor in vulnerability to alcohol and other drug use. Kumpfer provides extensive empirical data supporting the idea that psychosocial risk factors cluster in the following areas: parental dysfunction, family dysfunction, parenting dysfunction, community and social environment dysfunction for the family, and school environmental dysfunction. Table 1 gives more detail.

Risk Factors vs. Protective Factors

The more risk factors a child endures, the higher the risk of later problems (Schorr 1988). Several researchers on risk and protective factors (Garmezy and Rutter 1983; Werner 1986) stress that the development of such problem behavior as alcohol or other drug use or delinquency is a dynamic process as an individual constantly adapts to stressful life events. Reinforcing the protective, nurturing factors can redress the balance and increase the resiliency of a vulnerable child.

Tables 2 and 3 list a number of the most often cited risk factors, as well as the factors that seem to protect so-called "resilient" children. In addition, Kumpfer and DeMarsh (1986) pinpoint the following factors as those most likely to influence the risk of children of alcoholics and children of drug abusers:

- Age of the child when the family becomes significantly involved in the alcohol/other drug use of the parent or parents

- Degree of involvement in alcohol/other drug use of the primary caretaker and nonfulfillment of parental responsibilities

- Severity of emotional, physical, educational, and spiritual neglect or abuse

- Temperament of the child and role the child assumes in the family

- Social isolation of the child and family

- Degree of family stress arising from inconsistency in rules, rituals, discipline, etc.

- Degree of family conflict and lack of cooperative, supportive behavior

- Degree of open modeling of alcohol or other drug abuse by parents and siblings.

Narrowing the Target Audience

The previous section on family risk factors describes the kinds of family situations in which those with alcohol and other drug problems are more likely

Table 1. Family Risk Factors Found in Children Vulnerable to Chemical Dependency*

Dysfunction of Parents

- Increased alcoholism, drug abuse, and nicotine dependency in parents (Vaillant; Kumpfer and DeMarsh; Cotton; Goodwin)

- Increased antisocial or sexually deviant behavior in these parents (McCord and McCord; Robins) resulting in jail and prison terms (Booz-Allen and Hamilton)

- Increased mental and emotional problems, including depression and narcissism (Kumpfer and DeMarsh)

- Increased marital conflict (McCord and McCord; Robins, Bates, and O'Neal; Robins; Jones; Vaillant and Milofsky)

- Increased parental absenteeism due to separation (Nylander), divorce, and death

Dysfunction of family

- High level of family conflict (Kumpfer and DeMarsh; Booz-Allen and Hamilton; Vaillant and Milofsky; Ackerman; Moos, Bromet, Tsu, and Moos), especially verbal abuse and such negative communication patterns as threatening, blaming, belittling, and criticizing (Reilly)

- Decreased family organization and home management skills (e.g., disorganized households, fewer rules, unpredictable schedules) (Kumpfer and DeMarsh)

- Decreased family rituals (Wolin, Bennett, Noonan, and Teitelbaum; Bennett and Wolin)

- Decreased family cohesion (Vaillant and Milofsky; Kumpfer and DeMarsh)

- Increased family social isolation (Kumpfer and DeMarsh)

- Frequent family moves (Vaillant and Milofsky)

- Increased family stress, including work strain, illness strain, losses, transitions, family and marital strain, and financial strain (Kumpfer and DeMarsh) and low income (El-Guebaly and Offord)

- For girls only, unstructured and laissez-faire home environments with few strict rules and little pressure to achieve, combined with fostering of autonomy, and little emphasis on propriety, conventions, and religion (Block, Block, and Keyes)

Table 1. Family Risk Factors Found in Children Vulnerable to Chemical Dependency* (continued)

Dysfunction in Parenting

- Lack of knowledge about effective behavioral discipline methods from their own upbringing, with tendency toward coercive discipline procedures modeled by their parents (Kumpfer and DeMarsh)

- Deficiencies in parenting and discipline passed cross-generationally (grandparent to parent), correlated with antisocial offspring (parent to child) (Elder, Caspi, and Downey; Huesmann, Eron, Lefkowitz, and Walder)

- Decreased family management skills (Loeber and Dishion; Rutter and Giller; Patterson)

- Decreased parenting skills, including decreased knowledge of parenting skills and decreased appropriate discipline techniques or inconsistent or lax discipline (Kumpfer and DeMarsh; Baumrind; Braucht; Black; Blum; Vaillant and Milofsky; McCord and McCord; Jones); parents tend to be either strict or permissive (Sowder and Burt)

- Decreased monitoring and supervision of children as shown by less contact or time spent with the children (Kumpfer and DeMarsh; Kumpfer; Sowder and Burt; Dishion, Patterson, and Reid)

- Decreased positive responses and reinforcement of children (Kumpfer and DeMarsh; Kumpfer), particularly emotional neglect (Booz-Allen and Hamilton)

- Decreased parental involvement with the child and decreased parent/child attachment (Vaillant and Milofsky; McCord and McCord; Chein)

- Home environments of drug abusers characterized as cool and hostile, with weak parent/child relationships (Chein)

- Home environments of drug-abusing children described as fathers being disengaged and mothers being enmeshed (Kaufman and Kaufman)

Dysfunction of Community and Social Environment

- Poorer environmental support systems (Vaillant and Milofsky)

- Decreased family involvement in recreational, religious, and cultural activities (Kumpfer and DeMarsh)

- Decreased social networks (Fraser and Hawkins), with parents in drug-abusing families having fewer friends (Kumpfer)

---

*Citations that appear in this table will be found in Kumpfer (1987a and b), pp. 28–36, 51–71.

Table 2. Checklist: Youth Risk Factors*

1. *Ecological Environment*

   Poverty/lack of resources

   Living in an economically depressed area with:

   environmental toxicity

   high unemployment

   inadequate housing

   poor schools

   lack of perinatal care (prenatal, neonatal, postnatal)

   inadequate health and social services

   lack of opportunity/alternatives for meaningful tasks

   high prevalence of crime

   high prevalence of illegal drug use and neighborhood drug dealing

   social support for drug dealing as a legitimate source of income

   Minority status involving:

   racial discrimination

   culture devalued in American society

   differing generational levels of assimilation

   cultural and language barriers to getting adequate health care and other social services

   low educational levels

   low achievement expectations from society

2. *Family Environment*

   Alcohol and other drug dependency of parent(s)

   Parental abuse and neglect of children

   Antisocial, sexually deviant, or mentally ill parents

   High levels of family stress, including financial strain

   Large, overcrowded family

   Unemployed or underemployed parents

   Parents with little education

   Socially isolated parents

   Lack of social bonds and supports (significant others, kinship network)

   Single female parent without family/other support

   Family instability

   High level of marital and family conflict and/or family violence

   Parental absenteeism due to separation, divorce, or death

   Lack of family rituals

   Inadequate parenting and low parent/child contact

   Frequent family moves

Table 2. Checklist: Youth Risk Factors* (continued)

3. *Constitutional Vulnerability of the Child*

Child of an alcohol or other drug abuser
Less than 2 years between the child and its older/younger siblings
Birth defects, including possible neurological and neurochemical dysfunctions
Neuropsychological vulnerabilities
Physically handicapped
Physical or mental health problems
Learning disability

4. *Early Behavioral Problems*

Aggressiveness combined with shyness
Aggressiveness
Decreased social inhibition
Emotional problems
Inability to express feelings appropriately
Hypersensitivity
Hyperactivity
Inability to cope with stress
Problems with relationships
Cognitive problems
Low self-esteem
Difficult temperament
Personality characteristics of ego undercontrol; rapid tempo, inability to delay gratification, over-reacting, etc.

5. *Adolescent Problems*

School failure and dropout
At risk of dropping out
Delinquency
Violent acts
Gateway drug use (cigarettes, alcohol, marijuana)
Other drug use
Early unprotected sexual activity
Teenage pregnancy/teen parenthood
Unemployed or underemployed
At risk of being unemployed
Mental health problems
Suicidal

6. *Negative Adolescent Behavior and Experiences*

Lack of bonding to society (family, school, and community)
Rebelliousness and nonconformity
Deviance
Resistance to authority
Strong need for independence
Cultural alienation
Fragile ego
Feelings of failure
Present versus future orientation
Hopelessness
Lack of self-efficacy
Low self-esteem
Inability to form positive close relationships
Vulnerability to negative peer pressure

*Sources are listed in a separate reference list at the end of this chapter.

Table 3. Checklist: Youth Protective Factors*

1. *Ecological Environment*
   Middle or upper class
   Low unemployment
   Adequate housing
   Pleasant neighborhood
   Low prevalence of neighborhood crime
   Good schools
   A school climate that promotes learning, participation, and responsibility
   High-quality health care
   Easy access to adequate social services
   Flexible social service providers who put clients' needs first

2. *Family Environment*
   Adequate family income
   Structured and nurturing family
   Parents promote learning
   Fewer than four children in family
   Two or more years between the birth of each child
   Few chronic stressful life events
   Multigenerational kinship network
   Non-kin support network, e.g., supportive role models, dependable substitute childcare
   Warm, close personal relationship with parent(s) and/or other adult(s)
   Little marital conflict
   Family stability and cohesiveness

   Plenty of attention during first year of life
   Sibling as caretaker/confidante
   Clear behavior guideline

3. *Constitutional Strengths*
   Adequate early sensorimotor and language development
   High intelligence
   Physically robust
   No emotional or temperamental impairments

4. *Personality of the Child*
   Affectionate/endearing
   Easy temperament
   Autonomous
   Adaptable and flexible
   Positive outlook
   Healthy expectations
   Self-efficacy
   Self-discipline
   Internal locus of control
   Problem-solving skills
   Socially adept
   Tolerance of people and situations

*Sources are listed in a separate reference list at the end of this chapter.

to grow up. What about the children themselves? What signs during childhood may predict potential high risk of alcohol and other drug use problems either as teenagers or adults? Throughout the research literature, two particularly strong threads are apparent. Serious adolescent drinking and drug dependency occur at higher levels among the following:

- Children with conduct disorders and with social deviancy during adolescence

- Children of alcoholics (CoAs) and children of drug abusers (CoDAs)

Children with conduct disorders

The association of antisocial personality and chemical dependency is one of the strongest, most consistent correlations throughout the literature. Research shows that

- Chronic serious delinquency and adolescent drug use share many common risk factors (Hawkins et al. 1985, 1986); nearly 50 percent of serious juvenile offenders in the National Youth Survey report using multiple illicit drugs and over 80 percent report using one illicit drug (Elliott and Huizinga 1984).

- Early initiation into alcohol and other drug use (by age 14) predicts early chemical dependency and abuse (Robins and Pryzbeck 1985) and is associated with general deviance and other antisocial and problem behaviors (Johnston et al. 1978; Jessor and Jessor 1978).

- As part of a constellation of antisocial behavior patterns, drug use can be predicted by personality/behavior characteristics that can be identified in early childhood and remain consistent over time (Hawkins et al. 1986; Block et al. 1988).

Children who manifest conduct disorders in their early years and antisocial characteristics later are more likely to use alcohol and other drugs early and frequently. These preteen children, who have trouble with prosocial bonding to family, school, friends, and society, often join other alienated, isolated youngsters in a peer group that shares drinking and possibly other antisocial activities (Hawkins et al. 1986). The personality factors exhibited by these children seem sufficient to explain why they initiate early use. These young people often are rebellious, resist traditional authority and traditional values, and have a high tolerance for deviance and a strong need for independence (Jessor and Jessor 1978). Some research suggests marijuana-using youth have a sensation-seeking orientation and a willingness to risk injury and illness (Penning and Barnes 1982). Also, ninth-grade drug users perceive their parents as less caring and more rejecting than do nonusers (Norem-Hebeisen et al.

1984). This suggests a motive for turning from parents to peer influence at an early age.

The literature on adolescent alcohol and other drug use reflects the fact that, as part of a constellation of antisocial behavior problems, alcohol and other drug use can be predicted by previous patterns of antisocial behavior. Problematic conduct early in life continues for certain groups of children, as shown by numerous studies. A longitudinal study of high-risk early signs of delinquency (Spivack 1983) revealed that conduct disturbances in adolescence could be predicted from kindergarten and first grade; signs included

- Acting out
- Overinvolvement in socially disturbing behaviors
- Impatience
- Impulsiveness
- Defiance and negativity.

In summarizing a large body of information on this subject, Hawkins et al. (1986) state that "the evidence of a positive relationship between childhood antisocial behavior and subsequent drug use is relatively consistent." *Important caveats include*

- It is not clear what is the earliest age at which childhood antisocial behavior can be reliably identified as predicting drug use.
- Although serious antisocial behaviors in childhood appear to be virtually a prerequisite for serious antisocial behaviors (including drug use) in later life, less than half the children with serious behavior problems manifest such problems later.
- Virtually nothing is known about the effect of peer groups in the early childhood years.

The review of all pertinent longitudinal studies by Zucker and Lisansky Gomberg (1986) lists several convergent findings pertaining to the childhood predictors of later alcohol and other drug users. These findings include

- Childhood antisocial behavior is consistently related to later alcoholic outcome, encompassing greater amounts of antisocial and aggressive activity, and more rebelliousness.
- More childhood difficulty in achievement-related activity is consistently found in later-to-be alcoholics, including poorer school performance, less productivity in high school, completion of fewer years of schooling, and more school truancy.

- A greater activity level is a possible etiological factor, including more hyperactivity, greater likelihood of rapid tempo, and more neural disorders, such as infant nervousness and fretfulness and poorer physical coordination.

- Males who later become alcoholics are more loosely tied to others, less dependent, less considerate, earlier to leave home, more indifferent to their mothers, and more indifferent to siblings.

Several reviews of the longitudinal research, including sophisticated recent studies starting in early childhood, appear in Hawkins et al. (1985, 1986), Kumpfer (1987b), and Block et al. (1988). For boys who develop adolescent drug problems, childhood characteristics seem to focus around a pure form of "under-control" (Block et al. 1988). Kellam et al. (1983) found that the boys at highest risk were aggressive and shy; boys at somewhat less risk were those characterized only by aggression without shyness.

A recent study (Block et al. 1988) reports on 100 personality factors in 54 girls and 51 boys assessed at ages 3, 4, 5, 11, 14, and 18. Drug use at age 14 was related to concurrent and preschool personality characteristics. A simple review of the characteristics of these children dramatizes why they have so much difficulty in school, in making friends, and in their homes. (For a listing of the nursery school correlates of marijuana use at age 14, see table 4.)

By age 14, the adolescent girl marijuana user seems to be "uneasy with self, uneasy with people, self-protective, unexpressive, detached from others, devious and even hostile, and generally unlikable." The same researchers suggest that these girls' "contorted, convoluted, desperate, and despairing personality mode...constrains their potential" (Block et al. 1988).

Boy marijuana users at age 14 appear "undependable, not submissive, directly hostile, not protective of others, negativistic, not sympathetic to others, guileful, without a clear-cut personality, ungiving, unethical, unconventional, overreactive to frustration, lacking in guilt, and unpredictable."

Risk factors associated with youthful alcohol and drug use, as compiled by several researchers, are listed in table 4. **It is extremely important to understand that risk factors do not predict the certainty of problems for any given child.** Risk factors refer only to the statistical probability that a problem may occur. Among children with conduct disorders, more than half will *not* go on to develop adult behavioral problems (Hawkins 1986). Risk factors are a useful way to identify children who may need help. They do not predict an adverse outcome for any particular child.

Table 4. Risk Factor Research on Adolescent Chemical Dependency*

Biological Vulnerabilities

- Alcoholism or drug abuse in a first-generation relative (parent, sibling) carrying four to five times the risk of alcoholism found for the general population (Goodwin)

- In boys, father with male-limited alcoholism (nine times normal vulnerability) (Bohman; Cloninger), a type of alcoholism affecting 25 percent of male alcoholics

- In boys, antisocial personality inherited as part of a male-limited syndrome— a serious type of alcoholism with early onset that seems related to the "St. Louisian Triad Syndrome," which includes Briquet's Syndrome (Bohman, Cloninger, von Knorring, and Sigvardsson)

- In girls, increased Briquet's Syndrome (a syndrome with frequent pain, without apparent physiological conditions) associated with male-limited alcoholism (Bohman, Cloninger, von Knorring, and Sigvardsson)

- In utero exposure to alcohol and drugs, resulting in Fetal Alcohol Effects, Fetal Alcohol Syndrome, or Fetal Drug Effects (Bohman, Cloninger, von Knorring, and Sigvardsson)

- Temperament vulnerabilities, such as excessively high activity level or hyperactivity (Morrison and Stewart; Cantwell); decreased attention-span persistence and possible attention deficit disorder (Tarter, Hegedus, Goldstein, Shelly, and Alterman)

- Possible brain activity dysfunction (neurological) (in research stage)

- Hypothesized neurochemical dysfunctions (in research stage)

- Possible neuropsychological vulnerabilities, such as decreased I.Q. in 3- to 7-year-old children of methadone-maintained mothers (Sowder and Burt); decreased abstraction and problem-solving capability (Noll and Zucker)

Personality Factors

- Constellation of personality characteristics encompassed by the concept of ego undercontrol (inability to delay gratification, rapid tempo, emotional expressiveness, mood ability, overreactivity) (Block, Block, and Keyes)

- In girls only, an absence of ego-resiliency (i.e., an insufficiency in the ability to adapt that leads to personal vulnerability) (Block, Block, and Keyes)

Table 4. Risk Factor Research on Adolescent Chemical Dependency (continued)

- In nursery school children, personality antecedents of drug use at age 14 include restlessness and fidgeting, emotional lability, inconsiderateness, nonobedience, lack of calmness, domineeringness, uncooperativeness, immature behavior under stress, reluctance to yield and give in, aggressivity, overreactivity to frustrations, reluctance to seek help from adults, lack of neatness, open expression of negative feelings, efforts to take advantage of others, readiness to cry, teasing, inability to recoup after stressful experiences (Block, Block, and Keyes)

- In nursery school girls only, additional personality antecedents of drug use at age 14 include being afraid of being deprived, being cautious, being sulky and whiny, jealous and envious, selfish, having poor coordination and a tendency to daydream (Block, Block, and Keyes)

- In nursery school boys only, additional personality antecedents of drug use at age 14 include risk-taking; competitiveness; awareness of and direct expression of negative feelings; an absence of shyness and introspectiveness; having a rapid tempo; being talkative; being physically active, energetic, and well-coordinated (Block, Block, and Keyes)

- By adolescence, antisocial personality factors include

  — Rebelliousness (Block, Keyes, and Block; Kandel; Bachman; Johnston and O'Malley; Goldstein and Sappington; Smith and Fogg; Green; Block, Block, and Keyes)

  — Nonconformity to traditional values (Gorsuch and Butler; Jessor and Jessor; Block, Block, and Keyes)

  — High tolerance of deviance (Brook, Lukoff, and Whiteman; Jessor and Jessor; Block, Block, and Keyes)

  — Resistance to traditional authority (Goldstein and Sappington)

  — Strong need for independence (Jessor; Segal; Block, Block, and Keyes) and normlessness (Paton and Kandel)

  — Low scores on measures of personal competence and social responsibility, such as obedience, diligence, and achievement orientation (Smith and Fogg)

  — Lower scores on measures of well-being, responsibility, socialization, self-control, tolerance, achievement, and intellectual efficacy (Wexler)

Table 4. Risk Factor Research on Adolescent Chemical Dependency (continued)

Psychosocial Factors

- Early antisocial behavior (Robins; Johnston, O'Malley, and Evelard; Kandel; Jessor and Jessor; Wechsler and Thum)

- Male aggressiveness in first grade, especially when combined with shyness (reluctance to raise hand in class; tendency to withdraw socially) (Kellam, Simon, and Ensminger)

- Early aggressiveness combined with irritability (Lewis, Robins, and Rice; Nylander)

- Difficult temperament, including frequent negative mood states and withdrawal (Lerner and Vicary)

- By adolescence, a lack of social bonding to society (Hawkins, Lishner, Catalano, and Howard)

- Early onset of drug use (by age 15) (Robins and Przybeck)

- Extent of adolescent proneness to problem behaviors, including use of tobacco (Jessor and Jessor; Kandel; Labouvie and McGee; Block, Block, and Keyes)

School Factors

- Decreased school attendance with increased tardiness and truancy (Kumpfer and DeMarsh; Holmberg)

- Learning problems, only if combined with aggressiveness (Kellam, Brown, Rubin, and Ensminger)

- Low degree of commitment to education (Hirshi; Elliott and Voss; Kim; Friedman; Galli and Stone; Robins; Brook, Lukoff, and Whiteman; Holmberg)

- Increased academic and behavioral problems in school (Herjanic, Barredo, Herjanic, and Tomelleri; Rimmer; Kumpfer and DeMarsh)

- Increased placement in special education or alternative schools, early school dropout (Holmberg)

- By end of elementary school, poor school performance (Smith and Fogg) and school failure (Robins; Anhalt and Klein; Jessor; Brook, Lukoff, and Whiteman)

*Based on Kumpfer 1987 a and b; Hawkins, Lishner, Catalano, and Howard 1986; Block, Block, and Keyes 1988; Benard 1987.

Children of alcoholics and other drug abusers

Children of alcoholics and other drug abusers make up a second major group at high risk for alcohol and other drug use problems. Many of these children have the conduct disorder and social deviancy problems described in the previous section (Nylander 1960; Woodside 1982). Children of alcoholics and other drug abusers are found at very high rates among juvenile delinquents, runaway youth, and children in foster care (Brown and Mills 1987), as well as among children with a history of being physically and sexually abused (Behling 1979).

It is essential to reach this audience, because they are at increased risk of alcoholism during both adolescence and adulthood. A strong association also has been found between a family history of problem drinking and the development of alcoholism at an early age; this association cannot be explained by differences in age at the onset of drinking (Volicer et al. 1983). Clinicians and researchers report the following:

- About 70 percent of youth in treatment for chemical addiction come from alcoholic or drug-abusing homes (Heuer 1986).

- In one intensive study of juvenile delinquents who were problem or addictive drinkers (17 boys and 3 girls), 100 percent of the youths had an alcoholic father and some also had an alcoholic mother (MacKay 1963).

- In adulthood, more than one-third of children from alcoholic families will themselves be heavy abusers of alcohol (Miller and Jang 1977).

However, many children of alcoholics and other drug abusers do not fit this picture of antisocial behavior and multiple overt problems. Children of alcoholics are often high achievers, bright, and over-responsible. Because of their stressful home environment, these nonacting-out children also need attention.

A growing body of literature attests to the heavy emotional load that children of alcoholics carry into adulthood (Russell et al. 1985). Having grown up in a home atmosphere of confusion, inconsistency, and isolation, adult CoAs may find trouble with bonding and attachments in intimate adult relationships. Clinicians report that they learned "don't talk, don't feel, don't trust" at an early age, and their sense of isolation and abandonment produces shame. Many cannot play or attain a sense of mastery over their lives. For these children, reducing the number of risk factors in their lives and augmenting the protective factors may be of great help to achieving a satisfactory adult life.

Knowledge, Attitudes, and Practices of Children

Children in the general population

- Are all aware of alcohol, through television and advertisements
- Do not know that alcoholism is a disease but think it is a bad habit (5th–7th graders)
- Say alcoholics need help to stop drinking (5th–7th graders)
- Have increasingly negative attitudes toward drinking until about age 10, then begin to shift toward positive attitudes
- Have their first drinking experience at about age 12
- May drink heavily at times, having five or more drinks on one occasion (8th–10th graders)
- May have tried marijuana or cocaine (10th graders).

Children of alcoholics

- Have a heightened awareness of drunkenness
- Do not know what normal drinking is
- Perceive alcohol as the focus of life
- Associate alcohol with fighting, mistreatment, and neglect
- Feel that alcohol is more important to the parent than they themselves
- Feel guilty and responsible for the parent's drinking
- Learn to deny the problem
- Are more distressed by family conflicts associated with alcoholism than with the drinking per se
- Are determined that they themselves will never drink
- Deny that the parent's behavior may influence their own
- Have difficulty controlling drinking if they begin.

Very little research exists on the knowledge, attitudes, and practices of children from high-risk environments. Therefore, some of the information presented here refers more broadly to all children, and not specifically those at high risk.

Some data are available on the knowledge, attitudes, and practices of children of alcoholics. Family studies, despite their different samples with varying demographic characteristics, report very similar findings about how children in alcoholic homes say they feel and respond to events (Russell et al. 1985). Also, there is a small but growing body of information from the school- and treatment-based programs for children of alcoholics initiated over the last decade. Deutsch (1982) is a particularly good source for understanding how a child's perceptions about alcohol are distorted by living in an alcoholic home.

Awareness and Attitudes

All American children are aware of alcohol. By the time a child is of legal drinking age, he or she will have seen alcohol consumed an average of 90,000 times on television (Center for Science in the Public Interest 1987). A survey of children 12 or younger in the Washington, D.C., area found that children on average could name 5.2 alcoholic beverages but only 4.8 presidents (*The Alcoholism Report* 1988).

Kumpfer (1989) points out that children of substance abusers are very vulnerable to messages about alcohol or other drug use from the mass media (television, radio, music, and advertisements) because of the lack of buffering influence from their parents. Efforts that deglamorize the portrayal of alcohol and other drugs in the media should, therefore, help reduce the risk of use by these vulnerable children.

Educators report that most young children, if encouraged to think of situations and reasons for drinking that are not related to drunkenness, can name quite a few (Deutsch 1982). But for children of alcoholics, drinking means getting drunk. Because the nonalcoholic spouse is likely to condemn drinking and to avoid serving alcohol to friends, the children often do not see drinking except in the context of getting drunk. Deutsch points out that their earliest observations lead children of alcoholics to view alcohol differently from other children:

- Alcohol is perceived as the focus of life; everything in the home revolves around the alcoholic's drinking or, if recovering, his or her nondrinking.

- Alcohol is connected to fighting, mistreatment, neglect, and broken promises.

- Alcohol is perceived as more important than the child is to the parent, with even 6- or 7-year-old children recognizing that money is being spent on alcohol instead of on needed clothes or food for the family.

- Alcohol is very powerful, and can transform peace into chaos; it also may be the stimulus for unusual parental kindness and generosity.

Tests of fourth- to sixth-grade children suggest that the students know more about the properties of alcohol than about alcoholism (Lehr and Schrock 1987). The Children of Alcoholics (CoA) Foundation recently conducted field tests of their CoA awareness program among schoolchildren (Woodside 1988). Results indicated that 60 percent of students in fifth through seventh grade do not know alcoholism is a disease; they think it is a "bad habit." Most children (57 percent) think people become alcoholics because they don't care about themselves. Some children think alcoholics can stop drinking whenever they want, do not really want to stop, or can never stop; 79 percent say alcoholics need help to stop drinking.

The majority of children (78 percent) do know that children of alcoholics are more likely than others to become alcoholics, and most (82 percent) think those who live with alcoholism are lonely, angry, and sad. Less than half (48 percent) think children need help whether or not the parent stops drinking (Woodside 1988).

It is widely reported in the literature that children of alcoholics do not understand that alcoholism is a disease that they did not cause and cannot control or cure. Clinicians agree that CoAs usually feel guilty and responsible for their parents' alcoholism (Woodside 1988). They tend to blame themselves for their parents' drinking, equating the drinking problem with being unloved by their parents (Russell et al. 1985). The CoA Foundation study showed children in grades five to eight could suggest many ways in which they think they can make their parents drink, such as worrying them, getting in their way, upsetting them when they're tired, getting poor grades, staying out late, and drinking alcohol themselves (Woodside 1988).

The words "drinking" and "alcoholism" are either taboo in these households, never mentioned by either parent, or they may be fearful words, associated with violent arguments and mutual recriminations. The result is that children from alcoholic homes learn not to mention drinking and not to think about it. Deutsch (1982) believes that alcohol is so "freighted with terrifying power" that CoAs can't tolerate the evidence before their eyes. The children learn denial from their parents, which they then internalize and practice in their own lives.

What children of alcoholics do not know is also significant. Unless the parent is in recovery, those working with these children report they generally do *not* know:

- What normal drinking is
- That their alcoholic parent has a disease
- That troubles with the alcoholic parent are not their fault
- That they cannot stop the drinking
- That the alcoholic cannot just stop drinking
- That their alcoholic parent loves them

- That they are not the only ones who have this "family secret."

Cork (1982), in one of the few studies directly asking CoAs about their feelings concerning family life and parental drinking, interviewed 115 middle- and upper-class children aged 10 to 16 who were from intact homes. Every child felt in some way affected by a parent's drinking. More than 90 percent expressed a lack of self-confidence and feelings of being unloved and rejected by one or both parents. More than 50 percent felt anger and disrespect for the alcoholic parent. In most cases, there was also resentment toward the nonalcoholic parent, who was perceived as being responsible for the spouse's drinking and unresponsive to the child's needs.

Significantly, only 5 percent of these children reported that drunkenness or drinking was their main concern. For over 90 percent of the children, it was the parents' constant fighting and quarreling that was most distressing. Other studies of children also have found that the atmosphere of extreme tension and argumentativeness in alcoholic families seems more upsetting than the drinking per se (Wilson and Orford 1978).

In comparing their families to those of friends, CoAs felt they did not have a "real family" because their family did not have fun and do things together (Wilson and Orford 1978). Clinicians have observed that alcoholic families are socially isolated due to the shame associated with the drinking problem, the family's state of disorganization, and the inability of the family to conform to social expectations (Morehouse 1979; Barnes 1977).

In terms of attitudes toward personal use, considerable research has shown that a change in attitude occurs before children start using a mind-altering substance outside of parental supervision. The child's underlying attitude changes from opposing to favoring use. Several researchers have found that young children in general are mildly negative toward using alcohol and that they become increasingly negative until about age 10. Between grades five and six (ages 10 to 11) a significant shift starts to occur toward more positive attitudes about drinking alcohol (Pisano and Rooney 1988). At the same time, children also become more receptive to the influence of their peers (Pisano and Rooney 1988).

This same type of shift in attitude is presumably occurring among children of alcoholics and other drug users. Deutsch (1982) states that the different attitudes of CoAs toward alcohol can be seen in children at very early ages; the differences are so marked that they can be used to identify CoAs with surprising accuracy. One of these differences is that these children are determined that this will never happen to them; that they themselves will never drink.

Other differences in the young, preadolescent CoAs' attitudes, according to Deutsch (1982), include the following: a heightened awareness of drunkenness, the inability to recognize as drinking any intake of alcohol that does not result in drunkenness, and a mixture of fear and fascination—probably mainly fear—that leads them to believe that alcohol is evil and should be banned. Alcohol may always be an emotionally loaded topic for these children, unless they receive help in dealing with it. Because of the "don't talk" rule and the denial in many alcoholic families, CoAs are unlikely to talk at home about their vulnerability to alcoholism or their other concerns about chemical dependency (Lehr and Schrock 1987).

Deutsch (1982) reports that 8-year-olds acknowledge their fear that alcohol will do to them what it did to their parents. Teenagers will not acknowledge this fear. Adolescents, because of their developmental need for independence and individuation from the parent, deny that the parent's behavior may influence their own. The teenager, feeling invulnerable, shrugs off the fear of being an alcoholic like the parent.

Behavioral Intentions and Practices

American children in general start drinking at younger ages than in the past. According to Gordon and McAlister (1982), the first drinking experience usually occurs around age 12 in contrast to ages 13 to 14 in the 1940s and 1950s. Some children as young as 10 to 12 years old have serious alcohol problems.

Discouraging facts emerged from a recent survey about the health knowledge, attitudes, and behavior of America's teenagers (Marwick 1988). This survey of 11,419 students in grades 8 and 10 in 217 schools indicates that many young people do not make the right health decisions. They are careless about avoiding injury, frequently consider suicide, are fundamentally ignorant about sexually transmitted diseases, and use alcohol and other drugs and tobacco despite warnings.

Although adolescent use of alcohol and other drugs has decreased since the 1970s, more than one-fourth of eighth-grade students and more than one-third of tenth-grade students say they have had five or more drinks on a single occasion within the 2 weeks preceding the survey (Marwick 1988). Among tenth-grade students, 35 percent say they have tried marijuana and 9 percent report they have tried cocaine. Other researchers (Ahmed et al. 1984) report that among teenagers the willingness to risk injury and illness predict the intent to use and actual use of alcohol and cigarettes; willingness to risk illness is also associated with the intent to use and actual use of marijuana.

There is no evidence that the percent of CoAs who start using alcohol during their teenage years is any higher than in the general population. In Cork's study of 10- to 16-year-old CoAs, more than half the children said they would not drink, the major reasons being fear of becoming like the alcoholic parent, belief that drinking disrupts family life, belief that drinking is wrong on health or moral grounds or because it hurts other people. More than one-third of the children intended to drink as adults or were already drinking; Cork (1982) felt that these children were among the most disturbed in the study and among those most likely, without outside help, to misuse alcohol or become dependent on it.

Once they start drinking, vulnerable children of alcoholics or drug abusers may find that they have a hard time controlling their use of alcohol and other drugs. These children may be firmly convinced that alcoholism or other drug addiction will never happen to them, yet they have no clear idea of how much is too much. Some of these youths are depressed and find that alcohol helps them "feel normal" (Kumpfer 1987a). Based on the medical literature concerning the differences in the effect of alcohol on children of alcoholics or drug abusers versus other youth, Kumpfer (1987a) thinks it possible that "children from substance-abusing families may outperform other kids when under the influence. 'Cool,' competent, normal kids become sloppy and funny, while shy, unsocial children from substance-abusing families become brave and confident" (p. 3).

Youth in treatment for chemical dependency are more likely to come from alcoholic homes. One study of 1,900 patients in treatment for alcoholism (about one-fourth of them women) looked at the progress of the alcoholism in terms of family history (McKenna and Pickens 1980). Children of two alcoholics were more likely than children of one alcoholic, who in turn were more likely than children of nonalcoholics, to be younger when first intoxicated, to show a more rapid course between first intoxication and admission to treatment, and to have more pretreatment behavioral problems. The number of alcoholic parents was directly related to the severity of the alcoholism and to such increased psychopathology as aggressiveness and depression (McKenna and Pickens 1981).

The teenage child of an alcoholic, according to Deutsch (1982), drinks alcohol as he or she has learned to drink it—abusively. Some of these children may be like the recovered alcoholic; they may simply not be able to pick up a drink without calling forth their whole unresolved relationship with alcohol. For children from chemical-abusing homes, alcohol may be serving a number of functions, including

- A chance to release pent-up feelings of anger and aggression and to strike back at both parents

- A chance to obliterate feelings of depression as well as guilt over how nonabusing family members will feel about the drinking

- An opportunity to attract the family's attention and perhaps bring them together

- A chance to excel with friends and gain their approval (one sign of vulnerability to alcoholism is the ability to "hold one's liquor" without visibly being affected, a trait that can be much admired among the young)

- A chance to become a different person (both alcoholics and teenage problem drinkers tend to have very different personalities when they are drunk than when they are sober, so the shy, uncertain person may become jovial and fun-loving).

Deutsch (1982) also explains the vicious cycle that develops for the child of an alcoholic who is abusing alcohol. Friends who use alcohol occasionally will begin to distance themselves from the CoA who is drinking abusively and often. The child is often not aware that he or she has lost friends because of the drinking. New friends need to be found, and they are chosen for the way they drink.

CoAs often do not think drinking is a problem even though they have been in trouble with the law on several occasions; they need to overlook any connection between the drinking and their problems. They need to believe the lie that they could quit drinking if they wanted to. In the alcoholic home, denial was a habit learned and internalized—a long-standing way of protecting the self from actual events. Deutsch recommends that CoAs be given help in understanding their parents' denial about alcohol, so that they have a chance to see in advance the tricks and turns that a person uses to deny drinking problems. Really confronting denial—their own and their families'—would then help them see these tactics in themselves if they should develop drinking problems later.

For some adolescent CoAs, there may be a temporary protective factor in having an alcoholic parent, the children having vowed never to be like their alcoholic parent. However, they may become prone to alcohol or other drug use in later adolescence or early adulthood because of depression and stress (Russell et al. 1985). As adults, about 30 percent of the children of alcoholics are alcoholic themselves (Miller and Jang 1977).

Research Needs

The state of knowledge about those at risk for alcohol and other drug use somewhat resembles the pioneers' knowledge about the American West. The pioneers' destination and direction were clear, but they knew little about the particular routes for getting from one coast to the other. We don't know enough about the various paths to alcohol and other drug problems, especially for the general population. Alcoholism has many causes; moreover, the nature of the different types of alcoholism and their specific precursors have not been defined. Also, more research is needed to differentiate the risk factors related to infrequent, illegal drug use from those related to compulsive, dysfunctional drug use (Battjes and Jones 1985).

The list of factors placing a person at higher risk for alcohol and other drug problems is a long one, and research does indicate which factors seem to be the more serious. While the constellation of risks seems undisputed, the process of interrelationship among these risks has not been clarified. Which problems precede and which follow, and for which types of alcoholism and drug use? Does depression, for example, precede some types of parental dysfunction? The action and interaction of risk factors over time, from early childhood, need to be clarified.

Some of the questions that lack definitive answers include the following:

- What are the patterns of risk for minorities and cultural groups, and how do these differ from the patterns of those with Northern European ancestry—a group at particular risk for alcohol problems?

- Who are the children most at risk for marijuana and other illegal drug use, and prescription drug misuse?

- What are the biomedical risk factors for alcohol and for the many other different drugs used and abused?

- How is sensation-seeking related to adolescent drug use?

- Does use of crack, because of its fast addictive properties, pose a greater risk for the general population than alcohol use?

- What protective factors will be most influential for helping particular types of children?

- Based on the "stages" theory of use, can one prevent more extreme drug use by preventing use of a "precursor" substance (such as tobacco)?

- What are the key factors for young children in developing the "intent to use" that begins to emerge in later elementary school years? How do children's health orientations and behavior in general develop over those early years?

- In a society where alcohol use is widely accepted and heavily promoted, is it possible to stop initial use by the teenagers who are most at risk—those who find they feel better physically or emotionally when they drink and, therefore, cannot stop? How can nonuse messages be made acceptable?

- How can preventionists reduce risk factors—that is, deal with the attitudes and behaviors that promote problems, not just the drug use, which may be symptomatic of underlying problems?

- What are the knowledge, attitudes, and behaviors of specific subgroups of youth (e.g., low socioeconomic status and ethnic minorities)?

Insufficient information exists to provide a reliable basis for developing communications strategies.

- How can promising strategies be tested? Demonstrations or similar efforts may begin to provide clues to what knowledge is needed, which attitudes may be shaped, and which behaviors should be targeted to prevent alcohol and other drug problems, especially among high-risk youth.

- Are high-risk youth more susceptible to pro-use advertising and promotions, and, if so, from what sources—the media, peers (which?), older siblings, etc.?

- Are they receptive to nonuse messages and, if so, from whom and through which channels? Research is needed with regard to what makes high-risk audiences become receptive to any alcohol and other drug messages.

- Should specific gender-related issues regarding high-risk youth be considered? (For example, should male-specific messages be designed for those antisocial boys who are at high risk, and, if so, should they be aimed at elementary-age boys when this behavior pattern is first emerging?)

Planning Considerations

Target audiences. Segment the audience according to

- Type of risk—children who fall into one or more of the categories identified by P.L. 99-750, including children with conduct disorders and children of alcoholics and other drug abusers

- Age—consider educational and emotional level as well as chronological age

- Gender—for messages to older youth in particular

- Socioeconomic status

- Ethnic background

- Drinking/drug use status

- Substance used

- Type of family dysfunction—CoAs and CoDAs may have different needs.

Channels

- Schools, including alternative schools

- National organizations, especially those with local affiliates

- Businesses in high-risk, urban environments
- Community resources, such as WIC sites, convenience stores, laundromats
- Media, including daytime entertainment programming, TV curricula, PSAs, docudramas
- Health care sites.

Sources

- Parents (for younger children)
- Peers (for children in intermediate and high schools)
- Teachers and counselors
- Athletes
- Law enforcement personnel
- Ministers and other spiritual leaders
- Youth group and other community leaders.

Materials

- Available materials include
    - Videotapes, books, booklets, brochures, comics, coloring books, posters, curricula
    - Materials targeted primarily to a broad audience
    - Some materials targeted to CoAs, including videotapes, comics, coloring books, and puppets.
- Needed are
    - Materials targeted to specific, high-risk populations
    - Low-literacy materials
    - Materials for fathers
    - Training materials.

Messages

- Messages for families should
    - Acknowledge the difficulty of parenting
    - Stress the support parents can give each other

— Approach parents as partners

— Present a balanced view of children

— Provide sample parent-child dialogues

— Define what is overly strict and overly permissive

— Demonstrate positive parenting

— Provide information to parents about risk factors and how to detect risk in their children

— Provide information that empowers parents and children to ask for help

— Identify appropriate resources

— Avoid blaming or stigmatizing the family.

• Messages for high-risk youth should

— Give as complete a message as possible

— Develop materials that help develop skills, such as social skills and refusal skills

— Instill reasons for not using alcohol and other drugs

— Suggest positive alternatives to alcohol and other drug use in order to influence behavior

— Combine a variety of messages and strategies for each high-risk group that is targeted

— Provide information about resources

— Avoid stigmatizing CoAs and CoDAs and other children from high-risk environments.

Concentrated focus on children at high risk for alcohol and other drug problems began only in the mid-1980s. Yet already, there is an impressive level of consensus on guidelines for reaching this population. Over and over, in telephone interviews with researchers and clinicians and in research reports, the following points are made about planning communications programs for this audience:

• *Use multiple interventions.* There is not going to be any simple communications message—any "magic bullet"—that can stop the vulnerability of the high-risk child. Most dysfunctional families have a cluster of interrelated problems (risk factors). Communications and change strategies should be designed to address as many risk factors as possible, with multiple interventions through the media, school, community, and interpersonal contacts.

- *Pretest all messages and materials.* It is suspected that high-risk youth may hear and interpret messages differently from message developers or other children. Messages designed for "mainstream" youth (such as "just say no") may be ineffective or even counterproductive for the high-risk child.

- *Conceptualize problems and strategies in three areas:* (a) dysfunction of the family; (b) dysfunction of parents; and (c) dysfunction of the parenting role. These distinctions are important for designing messages that enlist positive parental involvement, rather than generating resistance.

- *Begin with motivation and information, leading to the building and practice of skills,* such as family management. Media communications strategies may be particularly valuable in the early stages of this process and in later reinforcement.

- *Develop long-term programs.* Intervention strategies should have continuity instead of being one-shot approaches; there need to be follow-through and skill-building with goals and expectations that are both realistic and meaningful to the high-risk child and family.

Audience Segments

An understanding of the great diversity in high-risk children and their families is essential for all communications planning. Although there is a need to identify those themes that matter to all families, whether rich or poor, urban or rural, professional or unskilled, many materials, even on the same topics, will need to be tailored to a specific segment of the high-risk audience. Based on input received from professionals working in the field, high-risk families can be segmented according to the following factors:

- *Age.* Communications should be appropriate for the youth's cognitive, educational, and developmental level. Older children have more complex ways of viewing the world, can conceptualize, and can generalize and think in abstractions. High-risk youth, however, may have low literacy skills and relatively poor role models for inductive or deductive reasoning, and may therefore, even as older youth, have difficulty dealing with abstractions.

- *Gender.* Messages, images, and other appeals may begin to be male- and female-specific as youth go through puberty, and special messages are appropriate for teenage boys and girls.

- *Socioeconomic status.* Messages, images, and appeals need to be appropriate for youth according to socioeconomic status. For example, affluent teenagers react negatively to street communication messages and images, and vice versa.

- *Ethnic background.* Little is known about the different perception of messages by teenagers from varying cultural and ethnic backgrounds.

- *Drinking/drug use status.* At-risk youth who are nonusers need to be differentiated, for communications purposes, from at-risk youth who are using alcohol and other drugs. Some experts believe that nonuse messages, especially for high-risk youth, are perceived by them as showing caring and protection; others believe that strong nonuse messages may be perceived by high-risk youth as issues to rebel against.

- *Substance used.* Information is needed for youth that classifies the effects of drugs, rather than giving information on specific drugs. The music groups to which teenagers listen help show what drugs they use, and may help to identify which youth are likely to use which drugs.

- *Type of family dysfunction.* Children from alcohol-abusing and drug-abusing families face somewhat different problems, such as whether illegality, crime, and jail are involved for the parent. Some believe, for instance, that CoAs have an overdeveloped conscience (always wanting to do the "right" thing), whereas they believe that CoDAs may have underdeveloped consciences (e.g., "I don't care who I hurt").

- *Type of risk.* Children who fall into one of the categories identified by P.L. 99-750 as amended (see introduction to this chapter) could be targeted. Children with conduct disorders and children of alcoholics or drug abusers are also important audience segments.

Channels

National organizations

Communications planners should consider expanding the roster of organizations that are usually involved in alcohol and other drug use prevention, intervention, and treatment issues. Many national organizations have issues affecting multiproblem children and families as their primary agenda. The significance of alcohol and other drug use in other problem behavior, such as juvenile delinquency, child abuse, sexual abuse, teen pregnancy, traffic fatalities, crime, homelessness, and youth suicide, is often not recognized by these organizations. It is likely that many organizations not currently involved in alcohol and other drug communications efforts could be mobilized to participate.

Local organizations may be fearful about implementing strategies for high-risk children, stereotyping them as violent and out of control. Alcohol and other drug organizations may be able to address and allay these fears, and to ensure that such stereotyping does not occur. Local leaders may need to be told that they already have many high-risk youth in their group.

See chapter 6 for a detailed discussion of working with intermediaries and appendix E for a list of specific intermediary organizations that could be approached.

Businesses

Local businesses and corporations are extremely important to enlist in intermediary efforts. Many businesses need motivated and prosocial youth and young adults to fill their current need for employees. Some of the most innovative ideas for helping disadvantaged young people have come from those in businesses, and high-risk young people in high-density urban areas desperately need the skills motivation and job training—and the jobs—that industry can provide. In addition, worksites may offer opportunities for communicating with parents and improving their parenting skills (i.e., lunchtime seminars). In addition, industry's employee assistance programs (EAPs) can help intervene with problem drinkers, getting them into treatment and reinforcing their recovery. Through EAP programs, the spouses and children of alcoholics and other drug abusers also may be reached directly and indirectly.

Community channels

Community channels may be used to encourage and motivate high-risk families to seek help, but only if community resources exist to provide this help, even for low-income residents. This help may include addressing underlying factors such as parenting, job skills, and improved nutrition. Alcohol and other drug messages, per se, may be ignored until other, more immediately pressing issues are resolved.

For well-educated or high-literacy high-risk families, community channels might include bulletin boards and printed information generated by community sources. Locations where the information can be placed may include

- Public and parochial schools
- Adult education sites
- Community colleges
- Public libraries
- Women's resource centers
- Women's studies centers
- City/county parks and recreation departments

- YMCAs
- YWCAs
- Jewish community centers.

Early innovators may live in housing projects as well as in middle-income homes. For example, a mother in the Alexandria, Virginia, Cameron Valley public housing development became concerned when 17 project children "failed" in elementary school. Realizing the problem was lack of preschool experience for the public housing children, she helped organize a housing project preschool that, with financial help from a church congregation, has thrived for 4 years and ended school failure for the project's first graders (*The Washington Post*, March 23, 1988). Media that reach women in the projects can help empower them to take action. Appropriate media channels might be daytime television for those who do not work, Black radio stations, signs on buses, or materials distributed by churches or by tenants' associations in housing project meeting rooms.

Community resources where lower income families may see notices, bulletins, or information include

- Housing projects
- Administration for Children, Youth, and Families offices
- WIC centers; youth and drug agencies
- Methadone and health care clinics
- Grocery, convenience, liquor, and thrift stores
- Child protective services
- Lunch counters, diners, and bars
- Laundromats
- Movie theaters
- Recreation centers (e.g., basketball courts, bowling alleys)
- Beauty parlors and barber shops
- Churches and other religious settings
- Herbalists
- Shelters.

Communications strategies may be used to convince many agencies to become involved; a multiple approach is called for because high-risk environments produce multiproblem families and youth. These strategies may also help to overcome some of the fears of teachers, social workers, and others who deal with those from high-risk environments (e.g., help a teacher to understand that an overly aggressive boy may have developed this behavior as a coping mechanism to deal with a father who molests him, and then provide knowledge to help the boy develop more appropriate skills for dealing with such threatening situations).

The media

Media gatekeepers are an essential target for communications strategies. The media can be especially valuable in two key areas. First, both broadcast and print media can be used to motivate parents and youth to get help and can provide some initial information on skills. Second, television can help to reinforce healthy and safe behaviors. Media also can be very valuable in telling citizens about successful programs and raising public awareness and commitment for local programs.

High-risk families with low literacy skills may best be reached through the electronic media. For example, children and their parents, if unemployed, may watch daytime commercial television; they may not be reached effectively by printed media geared to audiences at a higher reading level. Improving literacy level, in and of itself, may be an important prevention strategy that could be tested using appropriate research methodologies. Radio is also a viable communications medium, particularly if the material has been targeted according to specific listening patterns.

Television is a major information resource for families. (See chapter 4, Reaching Parents, for more information on viewing habits.) Here is a sampling of television programs that could be useful in a communications program to prevent youthful alcohol and other drug use.

- Television programs focused on how to prevent children from using drugs (model: Preparing for the Drug-Free Years, which discusses setting firm but reasonable expectations and getting families involved in activities; Hawkins et al. 1987a)

- Parenting workshops on television in conjunction with docudramas on families whose teenagers have drug problems; followup can be community workshops conducted by trainers

- Television curricula (model: the Nova series on the brain)

- Television homework assignments for parents/children in conjunction with outstanding television programs on drugs; could include teacher guides and parent/child workshops

- Inclusion of high-risk issues in segments of television documentary or dramatic series

- Commercials or PSAs—for example, OSAP grantees talking about parenting and urging families to participate in community family training programs.

Many more uses of television may be appropriate, and as more creative uses of television are developed, such as programs fed directly into schools, the uses may expand.

Newspapers and magazines offer the advantage of space to discuss often complex high-risk issues in greater depth, either in one feature article or through a series of articles. Such coverage can include the problem and suggested solutions, including referral to community resources for help. Through concerted community efforts, a special newspaper supplement could be sponsored by a group of concerned businesses and agencies. Unlike television and radio coverage, this printed information can be saved and shared or read again.

Schools

The schools are the only U.S. institution that consistently reaches most young children. Schools are a setting where children can be helped directly and effectively. Experts stress the importance of encouraging schools to provide more help to high-risk children.

Once students drop out of school, it becomes very difficult to reach them. For such youth, alternative schools can be a promising institutional channel. The Street Academy Model, Cities-in-Schools, and the Rich's Department Store alternative school in Atlanta, Georgia, offer demonstrations of this concept. Channels for reaching youth in trouble can be community organizations (e.g., the Boys Club Targeted Outreach and Smart Moves programs). Traditional community groups can be successfully set up in juvenile justice settings (model: Boy Scout troops in juvenile detention centers). Not all young people who are in trouble with school or the law are involved in acting-out behavior; many are looking for structure in their lives. Others may be acting out as a way of asking for structure.

Health care sites

Physicians' offices, clinics, hospital waiting areas, and community health centers are logical and useful settings for distributing information and for carrying out communications programs. More information on reaching health professionals will be found in chapter 5.

Interpersonal channels

The channels listed above all represent fairly traditional avenues for reaching general populations who are at least somewhat motivated to receive or seek out information or services. They may not, however, be the best channels for reaching families and youth who are often disconnected, isolated, fearful, alienated, and distrusting of much considered to be mainstream. Such families may perceive their current lifestyles as relatively comfortable because they are at least familiar. Many of these families appear to be resistant to asking for help, perhaps because of an overwhelming sense of shame, guilt, or embarrassment or because of cultural mores that view asking for help as a sign of weakness. These barriers, identified most often in retrospect by experts working with high-risk families, suggest that interpersonal, one-on-one channels may be more effective than traditional channels. The channel, as well as the message and source, must be culturally sensitive and appropriate.

Sources

The credibility of sources may vary with target audience age. Parents are generally a key source of information during early years, with peers becoming more influential at about the junior high level. (However, parents can continue to be a strong influence on teenagers, particularly when parent/child bonds are close.) High-risk youth, on the other hand, even at younger ages, may not view parents as credible sources of information. They may be more receptive to messages from any adult they perceive to be caring or loving toward them (e.g., a teacher, scout leader, or minister). However, more research is needed.

Social service providers may also serve as sources. The high-risk child or parent may be identified at any of many points within the community social, health, or juvenile justice service network, and may need help from a number of different agencies simultaneously. For example, a high-risk single parent may be an immature teenager, dependent on drugs, in need of health care, under-educated, unemployed, threatened with homelessness, and having little family support.

Many types of social service providers can act as gatekeepers for programs to reach youth, including those reaching others through education, welfare and social services, religious institutions, recreation activities, transportation, juvenile justice, or health and wellness services. Even a local Department of Motor Vehicles, as part of its effort to reduce traffic fatalities, may be persuaded to assist in these efforts.

Gatekeepers could include

- Counselors/trainers in parenting education
- Day-care/preschool/Head Start personnel
- School personnel, including nurses, maintenance engineers, and coaches

- Drug/alcohol treatment personnel
- Youth organization leaders (e.g., Boy Scouts, Girls and Boys Clubs, Big Brother/Big Sister, 4-H Club)
- Summer camp and recreation counselors
- Law enforcement officers
- Probation officers
- Welfare agency personnel
- Staff at clinics serving teenage girls
- Mental health personnel
- Motor vehicle personnel
- A parolee who can convince others that "doing time" is not a status symbol
- Valued athletes
- Nutritionists and herbalists
- Spiritual leaders
- Politicians
- Other helpers such as the local barber
- Sororities/fraternities
- Extended family members
- Peers with positive attitudes.

Materials Review

Availability

A nationwide search for alcohol and other drug education materials located an abundance of products pertaining to high-risk parents and children (for tally, see table 5).* Materials came from all major alcohol/drug organizations and sources (e.g., the National Council on Alcoholism, Alcoholics Anonymous, the Johnson Institute), from State agencies, from many commercial publishing firms, and from small, dedicated vendors (e.g., the Feelings Factory in North Carolina).

---

*More information on these materials is available from the National Clearinghouse for Alcohol and Drug Information (NCADI); see appendix E.

Table 5. High-Risk Families/Youth Product Tally

Total Products Received: 731			
Videotapes	185	Comic books	6
Brochures	106	Newsletters	6
Books	92	Articles	6
Booklets	85	Card games	6
Posters	44	Information packages	5
PSAs	43	TV transcripts	5
Workbooks	28	Overhead transparencies	4
Curricula	26	Games	2
Fact Sheets	15	Script	1
Reports	15	Other	7
Classroom material	11	Dolls Puppets	
Audiotapes	10	Coloring books Bookmarks	
Magazines	9	Conference proceedings	
Software	8		

Overall, the quality of the materials was high. The technical quality of the videos was especially gratifying; a number moved beyond information delivery to present compelling, believable, and often touching messages and stories. In general, the finest products came from sources that are actively involved in alcohol/other drug prevention or treatment programs, where hands-on experience had been combined with professional video or print production. One example of such a product is the family activity workbook *Preparing for the Drug-Free Years* (Hawkins et al. 1987a). Another is the Johnson Institute's book *Choices and Consequences* (Schaefer 1987), which describes a coordinated intervention strategy for schools involving parents and the criminal justice system.

Commercially produced materials tended to be targeted to a broad, general audience and to focus on awareness and information. Many basic, short information pieces were received on both alcohol and drugs.

Many small, inexpensive products describing the intervention process with adult alcoholic family members were received from Al-Anon Family Group Headquarters and other sources. Several clear, compassionate, and upbeat booklets and videos are available on this topic. Several books and videos for caregivers on the treatment of teenagers and their families were received, and these reflect recent treatment approaches. One Canadian relapse-prevention program for adults—with videos and manuals—might be a model for adaptation with teenagers (Alberta Alcohol and Drug Abuse Commission 1987).

One series of videotapes from the Massachusetts's Governor's Youth Alliance Against Drug Abuse (Boston Neighborhood Network Television 1986–1987) portrays realistic youth scenes involving drug problems, such as a sixteenth birthday party and a victory celebration. Part one of each tape shows teens acting out a problem scenario; part two shows community forums in which teens discuss issues raised in the part one scenario. Tapes can be shown with just the first story, to trigger discussion, or with the forum included.

Many materials for children of alcoholics, especially of elementary school age, have been developed since 1980. These are often colorful and upbeat, and provide helpful, reassuring messages. Examples include videos, comic books, coloring books, puppets, activity guides, posters, and group-session curricula. Some sources include the Johnson Institute, Alcoholics Anonymous, and Al-Anon Family Group Headquarters. The Children of Alcoholics Foundation has several colorful, practical brochures about how specifically to help CoAs, and the National Association for Children of Alcoholics (NACoA) is an excellent source of information on available materials. A comprehensive resource list of materials for elementary school CoAs has been compiled by OSAP and is available through the NCADI (see appendix E).

An elementary school resource list is also included in a new guide for elementary schools, available from NACoA (see appendix E for address). Called *It's Elementary: Meeting the Needs of High-Risk Youth in the School Setting*, this new guidebook is part of a series of materials in the NACoA "It's Elementary" project. Other materials include a teacher's guide for CoAs, a Spider Man comic book for children on emotional abuse, and a series of Marvel Comics posters carrying the message, "Some Moms and Dads drink too much...and it hurts." A school-based training film, now in the planning stage, will be available by 1990; a training program for elementary schools is also being developed. The Children of Alcoholics Foundation sponsors a traveling exhibit of art by CoAs available for schools in fall 1989.

Gaps in what is available

The collection process brought in few hands-on materials for program directors to use in carrying out workshops, group sessions, and training, and there was a severe shortage of materials aimed toward working with minority cultures. Most workbooks and group session guides that were received reflected current prevention techniques. Predominant topics included how to handle peer pressure, build social and decisionmaking skills, and teach assertiveness and refusal skills.

No materials were received addressed to fathers, foster parents, or adoptive parents. A few items, including a videotape, pertained to latchkey children home alone but dealt strictly with safety issues and did not include alcohol or other drug matters. Almost no materials were located for parents of preschool children on identifying risk factors in young children and on communicating with them in ways designed to help reduce later drug/alcohol problems. Very few materials are now available for single parents and for low-income parents. (For a review and description of parent training curricula, including those for minority groups and substance-abusing parents, see DeMarsh and Kumpfer 1986.)

Information about what puts a young child at special risk of alcohol or other drug use, and how to help the child, is not available in the popular literature for parents. All types of materials are needed, from videos that demonstrate high-risk behavior to brochures and checklists for parents.

Some brochures are available on recognizing the signs of alcohol or other drug use in children and youth, but there is little concrete material for parents on how to choose treatment or find a counselor. Materials of the Toughlove parent support groups provide excellent hands-on help to parents of youth who are out of control; this approach seems to be a suitable one for families with younger children who need to be protected. Materials from the Johnson Institute provide excellent intervention guidance for parents or those working with alcohol- or drug-dependent youth.

Very few materials, except for those available from the Johnson Institute and Toughlove (York et al. 1982), address the intervention process with teenagers. Almost no materials were received for gatekeepers or parents dealing with teenage treatment issues, and none were received on relapse prevention for teens.

Appropriate messages for high-risk, acting-out teenagers tend to be embedded in materials for general youth audiences. Almost nothing specifically targets the teenager who is at risk because of his or her own behavior and who needs to know the effects of alcohol on depression and anxiety.

Areas in which materials need to be developed include the following:

- Materials for parents on raising children in high-risk environments
- Materials for low-literacy groups (the general reading level of material received was about twelfth grade), such as illustrated pamphlets for the low-literacy, pregnant teenager on parenting skills and how to get help
- Materials for out-of-school, alienated teenagers
- Upbeat, exciting media materials for kids who are already using alcohol or other drugs
- Materials targeted to fathers
- Materials for the single-parent family or two-parent working family on prevention with the latchkey child
- Posters (the limited number received came from only a few sources)
- Trigger films (open-ended films used to stimulate discussion)
- Information on project ideas and successful models for hard-to-reach, high-risk kids
- Information on risk factors/protective factors for parents, teachers, and caregivers
- Materials that deal with the importance of alcohol/drugs in family dysfunction, including emotional and physical child abuse, sexual abuse, juvenile delinquency, traffic accidents, family violence, teenage suicide, and runaways
- Training and other materials for gatekeepers and caregivers (Examples include videos showing teachers how to communicate with a troubled child who is timidly seeking assistance; videos demonstrating to parents and to preschool caregivers the behavioral signs of a child who is at high risk; fact sheets for social workers who deal with family violence or runaways on the relationship of these problems to family alcohol and other drug use.)
- Information on the genetic/familial vulnerability of some children to alcohol and other drug problems
- Materials for minority groups
- Information on the intervention and treatment process with teenagers.

Subsequent chapters contain more detailed discussions of materials available and needed for specific audiences.

Messages

Messages for families

Many parents who have alcohol and other drug problems will be in a state of denial about the personal and family difficulties caused by this behavior. In addition to this form of denial, stressed and dysfunctional parents in general may be resistant to direct parent training. Parents may not want to hear that they could be responsible for their children's problems or that they are not rearing their children correctly. High-risk, troubled parents may not want to admit they are failing as parents.

For these reasons, it may be advisable to approach parents as partners—to offer a "parent partnership," not parent training. "Family training" can also be used as a euphemism for parent training. Help to families can be couched in terms of "helping children succeed in school" or "preparing children for the drug-free years" (Hawkins et al. 1987a). Parents welcome information about how to help their children, and parenting skills can be built within that framework. This sort of approach also avoids stigmatizing the high-risk or troubled family, an important consideration.

A range of messages and strategies for parents has been suggested. These include the following:

- Stress the community of parents: "Parenting can be confusing...can be fun," "Let's talk about kids—all kids—my kids, your kids, his kids, her kids."

- Present a balanced view of children—the positive and negative sides, the discouragement and the joy.

- Stress that all parenting is hard—"You're a success if you don't give up."

- Communicate sample dialogues, such as some of those in the "Talking With Your Kids About Alcohol" (TWYKA) curriculum (Prevention Research Institute, Lexington, Kentucky).

- Define what is meant by "overly strict" and "overly permissive" parenting, recommending specific rules and consequences (models: Hawkins, *Preparing for the Drug-Free Years*; Glenn, *Developing Capable Young People*).

- Teach parents to be "play therapists," using observations (model: Guerney Filial Therapy Program).

- Help families plan family activities, including how to conduct a family meeting (model: Hawkins, *Preparing for the Drug-Free Years*).

- Provide guidelines on what are reasonable expectations for children at different ages.

- Appeal to all parents' natural wish to see their children happy and successful.

In addition, for the family with a high-risk child, one message may be, "You can be a great parent for your other kids, but still need help with your special-needs child." It is important to combat the parents' feeling that they are bad parents. Parents with adopted children who may be genetically vulnerable to addiction may need special help in knowing both protective factors and danger signs.

Messages for youth

Those developing materials and messages for all children must be careful not to stigmatize or label the child. This is particularly true of CoAs and CoDAs who may already feel different and isolated from mainstream society. In developing communications messages and campaigns for young people, experts make the following recommendations:

- Give as complete a message as possible.

- To be complete, go beyond giving knowledge alone.

- Provide information about resources.

- Develop materials that help develop skills, such as social skills and refusal skills.

- Instill reasons for not using alcohol and other drugs.

- Suggest positive alternatives to alcohol and other drug use in order to influence behavior.

- Combine a variety of messages and strategies for each high-risk group that is targeted.

- Include where to go for help, such as hotlines or local prevention/treatment programs, on all media announcements or segments addressed to youth.

- Avoid being overly heterosexist. There is a higher incidence of alcohol and other drug problems among homosexual populations, but messages designed exclusively for heterosexual populations are less likely to be accepted by this at-risk population.

- Combat cultural stereotypes; e.g., media messages might show Black youth who are extremely successful.

Chapters 2 and 3 have more detailed recommendations for developing positive messages for minority youth.

Research is only beginning on how different ethnic/racial groups perceive messages, and too little is known at present. It appears, for example, that some of the current drug education efforts are more acceptable to Black youth than to other groups (Bass, internal communication, OSAP 1988). Focus groups are needed to identify credible sources for messages and to test messages for their power and acceptability with specific ethnic groups.

Barriers to successful communication

Obstacles at many differing levels may impede the delivery and acceptance of communications messages. High-risk families and youth are recognized as a group that is hard to reach, may be resistant to accepting help, and may find behavior change very difficult because of deep-seated and even multigenerational behavior patterns. Those working with high-risk families mention the following as obstacles to be considered in designing communications strategies:

- Lack of credible message sources for families from cultural/racial minority groups (treatment with caregivers of a different cultural/racial background is also difficult)

- Distrust of the "system"

- Denial by families of their family dysfunction and of alcohol and other drug use

- Fear of being stigmatized and of loss of confidentiality

- Lack of concern or respect for experts' opinions about alcohol, since most people have their own personal experience to judge by

- Skepticism about messages that do not fit parents' own experiences around alcohol and/or other drugs

- Distortion of messages heard, because a person's perception of a new message is colored by his or her attitudes and biases, varying experiences, beliefs about what is acceptable, and degree of current use

- Narcissism of parents

- Lack of resources for parenting or counseling services, books, and other aids

- Lack of energy and time to handle anything more on the part of exhausted working parents.

Recommendations

Increase public awareness and support

- Encourage volunteerism
- Alter negative perceptions of high-risk children
- Convey messages of hope
- Build community and social support.

Raise awareness among community organizations and caregivers

- Promote information exchange among communities
- Conduct a community needs assessment and publicize the results
- Announce and reward the network of organizations involved
- Convene groups' leaders in inner-city programs and widely publish their recommendations
- Provide training materials for social service providers to communicate with high-risk youth and families
- Develop materials for day-care providers.

Raise family awareness

- Target high-risk, dysfunctional families
- Target families with very young children
- Develop materials targeted to parents
- Incorporate interpersonal communication components into programs
- Convey messages that focus on family risk factors
- Raise awareness of protective factors.

Develop programs for high-risk youth

- Research and develop effective messages
- Educate all children
- Distribute materials targeted to CoAs and CoDAs
- Incorporate CoA and CoDA information into curricula.

Communications activities can be designed to accomplish several major goals:

- To increase knowledge and understanding about both the risk factors and the protective factors for high-risk families, as well as to encourage ameliorative actions by everyone concerned about these children, whether they are professionals, parents, neighbors, or businesses

- To increase knowledge among community gatekeepers (and individuals) of ideas and programs being adopted by others, and about how to become involved

- To provide a community forum and mobilizing center

- To provide new and expanded opportunities through media and community channels for parents to learn about the effects on families of alcohol and other drugs, to enhance their parenting and family management skills, and, as appropriate, to obtain help for themselves

- To increase both the number and intensity of informal and formal supports (from individuals and institutions) working at the community level to help high-risk children and their families

- To provide motivation and encouragement for ordinary people to contribute to efforts to help families and youth in high-risk environments.

To reach goals such as these, consider the recommendations that follow. These recommendations have emerged from reviews of the literature cited in previous sections and from meetings with the experts who are listed at the end of this chapter. Some ideas pertain particularly to national initiatives; others would be more appropriate at the local or State level. These recommendations do not constitute a systematic program, nor are they prioritized; rather, they are intended to provide program planners with ideas that they can adapt to their own communities, constituencies, and resources.

These fall into four major categories: (1) increasing public awareness and support, (2) raising awareness among community organizations and caregivers, (3) raising family awareness, and (4) developing programs for high-risk children and youth.

Increase Public Awareness and Support

A communications program can raise public awareness and support and mobilize opinion leaders or early innovators. Using the mass media, such a campaign can

- Raise the awareness of citizens about which children are at special risk of alcohol and other drug problems and about the ways in which these children can be helped

- Make people feel personally affected and motivated to do something about the plight of children, and especially the plight of children from high-risk environments

- Suggest the concrete steps people can take as individuals to help these children

- Inform people about positive programs that require collective efforts at the community level.

The public needs to understand that any child—whether rich or poor, living in a city, suburb, or rural area—can be at risk for alcohol and other drug problems. This particular problem, which affects children at all socioeconomic levels, may be used as a rallying point for subsequently helping disadvantaged children.

Recommendations for raising public awareness are discussed below. They include

- Encourage volunteerism

- Alter negative perceptions of high-risk children

- Convey messages of hope

- Build community and social support.

Encourage volunteerism

Professionals, along with caring neighbors and other natural community leaders, need to be able to recognize, and to be motivated to reach out and help, vulnerable children. On the island of Kauai, Werner (1986) found that informal support from a caring relative or friend was more effective than professional help in protecting children from adverse consequences.

It is possible that the Volunteer Office of the Executive Office of the President could be enlisted to organize a program that would use individual volunteers for helping families. Like ACTION's Foster Grandmother program, a national (or local) "Adopt a Family" or "Help One Family" or "Help One Child" program could provide a specific mechanism for help by individuals to individuals. A specific theme, such as "Count On Me," could provide the type of message most helpful to high-risk youth.

However, nothing this organized or ambitious is required. Individuals can be encouraged to invite a child to the zoo, to dinner, to a family outing. Small, kindly gestures that show caring really matter to the high-risk child; the public needs to be aware that such caring can make a tremendous difference in the quality of life for such a child. Parents, grandparents, teachers, older athletes, sorority sisters, rabbis, ministers, tribal chiefs, social service workers, telephone installers, neighbors—what each can do is different. All sectors can use information on this topic—from brief information pieces to videos to workshops to support groups—and can apply the knowledge to make a difference for a child.

Alter negative perceptions of high-risk children

Prevention and treatment experts recommend that communications efforts be directed at transforming certain prevailing social attitudes about high-risk youth, arousing public concern about their plight, and getting people involved in helping them. Negative social attitudes include

- *A sense of hopelessness about these children and about the possibility of helping them.* Several key messages could be developed to influence both opinion leaders and the broader society, such as the following:

  — These children are young and growing and can, therefore, change; working with these children is a hopeful field full of promise.

  — You as an individual can make a tremendous and lifelong difference for a high-risk child; the turning point for a child can be one person who cares.

  — It may take only one event to turn around the life of a child.

  — Many high-risk children, against great odds, grow up into healthy, contributing citizens; with a boost from their schools and their communities, many more of our children can grow up to lead healthy, productive lives.

  — Children from high-risk families often have lots of energy and work very hard (even if it is at defending themselves). This energy could be more positively channeled for increased productivity, decreased health care costs, etc.

- *A rejection of responsibility for these children; lack of concern for the "have nots" by the "haves."* Messages need to instill the sense that each individual can help by taking responsibility for helping a child or for providing some service. Some messages could be these:

  — High-risk youth learn many skills (e.g., negotiation skills) that can be applied to improving productivity for the United States.

  — High-risk children who are cared for are, in turn, more often motivated to help others.

  — Help to a high-risk child today buys all of us a better tomorrow.

- *A perception of high-risk children as unappealing.* Many high-risk youngsters are vulnerable and dependent and do not fit the tough, dangerous stereotype. Messages could include these:

  — Every youth group already includes unidentified young people from high-risk environments.

  — Even an apparently tough street kid often masks a vulnerable, frightened child beneath this facade.

People may become involved only if the message includes concrete actions that they can take. Ideas for such involvement could be to "Adopt a Family," "Adopt a Neighborhood," or be an advocate for a family that needs help in locating community services. Building on the positive attributes developed as a result of living in a high-risk environment could, in fact, contribute to a renewed energy in America.

Convey messages of hope

Communities developing new communications strategies can counteract the sense of hopelessness that so many people feel about drug problems. Extraordinary progress has been made in the last 20 years. Children at risk can be helped. The lives of vulnerable children can be changed. Messages of hope and optimism that can be conveyed to the public include the following:

- *Risk factors are known and many can be eliminated.* Many events and conditions that put children at risk have been identified; the greater the number of risks the child endures, the more vulnerable the child. Many of these risk factors are amenable to change.

- *Protective factors are known; individuals can make a difference.* Many children at high risk grow up to lead useful, healthy lives.

- *Many children at risk for alcohol and other drug problems can be identified and helped early*—at the preschool and early elementary school stage.

- *Preschools can work in breaking the cycle of hopelessness for disadvantaged children.* Project Head Start is an outstanding success story (Schorr 1988).

- *Parents can take actions within their families to reduce the risk of chemical problems in their children.*

- *Alcoholics do not need to hit bottom before they can be helped.* New methods of intervening with the alcoholic have been developed that increase the likelihood that the person will enter treatment.

- *If you are the child of an alcoholic, if you have an alcohol or drug problem yourself, you do not have to face it alone.* Thousands share this problem, and there are support groups with welcoming, caring people to help all over the country. A community hotline would be useful as an ongoing, central reference point for teenagers who may be shy or ashamed or not know how to seek local helping resources aggressively.

- *New intervention and treatment methods have been developed to help the teenager who is abusing alcohol or drugs.* There are now models for parents, schools, and juvenile justice systems to work together in the interest of the child.

- *Help is available for families.* If someone in your family—a husband, wife, child—has a drinking or a drug problem, or if you are worried that someone could be hurt when family members lose their temper—you can do something about it. For this message, a hotline or other referral mechanism would offer families a resource to contact for help.

Build community and social support

Another communications goal related to the general public is to change social norms that implicitly promote alcohol use and encourage abstinence for high-risk and other children.

In the last decade, U.S. attitudes toward youth drinking have crystalized. Instead of State-by-State legal drinking ages, which promoted ambivalence, all States now allow use of alcohol only for those over 21. This public policy of nonuse of alcohol by youth should not be interpreted to mean that "good" kids do not drink and "bad" kids do. The goal for young people is to discourage all drinking because it is illegal for those under age 21. Also, drinking during the early teenage years is particularly dangerous, since more early drinkers develop serious problems with alcohol and with progressing to marijuana and other drugs.

Table 6 shows strategies and potential messages and materials for changing social norms pertaining to children of alcoholics and drug abusers.

Raise Awareness Among Community Organizations and Caregivers

A second broad goal is to raise awareness among organizations and caregivers in order to expand the number of organizations involved in alcohol and other drug communication activities. Recommended strategies include

- Promote information exchange among communities
- Conduct a community needs assessment and publicize the results

Table 6. Increasing Public Awareness and Support

GOAL 1: To raise public awareness and motivate individuals to help high-risk children and their families

SAMPLE THEMES: Lots of kids today need help and you can make a difference ("Be a Friend, Befriend a Child Who Needs You")
"Help a kid off his knees today and that child can stand tall for the rest of his life"
Families are our future: Show that our community cares

COMMUNICATIONS STRATEGIES:

- Increase awareness of the need to help troubled children and motivate a sense of individual responsibility for these children

- Personalize high-risk children, so people do not fear them as only rebellious, difficult kids

- Provide concrete ideas on how to support and help the high-risk child from an alcoholic or other drug-abusing home

- Encourage citizens to participate in community programs for high-risk youth and families

- Instill the sense that all families rearing children need support, be it from friends, relatives, neighbors, or more organized sources

Potential Materials

Short television/video vignettes (with local telephone number) showing what-to-do scenarios (e.g., when you hear a child being beaten through your wall, when you see a child socked by a parent at the grocery store, when you see your neighbor let her child out of her car and walk unsteadily to her front door, etc.); design for use as television segments or as trigger films

Newspaper columns on individuals who are making a difference in people's lives (sample: corner store owner reported in *Washington Post* who gives inner-city children rewards for report cards); provide these sources for television program commentators; send sample clips to trade publications; approach nationally disseminated magazines such as *Reader's Digest*

National or local award for a Helping Neighbor of the Year: nominated like Teachers of the Year by schoolchildren and given national visibility and publicity; also investigate existing Governors' awards and community awards for outstanding citizen volunteers

PSAs showing programs that work, kids in action, promoting idea of helping them and urging individuals to volunteer

Table 6. Increasing Public Awareness and Support (continued)

PSAs by some successful adults who were high-risk children, telling about people who made a difference for them and urging individuals to volunteer or to help a child they know (NACoA could help identify credible spokespersons)

Package for individuals on how to help a child who is a CoA (include brochures, for example, from CoA Foundation)

Brochures/fact sheets on protective factors that neighbors, grandmothers, teachers, and others can carry out

GOAL 2: To change social norms that implicitly promote alcohol use and to encourage abstinence for high-risk and other children

COMMUNICATIONS STRATEGIES:

- Increase the awareness of the public, parents, and children about the familial and genetic vulnerability of CoAs and children of drug abusers (CoDAs)
- Prevent use of alcohol and other drugs in children, particularly CoAs and CoDAs
- Encourage social support for nondrinking by peers

Potential Materials

Develop PSA series on alcoholism and families (model: New York State campaign)

Recycle alcoholism heredity segment of PBS *Brain* series for use as trigger film

Encourage NOVA or other PBS programs to create longer film on heredity issue

Provide technical assistance for storyline on peer pressure/CoA/CoDA vulnerability for television Afterschool Specials series

Develop and publicize brochure for parents on genetic vulnerability combined with protective family factors (model available: New York State)

Encourage articles in layperson's terms in publications such as *Parade, Parents*, and syndicated newspaper health sections

Create fact sheet on vulnerability, including onset of drinking age, and arrange widespread distribution through such vehicles as Prevention Pipeline, National Prevention Network, and the NACoA newsletter

Develop a "Be a Good Buddy" package for kids, using such materials as Children of Alcoholics Foundation brochure on how to help a friend who is a CoA; include new material on vulnerability, and perhaps a "Be a Buddy" sticker, pin, or poster

Arrange an article on peers and CoAs to appear in *My Weekly Reader* or other publications directed to children

- Announce and reward the network of organizations involved
- Convene group leaders in inner-city programs and widely publish recommendations for messages, materials, formats, etc.
- Provide training materials for social service providers to communicate with high-risk youth and families
- Develop materials for day-care providers.

Promote information exchange among communities

Communities differ, and each involved community must determine its own needs, priorities, and resources. At the national level, materials could be designed to share information about what other communities are doing and about what programs and strategies appear to be the most effective. For example, the OSAP High-Risk Demonstration Program grantees are currently developing many strategies and materials that could be shared with other communities. The evaluation of these grants, now underway, will provide much useful information about which strategies seem most successful and can be endorsed by OSAP. The demonstration grants have a strong emphasis on programs for minority and other disadvantaged groups, CoAs and CoDAs, and adolescent gateway drug users. They also include a number of programs for very young children.

Conduct a community needs assessment

Although this report specifically focuses on communications, it is important to recognize that communities need to address many other issues, such as provision of services, social norms, or public policies. A needs assessment can help identify what the community needs most and what role communications can play in meeting those needs. Communicators can promote, disseminate, and use the findings to raise support for programs to address the needs that were identified.

Expand the number of organizations involved

Local companies and foundations may be willing to help fund youth-targeted prevention and treatment programs. A recent survey of grantmakers by Louis Harris and Associates reported a highly positive response (Boys Clubs of America 1988). More than half the grantmakers were currently funding prevention or treatment programs and estimated they would triple their current rate of giving if their requirements for parental involvement and for better information about effective prevention strategies could be met. One-quarter of grantmakers had never been approached for funds on this topic.

The Harris survey found considerable optimism that prevention can make a difference in reducing youth drug and alcohol problems. Business and union leaders and foundations tended to be less aware about prevention activities than those in youth-serving agencies or in the substance abuse counseling field. Grantmakers favored initiating prevention efforts by at least age 10 (experts in the field said prevention should begin by age 6 or younger). Only 20 percent of grantmakers and community leaders thought that genetic predisposition plays a major role in alcohol addiction.

Based on the Harris survey results, the Boys Club report suggests that communications to funding sources and community leaders need to include the following:

- Specific, expert information about up-to-date, effective prevention programs and models

- Plans that involve parents and community leadership

- A focus on the links between youth alcohol and other drug use and other social problems

- As strong an emphasis on alcohol as on other drugs

- An emphasis on the need to start prevention at an early age

- Information about the genetic predisposition to substance abuse

Table 7 provides ideas for raising public awareness through intermediaries.

Provide training materials for social service providers to communicate with high-risk youth and families

In many cases, there is a lack of interdisciplinary exchange among professionals within a community. For example, prevention specialists may not be conversant with social work issues; counselors working with CoAs may miss opportunities for support because they are not familiar with the mental health system. Specific messages might include information on the relationship between alcohol and other drug use as a major factor in much family/youth dysfunction and practical strategies for intervention.

Table 8 offers more suggestions for increasing professional awareness among social service providers.

Table 7. Community Organization/Caregiver Awareness: Networking

GOAL: To increase awareness of the types of communications efforts that would be appropriate in a given community

COMMUNICATIONS STRATEGIES:

- Contact organizations with a high-risk youth agenda, such as child abuse, and mobilize appropriate groups to to help develop communications programs, messages, formats, etc.; widely disseminate the report

- Contact organizations involved in child and family development issues, promoting their participation in the above activity

- Increase awareness by community and professional groups of the strong relationship between alcohol/other drug problems and other social issues, including delinquency, traffic safety, runaways, criminality, child abuse, incest, domestic violence, suicide, and poverty

- Identify the needs for risk-related materials and media support expressed by community, volunteer, and professional groups

Potential Materials

A series of fact sheets showing research findings on the correlation between alcohol/other drugs and other social problems

Products identified or developed in response to organization needs; for example, family drug training/information materials for counselors at such runaway shelters as those run by the Administration for Children, Youth, and Families (ACYF)

Identification of a communications vehicle that could be sent regularly to organizations (e.g., the Learning Community newsletter, updates on a public awareness campaign)

GOAL: To communicate the importance of coordinated prevention services for high-risk families

COMMUNICATIONS STRATEGIES:

- Conduct a community needs assessment and promote/disseminate it widely

- Carry out a two-stage community mobilization campaign using television, town meetings, television closed-circuit conferences

- Explode the myth that nothing works, through television, radio, billboards, bus cards, and other appropriate channels

- Provide guidelines for gatekeepers and for strengthening families

Table 7. Community Organization/Caregiver Awareness: Networking (continued)

Potential Materials

Two 1/2-hour television specials followed by town meetings (models: *The Chemical People*, National Assembly of National Voluntary and Social Welfare Organizations, Inc., program *Making the Grade*) on the theme of what different programs are doing to help families and high-risk children

Followup of national television closed-circuit conferences, with experts on particular categories of high-risk programs, such as CoA groups in schools, family management training in housing projects and welfare agencies, parenting training for pregnant teenagers, etc., with telephone calls from the closed-circuit community sites (model: Brown University High-Risk Youth Video/Teleconferences)

Community planning materials: needs assessment instruments (models available); checklist of types of family services possible; brief list of factors important for success with high-risk families and descriptions of successful models (some sources of information: L. Schorr's *Within Our Reach*, L. Kaplan's *Working With Multiproblem Families*, OSAP's High-Risk Youth Demonstration Program, The Committee for Economic Development's *Children in Need*, and Kumpfer 1986)

Package of materials for communities to use in their education/mobilization efforts: video vignettes of successful programs in action, selected materials produced by OSAP, brochures/fact sheets developed on risk and protective factors

Parenting training models: Compiled from OSAP's technical assistance project (The Circle) assessing/categorizing parent training models and from Office of Juvenile Justice Delinquency Prevention (OJJDP) project (Kumpfer) assessing parent/family models for high risk, delinquent youth

Fact sheet/guidelines for policymakers on the cost savings of prevention programs for children, showing that prevention is a bargain compared to the current cost of our failures (sources of information: *Within Our Reach* by L. Schorr, *Children in Need* by the Committee for Economic Development, NIAAA's *Sixth Special Report to Congress*, Children's Defense Fund, OJJDP cost estimates on delinquency and drugs, etc.)

Fact sheet on foundations now funding or willing to fund prevention programs, reprinted from Louis Harris survey of grantmakers

Package for grantmakers including list of factors important to success (see community planning materials above), descriptions of models for success (see above), new OSAP grant summaries book (in process), briefing paper on value of research in high-risk youth and families field, data sheets on number of youth in high-risk categories (Source: J.G. Dryfoos, *Youth at Risk: One in Four in Jeopardy*, draft report to the Carnegie Corporation of New York)

Table 7. Community Organization/Caregiver Awareness: Networking (continued)

Potential Materials Specifically Addressing Adolescents

Information/products compiled from organizations with adolescent-focused chemical abuse components, such as Carnegie Corporation of New York's Council on Adolescent Development, National Collaboration for Youth (*Making the Grade*), Harvard Center for Health Communications, Scott Newman Foundation, National Council on Alcoholism, OJJPP/OSAP youth-gang project, and OJJDP (Pacific Institute for Research and Evaluation) project to develop a coordinated community services model for youth in trouble

Package on treatment options for youth, containing reprints of articles (e.g., *Update* 6(4), 1988), resource list of training and participant materials, potential reprints or summary of in-process Federal study on adolescent treatment options (Howard Liddle, Ph.D., University of California at San Francisco), a potential listing of 1,900+ inpatient/outpatient adolescent drug-abuse treatment programs (National Association of Addiction Treatment Providers)

Package on intervention with youth for caregivers containing reprints (excerpts from *Choices and Consequences*, Johnson Institute video), flyers advertising manuals on school-based intervention from Student Assistance Programs, reprints of articles on intervention with youth, guidelines for coordinating community intervention services)

Table 8. Professional Awareness
(Technology Transfer and Interdisciplinary Cooperation)

GOAL 1: To raise awareness among service providers about alcohol/drug abuse as a major factor in family/youth dysfunction

COMMUNICATIONS STRATEGIES:

- Raise awareness of both lay and professional people about specific risk and protective factors in children related to later alcohol and other drug problems

- Promote interdisciplinary awareness about the significance of family alcohol/other drug issues in prevention of adolescent suicide, school failure, child abuse, and other major problems

- Expand knowledge about mental health issues among CoA/CoDA gatekeepers and about codependency issues among mental health gatekeepers

- Provide specific practical messages for gatekeepers to use

- Motivate gatekeepers to teach parenting skills to high-risk parents and low socioeconomic groups—groups not effectively served at present

- Raise awareness of the need for a body of interdisciplinary research in the field of high-risk youth and families

- Motivate alcohol/other drug field professionals to coordinate/outreach with other social service providers

GOAL 2: To transfer research findings and knowledge of successful strategies to media professionals (possible mechanisms: conference by Entertainment Industry Council; roster of expert program consultants/interviewees for news and information shows; advisory group on story plots for television/radio situation shows and dramas [model: NIDA AIDS Project described in Backer 1988])

COMMUNICATIONS STRATEGIES:

- Raise awareness of media about what programs and strategies work and about promising new directions

- Provide expert and consistent message resources for television, radio, and print media

- Expand coverage of prevention messages within the news and entertainment arenas

Table 8. Professional Awareness
(Technology Transfer and Interdisciplinary Cooperation)
(continued)

Potential Materials

Slide presentations on significance of alcohol/other drug problems in high-risk youth and families for use at professional conferences

Basic information pieces for CoA field in brief, catchy entertaining formats

Professional conference exhibits/pamphlets re: relation of alcohol/other drug problems to youth suicide, runaways, foster care, and to family child abuse, incest, violence, and other dysfunctional behavior

Fact sheet developed and disseminated to graduate schools of social work

Articles prepared for publication in professional journals

Develop materials for day-care providers

Day-care providers require a range of materials, depending on whether they are professionals or untrained workers at low wages. Some excellent new hands-on material may be developed by grantees in the OSAP High-Risk Youth Demonstration Program.

Raise Family Awareness

This section suggests communications strategies for reaching families, discusses obstacles and how to overcome them, and presents ideas about useful messages, channels, and materials. Table 9 summarizes some of these topics. The overall goals of communications with parents of high-risk children include the following:

- To raise the awareness of parents about high-risk factors and protective factors that affect their children

- To make parents aware of parenting styles and techniques and family management practices that help protect children from later alcohol and other drug use

- To encourage parents to seek help for their own problems, particularly those with family alcohol or other drug use problems.

A communications plan will involve two phases. The first step is to raise the awareness of high-risk parents about risks and motivate them to take action. The second phase involves building skills for parents.

Skill-building can occur through a variety of vehicles—written materials, television workshops, training groups in the community, case management in clinics, neighborhood or school discussion groups, and mutual support groups.

Materials, strategies, and programs all should provide incentives and positive experiences for parents. Dinners, prizes, and outings planned for the entire family are sample incentives. For poor neighborhoods, vans can pick up families for such events as baseball games. Meals for children and their parents will also attract families. Paying the parents can be an incentive; lack of money in low-income families may be an excuse that masks their fear of participating in new activities. These parents, often single mothers, need help in learning about and structuring activities—in using public transportation, finding free community events, and building the confidence to plan and carry out leisure events. They may also need more resources for the development of supportive networks, treatment, and related services.

Although parents will be drawn into programs initially by their children's needs, the strategies should also serve the parents as people. The support

Table 9. Strategies to Reach Parents and Families

Obstacles	Credible Sources	Media Channels
Denial by family of family dysfunction and alcohol/drug problems	Respected individuals who have successfully raised families	Television news, documentaries, skills-training workshops
Fear of being stigmatized	Locally known and respected individuals may have more power/credibility than media celebrities	Educational TV
Fear of loss of confidentiality		Cable TV
Narcissism of parents		Daytime TV
Lack of insurance resources for parenting/counseling services		Radio—segmented for audience
Lack of energy/time by parents		Print
Distrust of the "system"		Newspapers
Lack of credible message sources for cultural/racial minority groups		Magazines
Lack of concern/respect for expert's opinions on alcohol		Bus/subway posters
Skepticism about alcohol/drug messages that don't fit parents' own experience		Storefront posters
Distortion of messages heard by parents' attitudes, biases, experience, degree of use		Religious newsletters
Assumption by parents that children's alcohol/drug use will be okay		Videotapes
Distorted, depressed view of life by dysfunctional families		Audiotapes
Lack of awareness of community resources, discomfort with middle-class settings		
Overwhelming need for services for basic survival		
Cultural mores		

Note: In high-risk communities, many informal networks of other helpers often exist. They may or may not include the more traditional gatekeepers as listed above. It's important to identify and seek out the assistance of these in this informal network.

Table 9. Strategies to Reach Parents and Families (continued)

One-on-One Institutional Channels	One-on-One/Group Community Channels	Gatekeepers
Settings for family skills and parenting training:	Organizations	Counselors/trainers in parent education
Schools	Alafam	School personnel
Worksites (lunchtime programs)	Alcoholics Anonymous	Mental health personnel
Daycare settings	Al-Anon	Counselors in alcohol/drug treatment centers
Libraries	Narcotics Anonymous	Community youth workers
Community colleges	Cocaine Anonymous	Spiritualists
Hospitals	Parents Anonymous	Case workers in juvenile justice/welfare systems
Women's centers	Families Anonymous	Teen pregnancy clinic personnel
Community centers	National Association for Children of Alcoholics chapters (NACoA)	Sorority/fraternity members
Churches	National Association of Native American Children of Alcoholics (NANACoA)	Hospital/clinic personnel
Settings for family and parenting training among disadvantaged groups:	Parents Without Partners	Head Start/daycare personnel
Project Head Start programs	Local community parent skills training workshops	Social service workers
Welfare offices	Community-focused	Local pharmacists
Teen pregnancy clinics	Bulletin boards	Beauticians/barbers
School programs for teen mothers	Libraries	Corner grocery proprietors
Public housing facilities	Schools (parent resource centers)	Ministers
Visiting nurse programs	Community colleges	Media
Alcohol/other drug treatment clinics	Hospital education programs	TV managers
Public health clinics	Parks/recreation departments	Radio station managers
ACYF offices	Community centers	Newspaper, magazine editors
WIC offices	Worksites	Public relations personnel in school systems/county governments
Youth/drug agencies	Daycare settings	
Child protective services	Housing projects	
Family housing shelters	Grocery and convenience stores	
Women's shelters	Thrift stores	
	Lunch counters, diners, bars	
	Laundromats	

provided within parents' groups can help adults become bonded to something and can give parents a chance to talk about their own needs. In families with chemically dependent children, the parents often end up seeking marital counseling.

Some strategies for raising family awareness are discussed below. They include

- Target high-risk, dysfunctional families
- Target families with very young children
- Develop materials targeted to parents
- Incorporate interpersonal communication components into programs
- Convey messages that focus on family risk factors
- Raise awareness of protective factors.

Target high-risk, dysfunctional families

Many prevention and treatment experts recommend that communications efforts should focus first on the high-risk dysfunctional family. The following types of families may be considered as priority groups:

- Dysfunctional families, including those characterized by parental alcohol and other drug abuse, physical or sexual abuse of their children, emotional neglect, or mental disturbance
- Alcohol-abusing families (both active and recovering)
- Other drug-abusing families (both active and recovering)
- Single parents facing multiple socioeconomic hardships, such as lack of family support, poverty, low educational levels, and teenage parenthood
- Functional families with a special-needs child.

Current studies show that a poor early family environment is an important factor in vulnerability to alcohol and other drug use (Hawkins et al. 1985; Kandel 1974; Zucker and Lisansky Gomberg 1986). The currently studied risk factors cluster around psychosocial dysfunction in a number of areas: in the individual parent, in the parenting role, and in problems related to the social, community, and school environment (see table 1). Many studies have found similar patterns in the early families of problem drinkers, with these adults remembering a high level of marital conflict in their childhood homes, unsatisfying parent-child interaction because of inadequate parenting or parental disinterest and neglect, and parents who were inadequate role models because of alcoholism or social deviancy (Zucker and Lisansky Gomberg 1986).

This recommendation should in no way be interpreted to mean that the family environment alone causes alcohol and other drug problems. It is recognized that factors beyond the family—accessibility, policies, laws, economic conditions, social norms, cultural patterns, genetics, and other circumstances—contribute to the extensive alcohol and other drug problems found in the United States, and as more becomes known about them, communications strategies need to be developed.

Target families with very young children

Experts contributing to this report, such as Drs. Jeannette Johnson, Karol Kumpfer, and others listed at the end of this chapter, strongly recommend that children up to third grade, along with their parents, be the first priority in communications efforts. These are the reasons:

- Many constitutionally or emotionally vulnerable children begin to encounter difficulties at birth or soon thereafter.

- Parents of a young child are more hopeful and flexible than those discouraged by years of dealing with a difficult child.

- Children change more easily at younger ages; the younger child may be helped to develop social skills before problems with school, friendships, or authorities begin.

- Some children at high risk for alcohol and other drug use and other serious antisocial behavior can now be identified early; these findings are based on risk factors identified through both longitudinal and cross-sectional research (Kumpfer and DeMarsh 1986; Garmezy and Rutter 1983; Robins 1978; Block et al. 1988). IMPORTANT CAVEAT: These are risk factors, not predictions; roughly half of the children identified as high risk for antisocial behavior will develop later problems, while the other half will live normal lives (Hawkins et al. 1986).

- Many high-risk youth become part of an antisocial, drug-abusing peer group by the time they are teenagers; these youth will be difficult to reach through either communications strategies or conventional community programs, and it is too late for primary prevention efforts.

- Early help to young children can save them years of unhappiness and misery; in addition, community caregivers may more readily support efforts addressed to younger children than programs for alienated, antisocial teenagers.

Table 10 presents specific strategies for approaching parents of young children.

Table 10. Family Awareness (Parents of Young Children)

GOAL: To expand awareness of high-risk families on how to prepare children for teenage alcohol- and drug-free years

COMMUNICATIONS STRATEGIES:

- Provide parents with demonstrations of good family communication on alcohol/other drug issues
- Raise parents' awareness about risk factors and protective factors for their children
- Provide an educational/cooperative experience between the child, parents, and school
- Offer special guidelines to single parents and families with alcohol/ other drug abuse
- Demonstrate positive parenting styles to parents through community workshops or closed-circuit television teleconferences

  (OSAP manual available on training of trainers for parenting skills workshops; OSAP-sponsored workshops available in 1989)
- Motivate parents to seek help through training and support groups

Potential Materials

Television program on setting firm but reasonable expectations and getting families involved in activities (model: Hawkins et al., *Preparing for the Drug-Free Years*)

Television parenting workshops in conjunction with docudramas on a family whose teenager has a drug problem, with followup community workshops conducted by trainers

Television homework assignments for parents/children together, with questions on drugs; could include teacher's guide and parent/child workshops

Television commercial plugs by researchers or OSAP grantees talking about parenting and urging families to participate in family training programs

Flyers and free loan video about parenting for low-literacy parents

Packet on guidelines for single parents (several research articles available for reprint/reformatting)

Fact sheet on single parenting skills to be promoted through such organizations as Parents Without Partners

Videotapes on parenting (potential models: American Training Institute; OSAP grantees); check for possible renting through retail video outlets

Checklist for parents on risk factors in children (models: King Broadcasting Co., "Drug Abuse Risk Check for Your Child;" and Hawkins et al., *Preparing for the Drug-Free Years*)

Parent training modules on alcohol/other drugs identified through OSAP demonstration grants or technical assistance program and available for wide dissemination to generic parenting programs

Develop materials targeted to parents

Parents need simple, quick, easy-to-read information about risks and protection factors pertaining to their children. A review of existing educational material located few targeted to minority parents or low-literacy audiences. In general, there is great need for colorful, attractive materials for parents that give specific information on how to raise their high-risk, vulnerable children, without, of course, labeling or stereotyping. More information on needed materials appears earlier in this chapter under "Planning Considerations."

Incorporate interpersonal communication components into programs

Parenting skills, which are currently believed to help prevent alcohol and other drug problems, are most likely to be learned if they can be seen and practiced, so communications methods that allow this kind of personal interaction need to be explored. Interactive television programs, especially in conjunction with schools, can usefully demonstrate good parenting and family management skills.

The television docudrama and interactive learning programs (e.g., with accompanying checklist on child risk factors) will also act as an incentive to parents to seek parenting classes. The community awareness phase of a campaign should assist communities in setting up and publicizing their parent and family skills training and support groups. Also, the innovators (parents already in treatment or in parent groups) will be encouraged to bring in their neighbors and friends who can also benefit from skills training and support groups.

Convey messages that focus on family risk factors

Experts contributing to this report also felt that communications planners should consider addressing factors putting families at high risk instead of focusing on family categories. Task force members suggested that communities do the following as they prepare messages:

- Explain that risk factors are simply factors placing the family and child at risk—they are not absolute predictors and do not mean that a problem will necessarily occur.

- Link risk factors and protective factors together and organize them according to factors pertinent to schools, communities, and families.

- Classify risk factors (i.e., dysfunction of family, dysfunction of parents, and dysfunction of parenting role).

- If possible, rank risk factors (and develop strategies) according to whether they are primary or secondary (e.g., depression may occur as a precursor to stress).

- Do not attempt to rate factors according to bad versus worse; state simply that "these factors need to be considered."

- Emphasize that risk factors cluster together and should therefore be dealt with together rather than as separate factors.

- Provide lists of (child, parent, and family) risk factors for the gatekeeper or parent to measure on a scale of 1 to 5 or 1 to 9, with extent of the problem determining whether the child, parent, and/or family is "at risk," at "high risk," or at "highest risk" for alcohol or other drug problems.

Besides the risk factor lists in this chapter, another useful resource soon available is *Stopping Alcohol and Other Drug Use Before It Starts: The Future of Prevention*, a Report of a Committee of the Institute for Behavior and Health, Inc., edited by Robert L. DuPont, M.D. (in press through OSAP). *Preparing for the Drug-Free Years* by Hawkins et al. also contains a risk checklist.

Kumpfer (1989) recommends that public awareness campaigns include the increased risk of problems for CoAs/CoDAs and the risk factors to watch for, including the following specific messages:

- Substance-abusing parents should be made aware of their increased likelihood for raising antisocial and drug-abusing children.

- Genetic counseling should include information, based on the family history, about risk, vulnerability, and the chance of passing on the disease of chemical dependency.

- Parents and all those interacting with CoAs/CoDAs (teachers, youth group leaders, physicians) should be informed about the indicators of developing problems, so children may be referred to treatment, if services exist, for such risk factors as hyperactivity, learning disorders, academic problems, social incompetencies, emotional disorders, and depression.

Raise awareness of protective factors

Although less is known about protective factors than about risks, this is a very promising area for communications messages. Many children who live in high-risk families manage to grow up into adulthood as healthy, fully functioning human beings. Why are these children resilient? What protective factors worked to their benefit? Several studies (Werner 1986; Rutter 1984; Benard 1987) suggest that children have a chance to grow up into healthy adults if they

- Can learn to do one thing well that is valued by themselves, their friends, and the community

- Are required to be helpful as they grow up

- Are able to ask for help for themselves

- Are able to elicit positive responses from others in their environment

- Are able to distance themselves from their dysfunctional families so that the family is not their sole frame of reference

- Are able to bond with some socially valued, positive entity, such as the family, school, community groups, church, etc.

- Are able to interact with a (perceived to be) caring adult who provides consistent caring responses.

Resiliency factors, along with risk factors, need to be more widely publicized for the use of parents and gatekeepers. Another protective factor mentioned by experts contributing to this report is the perception of the mother that her infant is "cuddleable." Risk factor and protective factor lists for children and adolescents are shown in tables 2, 3, and 4.

Develop Programs for High-Risk Youth

Broad strategies for reaching high-risk youth include the following:

- Research and develop effective messages

- Educate all children

- Distribute materials targeted to CoAs and CoDAs

- Incorporate CoA and CoDA information into school curricula.

Research and develop messages for high-risk youth

More basic research is needed on what communications strategies will work with children from high-risk environments.

Table 11, Needed Communications Research on High-Risk Children and Youth, lists some of the questions that could help develop more targeted messages for both young children of alcoholics and other drug abusers and that group of high-risk, alienated teenage youth who may already be in trouble with alcohol or other drugs.

More research also is needed on bonding to seriously dysfunctional parents. The presumption is that youth need to bond first to their families. Then, based on the trust and respect they have experienced with parents, these youth will want and be able to bond to some other positive element of society, such as the school. Programs that build family skills and strengthen families (DeMarsh and Kumpfer 1986) do help bond children to their parents. The unresolved question, however, is whether to encourage bonding of children with seriously dysfunctional parents. Is it desirable, for example, to encourage a child to bond with a drug-abusing parent who is involved in criminal behavior, thereby strengthening

Table 11. Needed Communications Research on High-Risk Children and Youth

GOAL: To identify messages with potential for modifying alcohol/other drug behavior of high-risk children

COMMUNICATIONS STRATEGIES:

- Conduct research regarding knowledge/attitude/practices of children of alcohol and drug abusers (CoAs, CoDAs)

  — Determine the influence of peer groups on young CoA/CoDA children's attitudes/behavior

  — Explore how to prevent the change from "intend not to use" by young children to "intend to use," which occurs by about sixth grade

  — Assess whether messages/strategies can reinforce the CoAs/CoDAs' determination not to drink or use drugs like the parent (e.g., does the child focus on marital strife as the problem and not perceive drinking as the cause of strife?)

  — Assess the influence of peers' perceived and actual drinking on the initiation of CoAs/CoDAs into use

  — Assess what parental messages will reinforce abstinence by youth (e.g., Cork's suggestion that codependents' stronger feelings against drinking than those of the children may be a possible source of conflict and encourage use)

- Conduct focus groups or other qualitative research to help develop and test messages and themes with high-risk teenagers

  — Identify credible sources and prevention/early intervention messages with youth showing signs of alienation and school failure

  — Identify credible sources and intervention messages for youth already in trouble with alcohol/other drugs

  — Identify possible models/messages/materials for relapse prevention with teenagers; test concepts and messages with recovering adolescents

Potential Materials

Easy-to-read reports that translate the research findings into recommendations for communications

All types of materials with tested messages/strategies targeted to CoAs/CoDAs the parent's power as a role model? In some delinquent populations (e.g., sex offenders), there is already an enmeshment of children with their dysfunctional parents.

What is certain, according to experts consulted for this report, is that children from dysfunctional families who are successfully taught social skills will be better able to find mentors outside the family. Training parents to function better as parents also helps children to function better and to be better behaved.

Educate all children

Experts contributing to this report stress how important it is for all children to receive basic information about alcoholism and the family. The child from an alcohol- or other drug-abusing family needs support and understanding from his or her friends. As a CoA Foundation pamphlet (Woodside 1988) about young children makes clear, all children need to know the following:

- Alcoholism is a disease, and it affects all family members.
- Children in alcohol- or drug-abusing homes are not causing their parent's drinking or drug problem, and they can do nothing to stop it.
- All children from these homes deserve help for themselves.
- Children from alcohol- or drug-abusing homes are at increased risk of dependence or addiction if they start to use.
- Youngsters can do a lot to support and help their friends who come from these troubled homes.

Distribute materials targeted to CoAs

Children from substance-abusing families need to be given much more information about their own vulnerability than they are currently getting. The message "there are many people who cannot drink at all" needs to be transmitted more widely. With appropriate handling, the vulnerability message should not become a self-fulfilling prophecy. As with other inherited vulnerabilities, such as a family history of diabetes, knowledge can be a protective factor by encouraging preventive, self-monitoring behaviors.

Incorporate CoA/CoDA targeted materials into standard alcohol and other drug education curricula

Very few school curricula currently contain such information about CoAs/CoDAs, which is information needed by and appropriately taught to all children. The CASPAR alcohol and drug education program of Somerville, Massachusetts, is one of the oldest and most carefully evaluated of these curricula, but it is geared specifically for heavy-drinking, primarily blue-collar communities.

Children of alcoholics appear to learn more than other youth during school alcohol and other drug education programs (Kumpfer 1989). Children of alcoholics are particularly receptive to

- Information about substance abuse as a "family disease"
- Indicators of being at risk
- Coping strategies for living with substance-abusing parents.

Educational interventions targeted to children of substance abusers need to be paced slowly. Because of fear and embarrassment, many of these youth tend to learn more slowly than others. They are apt to feel very self-conscious in groups dealing with alcohol and other drug issues, wondering whether they are asking too many questions and appearing too interested or agitated.

Evaluation studies found that CoAs expected to drink less, and were drinking less than non-CoAs after participation in the CASPAR school alcohol education program. CoAs profited more than others from after-school, peer-led CoA groups but were reluctant to be identified with the CoA group.

Since the design of alcohol and other drug communication strategies for high-risk youth represents a relatively new arena, those individuals and organizations developing materials need to proceed with care. High-risk children may not hear and interpret messages the same way as other youngsters and, in addition, such children need special messages. For example, the common message "crack kills" may terrify the youngster whose parent uses crack. Since fear can trigger denial, the child is likely to forget this message. Different messages will be needed to avoid such denial by children living with their own or with family chemical addiction problems.

The need for training of teachers and school staff, as well as the kind of training to provide, also requires careful research. The National Association for Children of Alcoholics (NACoA) has several small, useful guides for elementary schools that are setting up CoA groups. Resource lists may be obtained from NACoA or from the National Clearinghouse for Alcohol and Drug Information (see appendix E).

Table 12 suggests strategies for incorporating CoA and CoDA information into school curricula.

Table 12. Communications Programs For Children of Alcoholics and Other Drug Abusers (Schools)

GOAL: Incorporate CoA/CoDA information into appropriate curricula within schools

COMMUNICATIONS STRATEGIES:

- Assist NACoA with outreach on the new *It's Elementary* book and provide technical assistance with their planned development of training materials/videos

- Assess opportunities for incorporating CoA Foundation efforts with CoA children into school-based activities

- Promote involvement of schools in national, State, and local community organization campaigns

Potential Materials

Resource list of books/training materials/resources for elementary-school CoAs and school staff

Package on Student Assistance Programs (SAP): (contents: reprints from Ellen Morehouse's book on the Westchester County SAP, NCADI fact sheet on different SAP models and their advantages, order forms for Wisconsin and other handbooks on SAPs, student survey form for assessing student needs and other materials)

Posters for teenage CoAs/CoDAs (none identified to date)

Guide/resource list for setting up Parent Resource Libraries in schools

Resource list of videos/educational aids/written materials for junior/senior high CoAs

Articles written by an expert on reasons for schools to sponsor parent training groups and to add CoA/CoDA units to their prevention education; arrangements made for publication in professional education journals

Package for elementary school teachers (National Association for Children of Alcoholics' guidebook *It's Elementary*, Questions and Answers on identifying CoA kids in the classroom, the announcement of video being produced by an OSAP demonstration grantee that shows high-risk early childhood behavior, list of elementary school curricula that contain CoA components)

Addendum: High-Risk Teenagers

Following recommendations from many sources, this monograph focuses on strategies for reaching young children and their parents. But to focus exclusively on younger children would mean passing over possible help to high-risk older children, from ages 10 to 16, who are already in trouble at school or with the law and are starting to use alcohol and other drugs at early ages. The younger age contingent, sometimes called "garbage heads," go out every night and on weekends and drink or may use other drugs. The philosophy of this population is to "party their brains out," to "live fast, die young, have a good-looking corpse" in preference to "dying as a nerd." These young people can be found in nightclubs, parking lots of malls, parks, or in walk-in centers if they are living on the streets.

This section suggests possible communications strategies for reaching troubled teenagers and discusses obstacles, messages, channels, and materials. Table 13 summarizes some of these topics.

Many of these youth have been having difficulties all their lives in fitting in and belonging anywhere—with their families, at school, and in making friends. Many of them came from families where there is alcohol or other drug use. They are often alienated, isolated youngsters who are rebellious, resist traditional authority and traditional values, and have a strong need for independence along with a high tolerance for deviance. In ninth grade, drug users perceive their parents as less caring and more rejecting than do nonusers (Norem-Hebeisen et al. 1984). These children turn away early from their parents' influence and join other alienated kids in peer groups that drink, hang out, and engage in antisocial activities.

Not all young people who are in trouble with school or the law are involved in acting-out behavior. Many are looking for structure in their lives. Once they start drinking, however, young people who are genetically or emotionally vulnerable may find they have a hard time controlling their use of alcohol or drugs. Some are depressed and find that alcohol helps them just to feel normal. Others may be drinking to allay fears and social anxieties.

A core problem for troubled youth is their sense of alienation and isolation; above all, these young people may need help in building social skills so that they can bond with their schools and their communities. These children already feel that they are "bad" or "good for nothing." In some places, the "no drinking by youth under age 21" policy is being distorted to create a moralistic environment of "good" (nondrinkers) versus "bad" (drinkers).

Youth who are in trouble from alcohol or drug use need to be approached on this basis: that alcohol or other drug use by young people should be stopped because it is illegal and harmful; it matters to the community (and to the

Table 13. Strategies to Reach High-Risk Teenagers

Obstacles	Credible Sources	Media Channels
Reject help out of	Local sports heroes	TV shows
• Fear	Popular media/music celebrities who are drug-free (*not* ex-alcoholics or ex-drug addicts)	• Afternoon soaps
• Lack of trust	Older peers ("non-nerds")	• Oprah Winfrey
• False bravado	People whom the teenager knows may have more influence and credibility than media celebrities	• "All My Children"
• Experience of repeated rejection		• "Hot" shows
Conflicting social messages on alcohol use, causing		• Music TV
• Ambivalence		• Cable TV (especially for Hispanics, Native Americans on reservations)
• Confusion		Radio shows
Skepticism and distrust because of		• "Hot" teenage stations
• Previous history of treatment		Subway ads
• Old promises that did not come true		Posters at skating rinks, teen hangouts
• Strategies that failed		
Low literacy		
Lack of institutional settings for reaching school drop-outs		

Table 13. Strategies to Reach High-Risk Teenagers (continued)

One-on-One Institutional Channels	One-on-One/Group Community Channels	Gatekeepers
School programs	Boys and Girls Clubs	Social service workers
• Project STATUS, Pasadena, California	• Smart Moves Program	School personnel
• Project PATHE	• Targeted Outreach Program	Youth organization leaders
• Student Assistance Programs	Big Brothers/Big Sisters	Law enforcement officers
• Newcomers and other support groups	4-H Club mainstreaming programs for troubled youth (Oregon State U.)	Church workers
• CoA student groups	Buddy programs (Denver)	Diversion personnel in juvenile justice system
• Pregnant teen student programs	YMCA/YWCA	Probation officers
Street academies, alternative schools	National Youth Alliance	Welfare agency personnel
• Cities in Schools	Alateen/Alcoholics Anonymous	Teen pregnancy clinic staffs
• Rich's Department Store Alternative School, Atlanta	Outdoor skills building	Mental health personnel
Juvenile justice system diversion programs	• Mt. Rainier in a Year	Beauticians/barbers
• Boy Scout troop	• Denver Wilderness Psychology Program	Proprietors of corner grocery and convenience stores
Teen shelter programs for homeless/runaways	Street theater/art program	
Comprehensive community youth center programs	• Soap opera writing	
Telephone hotlines	Vocational Skills Programs	
	• Building low-cost houses	
	Summer Recreation	
	• Camps	
	• Swimming pools	
	Malls/arcades	
	• Video games	
	• "Busted" computer game	
	• Alcohol IQ Video (Busch Creative Services)	

caregiver or parent or friend) that the young person not be hurt in this way. Communications strategies should convey the sense that adults understand stopping may not be easy. To make a decision to stop use, young people need help—not censure or blame. Messages to teenagers who are abusing alcohol or other drugs need implicitly to convey the sense that it is recognized a youngster may need help to stop, and that caring help is available. With help, a young person can find other ways to satisfy whatever need is being filled by alcohol or other drugs in that youngster's life.

Obstacles to Reaching High-Risk Teenagers

These youngsters are hard to reach because they resist traditional authority, often have a low literacy level, and may be on the streets instead of in school or in structured community settings. Their self-efficacy makes them less likely to respond to appeals based on caring about self, such as "take care of your health," or "don't take unnecessary risks that may hurt you." Also, these youth are already drinking and, in some cases, using multiple drugs at early ages. It is too late for "just say no" messages. Other obstacles include the following:

- Rejection of help because of fear and lack of trust or perhaps a false bravado

- Feelings of ambivalence and confusion about alcohol as a result of the many conflicting messages about alcohol use in U.S. society

- Skepticism and distrust based on the youth's history of treatment, of old promises that did not come true, and of previously tried strategies that failed

- Fear by children and youth of being rejected again

- Hopelessness by young people in inner cities about the possibility of ever having a worthwhile future with a decent job and a chance of achieving the "American dream"

- Presence in some inner-city neighborhoods of an open, accessible drug culture without apparent social sanctions and of large sums of money for youth who deal in drugs.

To reiterate, all message strategies need to be fully tested before being implemented. Focus groups need to test the message effects on *both* representatives of the youth target audience and any intermediary gatekeepers who will use the media or materials with youth.

Messages and Strategies

Prevention experts recommend that messages be developed within a framework that builds the self-efficacy of youth and lets them know they are cared about. The focus for strategies needs to be on the "four senses" (model: Boys Clubs programs) that matter to youth, including:

- A sense of belonging

- A sense of usefulness in life

- A sense of competency and of being valued by significant others

- A sense of influence and self-empowerment over one's own life.

Some considerations to be aware of in developing communications for high-risk youth include the following:

- Skepticism about danger messages—youth who have used alcohol or other drugs will laugh at exaggerated messages about the dangers of use ("it didn't happen to me").

- Focus on the positive—messages should be upbeat rather than negative in tone. If possible, messages should convey some sense of immediate gratification, focusing on youths' current social and interpersonal concerns as opposed to health, legal, or other long-term needs.

- Credible sources—celebrity ex-addicts and recovering people should *not* be used for prevention in general, but are particularly contraindicated for high-risk youth because these young people have a tendency toward negative identification (e.g., high-risk kids may forget the problem message and perceive instead "how terrific this ball player was even though he was on drugs").

- Reasons for drinking—youth drink for fun and to help them cope. These attitudes need to be considered in developing alternative messages.

- Sexualization—many high-risk young people will already be involved in sexual activity or will have been "sexualized" by their home life. Because inappropriate covert and overt sexual behavior by adults often occurs in chemically addicted families, many high-risk youngsters become aware of sexual messages early. The advertising media obviously understand that teenagers are receptive to messages about their physical and sexual appeal. Prevention messages might use this same approach as a possible way of getting attention from high-risk youth, e.g., being drug-free makes you more appealing to the opposite sex.

- Perceptions of drugs—young people tend to perceive alcohol, marijuana, and cocaine as improving sexual performance. Identifying such youth perceptions is important in developing messages to counter these myths.

- Depressive problems—many high-risk youth need help in learning to "tough out" the inevitable lows of life and control their impulses. This is different from the traditional prevention approach of helping youths find alternative highs.

- Status issues—youth in low-income drug cultures tend to value such visible signs of status as gold chains, a high-priced car, clothes, the number of girlfriends, and the amount of money a boyfriend has. Messages must somehow compete within this value system; current status symbols will change over time so the latest status signs need to be identified when developing a campaign message.

- The "non-nerd" factor—identifying "non-nerd" messages, such as those around sports, may be important for high-risk audiences; this, too, is something to test with the target audience to guarantee being on target.

- Delegitimizing the drug culture—messages are needed for youth in neighborhoods where drug sales are perceived as a legitimate source of income for legitimate reasons (e.g., paying the rent).

Types of messages that may appeal to teenagers include the following. It must be remembered, however, that what little is known about teenagers comes basically from formative research with youth not at high risk. Much greater levels of effort are required to even begin making "best guesses" that can then be pretested.

Peer Group Acceptance

For junior high and high school youth, their peer group is keenly influential. Kids have fun and "get high" in groups with their peers, and group settings are where most teenage drinking or other drug use occurs. Taking responsibility for one's friends is a message that appeals to youth, e.g., "If you care, you help your friends in trouble" or "If you have a friend who's strung out on alcohol and other drugs, pull your head outta the sand—find out how to help."

Many high-risk youth desperately want to belong (youth who transfer schools tend to be at high risk—a disproportionately large percentage come from alcohol- or drug-abusing families and the easiest peer group to gain acceptance in may be the alcohol and other drug users). A question to the young user could be: "How do you know the people you get high with are your friends? Maybe they just like you because you get high with them." A PSA suggested on this theme involves the portrayal of two girls getting into a car (girl #1 thinks girl #2 is her best friend); another girl leans in the car window and says, "You two must be best friends, you're always together," and girl #2 replies "Friends? Oh, no, man. We just get high together." The first girl gets the message and may be ready for intervention efforts.

Children, like their parents, have unrealistic expectations based on the lifestyles seen on TV shows. These unreal expectations can depress them and create a feeling of failure. Youth may need to be presented with new definitions of success, e.g., the quote from Dag Hammarskjold might be used, "Life demands from you all the strength that you possess—the only great feat is not to give up."

Achieving One's Hopes

Youth who are using drugs can be approached with concrete, direct messages aimed at demystifying drugs. The message is, "Look at how your use is keeping you from getting what you really want. Look in the mirror. Look at your skin. Do you have the boyfriend (or girlfriend) whom you really want? How long has it been since you kissed somebody when you were straight? Is your kissing improving based on the feedback you get, or don't you care because you're stoned? As you get older, boys (or girls) are going to expect you to kiss better. How can you improve your technique if you're always high on drugs when you kiss someone?"

Physical appearance and vanity matter to youth more than the physiological effects of drugs. Undesirable physical effects, such as bad breath, may be an effective message. As an example, one prevention specialist commented on what a turn-off it had been when a good-looking date got drunk and vomited on his suit. Also, the Brooke Shields poster (National Council on Alcoholism) carrying the message that "alcohol is fattening" was perceived as effective.

The broader message here is that drug use can interfere with getting what the youngster really wants—can sabotage the youth's most cherished competencies and skills. The young person may be risking all his or her dreams and hopes and plans by using drugs. However, high-risk children are often such gamblers—formative research is needed to determine the content, tone, and format of effective messages.

Helping Others

It has also been suggested that we do not often enough ask the high-risk child to help someone else. We know that helping others, especially someone younger, boosts a person's self-efficacy and sense of value. The example of older peers and siblings who drink or use drugs is a major reason kids give for initiating use. Appealing to the high-risk youth's concern for younger kids, including brothers and sisters, is a promising prevention strategy. Examples of this message are the video "Brothers" from the Massachusetts Governor's Alliance Against Drug Abuse (Boston Neighborhood Network Television, 1986-1987) and a poster of a big girl and a little girl on bicycles at a stop sign from the Alberta, Canada, youth media campaign (Alcohol Prevention Programs for Adolescents, n.d.)

Control and Self-Empowerment

High-risk youth need to feel that they have the power to influence the important things in their own lives, that they are neither helpless nor without hope. Delinquent youth need strategies that help them feel bonded to their families and their communities; a message that has been used successfully with this group is "getting on with my family, and getting out with my family."

Another message might be an attractive girl saying "I decided to be drug-free" with "I decided" being the critical element. Girls could be told what happens in a crack house, where girls prostitute themselves for crack.

Messages could be developed suggesting "Drug-free is sexy," "Drug-free is the way to have fun," "Everything you do for fun you can do without drugs," "It's hip not to be high" (Dr. J.: Boys Clubs). (In conjunction with this, muscle tone is "in" at the moment; what's "in" needs to be tested at the time of message development.)

For "hip," "cool" children, finding meaningful communication strategies can be very difficult. Some juvenile delinquents will join only nonstructured groups, because that's what they're accustomed to. Creative opportunities need to be identified within the given city or region that can offer excitement, interest, the chance for the young person to develop self-efficacy and the four major "senses"—the sense of belonging, of usefulness in life, of competency, of personal influence over his or her own life. Types of activities that can meet these criteria may include the following:

- Buddy relationship activities (model: the Denver program, similar to Big Brother/Big Sister, which involves many exciting free activities for both youth and the older person)

- Outdoor skills building and mountain climbing programs (models: "[Mt.] Rainier in a Year" and the Denver wilderness psychotherapy program)

- Street Theater program

- Art programs; rap music contests; writing and acting videotape scenes and dramas about alcohol and other drug issues

- Vocational construction programs (e.g., building low-cost houses)

- Program to write soap operas.

A strategy that may be worth exploring is that of using summer recreation sites—summer camps and swimming pools. Both may be "great places" for teaching skills and alcohol and other drug information to children. No models were identified, but such activities could be initiated through city parks and recreation departments and sponsors of summer camps.

Materials for Teenagers

Messages and materials need to be developed for high-risk youth that provide them with more information on the fact that some people cannot handle alcohol and drugs at all. These vulnerable youth need to know the danger signs, the differences in tolerance levels, and the inability of some people to stop. The message is "Some people are different. Maybe you have a family history that seems vulnerable to alcohol or other drug use—but you can do something about it. You'll have to work harder, but you can achieve a healthy lifestyle." The healthy lifestyle messages of the wellness movement are important in this context, with youth encouraged to work on achieving a lifestyle balance to feel healthy and happy.

Particular kinds of information are needed for high-risk young people. Suggestions are to

- Address the effects of drugs rather than specific physiological facts, but do provide drug-specific information

- Classify the drug effects by type of drug (i.e., depressants, stimulants), since kids talk about "getting high" and often use more than one drug

- Explain what happens within the body's system when drugs are used, so young people can follow the process through the cycle and understand why they can become or may already be dependent

- Present information in terms of "Here are some things that may happen that you may not like"

- Develop written materials in a direct, conversational style that presents drug use prevention in a realistic, appealing way both in content and in graphics

- Keep the literacy level low

- Use humor and countermessages

- Use anonymous sources of information (e.g., telephone hotlines and "Dear Abby" letters).

A number of available commercial materials, especially videos, are aimed at teenagers who use drugs. Many of these, however, only warn about the dangers of use at very high levels and create the implicit message that lower levels of usage are acceptable and not hazardous for teenagers. This sends a potentially dangerous message for youth. Just as women are advised not to drink during pregnancy because a safe level has yet to be determined, there is no research that suggests there is a safe level of alcohol or other drugs for youth. As with the physician's pledge to do no harm, so the public health approach is to do no harm.

Very few materials are designed to appeal directly to high-risk, hard-to-reach teenagers who are in trouble and need to know how to get help. Essentially all types of materials are needed, from television PSAs to information booklets to videos and program manuals. There is abundant information about chemical substances; it is the specific what-to-do knowledge that is less available for youth just as it is less available for adults. One useful resource is the "Make the Most of You" Adolescent Alcohol Problem Prevention via the Media program run by the Alberta (Canada) Alcohol and Drug Abuse Commission. This long-term program has developed a number of appealing materials that focus on meeting the needs of youth, without using alcohol or other drugs to meet these needs. They include posters and the *Zoot Capri* magazine, with themes appropriate for high-risk teenagers.

Low-literacy materials are badly needed. So are materials for youth from all minority groups. The Toughlove program, in addition to their materials for parent groups, have tough-talking, no-holds-barred manuals designed for teenagers who are in trouble with the law and out of the control of their parents. Alcoholics Anonymous has several small brochures for teenagers in trouble with drinking, and the Johnson Institute has an excellent intervention manual for teenagers to use to test themselves. Needed are materials for teenagers who are going through the recovery process or trying to prevent relapse.

Fact Sheet: American Youth in Selected Categories at High Risk for Alcohol and Other Drug Problems

- More than 20 percent (nearly 12.5 million) of all U.S. children (43 percent of Black and 40 percent of Hispanic/Latino children) live at or below the poverty level.[1] Children living in extreme poverty and deprivation are more likely to become enmeshed in delinquent and drug-using behavior,[2] particularly persistent (as opposed to occasional) drug use and delinquent activity.[3]

- 54 percent of U.S. children in female-headed families with no husband present (6,700,000 children) live at or below the poverty level; this includes 45 percent of white children who are in female-headed families, 67 percent of Black children, and 72 percent of Hispanic/Latino children in such families.[1]

- 6.6 million children under age 18 live in a home with an alcoholic parent.[4]

- In 1988, more than 2.3 million reports of child physical and sexual abuse or neglect were filed with authorities, an increase of more than 300 percent since 1976; substance abuse was "the dominant characteristic" in 30 to 40 percent of child abuse cases, with nearly 90 percent of abused children in Washington, D.C., reported to be in the care of someone "on drugs or drink."[5]

- About 85 percent of child abuse cases in 1984 involved a parent-child relationship; in sexual abuse of children, 66 percent of offenders were parents and another 19 percent were other relatives.[6]

- More than 1 million young people run away from home or are homeless each year,[7] and runaways are at greater risk for alcohol and other drug problems.[8]

- 1 million students drop out of high school each year; 1 of every 4 ninth graders will not graduate—the dropout rate reaches 50 percent in some urban areas,[8] and those who drop out are more at risk for developing alcohol and other drug problems.[9]

- One of eight 17-year-olds in the United States is functionally illiterate;[8] at-risk adolescents with low skills who drop out of school are three times more likely than their more successful peers to become unwed parents.[10] Those youth headed for college are less likely to abuse drugs.[3]

- More than 1 million adolescents become pregnant annually; half of these young mothers will never complete high school.[8]

- In 1985, more than 1.7 million young people ages 14 to 17 were arrested for crimes, not including traffic violations.[11]

- Nearly 1,900 teens took their own lives in 1984, making suicide the third leading cause of death for young people ages 15 to 24[11,12]; up to 80 percent of all adolescent suicides have been reported to be children of alcoholics.[13]

- Approximately 4.6 million young people, nearly a third of all 14- to 17-year-olds, have serious problems with alcohol.[8,14]

- Epidemiological studies show that one in four American children ages 10 to 17 (approximately 7 million of 28 million children) are at high risk of multiple problem behaviors and negative long-term consequences because of their current behavior involving alcohol and other drug use, failure in school, early sexual activity and risk of pregnancy, and delinquency.[15]

Notes

1. U.S. Department of Commerce, Bureau of the Census, Current Population Reports, Series P-20, *Characteristics of the Populations Below the Poverty Level*, 1985, and *Money Income and Poverty Status of Families and Persons in the United States*, 1985.

2. D.C. Farrington, Predicting self reported and official delinquency, in D.P. Farrington and R. Tarling, eds., *Prediction in Criminology* (Albany: State University of New York Press, 1985); D.J. West and D.P. Farrington, *Who Becomes Delinquent?* (London: Heinemann, 1973).

3. J.D. Hawkins, D.M. Lishner, J.M. Jenson, and R.F. Catalano, Jr. Delinquents and drugs: What the evidence suggests about prevention and treatment programming, in B.S. Brown and A.R. Mills, eds., *Youth at High Risk for Substance Abuse*, National Institute on Drug Abuse, DHHS Pub. No. (ADM)87-1537 (Washington, D.C.: U.S. Government Printing Office, 1987), 81–131.

4. S.B. Blume, *Report of the Conference on Research Needs and Opportunities for Children of Alcoholics* (New York: Children of Alcoholics Foundation, Inc., 1984), 4–5.

5. State abuse figures collected by the American Association for Protecting Children, 1988.

6. National Study for Child Neglect and Abuse Reporting (Colo.: American Humane Association, 1984).

7. U.S. Department of Health and Human Services and Department of Labor, *Count Me In Youth 2000*, p. 2.

8. E.D. Farber, The adolescent who runs, in B.S. Brown and A.R. Mills, eds., *Youth at High Risk for Substance Abuse*, National Institute on Drug Abuse, DHHS Pub. No. (ADM)87-1537 (Washington, D.C.: U.S. Government Printing Office, 1987), 129–136.

9. M.B. Holmberg. Longitudinal studies of drug abuse in a fifteen-year-old population. *Acta Psychiatrica Scandinavica* 71 (1985):67–79.

10. A. Sum, Analyses of data on basic skills levels of teens from the *National Longitudinal Survey of Young Adults* (Boston: Center for Labor Market Studies, Northeastern University, 1986).

11. U.S. Department of Commerce, Bureau of the Census, *Statistical Abstract of the United States*, 1985.

12. National Association of Children's Hospitals and Related Institutes, *Profile of Child Health in the United States*, 1989.

13. National Institute on Alcohol Abuse and Alcoholism, Research Monograph 4, *Services for Children of Alcoholics*, DHHS Pub. No. (ADM)81-1007 (Washington, D.C.: U.S. Government Printing Office, 1981).

14. National Institute on Alcohol Abuse and Alcoholism, *Towards the Development of a National Plan to Combat Alcohol Abuse and Alcoholism* (Rockville, Md., 1986).

15. J.G. Dryfoos, *Youth at Risk: One in Four in Jeopardy*, report submitted to the Carnegie Corporation of New York (June 1987).

Fact Sheet: Delinquent Youth

- Frequent use and abuse of drugs is more common among youth who engage in chronic delinquent behavior than among other adolescents.[1]

- The National Youth Study (a self-report study among adolescents in 1980) found

Nearly 50 percent of serious juvenile offenders report using multiple illicit drugs (offenders in this category admitted committing three or more offenses during the preceding year).

82 percent of these serious juvenile offenders report use beyond experimentation of at least one illicit drug.

Incidence rates for drug use are significantly higher among serious delinquents than among nonoffenders: alcohol use is 4 to 9 times higher; marijuana use is 14 times higher; and rates for other illicit drugs are 6 to 36 times higher, depending on the drug.[2]

- In one study of juveniles sentenced for violent crimes, half reported use of alcohol or drugs prior to the violent behavior and 40 percent reported using drugs immediately before their violent offense.[3]

- Among 2,000 adult prisoners, 83 percent of those jailed for violent crimes had been taking drugs daily during the month preceding their offense.[4]

- An estimated 2 to 6 percent of youth continue both frequent drug use and serious criminal behavior into adult life,[2,4] at enormous social and economic cost to society; such offenders are responsible for 75 percent of all robberies and 50 percent of felony assaults.[5]

Notes

1. J.D. Hawkins, D.M. Lishner, J.M. Jenson, and R.F. Catalano, Jr. Delinquents and drugs: What the evidence suggests about prevention and treatment programming, in B.S. Brown and A.R. Mills, eds., *Youth at High Risk for Substance Abuse*, National Institute on Drug Abuse, DHHS Pub. No. (ADM)87-1537 (Washington, D.C.: U.S. Government Printing Office, 1987), 81–131.

2. D.S. Elliott and D. Huizinga, The relationship between delinquent behavior and ADM problem behaviors, paper prepared for the ADAMHA/OJJDP State of the Art Research Conference on Juvenile Offenders with Serious Drug/Alcohol and Mental Health Problems, Bethesda, Md., April 17–18, 1983.

3. E. Hartstone and K.V. Hansen, The violent juvenile offender: An empirical portrait, in R.A. Mathias, P. Demuro, and R.S. Allison, eds., *Violent Juvenile Offenders: An Anthology* (San Francisco: National Council on Crime and Delinquency, 1984), 83–112.

4. J. Chaiken and M.R. Chaiken, *Varieties of Criminal Behavior* (Santa Monica: The Rand Corporation, August 1982).

5. B. Johnson, E. Wish, and D. Huizinga, The concentration of delinquent offending: The contribution of serious drug involvement to high rate delinquency, paper presented at the American Society of Criminology, Denver, 1983.

Fact Sheet: Runaway Youth

- 1 in 8 youngsters from all socioeconomic levels run away before their 18th birthdays.[1]

- About 166,000 youth are served annually by 127 government shelters and one-time crisis centers.[2]

- More than three-fourths of runaway youth have been physically maltreated.[3] (24 percent of all fatalities and 41 percent of all serious injuries in reported child abuse cases happen to youth aged 12 to 17.)[3]

- Many runaway youth come from complex multiproblem families and demonstrate multiple serious problems, such as a history of foster care, juvenile delinquency, physical and sexual mistreatment, and learning disabilities.[3]

- Runaway youth in one study evidenced high levels of disturbance, including

70 percent with academic performance difficulties

52 percent with sleeping difficulties

31 percent who admit drug use

35 percent who reported aggressive behaviors and 41 percent who reported homicidal thinking

23 percent engaging in reckless behaviors

51 percent who had attempted or seriously considered suicide; 13 percent with a record of attempting suicide and an additional 38 percent who reported significant suicidal thinking.[4]

Notes

1. I. Nye and C. Edelbrock, Some social characteristics of runaways, *Journal of Family Issues* 1(1980):147–150.

2. D. Shaffer and C. Caton, *Runaway and Homeless Youth in New York City* (New York: Itelson Foundation Report, 1984).

3. E.D. Farber, The adolescent who runs, in B.S. Brown and A.R. Mills, eds., *Youth at High Risk for Substance Abuse*, National Institute on Drug Abuse, DHHS Pub. No. (ADM)87-1537 (Washington, D.C.: U.S. Government Printing Office, 1987), 129-136.

4. E. Farber, C. Kinast, W. McCord, and D. Faulkner, Violence in families of adolescent runaways, *Child Abuse and Neglect* 8(1984):295–299.

Fact Sheet: Children of Alcoholics (CoAs)

- Between 12 and 25 percent of CoAs develop substance-related problems.[1]

- 1 of every 8 Americans is the offspring of a parent who has a problem with alcohol and nearly 7 million are children under 18 years of age;[2] in a typical classroom of 25 students, 3 to 4 children will be living in alcoholic homes.

- In 1984, children of abusers accounted for 650,000 of U.S. admissions for alcohol treatment and 178,000 of admissions for drug treatment, creating a cost to Federal, State, and local funding sources of approximately $663 million.[3]

- Studies consistently find that CoAs have more than average difficulty with achievement in school.[4]

- Children growing up in alcohol-troubled homes are at risk for serious medical, psychological, and substance abuse problems. Problems that CoAs face at a higher rate than the general population include fetal alcohol syndrome, hyperactivity, enuresis, school difficulties, school phobia, psychosomatic ailments such as stomachaches and headaches, child abuse and neglect, suicide, and incest.[5]

- Extensive literature review[1] shows children of substance abusers are over-represented among children needing special services:

Adoption or foster care

Services for juvenile delinquents and runaway youth

Intensive care for birth defects and fetal alcohol syndrome

Treatment for attention deficit disorder, hyperactivity, and aggressive conduct disorders

Public school classes for emotionally disturbed or handicapped children

Child abuse counseling programs

Adolescent psychiatric inpatient programs and child psychiatric outpatient programs

Hospital treatment for somatic complaints

Teenage mother pregnancy programs

Adolescent and adult substance abuse treatment programs.[6]

- Lack of acceptance at school is a significant risk factor in CoAs. Children who are unable to become attached to teachers or other children at school or have low

- commitment to school are more likely to develop chemical dependency problems.[6]

- Many children of alcoholics endure physical, emotional, and sexual abuse at home. In one study of 51 abused children, 35 (69 percent) had at least one parent and 32 (63 percent) had at least one grandparent with a history of alcoholism or alcohol abuse.[6]

- The problems of most children of alcoholics remain invisible because their coping behavior tends to be approval-seeking and socially acceptable. But these children may experience a range of psychological difficulties, including learning disabilities, anxiety, suicide, eating disorders, and compulsive achieving.[7]

- As adults, children of alcoholics are more likely to experience

Persistent depression

Work difficulties, often stemming in part from early emotional conflicts and school-related problems

Health problems related to stress, such as chronic fatigue

A tendency to be overly responsible about work and duties, often accompanied by an inability to relax.[8]

- Chemical dependency runs in families. By adulthood, children with a parent or sibling who abuses alcohol or other drugs are 4 to 5 times more likely than the general population to be alcoholics themselves;[9] grandchildren of alcoholics are 3 times more likely to become alcoholics.[10]

Notes

1. K.L. Kumpfer, Special populations: Etiology and prevention of vulnerability to chemical dependency in children of substance abusers, in B.S. Brown and A.R. Mills, eds., *Youth at High Risk for Substance Abuse*, National Institute on Drug Abuse, DHHS Pub. No. (ADM)87-1537 (Washington, D.C.: U.S. Government Printing Office, 1987), 1–72.

2. S.B. Blume, *Report of the Conference on Research Needs and Opportunities for Children of Alcoholics* (New York: Children of Alcoholics Foundation, Inc., 1984), 4–5.

3. W. Butynski, N. Record, and J. Yates, *State Resources and Services Related to Alcohol and Drug Abuse Problems: An Analysis of State Alcohol and Drug Abuse Profile Data FY 1984* (Washington, D.C.: National Association of State Alcohol and Drug Abuse Directors, Inc., 1985).

4. R.A. Zucker and R.B. Noll, Precursors and developmental influences on drinking and alcoholism: Etiology from a longitudinal perspective, in *Alcohol Consumption and Related Problems*, Alcohol and Health Monograph No. 1, National Institute on Alcohol

Abuse and Alcoholism, DHHS Pub. No. (ADM)82-1190 (Washington, D.C.: U.S. Government Printing Office, 1982), 289–327.

5. M. Woodside. *Children of Alcoholics: A Report to Hugh L. Carey, Governor, State of New York* (New York: State Division of Alcoholism and Alcohol Abuse, July 1982).

6. D.W. Behling, Alcohol abuse as encountered in 51 instances of reported child abuse, *Clinical Pediatrics* 18, no. 2 (1979):87–91.

7. Charter Statement, National Association for Children of Alcoholics, 1984.

8. C. Deutsch, *For the One in Eight Americans Who Is the Child of an Alcoholic* (New York: Children of Alcoholics Foundation, Inc., 1986).

9. D.W. Goodwin, Alcoholism and genetics: The sins of the fathers, *Archives of General Psychiatry* 6(1985):171–174.

10. L. Kaij and J. Dock, Grandsons of alcoholics, *Archives of General Psychiatry* 2(1975):379–381.

Bibliography

A separate list of references for the risk factor and protective factor tables follows this bibliography.

Ackerman, N.W. Childhood disorders and interlocking pathology in family relationships. In: Anthony, E.J., and Koupernik, C., eds. *The Child in His Family* (The international yearbook for child psychiatry and allied disciplines, Vol. 1). New York: Wiley & Sons, 1970.

Ahmed, S.W.; Bush, P.J.; Davidson, F.R.; and Iannotti, R.J. "Predicting children's use and intentions to use abusable substances." Paper presented at the Annual Meeting of the American Public Health Association. Anaheim, Calif., 1984.

Alberta (Canada) Alcohol and Drug Abuse Commission. *Planning for Success: Preventing Relapse.* Program kit. 1987.

The Alcoholism Report. Survey: Children know more booze brands than presidents. September 13:6, 1988.

Alcohol Prevention Programs for Adolescents. Edmonton, Alberta, Canada: Alberta Alcohol and Drug Abuse Commission, n.d.

Backer, T.E. Health professionals' and mass media's campaigns to prevent AIDS and drug use. *Counseling and Human Development* 20(7):1–10, 1988.

Barnes, G.M. The development of adolescent drinking behavior: An evaluative review of the impact of the socialization process within the family. *Adolescence* 12(48):571–591, 1977.

Battjes, R.J., and Jones, C.L. Implications of etiological research for preventive interventions and future research. In: Jones, C.L., and Battjes, R.J., eds. *Etiology of Drug Use: Implications for Prevention.* National Institute on Drug Abuse, Research Monograph No. 56, DHHS Pub. No. (ADM)85-1335. Washington, D.C.: Supt. of Docs., U.S. Govt. Print. Off., 1985, pp. 269–276.

Baumrind, D. "Why adolescents take chances—and why they don't." Paper presented at the National Institute for Child Health and Human Development. Bethesda, Md., 1983.

Behling, D.W. Alcohol abuse as encountered in 51 instances of reported child abuse. *Clinical Pediatrics* 18(2):87–91, 1979.

Benard, B. Protective factor research: What we can learn from resilient children. *Bonnie's Research Corner.* Chicago, Ill.: Awareness House Training and Development Systems Prevention Resources Center, 1987, pp. 3–10.

Block, J.; Block, J.H.; and Keyes, S. Longitudinal studies foretelling drug usage in adolescence: Early childhood personality and environmental precursors. *Child Development* 59:336–355, 1988.

Boston Neighborhood Network Television. *The Drug Dilemma.* Cambridge, Mass.: Bay State Health Care and Massachusetts Governor's Alliance Against Drugs, 1986–1987.

Brook, J.S.; Lukoff, I.F.; and Whiteman, M. Initiation into adolescent marijuana use. *Journal of Genetic Psychology* 137:133–142, 1988.

Brown, B.S., and Mills, A.R., eds. *Youth at High Risk for Substance Abuse.* National Institute on Drug Abuse, DHHS Pub. No. (ADM)87-1537. Washington, D.C.: Supt. of Docs., U.S. Govt. Print. Off., 1987.

Center for Science in the Public Interest, Washington, D.C., 1987.

Cloninger, C.R.; Bohman, M.; and Sigvardsson, S. Inheritance of alcohol abuse: Cross-fostering analysis of adopted men. *Archives of General Psychiatry* 38:861–868, 1981.

Cloninger, C.R.; Sigvardsson, S.; Reich, T.; and Bohman, M. Inheritance of risk to develop alcoholism. In: *Genetic and Biological Markers in Drug Use and Alcoholism.* National Institute on Drug Abuse, Research Monograph No. 66, DHHS Pub. No. (ADM)86-01444. Washington, D.C.: Supt. of Docs., U.S. Govt. Print. Off., 1986, pp. 86–96.

Colton, M.E. A comparison of heroin-addicted and non-addicted mothers: Their attitudes, beliefs, and parenting experiences. In: *Heroin-addicted Parents and their Children: Two Reports.* National Institute on Drug Abuse, Services Research Report, DHHS Pub. No. (ADM)81-1028. Washington, D.C.: Supt. of Docs., U.S. Govt. Print. Off., 1980.

Cork, R.M. *The Forgotten Children: A Study of Children with Alcoholic Parents.* Toronto: General Publishing Company Limited, in association with Addictions Research Foundation of Ontario, 1982.

Cotton, N.S. The familial incidence of alcoholism. *Journal of Studies on Alcohol* 40(1):89–116, 1979.

DeMarsh, J., and Kumpfer, K.L. Family-oriented interventions for the prevention of chemical dependency in childhood and adolescents. In: Ezekoye, S.; Kumpfer, K.; and Bukowski, W., eds. *Childhood and Chemical Abuse: Prevention and Intervention.* New York: Haworth Press, 1986, pp. 117–151.

Deutsch, C. *Broken Bottles, Broken Dreams: Understanding and Helping the Children of Alcoholics.* New York: Teachers College Press, 1982.

Deutsch, C. *For the One in Eight Americans Who Is the Child of an Alcoholic.* New York: Children of Alcoholics Foundation, Inc., 1986.

Dryfoos, J.G. *Youth at Risk: One in Four in Jeopardy.* Report submitted to the Carnegie Corporation of New York, June 1987.

Elder, G.H.; Caspi, A.; and Downey, G. Problem behavior and family relationships: Life course and intergenerational themes. In: Sherrod, L.; Sorensen, A.; and Weinert, F., eds. *Human Development: Interdisciplinary Perspective.* Hillsdale, N.J.: Erlbaum, 1985, pp. 293–340.

Elliott, D.S., and Huizinga, D. The relationship between delinquent behavior and ADM problem behaviors. Paper prepared for the ADAMHA/OJJDP State of the Art Research Conference on Juvenile Offenders with Serious Drug/Alcohol and Mental Health Problems. Bethesda, Md., April 17–18, 1984.

El-Guebaly, N. M.D., and Offord, D.R. The offspring of alcoholics: A critical review. *American Journal of Psychiatry* 134(4):357–365, 1977.

Flanzer, J. Alcohol abuse and family violence: The domestic chemical connection. *Family Focus and Chemical Dependency* 7(4):5–6, 1984.

Gallup Organization, Inc. Alcohol use and abuse in America. *The Gallup Report* No. 265, October 1987.

Garmezy, N., and Rutter, M. *Stress, Coping, and Development in Children.* New York: McGraw-Hill, 1983.

Goodwin, D.W. Alcoholism and genetics: The sins of the fathers. *Archives of General Psychiatry* 6:171–174, 1985.

Gordon, N.P., and McAlister, A. Adolescent drinking: Issues and research in. In: Coates, Thomas, ed. *Promoting Adolescent Health: A Dialogue in Research and Practice.* New York: Academic Press, 1982, pp. 201–210.

Gottfredson, D.C. Project PATHE: Second interim report. In: Gottfredson, G.D.; Gottfredson, D.C.; and Cook, M.S., eds. *The School Action Effectiveness Study: Second Interim Report* (No. 342). Baltimore, Md.: The Johns Hopkins University Center for Social Organization of Schools, 1983.

Gottfredson, D.C. *An Assessment of a Delinquency Prevention Demonstration With Both Individual and Environmental Interventions* (Report No. 361). Baltimore, Md.: The Johns Hopkins University Center for Social Organization of Schools, 1986a.

Gottfredson, D.C. An empirical test of school-based environmental and individual interventions to reduce the risk of delinquent behavior. *Criminology* 24:705–731, 1986b.

Gottfredson, D.C. "Changing school structures to benefit high-risk youths." Paper prepared for Symposium on Structural Change in Secondary Education, National Center on Effective Secondary Schools, Madison, Wis., May 12, 1987.

Hawkins, J.D.; Catalano, R.F., Jr.; Brown, E.O.; and Vodasy, P.F. *Preparing for the Drug-Free Years: A Family Activity Book.* Developmental Research and Programs, Inc.; Roberts, Fitzmahan and Associates; Comprehensive Health Education Foundation, Seattle, Washington, 1987a.

Hawkins, J.D.; Lishner, D.M.; Jenson, J.M.; and Catalano, R.F., Jr. Delinquents and drugs: What the evidence suggests about prevention and treatment programming. In: Brown, B.S., and Mills, A.R., eds. *Youth at High Risk for Substance Abuse.* National Institute on Drug Abuse, DHHS Pub. No. (ADM)87-1537. Washington, D.C.: Supt. of Docs., U.S. Govt. Print. Off., 1987b, pp. 81–131.

Hawkins, J.D.; Lishner, D.M.; and Catalano, R.F., Jr. Childhood predictors and the prevention of adolescent substance abuse. In: Jones, C.L., and Battjes, R.J., eds. *Etiology of Drug Use: Implications for Prevention.* National Institute on Drug Abuse, Research Monograph No. 56, DHHS Pub. No. (ADM)85-1335. Washington, D.C.: Supt. of Docs., U.S. Govt. Print. Off., 1985, pp. 75–126.

Hawkins, J.D.; Lishner, D.M.; Catalano, R.F., Jr.; and Howard, M.O. Childhood predictors of adolescent substance abuse: Toward an empirically grounded theory. In: Ezekoye, S.; Kumpfer, K.; and Bukowski, W., eds. *Childhood and Chemical Abuse: Prevention and Intervention.* New York: Haworth Press, 1986, pp. 11–48.

Hesselbrock, V.M.; Hesselbrock, M.N.; and Stabenau, J.R. Alcoholism in men patients subtyped by family history and antisocial personality. *Journal of Studies on Alcohol* 46(1):59–64, 1985.

Heuer, M. *Happy Daze.* Denver: MAC Publishing, 1986.

Holmberg, M.B. Longitudinal studies of drug abuse in a fifteen-year-old population: 1. Drug career. *Acta Psychiatrica Scandinavica* 71:67–79, 1985a.

Holmberg, M.B. Longitudinal studies of drug abuse in a fifteen-year-old population: 2. Antecedents and consequences. *Acta Psychiatrica Scandinavica* 71:80–91, 1985b.

Jessor, R. Problem-behavior theory and adolescent drinking. *Brown University Digest of Addiction Theory and Application* 7:52–55, 1988.

Jessor, R., and Jessor, S.L. Adolescent development and the onset of drinking: A longitudinal study. *Journal of Studies on Alcohol* 36:27–51, 1975.

Jessor, R., and Jessor, S.L. Theory testing in longitudinal research on marihuana use. In: Kandel, D.B., ed. *Longitudinal Research on Drug Use:*

Empirical Findings and Methodological Issues. Washington, D.C.: Hemisphere Publishing Co., 1978, pp. 41–71.

Johnston, L.D.; O'Malley, P.M.; and Bachman, J.G. *Drug Use Among American High School Students, College Students, and Other Young Adults: National Trends Through 1985.* DHHS Pub. No. (ADM)86-1450. Rockville, Md.: Alcohol, Drug Abuse, and Mental Health Administration, 1986.

Johnston, L.D.; O'Malley, P.M.; and Eveland, L.K. Drugs and delinquency: A search for causal connections. In: Kandel, D.B., ed. *Longitudinal Research on Drug Use.* Washington, D.C.: Hemisphere Publishing Co., 1978, pp. 137–161.

Kaij, L., and Dock, J. Grandsons of alcoholics. *Archives of General Psychiatry* 2:379–381, 1975.

Kandel, D. Inter and intragenerational influences on adolescent marijuana use. *Journal of Social Issues* 30:107–135, 1974.

Kaplan, L. *Working With Multiproblem Families.* Lexington, Mass.: Lexington Books, 1986.

Kellam, S.G.; Brown, C.H.; Rubin, B.R.; and Ensminger, M.E. Paths leading to teenage psychiatric symptoms and substance use: Developmental epidemiological studies in Woodlawn. In: Greze, S.B.; Earls, F.J.; and Barrett, J.E., eds. *Childhood Psychopathology and Development.* New York: Raven Press, 1983, pp. 17–51.

Kellam, S.G.; Ensminger, M.E.; and Turner, R.J. Family structure and the mental health of children: Concurrent and longitudinal community-wide studies. *Archives of General Psychiatry* 34:1012–1022, 1977.

Krauthammer, C. Spare us the family librium. *Time,* September 19, 1988. p. 104.

Kumpfer, K.L. "Prevention of Substance Abuse: A Critical Review of Risk Factors and Prevention Strategies." Report prepared for the American Academy of Child Psychiatry's Project Prevention: An Intervention Initiative, October 1987a.

Kumpfer, K.L. Special populations: Etiology and prevention of vulnerability to chemical dependency in children of substance abusers. In: Brown, B.S., and Mills, A.R., eds. *Youth at High Risk for Substance Abuse.* National Institute on Drug Abuse, DHHS Pub. No. (ADM)87-1537. Washington, D.C.: Supt. of Docs., U.S. Govt. Print. Off., 1987b, pp. 1–72.

Kumpfer, K.L. Promising prevention strategies for children of substance abusers. *OSAP High Risk Youth Update* 2(1):1–3, 1989.

Kumpfer, K.L., and DeMarsh, J. Family environmental and genetic influences on children's future chemical dependency. In: Ezekoye, S.; Kumpfer, K.; and Bukowski, W., eds. *Childhood and Chemical Abuse: Prevention and Intervention.* New York: Haworth Press, 1986, pp. 49–91.

Labouvie, E.W., and McGee, C.R. Relation of personality to alcohol and drug use in adolescence. *Journal of Consulting and Clinical Psychology* 54:289–293, 1986.

Lehr, K.W., and Schrock, M.M. A school program for children of alcoholics. *Journal of School Health* 57(8):344–345, 1987.

Louis Harris and Associates. "Children's Needs and Public Responsibilities: A Survey of American Attitudes About the Problems and Prospects of American Children." Survey conducted for Group W—Westinghouse Broadcasting Co., Study No. 863009. New York, September 1986.

Louis Harris and Associates. *A Catalyst for Action: A National Survey to Mobilize Leadership and Resources for the Prevention of Alcohol and Other Drug Problems Among American Youth.* Report of survey for Boys Clubs of America, 1988.

MacKay, J.R. Problem drinking among juvenile delinquents. *Crime and Delinquency* 9:29–38, 1963.

Mainard, R.; deBerranger, P.; and Cadudal, J.L. Une consequence frequente et grave de l'alcoolisme parental—les services commis sur les enfants. *Revue de l'Alcoolisme* 17:21–31, 1971.

Mann, J. Vox Populi Sovietskaya. *The Washington Post*, March 22, 1989, p. B3.

Marwick, C. Even "knowing better" about smoking, other health risks may not deter adolescents. *Journal of the American Medical Association* 260(11):1512–1513, 1988.

McDermott, D. The relationship of parental drug use and parents' attitude concerning adolescent drug use to adolescent drug use. *Adolescence* 19(73):89–97, 1984.

McKenna, T., and Pickens, R. Personality characteristics of alcoholic children of alcoholics. *Journal of Studies on Alcohol* 44(4):688–700, 1980.

McKenna, T., and Pickens, R. Alcoholic children of alcoholics. *Journal of Studies on Alcohol* 42(11):1021–1029, 1981.

Miller, D., and Jang, M. Children of alcoholics: A 20-year longitudinal study. *Social Work Research Abstracts* 13(4):23–29, 1977.

Moos, R.H., and Billings, A.G. Children of alcoholics during the recovery process: Alcoholic and matched control families. *Addictive Behaviors* (Oxford) 7:155–163, 1982.

Morehouse, E. Working in the schools with children of alcoholic parents. *Health and Social Work* 4(4):144–162, 1979.

National Institute on Alcohol Abuse and Alcoholism. *Sixth Special Report to the U.S. Congress on Alcohol and Health.* U.S. Department of Health and Human Services, DHHS Pub. No. (ADM)87-1519. Washington, D.C.: Supt. of Docs., U.S. Govt. Print. Off., 1987.

Needle, R.; Lavee, Y.; Su, S.; Brown, P.; and Doherty, W. Familial, interpersonal, and intrapersonal correlates of drug use: A longitudinal comparison of adolescents in treatment, drug-using adolescents not in treatment, and nondrug-using adolescents. *International Journal of the Addictions* 23:211–1240, 1988.

Norem-Hebeisen, A.; Johnson, D.W.; Anderson, D.; and Johnson, R. Predictors and concomitants of changes in drug use patterns among teenagers. *Journal of Social Psychology* 124:43–50, 1984.

Nylander, I. Children of alcoholic fathers. *Acta Paediatrica Scandinavica* 49(Supplement 121):1–134, 1960.

Office for Substance Abuse Prevention. *Stopping Alcohol and Other Drug Use Before It Starts: The Future of Prevention,* Prevention Monograph 1. OSAP, DHHS Pub. No. (ADM)89-1645. Washington, D.C.: Supt. of Docs., U.S. Govt. Print. Off., 1989.

Parker, A., and Harford, T.C. Alcohol-related problems of children of heavy-drinking parents. *Journal of Studies on Alcohol* 48(3):265–268, 1987.

Penning, M., and Barnes, G.E. Adolescent marijuana use: A review. *International Journal of Addictions* 17:749–791, 1982.

Pisano, S., and Rooney, J.F. Predisposition to drug use in rural adolescents: Preliminary relationships and methodological considerations. *Journal of Drug Education* 18(1):1–11, 1988.

Research and Policy Committee of the Committee for Economic Development. *Children in Need: Investment Strategies for the Educationally Disadvantaged.* New York: Committee for Economic Development, 1987.

Robins, L.N. Sturdy childhood predictors of adult anti-social behavior: Replications from longitudinal studies. *Psychological Medicine* 8:611–622, 1978.

Robins, L.N., and Przybeck, T.R. Age of onset of drug use and other disorders. In: Jones, C.L., and Battjes, R.J., eds. *Etiology of Drug Abuse: Implications for*

Prevention. National Institute on Drug Abuse, Research Monograph No. 56, DHHS Pub. No. 85-1335. Washington, D.C.: Supt. of Docs., U.S. Govt. Print. Off., 1985, pp. 178–193.

Sanchez-Dirks, R. Reflections on family violence. *Alcohol Health and Research World* 4(1):12–16, 1979.

Schaefer, D. *Choices and Consequences: What To Do When a Teenager Uses Alcohol/Drugs.* Minneapolis: Johnson Institute Books, 1987.

Schorr, L.B., and Schorr, D. *Within Our Reach: Breaking the Cycle of Disadvantage.* New York: Doubleday, 1988.

Sowder, B.J.; Carnes, Y.M.; and Sherman, S.N. Children of addicts in surrogate care. Unpublished manuscript, prepared for NIDA Services Research Branch. Institute for Human Resources Research, April 1981.

Spivack, G. *High Risk Early Behaviors Indicating Vulnerability to Delinquency in the Community and School.* National Institute of Juvenile Justice and Delinquency Prevention. Washington, D.C.: Supt. of Docs., U.S. Gov. Print. Off., 1983.

Steele, B.F., and Pollock, C.B. A psychiatric study of parents who abuse infants and small children. In: Helfer, R.E., and Kempe, H.C., eds. *The Battered Child.* Chicago: University of Chicago Press, 1968, pp. 103–147.

Steinberg, L. Latchkey children and susceptibility to peer pressure: An ecological analysis. *Developmental Psychology* 22(4):433–439, 1986.

Steinberg, L. Single parents, stepparents, and the susceptibility of adolescents to antisocial peer pressure. *Child Development* 58:269–275, 1987.

Volicer, B.; Volicer, L.; and D'Angelo, N. Variation in length of time to development of alcoholism by family history of problem solving. *Drug and Alcohol Dependence* 12:69–83, 1983.

Werner, E. Resilient offspring of alcoholics: A longitudinal study from birth to age 18. *Journal of Studies on Alcohol* 47(1):34–40, 1986.

Wilson, W.J. *The Truly Disadvantaged: The Inner City, the Underclass, and Public Policy.* Chicago: University of Chicago Press, 1987.

Wolin, S.J.; Bennett, L.A.; Noonan, D.L.; and Teitelbaum, M.A. Disrupted family rituals: A factor in the intergenerational transmission of alcoholism. *Journal of Studies on Alcohol* 41:199–214, 1980.

Woodside, M. "Children of Alcoholics." A Report to Hugh L. Carey, Governor, State of New York. New York: State Division of Alcoholism and Alcohol Abuse, July 1982.

Yankelovich, Skelly, and White, Inc. "Youth Monitor." Nationwide survey of 1,200 children and teenagers conducted 1986-87. New York: Shulman, Inc., 1988.

York, P.; York, D.; and Wachtel, T. *Toughlove*. New York: Bantam Books, 1982.

Young, L. *Wednesday's Children: A Study of Child Neglect and Abuse*. London: McGraw-Hill, 1964.

Zucker, R.A., and Lisansky Gomberg, E.S. Etiology of alcoholism reconsidered: The case for a biopsychosocial process. *American Psychologist* 41:783–793, 1986.

Zucker, R.A., and Noll, R.B. Precursors and developmental influences on drinking and alcoholism: Etiology from a longitudinal perspective. National Institute on Alcohol Abuse and Alcoholism. In: *Alcohol Consumption and Related Problems*. Alcohol and Health Monograph No. 1. DHHS Pub. No. (ADM)82-1190. Washington, D.C.: Supt. of Docs., U.S. Govt. Print. Off., 1982, pp. 289–327.

Sources for High-Risk and Protective Factors Tables

Abel, E.L., ed. *Fetal Alcohol Syndrome II: Human Studies*. Boca Raton, Fla.: CRC Press, Inc., 1981.

Benard, B. Protective factor research: What we can learn from resilient children. *Bonnie's Research Corner*. Chicago, Ill.: Awareness House Training and Development Systems Prevention Resource Center, 1987.

Clark, R. *Family Life and School Achievement: Why Poor Black Children Succeed or Fail*. Chicago: University of Chicago Press, 1983.

Feiner, R. Vulnerability in childhood. In: Roberts, M.C., and Peterson, L., eds. *Prevention of Problems in Childhood*. New York: Wiley & Sons, 1984, pp. 133–168.

Garmezy, N. The study of competence in children at risk for severe psychopathology. In: Anthony, E.J., and Koupernik, C., eds. *The Child in His Family, Vol 3: Children at Psychiatric Risk*. New York: Wiley & Sons, 1974, pp. 77–98.

Garmezy, N., and Rutter, M. *Stress, Coping and Development in Children*. New York: McGraw-Hill, 1983.

Jacob, T.; Favorini, A.; Meisel, S.; and Anderson, C. The spouse, children, and family interactions of the alcoholic: substantive findings and methodological issues. *Journal of Studies on Alcohol* 39:1231–1251, 1978.

Kumpfer, K.L. Special populations: Etiology and prevention of vulnerability to chemical dependency in children of substance abusers. In: Brown, B.S., and Mills, A.R., eds. *Youth at High Risk for Substance Abuse.* National Institute on Drug Abuse, DHHS Pub. No. (ADM)87-1537. Washington, D.C.: Supt. of Docs., U.S. Govt. Print. Off., 1987, pp. 1–72.

Kumpfer, K.L., and DeMarsh, J.P. Family-oriented interventions for the prevention of chemical dependency in children and adolescents. In: Ezekoye, S.; Kumpfer, K.; and Bukoski, W., eds. *Childhood and Chemical Abuse: Prevention and Intervention.* New York: Haworth Press, 1986a.

Kumpfer, K.L., and DeMarsh, J.P. Prevention strategies for children of drug abusing families. In: *Proceedings of the 34th Annual International Congress on Alcoholism and Drug Dependency.* Calgary, Canada, 1986b.

Patterson, G.R. Maternal rejection: Determinant or product for deviant child behavior? In: Hartup, W., and Rubin, Z., eds. *Relationships and Development.* Hillsdale, N.J.: Erlbaum, 1986.

Robins, L.N. Study of childhood predictors of adult antisocial behavior: Replications from longitudinal studies. *Psychological Medicine* 8:611–622, 1978.

Rutter, M. *Changing Youth in a Changing Society: Patterns of Adolescent Development and Disorders.* Cambridge, Mass.: Harvard University Press, 1979.

Rutter, M. Resilient children. *Psychology Today,* March 1984, pp. 57–65.

Thomas A., and Chess, S. Genesis and evolution of behavioral disorders: From infancy to early adult life. *American Journal of Psychiatry* 141:1–9, 1984.

Wahler, R.; Leske, G.; and Rogers, E. The insular family: A deviance support system for oppositional children. In: Hamerlynch, L.S., ed. *Behavioral Systems for the Developmentally Disabled. 1: School and Family Environments. New York: Bruner/Mazel, 1979.*

Werner, E. Resilient offspring of alcoholics: A longitudinal study from birth to age 18. *Journal of Studies on Alcohol* 47(1):34–40, 1986.

Wilson, C., and Orford, J. Children of alcoholics: Report of a preliminary study and comments on the literature. *Journal of Studies on Alcohol* 39:121–142, 1978.

Wolin, S.J.; Bennett, L.A.; Noonan, D.L.; and Teitelbaum, M.D. Disrupted family rituals: A factor in the intergenerational transmission of alcoholism. *Journal of Studies on Alcohol* 41(3):199–214, 1980.

Woodside, M. "Children of Alcoholics." A report to Hugh L. Carey, Governor, State of New York. New York. State Division of Alcoholism and Alcohol Abuse, July 1982.

Zucker, R.A., and Lisansky Gomberg, E.S. Etiology of alcoholism reconsidered: The case for a bio-psychosocial process. *American Psychologist* 41:783–793, 1986.

Experts Contributing to This Chapter

Elaine Bratic Arkin
Health Communications
  Consultant
3435 N. 14th Street
Arlington, VA 22201

Kathryn Begaye
Arizona Department of Education
1535 W. Jefferson Street
Phoenix, AZ 85007

Peter Bell
Institute on Black Chemical Abuse
2614 Nicollet Avenue
Minneapolis, MN 55408

Bernie Boswell, Executive Director
Family Research Center
736 South 500 East
Salt Lake City, UT 84102

James Bradley
Texas Commission on Alcohol and
  Drug Abuse
1705 Guadelupe
Austin, TX 78701-1214

Rudy Canter
PADRES Project
Parents Association for Drug
  Rehabilitation
1213 Sante Fe
Corpus Christi, TX 78404

Lynn Craig
Kansas Schools Teaming for
  Substance Abuse Prevention and
  Intervention
217 N. Water Street
Wichita, KS 67202

Lawrence Dolan, Ph.D.
Dept. of Mental Hygiene
Johns Hopkins School of Hygiene
  and Public Health
615 N. Wolfe St.
Baltimore, MD 21205

Judith E. Funkhouser
Deputy Director
Division of Communications
  Programs
Office of Substance Abuse
  Prevention
Parklawn Bldg., Room 13A-54
5600 Fisher Lane
Rockville, MD 20857

Robert Hassin
Assistant Executive Vice President
Boys and Girls Clubs of Greater
  Washington
7600 Georgia Avenue, N.W.
Suite 308
Washington, DC 20012

Jeannette Johnson, Ph.D.
National Institute on Drug Abuse
Addiction Research Center
4940 Eastern Avenue
Bldg. C, Room 261
Baltimore, MD 21224

Pat Kassebaum
MAXIMA Corporation
2101 E. Jefferson St.
  Executive Blvd.
Rockville, MD 20852

Karol Kumpfer, Ph.D.
Graduate School of Social Work
Social Work Building
University of Utah
Salt Lake City, UT 84112

Ellen Morehouse
Student Assistance Services, Inc.
300 Farm Road
Ardsley, NY 10502

Gerald S. Myers
Executive Director
National Association for Children
of Alcoholics
31582 Coast Highway, Suite B
South Laguna, CA 92677

Emma Redmond
Illinois Department of Alcoholism
and Substance Abuse
100 W. Randolph Street, Suite 5-
600
Chicago, IL 60601

Betsy Wells, Ph.D.
School of Social Work, JH30
University of Washington
Seattle, WA 98195

CHAPTER 2

Reaching Black Inner-City Youth

Understanding the Audience

Environmental factors - These children may often

- Live in substandard housing
- Live in single-parent households
- Be surrounded by crime and violence
- Lack positive male role models
- Attend overcrowded schools
- Drop out of school
- Have lower reading levels than white children of the same age
- Receive inadequate health care
- Have a higher mortality rate from disease and violence than white children
- Be placed more frequently than whites in foster care and institutions.

Psychosocial factors - These children may often

- Be highly aware of skin color and racial differences
- Have a sense of self-reliance
- Easily maintain contact with several adults and siblings or peers
- Have well-developed motor and verbal skills
- Have little faith in their chances of economic or educational achievement in the mainstream society.

Among high-risk youth, a subgroup consisting of Black urban children, aged 6 to 12, deserves special attention. Because the drug culture surrounds and threatens these children at a very young age, it is essential to reach them at this stage. By the time they become teenagers, they are extremely vulnerable to the easy accessibility of alcohol and other drugs, the lure of quick money from drug dealing, and a dwindling hope in any other sort of future.

This chapter analyzes the environmental, economic, and cultural realities that must shape communications programs with Black children and their families.

Environmental Factors

Alcohol and other drug use among inner-city Black youth must be viewed in the context of the difficult socioeconomic conditions that still pervade the Black community: poverty, crime, unemployment, poor schools, disrupted families, teen pregnancy, and homelessness. No communications program alone can solve these problems, but no communications strategy to reach inner-city children can succeed without taking them into account.

Data summarized by McAdoo and McAdoo (1985) show that a higher proportion of Blacks (55.4 percent) live in central cities than whites (20.4 percent). Likewise, a higher proportion of poor Black children (57.5 percent) live in central cities than poor white children (27.1 percent).

In overall quality of life, the outlook for children in these communities is bleak. Compared with other populations, they suffer more than their share from any downward turn in the economy and from intractable problems in health, education, housing, and employment. In the mid-1980s, the poverty rate for Black children reached a 20-year high; one of every two was poor, compared with one in five of all American children (McAdoo and McAdoo 1985). In 1969, Black children lived in households with a median family income of $14,580 (in 1981 dollars), or 56.4 percent of the white median family income. By 1981, the median family income for Blacks had fallen to $12,173, or 51 percent of the white median family income (McAdoo and McAdoo 1985).

Black children living in the inner city are at high risk of alcohol and other drug abuse because of a number of negative environmental factors, including their home situation, educational and health status, risk of involvement in the drug trade, and the drug culture that surrounds them.

Home situation

Black children are four times more likely than white children to grow up in a poor, one-parent household; three out of five will experience family disruption because of separation, divorce, or death of a parent (McAdoo and McAdoo 1985). These children are also more likely than white children to live in crowded, substandard quarters, or with relatives other than their parents. Fifty-three percent of all Black children are born to single mothers; 60 percent under age 3 are not living with both parents. In 1982, 70 percent of such single-parent Black families with children were poor (McAdoo and McAdoo 1985).

The absence of a father or a father figure is particularly hard on boys, who experience the loss of a role model, loss of control of behavior, rejection at school, and possibly recruitment and exploitation by older males of the street culture. Girls are also negatively affected: they may get the message from their mothers that they too can cope "successfully" as single parents (Hare, ed. 1988).

Although life at home for these children may be bleak, it can be preferable to living in an institution. Census data from 1980 showed that Black children were housed in psychiatric and foster care facilities at a rate 75 percent higher than white children, and were incarcerated in correctional institutions at a rate 400 percent higher than white children (McAdoo and McAdoo 1985).

Educational status

Writing in *State of Black America,* 1988, a recognized expert notes an unquestionable decline in urban school systems serving Blacks: "The education of our youth in urban systems has become largely an exercise in social control and babysitting by outsiders" (Hare 1988). Differences in educational achievement between minority and nonminority children, as measured by standardized tests, have been noted by researchers for many years; for example, the average reading proficiency of minority 17-year olds is only slightly better than that of white 13-year-olds, according to Hare (1988). Also, in 1984, the average score of Black students on the Scholastic Aptitude Test had risen only to the level of the 16th percentile of nonminority students (Children's Defense Fund 1988). Most experts believe that these differences are attributable to such factors as overburdened school systems, unqualified teachers who resent teaching inner-city children, and the practice of assigning many Black students to lower achievement tracks in schools. Thus, "structured educational failure legitimatizes job discrimination while eliminating legal recourse" (Dewart 1988). Students taught (or not taught) under such conditions may be unduly self-critical and tend to accept a poor educational outcome as the inevitable consequence of their own deficiencies (Hare 1988).

McAdoo and McAdoo (1985) report other evidence of the poor educational status of Black children. For example, almost half of all Black school-age children are one full grade behind whites of the same age. In addition, in 1979-80, Black children were three times more likely than whites to be enrolled in classes for the mentally retarded, but only half as likely to be in classes for the gifted and talented. In 1979, one out of five Black students dropped out of school before high school graduation, and in inner-city neighborhoods, the dropout statistics are far higher. Of girls who drop out before graduation, 40 percent do so because of pregnancy. Another indicator of the declining quality of Black children's educational experiences is the fact that fewer are going on to college after high school. In 1977, 50 percent of all Black high school graduates and 51 percent of all white high school graduates matriculated at a college. By 1982, 52 percent of white graduates were college bound, but only 36 percent of Blacks—a 14 percent decline in just 5 years (McAdoo and McAdoo 1985).

Although school may be far from a fulfilling and productive experience for urban Black children, community leaders and many parents have continually fought the dropout phenomenon. A recent Louis Harris survey (1989) of Black inner-city families asked parents what hopes they had for their children. The most frequent response, mentioned by 59 percent of respondents, was "learning to stay in school."

Health status

National data (McAdoo and McAdoo 1985) show gross inequities in the health status of Black children: a Black infant is twice as likely as a white infant to die before age 1. One out of every 47 Black infants dies before his or her first birthday. Although declining, the mortality rate for Black infants is not falling fast enough to reach the level of white infants in the foreseeable future. The maternal mortality rate for Blacks is far greater than for whites, and Black mothers receive far less prenatal care. Black infants suffer low or very low birthweight at a rate far exceeding whites. They are more subject than whites to nutritional deficiencies, complications of low birthweight, pneumonia, sudden infant death syndrome, digestive disorders, and intestinal infections. They suffer more often than whites from elevated blood lead levels and tuberculosis. The death rate for Black children is many times higher than for whites in all age groups up to the 15 to 19 age group, when white children are more likely to die as a result of automobile accidents and suicides. Black children are four times as likely as white children to be murdered (McAdoo and McAdoo 1985; U.S. Department of Health and Human Services [DHHS] 1985).

Regarding routine health care, inequities again are evident. Black children make only two-thirds as many visits to the doctor as whites, and they receive significantly less dental care. In 1982, less than half of Black children ages 1 to 4 received DPT immunizations and only 39 percent received polio vaccines, while nearly 80 percent of white children received these treatments (McAdoo and McAdoo 1985; Children's Defense Fund 1988).

Alcohol and other drugs have a major impact on the health of Blacks. The DHHS Task Force on Black and Minority Health found, for example, that the incidence of esophageal cancer among Blacks was 10 times that of whites; that Blacks' mortality rates for chronic liver disease and cirrhosis were nearly twice those of whites; and that between 1982 and 1984, cocaine-related deaths among Blacks tripled, while they doubled among whites (U.S. Department of Health and Human Services 1985).

There are few hard data on the numbers of inner-city children who are children of substance abusers, but there are good indications that in some localities, the numbers are very high. Deren (1986), in a review of the literature, notes that the New York City Department of Health reported in 1984 that the rate of "births with narcotism mentioned" was as high as 9.5 per 1,000 live births and that researchers have estimated that there are 800,000 children in New York City whose mothers are regular drug users. Black and other minority children figure heavily in these statistics. A child with an addicted mother is at risk of numerous untoward health outcomes, both in infancy and early childhood, including impaired cognitive abilities, school problems, physiological problems, and an increased likelihood of using alcohol and other drugs (Deren 1986).

The drug culture

There is evidence that the impact of alcohol and other drug abuse in Black urban neighborhoods is much more devastating than comparable abuse in white, middle-class neighborhoods. The reasons for this disparity are painfully obvious, but nonetheless bear repeating. Blacks in 1989 face enormous social and financial hardships, which are exacerbated by alcohol and other drug abuse. A vicious cycle is at work: young Blacks faced with poverty, crime, unemployment, inadequate schools, family disintegration, and normal adolescent rebelliousness are easily enticed to turn to drugs for escape, and, in some cases, as an entrepreneurial option that helps support their mothers and siblings. This descent into the drug culture, however, inevitably leads to more crime, incarceration, fear, despair, and potentially death.

A phenomenon of American cities in the late 1980s is the involvement of young children in the drug trade. Although no hard statistics are available to document the full extent of this problem, no reader of a major national news magazine or city newspaper can doubt that it exists. In Baltimore, reporters talked to the mother of an 8-year-old girl who lamented the child's involvement in the drug trade. She had been arrested in school with cocaine hidden in a gym shoe. Older brothers had been caught earlier (*Baltimore Sun*, January 21, 1989). In Washington, columnist Courtland Milloy writes of a mother who found a jar containing PCP in her home, evidence that her 17- and 19-year-old sons had been recruited into the drug trade. Sporting new cars and hip clothes, they rejected the idea of working at McDonald's for spending money. How did these children get started? The dealers lent them money, then called in the loan by forcing the two boys to push drugs (Milloy 1987).

A recent lead story in *Time* (Lamar 1988) equates the crack trade with an unsanctioned job program for ghetto youths. With the advent of crack on the drug scene, juvenile arrests doubled in Detroit, tripled in New York City, and quadrupled in Washington, D.C. Despite the frequency of arrests, children are seldom held for long by the police and thus represent a "recyclable labor pool." To the children themselves, as well as their employers, the financial rewards may seem well worth the risk of arrest, for in New York City, a teenage drug dealer can make as much as $3,000 a day. Sheer greed cannot explain the phenomenon entirely: some children do use the money for clothes, cars, and jewelry; but others use it to put food on the table for their families. Children are involved not only as sellers but also, in many instances, as buyers. In *Time*, Lamar quotes a DEA official: "A sophisticated marketing analysis couldn't have come up with a more perfect drug for kids. Five years ago, a kid had to spend $80 for cocaine. Now a kid can get a vial of crack for $3 to $5. The high is instantaneous, the addiction complete." Families are often powerless to intervene; in some instances children have been literally kidnapped by older dealers. School officials are equally stymied. They point to "a glut, not a lack, of educational programs aimed at crack...," but deplore the uselessness of such programs to combat the lure of the drug trade. In view of the hopelessness of ghetto life, one school principal commented, "Just saying no doesn't cut it. What can we just say yes to?" (Lamar 1988).

Hare (1988) comments that children in the inner city are exposed to an "underground economy," composed of pimps, numbers runners, prostitutes, and dope dealers; and that these undesirables function, for many children, as role models of success, with easy access to money, cars, clothes, and the other symbols of a "good life" otherwise denied to inhabitants of the decayed urban core.

Wade Nobels, director of the Center for the Advanced Study of Black Family Life and Culture, views drug-trafficking as "a crisis in culture," where "the culture of drugs with its own rules, values, perceptions, and practices is vastly devitalizing the black community..." (Nobels et al. 1986). Traditional Black cultural values emphasize cooperation, adaptability, trust, respect, restraint, the family, and the community. In contrast, the value system of the drug culture is characterized by violence, selfishness, materialism, immediate gratification, and a nonfamily/noncommunity orientation. Unfortunately, in the absence of positive employment, educational, and recreational activities, "drug dealing and drug-related activity emerge as [a] viable economic enterprise for urban youth" (Nobels et al. 1986).

Facts About Black Youth

Black youth are overrepresented at the lowest socioeconomic levels of society. This makes them more vulnerable to alcohol and other drug problems (McAdoo and McAdoo 1985).

- In the mid-1980s the poverty rate for Black children reached a 20-year high; one of every two is poor, compared with one in five of all American children.

- Fifty-three percent of all Black youth are born to single mothers. In 1982, 70 percent of such single-parent Black families with children were poor.

- A Black infant is twice as likely as a white infant to die before age 1.

- The incidence of esophageal cancer among Blacks is 10 times that of whites; Blacks' mortality rates for chronic liver disease and cirrhosis is nearly twice that of whites; and between 1982 and 1984, cocaine-related deaths among Blacks tripled, while they doubled among whites (U.S. Department of Health and Human Services 1985).

Psychosocial Factors

Certain characteristics of Black children may be important to consider in planning communications. Alvey et al. (1981) identify the following traits:

- Skin color awareness or "color consciousness," and awareness of racial differences

- A sense of self-reliance

- A strong "people orientation"

- Sensitivity to nonverbal cues

- Well-developed verbal and motor skills

- An obvious bicultural socialization

- Ease in maintaining frequent contact with several adults

- Experience of more prolonged contacts with other siblings or other children, rather than just with their parents.

These findings suggest that Black children may be receptive to prevention messages and adept at passing them on to others.

Alvey et al. noted the high verbal capacities of Black youngsters when in a nurturing environment, observing that Black children have been socialized to be both verbally and physically responsive. These authors point out that Black children are subject to "linguistic vulnerability, due to differences between 'usual speech mode' and 'formal speech mode'" (Alvey et al. 1981). This is a signal that those developing prevention messages pay particular attention to language used and pretest it with the target audience.

Also important to consider is the susceptibility of the Black child to developing a negative self-image. According to Alvey et al. (1981), "The child has considerable exposure to both subtle and overt sexism and racism through television. He has received a message as to who he is, how he is supposed to behave, and how he and his family are viewed by others. For most of his short life, he has viewed a parade of negative cultural stereotypes on the tube. His behavior and cognitive world may be reflective of this experience."

Moreover, these authors note, young Black children "must often deal with uncertainties about meal time, time with parents, whether material needs will be met" and with "the recognition of differences in their family's lifestyles and those portrayed in books and on television" (Alvey et al. 1981).

Knowledge, Attitudes, and Practices

Children in the general population: National surveys of children in elementary school suggest that they

- Know that marijuana, cocaine, and alcohol are drugs

- Think that beer, wine, distilled spirits, and wine coolers are relatively innocuous

- Believe that fitting in with peers is the main reason some children use drugs

- Experience peer pressure to use drugs and alcohol as early as fourth grade

- Undergo a change in attitude toward alcohol and other drugs, from negative to more positive, as they mature

- Lose faith in parents' and teachers' knowledge of drugs as they grow older

- Say that presenting the facts about drugs and talking about problems are the most effective school-based prevention measures

- Say that teaching younger children about drugs is the most effective thing they as individuals could do to ameliorate the drug problem.

Black inner-city children: A study of Black children found that substantial proportions (22 to 32 percent) of those aged 9 to 12

- See drugs as one element in popularity and peer acceptance
- See drugs as part of growing up
- Do not believe cocaine use is risky
- Say they like being high on drugs
- Think that most people can stop drugs if they want
- Say that it is hard to say no to a friend.

Black teenagers: In the absence of more data on children, planners can turn to studies of Black teenagers showing that they

- Are overrepresented in treatment programs and alcohol- and drug-related hospital admissions and arrests
- Are underrepresented in national surveys of alcohol and other drug use
- Include a large proportion (53 percent) who have used marijuana
- Include substantial proportions who have used cocaine (22 percent) and crack (17 percent).

What do children aged 6 to 12 actually know about alcohol and other drugs? Data on this age group, particularly on Black inner-city children, are very sparse. The following discussion includes data on children in the general population, on Black children aged 9 to 12, and on Black teenagers.

Knowledge

By some measures, children seem to know a lot about alcohol and other drugs. For example, the Center for Science in the Public Interest, surveying a small sample of children in Washington, D.C., and Maryland, found that the average child could name more alcoholic beverage brands than U.S. presidents (*Alcoholism Report* 1988b).

Another indication: in early 1988, the *Drug Abuse Report* announced a new, expanded "Dictionary of Street Alcohol and Drug Terms," published by the University of South Carolina School of Medicine. In the 2 years between the publication of the first and second editions, the vocabulary for street drugs had doubled. This is a telling indicator that drugs are ever-present in the American consciousness (*The Drug Abuse Report* 1988a). Children are usually well attuned to the major themes and concerns of the culture in which they live.

Data on children's precise knowledge of alcohol and other drugs, although scarce, do exist. On the national level, the *Weekly Reader* Survey documents the knowledge of 136,000 elementary school children. The survey was conducted twice, in 1983 and 1987, thus allowing some trends to be observed. The survey did not contact a representative sample of school children throughout the U.S.; instead, it was a readership survey (i.e., readers of the *Weekly Reader*). Also, since confidentiality could not be guaranteed, the survey did not inquire about each child's own knowledge, attitudes, and practices concerning drugs, but rather what each respondent believed children his or her own age think about these subjects (Borton and Johnson 1987). Although limited in scope, the *Weekly Reader* Survey does provide valuable information on what children know and where they get their information about alcohol and other drugs.

A comparison of the two surveys showed the following changes took place between 1983 and 1987:

- In 1987, students in grades four to six cited schools as their primary source of information about the dangers of drug use, while in 1983, television, movies, and families were the leading sources of information on drugs.

- In 1987, the overwhelming majority of fourth to sixth graders believed marijuana was a drug. Many more in the 1987 survey believed cigarettes were drugs than in 1983. The percentage of those who thought beer, wine, and distilled spirits were drugs also increased significantly between 1983 and 1987.

- In both surveys, children believed that "fitting in with other kids" was the main reason that children might use drugs. However, the later survey showed a significant drop in perceived peer pressure to try marijuana. Perceived pressure to try beer, wine, and distilled spirits remained about the same in both surveys, but increased sharply by grade (36 percent of 4th graders reported pressure, compared to 76 percent of 7th to 12th graders).

The 1987 *Weekly Reader* Survey included some questions about cocaine and wine coolers that were not addressed in the earlier version.

- Of fourth to sixth graders, 93 percent thought that cocaine or crack is a drug; also, a substantial percentage of younger children (grades two and three) correctly identified cocaine as a drug. Alarmingly, only 21 percent thought of wine coolers as a drug.

- As with other drugs, children cited "fitting in with other kids" as the main reason for using crack. Of fourth graders, 35 percent cited this reason, compared to 40 percent of fifth graders, and 43 percent of sixth graders.

- Among fourth graders, 41 percent reported "some to a lot" of pressure to use cigarettes; 34 percent reported pressure to use wine coolers; and 24 percent reported pressure to use cocaine or crack. As with other drugs, reported pressure to use rose with each grade: 68 percent of 7th to 12th graders reported pressure to use cigarettes, 66 percent to use wine coolers, and 33 percent to use cocaine.

- Starting with the youngest children, 90 percent of second and third graders saw great harm in using cocaine daily, 88 percent in using marijuana, 46 percent in drinking beer, and 45 percent in drinking wine coolers. Among fourth to sixth graders, most saw great harm in using marijuana and cocaine daily, but substantially fewer perceived great harm in daily use of wine, beer, distilled spirits, or wine coolers. Among older children (grades 7 to 12), the perception that marijuana was very harmful had dropped to 66 percent, but cocaine continued to be regarded as very harmful.

- As might be expected, the perception that many children their age have tried different substances rose with the grade level of respondents. Of 4th graders, 26 percent thought that many children their age had tried beer, wine, distilled spirits, or wine coolers, compared to 40 percent of 6th graders, and 80 percent of 7th to 12th graders. However, throughout grades 4 to 12, less than 20 percent of respondents believed that many of their peers had tried cocaine, stimulants, barbiturates, or marijuana.

- Children were asked to rate the comparative effectiveness of various school antidrug measures (presenting the facts about drugs, engaging in alternate activities, talking to children about their problems, and setting strict rules about drug abuse). Children at all grade levels rated "presenting the facts about drugs" as the most effective school-based prevention measure, and rated "imposing strict rules" as the least effective. Children were also asked to rate the effectiveness of the same measures as parental prevention strategies. "Teaching the facts" and "talking with children about their problems" were rated first and second by children in grades four to six. In grades 7 to 12, children, veering somewhat from the cognitive to the affective realm, rated "talking about problems" first, and "teaching the facts" second.

- The survey showed that children's estimation of their parents' and teachers' drug knowledge declined as their grade level increased. Over 40 percent of 4th to 6th graders thought that adults know a lot about drugs, compared with only 20 percent of children in grades 7 to 12.

- Children were asked to rank the effectiveness of various things they might do themselves to ameliorate the drug and alcohol problem. Choices given were (1) learn the facts, (2) encourage other children to say no, (3) encourage children who are using to seek help; (4) report any selling to parents or principals, and (5) teach younger children about the dangers. By a healthy percentage, this last strategy—teaching younger children—was deemed most effective by survey respondents in grades 4 to 6 and in grades 7 to 12.

To what extent these findings are applicable to Black inner-city children is not known. Clearly, some findings shout for our attention:

- The tendency to regard beer, wine, distilled spirits, and wine coolers (see also Burkenne 1988) as relatively innocuous

- The decline of parents' and teachers' perceived knowledge (and presumably their credibility) as the child grows older

- The major force that peers play in a child's decisions about alcohol and other drugs

- The sense among children that they themselves can be most instrumental in helping younger children avoid alcohol and other drug problems.

According to the experts contributing to this report, these are findings that should be heeded in developing strategies for Black inner-city children.

Attitudes

In assessing Black attitudes toward alcohol and other drug abuse, it is important to consider both community and individual perspectives.

Community Attitudes

The *Washington Post* recently reported the emergence of a "two-tier" drug culture:

> While the news media have been reporting a uniformly bleak "plague" of drugs over the past 18 months, numerous surveys have shown that public attitudes toward illegal drugs have become progressively more hostile. Some surveys have shown that the use of cocaine and marijuana among many segments of the population, particularly middle-class professionals and college students, has declined sharply. Yet, this is by no means a sign of imminent victory in the drug war—or even cause for unbridled optimism. For, while the use of crack cocaine has been concentrating on the urban poor, it is this segment of the population that has the least chance of recovering from the ravages of drug addiction. In effect, researchers say that the Nation's drug culture has been moving in two directions, one inching slowly toward a relatively drug-free environment and the other speeding

down a bleak and vicious road of drug-related violence, addiction, and death. (Isikoff 1989)

The *Washington Post* article then cites data from the national cocaine help line, 1-800-COCAINE, in support of this argument. Six years ago, fully half the hotline callers had college degrees and high incomes; by 1988 the picture had altered radically: over half the hotline callers were unemployed, and barely 16 percent were college educated (see also Herridge and Gold 1988).

One noted expert comments on the acceptability of alcohol use in the Black community:

> Alcohol use and abuse is so common in the black community that it has become accepted behavior. Its availability in large urban areas is such that there is no great distance to walk to procure it; no effort required to procure it after hours, when official places of purchase are closed; and prices are such that purchase is not prohibitive. Panhandling and pooling of funds are commonplace and tolerated, as is evidenced by the manner in which we easily dole out quarters and larger sums to alcoholics who clean our windshields, even when their services are discouraged or unwanted. This lack of an enforced collective or individual social policy against this kind of behavior, results only in encouragement. (Primm, ed. 1987)

Another expert describes attitudes of the Black community toward alcohol use:

> In many black communities, homicide, accidents, disease, and heavy drinking are viewed as a way of life, due to the high prevalence of these phenomena. A party without liquor or a street rap without a bottle is often perceived as unimaginable. These attitudes about drinking are shaped as youth grow·up seeing liquor stores in their communities next to schools, churches, and homes. Liquor stores and bootleg dealers frequently permeate the black residential community, where in traditionally white communities, they are generally restricted to commercial or business zones. With liquor stores throughout the fabric of black residential life, black youth grow up seeing men drinking in the streets and relatives drinking at home. (Harper 1986)

The Minnesota Institute for Black Chemical Abuse (1986) offers the following reasons for the acceptance of alcoholism in the Black community:

- *Availability.* Liquor establishments are plentiful in the Black community, and distilled spirits are sold in more places, such as drug and grocery stores.

- *Social norms.* Many Black communities lack clear social norms for appropriately using alcohol, and have a high tolerance for dysfunctional behavior.

- *Treatment problems.* In many Black communities, treatment facilities are scarce or nonexistent. Also, Blacks have an historically high failure rate in treatment and often report negative treatment experiences, often because of the need for more social support and followup care.

- *Denial.* Denial is a typical reaction to alcoholism for most population groups. For Blacks, denial is compounded by the fear of being deemed "inferior" if they acknowledge the problem.

Without scapegoating the distilled spirits industry, it can be said that part of the alcohol problem in the Black community derives from enthusiastic distilled spirit marketing. Hacker, Collins, and Jacobsen (1987) show how Blacks are cleverly targeted by alcohol marketers. Alcohol producers are frequent sponsors of "worthwhile" promotional activities in their communities: concerts, sports, scholarships, community business organizations, and the like. The largesse of alcohol marketers puts the Black community in a bind: they feel indebted to marketers and loath to sacrifice revenue for much-needed projects. The authors estimate that more than $2 billion is spent annually in the United States to promote purchasing alcoholic beverages; tens of millions of this total is spent on campaigns targeting Blacks. (In contrast, the National Institute on Alcohol Abuse and Alcoholism [NIAAA] spent only $2 million in 1986 to study the drinking problems of all minorities, and only $500,000 on Blacks specifically.) It is not difficult to conclude that the anti-alcohol abuse message of public service announcements is overwhelmed by alcoholic beverage advertising.

Peter Bell (1986) asks communities to consider their own attitudes toward alcohol and other drugs. Have they established rules regarding use (e.g., ritualistic or social use is sanctioned, whereas use to medicate stress is not)? Have they established a method to communicate the rules? Who is carrying the message? Parents? Religious institutions? Bell believes the primary messenger regarding use is the marketer. Are there systems of accountability? What happens when someone crosses the line? Do they know what will happen? These are hard questions, but ones that a community bent upon prevention must consider.

Youth attitudes

Findings of the *Weekly Reader* Survey disclose a generally negative attitude toward alcohol and other drugs among children in the 6 to 12 age range. (Borton and Johnson 1987).

However, young adolescents are pressured to use alcohol and other drugs and acknowledge the importance of "fitting in" with a peer group (Borton and Johnson 1987). It appears that attitudes do begin to shift as children mature. In his study of teen attitudes, Black (1988a) found the following prodrug attitudes among Black 9- to 12-year-olds:

- 29 percent see drug abuse as popular
- 28 percent believe drugs are "just part of growing up"
- 25 percent believe marijuana "increases creativity"
- 22 percent report that they like being high on drugs
- 11 percent think it's okay to sell cocaine to a friend
- 10 percent would like to try crack "just once."

However, Black also found marked improvement in the attitudes of Black children (ages 9 to 12) studied in 1987 and 1988, as seen in the following table:

Table 1. Attitudes of Black Children Aged 9-12 Toward Drug Use

Attitudes of Black Children (Ages 9-12)	Percentage Who Agree		
	1987	1988	Variance
Smoking marijuana is okay.	21%	6%	-15
People who use drugs are no different.	28%	19%	-9
Would try drugs if a friend did.	12%	5%	-7
Most people can stop drugs if they want.	34%	28%	-6
Parties are more fun with drugs.	10%	5%	-5
It is hard to say no to friends.	37%	32%	-5
	n=58	n=151	

Source: Black 1988b.

Research conducted by the Media-Advertising Partnership for a Drug-Free America (1987) found that a prodrug attitude is ingrained in a significant percentage of Black teens. Of Black teens, 37 percent believe that marijuana users are popular, while 32 percent believe that using cocaine impresses the opposite sex. Twenty-nine percent see drugs as a good way to escape hard times; and 33 percent say that drugs help a person forget his or her troubles. Of Black youths who say they use drugs as part of their "macho" image, 26 percent believe there is no risk to "regularly" using crack or cocaine.

Again, a common thread throughout the research reviewed is the concern among young teens about what others think of them. If they think it is necessary to use alcohol or other drugs to "fit in," then that is what they will do. To youth, the risks of not belonging and not fitting in are worse than the perceived risks associated with alcohol and other drugs (Borton and Johnson 1987; Black 1988a; Media-Advertising Partnership for a Drug-Free America 1987).

Practices

For many years, popular wisdom held that use/misuse of alcohol and other drugs surfaced in middle to late adolescence and seldom infringed on the lives of younger children. Research of the past decade has convinced us otherwise. Major national studies—those that ask older persons to describe retrospectively their youthful first use of drugs—lead us to conclude that use of alcohol and other drugs by preadolescents is not uncommon.

However, hard data on actual, current use of alcohol and drugs by preadolescents are scarce, and obtaining such data is understandably difficult. Children are not often arrested and subjected to urine or blood screens for alcohol and other drugs. They are not often seen in drug treatment settings. Since their use is minimal compared with that of the older population, not many are seen in hospital admissions for drug- or alcohol-related reasons. Self reports of alcohol and other drug abuse by this population are fraught with difficulties. As minors, children are protected by many more legal restrictions to data collection. They may have more difficulty understanding the survey questions, and hence be more prone to erroneous reporting. As a group, children must be surveyed almost exclusively in school settings, which in itself presents a host of problems to surveyors.

A number of State and local studies of children's use of alcohol and other drugs have been done (Macro Systems 1986), but apart from the *Weekly Reader* Survey (which is not a study of prevalence of use, but of perceived prevalence), there are no national data. In the absence of national data on children ages 6 to 12, we must turn to data on older youth, to anticipate problems their juniors are likely to face. Many such studies have been conducted by public and private agencies and academic institutions; a few of the major national surveys are discussed below.

A consistent—but possibly misleading—finding of major national surveys of young people's use of alcohol and other drugs is a lower rate of use among Blacks than among whites for most drug categories. Among such surveys, the following are notable:

- Monitoring the Future (MF), an annual nationwide survey of 1,600 high school seniors, based on a self-administered questionnaire and conducted in a classroom setting. Because it is administered only to seniors, MF is known to underrepresent Black youth, many of whom have dropped out by the senior year.

- The National Household Survey on Drug Abuse (NHSDA), a nationwide survey of the general population, aged 12 and over, that excludes students living in dormitories and persons of no fixed address. The interview is administered face to face in a household setting (National Institute on Drug Abuse 1987a).

- The National Longitudinal Survey of Youth (NLSY), a survey of 12,000 young adults, aged 20-27, ongoing since 1979. This survey focuses mainly on labor market experience of youth, but does have a set of questions devoted to the use of alcohol and other drugs, designed to be comparable with information captured on the MF and NHSDA surveys. NLSY interviews are also administered face to face.

The NLSY survey is especially notable in its emphasis on those who are not well represented in other studies, including minority youth, dropouts, the unemployed, and economically disadvantaged people, all of whom are oversampled in NLSY. The NLSY sample was designed to provide better epidemiological data on minorities and school dropouts.

However, according to a recent study, compared with the other national surveys, the NLSY showed serious and unexpected underreporting of drug abuse. Further, the underreporting was not randomly distributed, but was more prominent among social and ethnic groups found in previous epidemiological surveys to have had lower prevalence rates than middle-class whites (Mensch and Kandel 1988).

Groups for whom underreporting was particularly severe included women and Blacks. Ethnicity was considered especially serious in underreporting. The authors point out that every study that has reported drug use rates by ethnicity shows lower rates for Blacks than whites, in almost all drug classes. These lower rates contrast with the overrepresentation of Blacks in treatment programs, general hospital admissions for drug problems, and arrests with positive urine samples.

Mensch and Kandel believe that, although the issue of underreporting in national surveys has not been treated extensively in literature, a consistent pattern is emerging: members of minority groups are more inclined to provide socially desirable responses to questions about alcohol and other drug abuse than are majority respondents. There are many possible reasons for this phenomenon: minority respondents may feel more threatened by possible consequences of acknowledging use and abuse; they may have less trust in the research process; or they may be more affected by field conditions, e.g., familiarity or unfamiliarity with the setting of the interview or the interviewer, the presence or absence of third parties (e.g., parents), or other factors.

Watts and Wright (1986/87) cite several possible reasons for a reported lower prevalence of drinking among Black adolescents, compared with whites. These reasons include the conservative Protestant upbringing of many Blacks, under-reporting of use by Blacks, exclusions of Blacks from many surveys, and the possibility of more late-onset drinking behaviors on the part of Blacks. These authors concur that more research is needed in this area.

Statistics that underestimate the use of alcohol and other drugs by Black youth are a great problem, according to Primm (1987), because such statistics figure heavily in allocating resources for prevention and treatment to specific States, communities, and population groups. In short, better epidemiologic data are needed to describe the actual scope of the problem of alcohol and other drug use by Black youths.

Some recent findings deserve mention. A national study conducted by the Media-Advertising Partnership for a Drug-Free America (1987) found that 53 percent of Blacks 12 years of age or older smoked marijuana at some time, and 35 percent used it within the last year. Nineteen percent of Black teens used cocaine in the past year; and 22 percent intended to use cocaine within the next 12 months. Of Black teens, 17 percent reported they used crack in the past 30 days, and intended to continue using it. One recognized expert (Harper 1986) reported that approximately 32 percent of Black youth age 13 to 20 in Washington, D.C., used illicit drugs from time to time. He also found that the homes of working parents were used for daytime parties involving cigarettes, illicit drugs, and alcohol.

Research Needs

Although the picture of young Black children and their knowledge, attitudes, and practices concerning alcohol and other drugs is becoming clearer, we still need more and better data to guide communications, prevention, and intervention strategies.

Some current programs for Black children are attempting to fill gaps in our understanding of what these children know and fail to know about alcohol and other drugs and are starting to design and test assessment instruments especially developed with the needs of this population in mind (Office for Substance Abuse Prevention [OSAP] 1988). Specific questions that still need to be answered include

- How does the knowledge of poor Black children about alcohol and other drugs compare with that of white middle-income children?

- What is the relationship between accurate and adequate knowledge of alcohol/other drugs and educational level?

- Are there myths or misconceptions about alcohol and other drugs—such as their availability, immediate effects, addictive properties, health hazards—that are more common among inner-city Black people and their children than among other population groups?

- What sources of information on alcohol and other drugs do Black children have? How do they rate these sources? Which sources do they consider most credible?

- What barriers prevent Black children from getting and using knowledge of alcohol and other drugs?

- How prevalent is alcohol and other drug use among Black inner-city children?

Planning Considerations

Audience segments

- Black males
- Children born to addicted or alcohol-dependent mothers
- Children growing up in alcohol- or other drug-abusing families
- Children of single mothers
- Children who are already using drugs
- Children involved with the drug trade
- Foster children.

Channels

- Black radio stations
- Black magazines
- Alternative media, e.g., videodocumentaries, community theater
- Black churches
- Recreation centers
- Neighborhood stores
- Movie theaters.

Sources

- Community role modes and mentors
- Older siblings
- Elderly relatives
- Radio disk jockeys
- Celebrities (carefully selected).

Materials

- Available are
  - brochures and fliers
  - some posters
  - some videotapes.
- Needed are
  - radio PSAs
  - billboards and posters
  - culturally appropriate curricula
  - low-literacy print materials.

Messages. Messages should:

- State clearly that no child should use alcohol or other drugs
- Be appropriate to lifestyle, language, and culture of the inner city
- Emphasize the immediate as well as the long-range benefits of nonuse
- Promote other rewarding activities.

When designing communications programs, it is important to select components that are meaningful to and appropriate for the target audience. In the past, programs designed to speak to white middle-class youth have been less than successful in reaching poor urban Black youth. NIAAA researchers noted

> A concern of many black and minority communities is the extent to which culture is infused into prevention projects. Since ethnic background, culture, and custom influence drinking behavior, then the inclusion of culture, customs, and ethnic heritage must be a part of prevention.

Black Americans represent the largest ethnic minority group in the United States, yet alcohol programming for this group has been limited and is often not sensitive to cultural differences and values. In particular, black youth programming has been inadequate with few available materials to guide the planning and implementation of these efforts. (Scott and Miranda 1981)

Black youth use and respond to different media and, in some cases, have created totally new means of communications, e.g., rap music. To reach these young people with effective prevention messages and materials, it is important to get inside their culture and listen to their personal stories of struggle, survival, and success.

The following discussion of audiences, channels, materials, and messages that may help reach Black inner-city children is based on research reports and the opinions of experts who contributed to this chapter.

Audiences

While our general target audience for this discussion is Black inner-city youth, ages 6 to 12, the point must be made that there are subgroups of Black children who face a variety of challenges that tend to exacerbate their already high-risk status. These subgroups include

- Black males

- Children born to addicted or alcohol-dependent mothers

- Children growing up in alcohol- or other drug-abusing families

- Children of single mothers

- Children who are already using drugs

- Children involved with the drug trade

- Foster children.

Many of these subgroup characteristics are identified as predictors of high-risk behavior in the 1986 Anti-Drug Abuse Act (PL 99-570); chapter 1 of this monograph specifically discusses youth who can be characterized as high-risk. Other characteristics mentioned above have been identified by experts and through anecdotal evidence as possible factors in alcohol and other drug use by urban Black youth.

Channels

Television and advertising

Research indicates that Black households watch more television than non-Black households (HDM/Dawson Johns and Black 1988), and that the children in these households appear to have a voracious appetite for television. A January/February 1987 Nielson television index reported a 45-percent greater viewing rate for 2- to 17-year-old Black youth than for their non-Black counterparts. And while television is viewed as a benign, albeit intrusive, medium by most people, there are some Black observers who view it as a major factor in the poor social and self-image of Blacks. Bruce Hare writes:

> Aside from the exploitation of youthful insecurities by commercials, creating diseases to sell cures, such as perpetuating the need to "relax" one's hair, prevent chapped lips, and wear designer jeans, the tube serves to condition the population. Television tells youth what to want, whom to like, how to be, and what to think. It romanticizes greed, crime, infidelity, materialism, and individualism. Furthermore, it not only provides white America with distorted images of black people and black communities, but creates gross misconceptions of the world for Black America as well. While comic treatment of whites on the tube is counterbalanced by serious treatment, it is hard for a viewer to conclude that the black family, for example, is anything other than a joke. It creates people who confuse reality and illusion, desensitizes people to violence, and programs all populations to a pro-male, white, and upper-class imitation pattern. (Hare 1988)

As harsh as that assessment may seem, it does not mention another problem, one that is discussed in *Marketing Booze to Blacks* (Hacker et al. 1987). This landmark publication contends that Black television viewers have become a particular target for beer advertisers and that many of the ads are an insult to the values held by most Black people. In describing a malt liquor campaign featuring a well-known Black actor, the authors state that the ad "suggests how to get women drunk and into bed." Moreover:

> As if promoting the high alcohol content of malt liquors and the chances of scoring with women were not enough, other aspects of the ad offend as well. The ad, replete with sexual innuendoes and a guarantee of sexual success, was seen on (among other shows) re-runs of the popular black-oriented family comedy show, "The Jeffersons" and was broadcast, in New York City, for example, in the early evening when (according to Arbitron) over 300,000 viewers (15 percent of the total) were under the age of 18. The insensitivity of the message—that women can be seduced if you get them drunk—is

heightened by the sad reality of high rates of unwed pregnancies among black teenagers.

Radio

Radio has always been a popular medium among Black youth. A recent survey by the Media-Advertising Partnership for a Drug-Free America (1987) found that 85 to 95 percent of all Blacks listen to Black-programmed and urban radio stations. Black radio serves as a prime source of information and, in many cases, as a voice of its community. The disk jockeys and talk show personalities command great attention, and Black audiences accord them a high degree of respect and credibility.

After television, radio is the second most common medium among Blacks, with 79 percent of the Partnership's survey respondents reporting that they use a radio at least two or three times per week (HDM 1988). The Partnership for a Drug-Free America strongly supports using radio to reach Black teens with prevention messages. Black radio has some substantial qualitative advantages. It develops a one-on-one relationship with the listener, it is believable, and it specifically targets the Black population.

Print

Magazines and newspapers are less popular than television and radio among Black urban communities. Sixty-eight percent report reading a magazine and 62 percent report reading a newspaper two or three times a week (HDM 1988). Several magazines address topics of particular importance to Blacks. The readers of these magazines, however, seem to be well educated and affluent.

While magazines and newspapers are less popular among urban Black youth, these media are still important information providers. Black publications, especially those targeted to preteens and teens, offer opportunities to target prevention messages specifically to Black youth. And while Black youth are less likely to read magazines like *Jet, Ebony, Black Enterprise*, and *Essence*, many of their parents read these publications and can pass on vital information to their children. Comic books may also be a useful vehicle.

The problem of low literacy among urban Black youth is an impediment to conveying prevention messages through the print media. The average reading proficiency of minority 17-year-olds is only slightly better than that of white 13-year-olds (Children's Defense Fund 1988). A national campaign to increase the literacy of Black youth could serve the dual purpose of increasing their chances for educational and employment achievement, while removing a crippling frustration that could be a factor in alcohol and other drug abuse.

Several other problems surround the role of the Black print media in the effort to convey alcohol and other drug use prevention messages to Black youth. First, Black magazines are read mostly by more affluent readers and so may miss the target audience altogether. Second, many Black publications depend heavily on alcohol and cigarette advertising to produce revenues. According to Hacker et al. (1987), in *Marketing Booze to Blacks*:

> In most of the leading Black-oriented magazines, alcohol ads are second in number to cosmetic and hair products. They usually outnumber cigarette and automobile ads. As with many Black ad agencies, Black magazines have become significantly dependent on alcohol ad revenues. The apparent price of this addiction to alcohol ad revenues has been a stunning silence about health risks associated with alcohol use.

Billboards

Driving through almost any Black inner-city neighborhood, one sees an extraordinary number of outdoor billboards, many of them advertising alcohol products. This proliferation of billboard advertising in Black communities has become an issue across the Nation, and efforts to control the use of billboards by alcohol advertisers have been undertaken. The Coalition for Scenic Beauty notes:

> The billboard industry is saturating low-income neighborhoods with billboards advertising tobacco and alcoholic beverages. This has resulted in thousands of new billboards being placed indiscriminately in ethnic neighborhoods. A much higher percentage of billboards in ethnic neighborhoods advertise alcohol and liquor products compared to billboards in other locations. For example, during the first nine months of 1986, liquor marketers spent nearly 16 times as much on 'junior billboards' directed at blacks as they spent on advertising to the general public. A 1987 survey conducted by the City of St. Louis found twice as many billboards in black neighborhoods as white. Almost 60 percent of the billboards in the black neighborhoods advertised cigarettes and alcoholic beverages. (Coalition for Scenic Beauty, no date)

Communications programs could use billboards for messages to prevent alcohol and other drug use, countering the pro-use messages of advertisers.

Alternative media

Social marketers, including alcohol and other drug prevention advocates, rely heavily on television and radio to increase awareness, change attitudes, and reinforce healthy behaviors. But the mass media may not adequately serve this purpose. According to *Washington Post* columnist George F. Will (1987), part of the problem is advertising clutter. The typical American is exposed to approximately 3,000 commercial messages—from newspapers to billboards—a day. It is said the average American spends a year and a half of his life watching television commercials. The number of messages transmitted by broadcast and print media doubled between 1967 and 1982 and may double again by 1997.

In fact, there has been such a heavy reliance on television by both commercial advertisers and nonprofit groups, recent research indicates, that even though people, and particularly young urban Blacks, may be watching more television than ever, they may also be reaching a saturation point resulting from the continuous bombardment of ads and public service announcements (PSAs). Will believes actual attention to the messages may be declining. Adding the proliferation of advertising and PSA messages that seem to spring up from every available space, both outdoors and in our homes, it is no wonder people are overwhelmed by sales pitches.

In the face of such an avalanche of information, it is clear that those involved in communicating prevention messages will have to be more creative both in message design and placement. While television will undoubtedly continue to be a prime medium for communicating alcohol and drug problem prevention messages to Black youth, other presently underused media may prove more effective in standing out from the clutter and, therefore, delivering more effective messages. Possible alternatives are community theater and videodocumentaries, which are discussed under "Recommendations."

Community channels

Alcohol and other drug abuse professionals have known for years that prevention requires a community-wide systems approach involving everyone from parents and teachers to community leaders, business and industry, existing support groups like churches and recreational facilities, and the media. The primary goal of the concerted application of all these resources is to help young people develop healthy attitudes about themselves, their families, and their communities—attitudes leading to positive lifestyles that do not include using alcohol and other drugs.

A prototype of a model for diffusing health information among minority groups was developed by the National Heart, Lung, and Blood Institute (NHLBI 1985). While NHLBI was concerned with diffusing information regarding high blood pressure and high blood cholesterol in Black communities, the principles and findings of its study have applicability to our effort for diffusing effective alcohol and other drug problem prevention messages among Black inner-city youth. The community diffusion model states, "Diffusion efforts aimed at culturally diverse populations should be most effective if planned and implemented at a community level...the model also acknowledges appropriate roles for individuals and organizations outside the core community" (NHLBI 1985).

Nine Critical Steps

An NHLBI study identified these steps for effective community diffusion programs for Blacks and other culturally diverse communities.

- *Establish Working Group of Co-Change Agents*—This process should be ongoing. While one or two key persons will provide overall program management, it is likely that the networks of co-change agents and opinion leaders involved in planning and implementing strategies will continue growing and evolving.

- *Recognize Problem, Seek Help*—This is a process of becoming aware or making others aware of a community problem or need that should be addressed.

- *Assess Community*—Knowledge of the target community is crucial for effective diffusion strategies.

- *Determine Measurable Goals*—This process is necessary for proper planning, monitoring, implementing, and evaluating diffusion strategies.

- *Plan Diffusion Activities*—This process is ongoing and should allow for changes in strategies resulting from continuous monitoring of program activities and evaluating program outcomes. Diffusion activities are especially important in culturally diverse populations, because different activities may be required to reach different audiences.

- *Prepare Communications Tools*—Communications tools are the actual written and/or audiovisual materials that are used to convey a message. Different audiences, again, may require different tools that may need to be developed.

- *Pretest*—Diffusion activities and communications tools should be pretested on a small sample of the target audience.

- *Implement and Monitor Plan*—Monitoring should be maintained throughout, so revisions can be made when needed.

- *Assess Final Results*—This documents program outcomes, which can be useful to other communities or for future diffusion projects.

Churches

The church still plays a major role in the Black community and is viewed by many as the most responsive and supportive institution accessible to Black people. While many people associate Black religion with gospel singing and Baptist revival meetings, there is a great diversity of religious practice among Blacks, which includes participation in virtually every Christian denomination, as well as other religions such as Islam, Judaism, and more secular or "New Age" movements. A hallmark of "the Black church" has been its traditional role as a catalyst and forum for social and political action within the Black community. It is no accident that two of the most powerful activist voices to come out of the Black community in the last 3 decades have belonged to clergymen: Martin Luther King, Jr., and Jesse Jackson. Both men rose to national prominence on the wave of their extraordinary influence, first among their religious constituencies and then in the larger community. The Black clergy, for the most part, still commands a high degree of respect and authority within the Black community.

According to experts, while the Black church and Black ministers have spoken out forcefully and effectively over the years on many issues, including civil rights, child care, and economic justice, many have been reluctant to speak out on one of the most devastating problems facing Black life—alcohol and other drug problems. For too long, they say, many Black churches have viewed alcohol and other drug abuse as a moral failing and have tended, like much of the larger society, to "blame the victim" and label him or her as undesirable. This appears to be changing as Black clergymen have become better educated and more likely to deal with the host of problems associated with alcohol and other drug use, particularly by young people.

Attempts could be made to galvanize the collective strength of the Black church throughout the country and apply its massive human and economic resources to fighting alcohol and other drug use among young, urban Blacks. The need for this involvement by the churches can be communicated through such forums as national church conventions, television and radio ministries, church newsletters, and pulpit sermons.

Voluntary and civic organizations

These include groups organized to fight alcohol and other drugs as well as other groups concerned with families and youth. Big Brothers/Big Sisters and Boys Clubs, for example, are active in some inner-city communities.

Efforts should also be made to involve the larger community, which includes Federal, State, and local government, as well as private, voluntary organizations. These groups can be helpful both in program collaboration and as funding sources for projects the community may want to implement. Some groups that have already been identified as having an interest in reducing the incidence of alcohol and other drug problems among inner-city Black youth include the following:

- NAACP
- National Urban League
- National Medical Association
- National Black Alcoholism Council
- Zeta Phi Beta Sorority, Inc.
- Operation PUSH

- Links, Inc.
- Institute on Black Chemical Abuse.

Community gathering spots

Many experts involved in this project agreed that typical surveys designed to assess the extent of alcohol and other drug use among youth understate the problem among urban Black youth, because so many of these young people are away from the mainstream. Most surveys are school based, while many youth at highest risk are on the street.

This is why strategies to reach these youth must include community outreach approaches. Approaches may include using more of the following channels to convey prevention messages:

- Recreation centers/basketball courts/roller rinks, etc.
- Shelters/soup kitchens
- Barber and beauty shops
- Community colleges
- Soul food restaurants
- Corner grocery stores and convenience stores
- Movie theaters.

The Smart Moves Program

A successful program that is undergirded by conscious message strategies targeted to urban Black youth is the Smart Moves Program of the Boys Clubs of America. Jim Cox, director of the Boys Club Smart Moves Program in the Hillside Public Housing Project in Milwaukee, described the following strategies that have proven promising in teaching inner-city Black youth the skills needed to recognize and resist media, peer, and other social pressures that encourage using alcohol and other drugs:

- Use positive role models
- Encourage alternative activities
- Encourage a sense of belonging
- Introduce prevention programs/communications through existing "trusted" community groups like Boys Clubs
- Use positive peer pressure (use older youth to counsel the younger ones).

Source: Cox 1989.

Sources

Celebrities

Well-known achievers in the sports, entertainment, business, or political fields command attention and may be effective spokespersons. It can be helpful to have these people talk with young people or have them appear on television, radio, or in printed public service announcements. However, experts consulted for this report agreed that, contrary to popular belief, celebrities, including sports figures, do not necessarily represent the most credible sources for delivering alcohol and other drug abuse prevention messages to inner-city Black youth, because they do not represent people with whom Black youth interact on a daily basis. There is also a danger in using recovering celebrities in that they may send mixed messages to youth: "If he once did drugs and came out on top, maybe I can too." This is not to suggest that celebrities should never be used, but that they should be chosen carefully, based on their own lifestyles, their honest commitment to alcohol and other drug use prevention among youth, and their acceptance by youth as role models.

Dawnn Lewis: Role Model and Spokesperson

Actress Dawnn Lewis has visited numerous schools throughout the Nation and volunteered her services to star in an OSAP television public service campaign. Ms. Lewis, who costars as Jaleesa Vinson on the popular television show *A Different World*, has demonstrated a real commitment to helping young people resist the temptation to engage in alcohol and other drug use. Coming from an inner-city background in Brooklyn, New York, Ms. Lewis, who dances, writes music, sings, and acts, urges young people to express their talents and allow their dreams to grow without the negative influences of alcohol and other drugs. Ms. Lewis is an example of the kind of positive role model/celebrity who can be used successfully to promote drug-free lifestyles for urban Black youth.

Community figures

A frequent lament among Black people who live in the inner city is that because a Black inner-city middle class no longer exists, there are few positive role models for youth. While this is regrettably true in many cases, numerous successful Blacks will, if asked, come back to their old neighborhoods to share their stories and encourage youth to aspire and work for success. For example, the *Washington Post* recently reported on the efforts of Navy Reserve pilot Drew Brown, who has visited some 350,000 students in cities throughout the Nation with a message urging Black youth to stay in school, to set ambitious goals, and not to use race or poverty as excuses for giving up (Barker 1988).

There is a compelling need for consistent, personal attention and involvement by local role models in the everyday lives of young, urban Blacks, many of whom live in female-headed, single-parent families. The experts consulted for this project agreed that young Black males, in particular, need consistent Black male role models to help them navigate through adolescence in the sometimes dangerous inner city.

Family members

Sociologist Bruce Hare has reviewed research showing that older siblings and peers exert an enormous influence on younger Blacks (Hare 1988). This older sibling/peer influence may be an important factor in Black families, many of which are headed by single women who work and need to leave the oldest child at home "in charge" of the younger ones. This older sibling assumes the role of a parent and may have an even greater influence on his or her charges than the real parent, say some of this project's expert consultants. Young children can be either negatively or positively influenced by this older sibling. Older siblings can convey alcohol and other drug use prevention messages both interpersonally and through such mass media as television and radio public service announcements, brochures, posters, and transit cards.

Despite the well-documented fragmentation and stresses affecting the Black family, there remains a deep-rooted respect among most Blacks for the family unit. Since the time of slavery, however, this dream of the typical husband-wife-child family unit has been undermined by such external factors as separating families during the slave trade for economic reasons, treating slaves as commodities, sexual abuse of Black women during slavery by their white masters, and the stresses associated with racism and urbanization during the post slavery era. Harper (1986) provides an indepth discussion of these historical phases of Black family life.

According to Harper, the family ideal was more fully realized by southern Blacks than by northern Blacks. This southern model, with grandmothers, uncles, cousins, and other relatives living either under the same roof or in the same small town, has become a part of the Black consciousness and reminds many Blacks of a time when unity was not just an ideal, but a reality of life. Experts on this project agreed that there is a great deal of respect among most Blacks for such family icons as the mother, grandmother, grandfather, and elderly aunt and uncle. They recommended that more use be made of these persons as credible sources for reaching Black inner-city youth with alcohol and other drug use prevention messages.

Materials Review

A search for educational materials related to the prevention of alcohol and other drug use among youth located more than a thousand items. Of these items, only 192 were targeted toward minorities and only about 60 to Blacks. These 60 included about 10 videotapes, approximately 10 posters, several curricula, and assorted booklets, brochures, and fact sheets. Sources were Federal and State agencies, voluntary groups, and private producers.*

Needs exist for the following:

- Simple visual materials with a clear "no use" message for underage youth

- Black radio PSAs

- Low-literacy brochures, pamphlets, and fliers

- Outdoor advertising, such as billboards, bus signs, etc., to counter the proliferation of tobacco and alcohol ads aimed at Blacks

- Materials for Black children of alcoholics, school dropouts, and single or teenage parents.

Messages

Understanding the language and lifestyle of the Black inner-city child is no easy task. As we approach the end of the 1980s, it is clear that there is an acceleration of creative expression within the Black community and the codes of cultural identity are undergoing almost constant change. From rap music to gold chains to haircuts known as "the fade" or "the box," everything is changing. Last week the word was "bite," meaning the act of copying or imitating something. This week the word is "word," used as an exclamation point to emphasize the truth or seriousness of a statement. It is hard enough for the parents of these hip and increasingly cynical, sometimes violent, young people to understand their ever-changing language and styles. How can we expect prevention agencies to keep up?

One strategy is to look beyond the popular language and symbols to more basic, underlying cultural themes, credible spokespersons, and communications channels that can be used to reach these youth. Understanding today's hip slang may be less important to prevention efforts than understanding the values, needs, and wants of this special youth group.

Experts contributing to this chapter recommended that messages to Black youth appeal to their cultural and familial ideals. Success stories need to be told. Role models need to be spotlighted. The historical underpinnings of

---

*More information is available from the National Clearinghouse for Alcohol and Drug Information; see appendix E.

positive cultural values in the Black experience need to be given a chance to breathe again.

There is practically unanimous consensus among prevention and treatment practitioners, as well as community leaders, that in the face of the myriad socioeconomic problems plaguing the Black community, the single most needed quality is a sense of hope and dignity. Examples can be found in the speeches of Black leaders:

"Down with dope! Up with hope!"

"I may not have a job, but I am somebody."

The Rev. Jesse Jackson

"We must not allow...any force to make us feel like we don't count. Maintain a sense of dignity and respect..."

Dr. Martin Luther King, Jr.

In addition, messages should attempt to counteract the lure of drugs by emphasizing the immediate as well as the long-range benefits of abstention and by promoting other activities.

Recommendations

- Encourage personal, one-on-one mentoring of young urban Blacks by positive role models.
- Call attention to the need for improved parenting skills and reduced teen pregnancies.
- Encourage Black churches to become involved.
- Communicate to young Blacks their rich cultural heritage.
- Persuade television program decisionmakers to be more sensitive in their portrayals of Blacks.
- Construct media messages that use older youth to deliver prevention messages.
- Use Black radio.
- Work with the business community, especially in high-density urban areas, to increase advertising for prevention messages.
- Mobilize local citizens to demand removal of offensive alcohol and other drug paraphernalia ads from billboards.

- Use media that involve youth.

- Make information available where youth congregate.

- Encourage corporations to take a more active role in communications efforts.

- Develop materials targeted to Black youth.

The following suggestions, gleaned from a review of existing literature as well as meetings and interviews with prevention experts, are not meant to exhaust the range of communications strategies (which themselves are only one part of the prevention agenda). They are a compendium of ideas, some old and some new, designed to stimulate action and further discussion. No effort was made to assign priorities among these recommendations. Direct discussions with youth and those who influence their knowledge, attitudes, and practices will be needed to clarify which of them are most likely to succeed in a particular community.

Encourage more personal, one-on-one mentoring of young urban Blacks by positive role models. There is an acute need for more Black men and women to volunteer to mentor urban youth. Community-wide mass media campaigns could urge more Blacks to serve as Big Brothers/Big Sisters or to become involved in youth organizations such as Boys Clubs (see sidebar below). In addition, men of Black churches could serve as mentors for youth in the community.

Call attention to the need for improved parenting skills and a reduction in teen pregnancies. With the proliferation of teenage pregnancy and poor, single-parent families, there is also a need to motivate young urban Blacks to reduce the risks of teenage pregnancies and, for those with children, to improve their parenting skills. Essential to the survival of urban Black youth is the need to be born to parents who want them and can provide for them. Without that love and commitment, the child is already at a disadvantage and begins to learn that survival can be a cruel, heartless game, played best in the streets. Too often, when young people start having babies before they are old enough to be loving parents, the cycle of poverty and alcohol and other drug abuse is refueled.

Adoption rates for Black children remain low. Without the love and nurturing of a dedicated adult, many orphaned Black children will never break the cycle of poverty, hopelessness, and alcohol and other drug abuse. While the need for people to come forth and adopt Black babies is acute, the demand for these babies remains low. Efforts must be redoubled at the local level to motivate Black adults and others to adopt these children.

Communications activities to curtail teen pregnancy, encourage adoption, and improve parenting skills may include

- Church-based parenting workshops

- Parenting seminars, using role-playing techniques, sponsored by tenant groups in public housing projects

- Localized mass media campaigns to raise awareness of the need for family planning and birth control

- Television documentaries and town meetings on the need for improved parenting skills-training in the Black community

- Television documentaries highlighting success stories of parents adopting Black children.

Chapter 4 discusses strategies for reaching parents.

Encourage more Black churches to become involved. In Philadelphia, the National Institute for Adolescent Pregnancy and Family Services has enlisted the help of three local churches that provide space for classes designed to help Black inner-city parents more effectively raise their children. The curriculum, which targets the parents of youth ages 9 to 12, includes information on alcohol and other drugs, as well as parenting and communications skills.

Other communications activities to increase the involvement of Black churches in the effort to reduce alcohol and other drug abuse among inner-city youth may include

- Convening a local alcohol and other drug abuse prevention seminar where Black ministers can exchange ideas and share experiences

- Using direct mail to urge churches to make mentoring a priority project.

Communicate to young Blacks their rich cultural heritage. All prevention and treatment programs need to communicate the inherent dignity of each human being and, in the case of young urban Blacks, the rich cultural heritage they share with African-ancestored people all over the world.

Two good examples of this approach, in an alcohol and other drug abuse prevention context, are the Winners program in Los Angeles and the Ethnic Heritage program in Chicago.

Both programs are in early stages of development and have not had time to be evaluated for effectiveness. However, both are reaching Black youth with curricula that have cultural relevance to them. The problem is that, without broader reinforcement from parents, teachers, and the media, the programs are expected to have limited long-term effect. Recognizing this, Darnell Bell, creator of the Winners program, is currently working on a parents' curriculum, as well as a parent-child workbook, which will outline culturally relevant community service projects that parents and children can do together, as an alternative to hopelessness and alcohol and other drug use by youth (personal communication, 1989).

Communicating Cultural Heritage: Two Case Studies

The Winners Program

The Winners program is an innovative prevention curriculum/workbook that "represents a 'pro-blackness' or strong racial identity strategy..." (Bell 1987). The two-volume curriculum, which is now being used in Los Angeles, targets elementary school-aged Black youth. The program features profiles of famous Black role models like Frederick Douglass, Count Basie, and Benjamin Bannecker, which are used to stimulate writing assignments where the students are encouraged to relate the good qualities of the role model to their own lives and experiences.

The Ethnic Heritage Program

The Ethnic Heritage Handbook was prepared by the Bobby E. Wright Comprehensive Community Mental Health Center for the Black Heritage Project. Used by Chicago's Greater Alliance of Prevention Systems (GAPS) in five GAPS sites on Chicago's West Side, the program has the following goals:

- Disseminate accurate information to youth on African and Black history and culture

- Expose youth in this community to African music and dance, drama, vocal and instrumental music, and creative writing

- Increase the awareness of youth about the negative impact that alcohol and other drug abuse has on the residents of their community, the temptations to abuse alcohol and other drugs by residents of their community, and the effect that poor diet and alcohol and other drug abuse have on the body

- Increase the sense of self-worth among youth living in the community, by making them proud of who they are as individuals and as an ethnic group, and by helping them to realize their hidden talents and untapped strengths

- Create an environment for self-actualization by youth living in the community, through creative expression and confidence-building activities; assign roles requiring that one account for his or her own actions and be responsible for what happens in the community.

Youth are encouraged to abide by the Ethnic Heritage Pledge, which reads, "I pledge myself to my people, to develop my mind, so that I may learn all I can in order to do my best; to keep my body physically fit, strong, and free from anything that would weaken me; to be kind and thoughtful; and to unselfishly share my knowledge in order to bring about the empowerment of my people!" (African American Heritage Project 1988).

Persuade television program decisionmakers to be more sensitive in their portrayals of Blacks. Especially because there is alcohol advertising targeted specifically to Black consumers, media strategies need to be developed to serve as countermeasures. According to the experts

- Television stations are very sensitive to public opinion. One letter from an irate viewer carries the weight of about 10,000 silent people. Citizens who are concerned by the quantity and content of alcohol advertisements targeted to Blacks may want to write or call their local stations to complain and encourage airing countermessages and information about the harmful consequences of alcohol use and abuse, particularly for young people.

- In the thoughtful consideration of using celebrities, the government may want to support and follow the lead of such groups as Black Artists Against Drugs, the Los Angeles-based group that has produced anti-alcohol and drug PSAs using such well-known Black celebrities as Bill Cosby, Run DMC, and LL Cool J.

- Advocacy groups and political leaders may want to seek to communicate about the benefits of equal time on television for messages about the risks associated with alcohol use and abuse.

- Greater use may be made of cable television, which offers unique public access channels in many communities.

Construct media messages that use older youth to deliver prevention messages. Messages should take advantage of the important role that older siblings play in many inner-city families, using their authority and credibility to deliver prevention messages. Traditional family icons, such as elderly relatives, could also be used as spokespersons in media messages.

Use Black radio. Radio, with its inherent close ties to the community, could be used more frequently by community leaders, prevention communicators, and citizens to urge urban Blacks to resist temptations of the drug culture, according to the experts. This could be done through the following activities:

- Talk show appearances
- Locally produced PSAs
- On-air advice and commentaries from DJs
- News coverage of positive, alternative activities by Black youth
- Letters and telephone calls to stations' general managers, urging more attention to the alcohol and other drug problems affecting the community.

Work with the business community, especially in high-density urban areas, to increase advertising for prevention messages. A number of Black organizations, including the National Black Alcoholism Council (NBAC), are beginning to focus on the issue of alcohol advertising targeted to Blacks. These organizations have begun an appeal to the Black media to rethink their ad content because of a concern about the high rate of alcohol and other drug problems in the Black community. While NBAC and others recognize that alcohol advertising is the bread and butter of most Black magazines, they want to begin working with the publications to explore ways that alcohol ads might be replaced with other product ads. This dialogue will necessarily expand to include a broad range of consumer-oriented advertisers who have historically neglected using Black media.

Mobilize local citizens to demand removal of offensive alcohol and other drug paraphernalia ads from billboards. As stated earlier, there is a growing movement to take steps to reduce billboard advertising because of the effect the ads have on young people. These young people see billboard ads every day on their way to and from school, and as they move within the community. Recently in Detroit, Michigan, Alberta Tensley-Williams, member of the Wayne County Board of Commissioners, led a protest against billboard ads for cigarette papers, a legal product now used mostly for rolling marijuana joints (De Ramus 1988). A similar protest was mounted recently in Dorchester, Massachusetts, where residents, citing historic, aesthetic, and public health reasons, sought a ban on billboard advertising (L. Brown 1988). Counteradvertising on billboards might also be an effective strategy.

Use media that involve youth. Greater use also could be made of the inherent creative talent of urban Black youth. This is a highly energetic group who does not get into trouble because of a lack of enthusiasm, but more often because of inadequate outlets to channel their verve. There are numerous ways to do this while simultaneously promoting alcohol and other drug-free lifestyles.

Video documentaries are being recognized as a powerful medium to focus on a topic like the dangers of alcohol and other drug abuse. One such documentary, "PCP Is Not For Me" (1987), was produced by a Washington, D.C., group called Public Interest Video Network. According to its producer, Arlen Slobodow, the success of the video is due largely to the active participation of actual neighborhood children in conceptualizing and executing the project. This strategy can be extended to a number of other "activity"-oriented communications projects such as poster and rap song contests, as well as music videos.

Community theater may also be an excellent vehicle to involve youth in delivering alcohol and other drug-free messages. In Washington, D.C., the Everyday Theater group puts on performances of such plays as "No Prisoners," a drama that aims to "shock, sadden, and deter District youth from drug dealing." According to an article in the *Washington Post*, "Participation in the play...functions partly as a dress rehearsal for unemployed or troubled youths eager to begin their lives anew. Some cast members are on probation or have been referred by social workers" (Sanchez 1988).

Make information available where youth congregate. There are also other communications channels located outside the home, in places where urban Black youth congregate. These locations include

- *Movie theaters.* Movie makers and theater owners can be encouraged to devote PSA space for alcohol and other drug abuse prevention messages as "leaders" to the feature presentation.

- *Recreation centers.* Many urban Black youth frequent recreation centers, including basketball courts, sports stadiums, community swimming pools, roller skating rinks, bowling alleys, etc. These centers are ideal places to distribute alcohol and other drug abuse prevention materials.

- *Corner grocery stores.* Many inner-city neighborhoods are served by small corner grocery stores. The storeowners can be enlisted to help distribute alcohol and other drug abuse prevention materials.

Encourage corporations to take a more active role in communications efforts. Some corporations are beginning to realize it is more cost effective to help urban Black youth develop into productive adults than to face the enormous economic and social consequences of benign neglect. Communications strategies can be developed to increase the awareness of business of the benefits of helping these youth.

Programs like Adopt-A-School, Summer Jobs, and other corporate outreach efforts need to be recognized, applauded, and expanded. It is increasingly apparent that the effort to save Black youth from the ravages of alcohol and other drug problems requires more than just government action. There is a need for total commitment from every sector—especially the business community. After all, urban Black youth can, if properly supported, motivated, and directed, provide tremendous creative and technical energy to corporate America. If neglected, however, these same potential contributors can become a drain on the Nation's economic and competitive goals, due to such factors as a decreased labor goal, crime, and higher taxes to support more prisons, welfare programs, and rehabilitation programs.

Government, corporate, and community leaders who understand the link between opportunity and motivation will want to publicize these corporate efforts, so that more youth might avail themselves of existing opportunities, and more corporations might initiate programs to give hope and opportunity to urban Black youth.

Table 2. Suggestions for Communications Programs
Black Inner-City Youth Aged 6 to 12

Channels

Community
- Schools
- Barber/beauty shops
- Movie theaters
- Convenience stores
- Corner grocery stores
- Soul food restaurants
- Churches
- Emergency medical facilities
- WIC offices
- Tenant groups
- Shelters
- Soup kitchens
- Adoption agencies
- Community colleges
- Recreation centers
- Basketball courts/swimming pools, etc.
- Cities in schools
- Video stores

Media
- Black radio stations
- Public access cable television
- Television/radio ministers
- Black magazines
- Community theater

Spokespersons
- Celebrities (carefully selected)
- Big Brothers/Big Sisters
- Men of the church
- Older youth
- Older family members
- Clergy
- Radio disk jockeys
- Sports coaches

Activities

- Step 1: Gather the formal and informal opinion leaders together with members of the target audience to solicit a long-term commitment for an intensive, system-wide approach to prevention. Use all communications mechanisms to motivate, persuade, and convince people that there is hope, prevention can work, and they can make a difference.
- Convene meetings of business leaders
- Hold seminars for clergy
- Organize "Kid's Congress"
- Hold parenting workshops
- Arrange peer counseling programs
- Give presentations to neighborhood meetings
- Teach about African heritage
- Conduct letter-writing campaigns to radio/television stations
- Develop PSAs
- Develop magazine articles
- Mount counteradvertising billboards
- Organize summer jobs program with businesses
- Support small business ventures by youth
- Debunk myth that drug dealing is lucrative option
- Encourage successful role models to give school assemblies as reinforcement to more intensive school-based curricula
- Involve youth in creating videotape documentaries, music videos
- Hold poster or rap song contests
- Involve youth in community theater
- Ask for volunteers for specific tasks
- Ask radio stations to run series of PSAs from groups to recruit volunteers

Table 2. Suggestions for Communications Programs
Black Inner-City Youth Aged 6 to 12
(continued)

Materials

- Simple visual materials
- Videotape documentaries
- Black radio PSAs
- Low-literacy brochures and pamphlets
- Counter outdoor advertising (billboards, bus cards)
- Materials targeted to children of alcoholics, school dropouts, single parents, and teenage mothers
- Community action manual with specific ideas for volunteers, businesses, parents, etc.
- Culturally appropriate curricula
- Adaptation of sorority/ fraternity materials

Messages

Messages specific to prevention should
- Give a clear, "no use" message for youth
- Emphasize the immediate as well as future benefits of not using drugs
- Emphasize that there are other satisfying activities

Messages to address basic issues should
- Emphasize that many successful Blacks do not use or abuse alcohol or other drugs
- Emphasize that Blacks have a rich ethnic heritage
- Encourage adoptions of Black children
- Support literacy programs
- Highlight the risks of teenage pregnancy
- Stimulate improved parenting skills

Develop materials targeted to Black youth. Although some materials exist for Black youth, there are definite gaps between what is available and what is needed. Experts cite the need for clear visual materials (posters, billboards) and verbal or audio materials (radio PSAs), as well as low-reading-level print materials. A discussion of available materials and needs appears above under "Planning Considerations."

Bibliography

African American Heritage Project. *Ethnic Heritage Program Handbook for the Alternative Activities Strategy of the Greater Alliance of Prevention Systems (GAPS).* Chicago: AAHP, 1988.

The Alcoholism Report. Survey shows alcohol and drug abuse as top concerns. May 24, 1988a. p.5.

The Alcoholism Report. Survey: Children know more booze brands than presidents. September 13, 1988b. p. 6.

The Alcoholism Report. Seventy-six percent of children in Texas secondary schools drink. September 13, 1988. p. 7.

Alvey, K.T. *Effective Black Parenting: A Review and Synthesis of Black Perspectives,* Grant Report MH 32905, Vol. 4. Rockville, Md.: National Institute of Mental Health, November 1981.

Alvey, K.T.; Harrison, D.S.; Cheek, D.K., et al. *The Culturally Adapted Parent Training Project: Recommendations for Adapting Parent Training Programs for Black Poverty-Level Parents of Preschool Children.* Grant Report MH 32905. Rockville, Md.: National Institute of Mental Health, February 1981.

Alvey, K.T.; Harrison, D.S.; Rosen, L.D.; and Fuentes, E.G. *Black Parenting: An Empirical Study With Implications for Parent Trainers and Therapists.* Grant Report MH 32905, Vol. 5. Rockville, Md.: National Institute of mental Health, July 1982.

Atkins, B.J.; Klein, M.A.; and Mosley, B. Black adolescents' attitudes toward and use of alcohol and other drugs. *International Journal of the Addictions* 22(12):1201–1211, 1987.

Austin, G.A.; Johnson, B.D.; Carroll, E.E.; and Lettieri, D., eds. *Drugs and Minorities. Research Issues 21,* DHEW Pub. No. (ADM)78-507. Rockville, Md.: National Institute on Drug Abuse, December 1977.

Baltimore Sun, Kimball gets 17 years, plus 15 on probation, 1989. p. B1.

Barker, K. Shoot for the moon, pilot urges city students. *Washington Post,* December 10, 1988. p. B1.

Bell, C.S., and Battjes, R. *Prevention Research: Deterring Drug Use Among Children and Adolescents.* National Institute on Drug Abuse, Research Monograph No. 63, DHHS Pub. No. (ADM)85-1334. Rockville, Md.: NIDA, 1985.

Bell, D. *Winners: A Culturally-Based, Values Clarification-Oriented, Creative Writing Primary Prevention Workbook for the Black Child.* Los Angeles: Darnell Bell, 1987.

Bell, P. Community-Based Prevention. In: *Proceedings of the First National Conference on Alcohol and Drug Abuse Prevention.* Rockville, Md.: National Institute on Alcohol Abuse and Alcoholism and National Institute on Drug Abuse, August 3–6, 1986.

Black, G.S. *The Attitudinal Basis of Drug Use.* Prepared for The Media-Advertising Partnership for a Drug-Free America, Inc., New York, 1988a.

Black, G.S. "Changing Attitudes Toward Drug Use: Executive Summary and Statistical Report." Prepared for The Media-Advertising Partnership for a Drug-Free America, Inc., New York, 1988b.

Borton, T., and Johnson, L., eds. *The Weekly Reader National Survey on Drugs and Drinking.* Middletown, Conn.: Field Publications, 1987.

Brisbane, F.L. Divided feelings of black alcoholic daughters: An exploratory study. *Alcohol Health and Research World* 2:2 (Winter): 48–50, 1986/87.

Brown, B.S., and Mills, A.R., eds. *Youth at High Risk for Substance Abuse.* National Institute on Drug Abuse, DHHS Publication No. (ADM)87-1537. Washington, D.C.: Supt. of Docs., U.S. Govt. Print. Off., 1987.

Brown, L. Dorchester billboards blasted: Alcohol ads come under mom's fire. *Boston Herald*, February 19, 1988.

Burkenne, R. Get 'em while they're young department: Wine chiller bars hit the market. San Francisco: The Trauma Foundation. In: *CAL Council Report*, 4:4, September 1988.

Chaplin, A.M. The new no generation. *Baltimore Sun*, November 24, 1987. p. B1.

Children's Defense Fund. *A Children's Defense Budget, FY 1989: An Analysis of Our Nation's Investment in Children.* Washington, D.C.: CDF, 1988.

Coalition for Scenic Beauty. *Fact Sheet: Alcohol and Tobacco Advertising on Billboards.* Washington, D.C.. n.d.

De Ramus, S. Citizens angry over billboard ads for rolling papers. *Detroit News*, January 12, 1988.

Deren, S. Children of substance abusers: A review of the literature. *Journal of Substance Abuse Treatment* 3:77–94, 1986.

Dewart, J., ed. *The State of Black America*. New York: National Urban League, Inc., 1987.

Dewart, J., ed. *The State of Black America*. New York: National Urban League, Inc., 1988.

The Drug Abuse Report. New dictionary of street drug terms appears. January 5:7, 1988a.

The Drug Abuse Report. Rangel committee releases GAO report blasting "Just say no." February 2:5, 1988b.

The Drug Abuse Report. OSAP grant supports peer role-model program. February 2:7, 1988c.

The Drug Abuse Report. Turn it around: New anti-drug slogan. February 2:8, 1988d.

The Drug Abuse Report. "Zero-tolerance" new Washington focus. April 19:6, 1988e.

The Drug Abuse Report. Users must be "personally and legally accountable." May 3:1, 1988f.

The Drug Abuse Report. "Zero-tolerance" document reveals philosophy. May 3:2, 1988g.

The Drug Abuse Report. "Just Say No" criticized again. May 31:7, 1988h.

The Drug Abuse Report. Dupont endorses zero-tolerance. May 31:8, 1988i.

Edmonds, T. "Justification paper for minorities task force." Paper presented to the Office for Substance Abuse Prevention under the Media and Materials Development Program. Rockville, Md.: OSAP, 1988a.

Edmonds, T. "Minorities task force meeting." Paper presented to the Office for Substance Abuse Prevention under the Media and Materials Development Program. Rockville, Md.: OSAP, 1988b.

Fein, E.B. Turning kids off drugs. *New York Times Magazine*, May 24, 1987, pp. 27–32.

Gallup Organization, Inc. Alcohol use and abuse in America. *The Gallup Report*. No. 165, October 1987.

Gilliam, D. The drug fight's need for an about-face. *Washington Post*, April 14, 1988. p. D3.

Globetti, G. Alcohol education programs and minority youth. *Journal of Drug Issues* 18(1) (Winter): 115–129, 1988.

Goodstadt, M.S. School-based drug education, what is wrong? *Education Digest*, Vol. 52 (February): 44–47, 1987.

Grant, D., and Moore, B. MIBCA-sponsored conference: Groundwork for future action. *Alcohol Health and Research World* 2:2 (Winter): 18-25, 1986–87.

Greene, D.I. Baltimoreans turn out for annual march against crime. *Baltimore Sun*, August 10, 1988. p. D1.

Griswold-Ezekoye, S.; Kumpfer, K.L.; and Bukoski, W.J., eds. *Childhood and Chemical Abuse: Prevention and Intervention.* New York: Haworth Press, 1986.

Hacker, G.A.; Collins, R.; and Jacobsen, M. *Marketing Booze to Blacks.* Washington, D.C.: Center for Science in the Public Interest, 1987.

Hare B.R., Ph.D. "Black youth at risk." In: Dewart, J., ed. *The State of Black America*, 1988. pp. 85–91.

Harper, F.D. *The Black Family and Substance Abuse.* Detroit: The Detroit Urban League, Inc., 1986.

Harrison, D.S., and Alvey, K.T. *The Context of Black Parenting.* Grant Report MH 32905, Vol. 3. Rockville, Md.: National Institute of Mental Health, November 1982.

HDM/Dawson Johns and Black. *Media Consumption Habits of Blacks.* Chicago: HDM, 1988.

Herridge, P., and Gold, M.S. The new user of cocaine: Evidence from 800-COCAINE. *Psychiatric Annals* 18(9): 521–522, 1988.

Isikoff, M. Two-tier drug culture seen emerging. *Washington Post*, January 3, 1989. p. A3.

Kondracke, M.M. The two black Americas. *The New Republic*, February 6, 1989. pp. 17–20.

Krone, K.V., and Lieberman, L. Drinking and smoking: Perceptions of children in grades one, two, and three. In: *Proceedings of the First National Conference on Alcohol and Drug Abuse Prevention.* Rockville, Md.: National Institute on Alcohol Abuse and Alcoholism and National Institute on Drug Abuse, August 3–6, 1986.

Lamar, J.V. Kids who sell crack. *Time*, May 9, 1988. pp. 20–33.

Lex, B.W.   Review of alcohol problems in ethnic minority groups. *Journal of Counseling and Clinical Psychology* 55(3): 2933-3000, 1987.

Lipscomb, W.R. "The black population drinking practices." Unpublished paper presented to the Alcohol Prevention Task Force, California State Department of Alcohol and Drug Programs. Berkeley, Calif.: The Source, n.d.

Louis Harris and Associates. "The unfinished agenda on race in America," Vol. I. Survey conducted for the NAACP Legal Defense and Educational Fund. New York: NAACP LDF, Inc., 1989.

Macro Systems, Inc. "Literature review on alcohol and youth." Prepared under contract No. ADM281-85-0015. Rockville, Md.: DHHS, ADAMHA, Office for Substance Abuse Prevention, November 1986.

Marwick, C. Even "knowing better" about smoking, other health risks, may not deter adolescents. *Journal of the American Medical Association* 260(1): 1512–1513, 1988.

McAdoo, H.P., and McAdoo, J.L. *Black Children: Social, Educational, and Parental Environments*. Beverly Hills, Calif.: Sage Publications, 1985.

Media-Advertising Partnership for a Drug-Free America. *Black Audience Strategic Plan*. New York: American Association of Advertising Agencies, 1987.

Mensch, B.S., and Kandel, D.B. Underreporting of substance use in a national longitudinal youth cohort. *Public Opinion Quarterly* 52:100–124, 1988.

Metropolitan Life. Alcohol use among children and adolescents. *Statistical Bulletin* 68:4 (October–December), 1987.

Miller, M. Drug use down, but not in the ghetto. *Newsweek*, November 23, 1987. p. 33.

Milloy, C. Mothers as fathers. *Washington Post*, January 3, 1989. p. D3.

Milloy, C. One youth's empowerment for success. *Washington Post*, April 3, 1988. p. D3.

Milloy, C. What's a mother to do about drug use. *Washington Post*, December 13, 1987. p. B3.

Minnesota Institute for Black Chemical Abuse. *Chemical Dependency and the Black Community: Strategies for Change*. A report on the conference sponsored by Minneapolis Institute on Black Chemical Abuse, Inc., and the Chemical Dependency Program Division, Minnesota Department of Human Services, Minneapolis, May 19–21, 1986.

National Heart, Lung, and Blood Institute. *Development of Diffusion Strategies Among Culturally Diverse Populations.* Prepared for NHLBI under Contract No. N01-HO-2-7003. Bethesda, Md.: NHLBI, 1985.

National Heart, Lung, and Blood Institute. *NHLBI Smoking Education Program: Strategy Development Workshop for Minorities.* Bethesda, Md.: NHLBI, March 1987.

National Institute on Drug Abuse. *A Guide to Mobilizing Ethnic Minority Communities for Drug Abuse Prevention.* DHHS Pub. No. (ADM)86-1465. Rockville, Md.: NIDA, 1986.

National Institute on Drug Abuse. *National Household Survey on Drug Abuse: Population Estimates 1985.* DHHS Pub. No. (ADM)87-1539. Rockville, Md.: NIDA, 1987a.

National Institute on Drug Abuse. "Executive Summary: Community Epidemiology Work Group." Unpublished. Rockville, Md.: NIDA, 1987b.

National Urban League. *Fact Sheet: The Black Teen Male.* Washington, D.C.: NUL, 1988.

Nobels, W., Ph.D.; Goddard, L.L.; Cavil (III), W.E.; George, P.Y. *A Clear and Present Danger and the Climate of Drugs and Service Delivery.* Oakland, Calif: Institute for the Advanced Study of Black Family Life and Culture, 1986.

Office for Substance Abuse Prevention. *Grantee Product Inventory.* Rockville, Md.: OSAP, 1988.

Orford, D.R. *Conduct Disorder: Risk Factors and Prevention.* Prepared for the Prevention Project, American Academy of Child Psychiatry, 1987, revised 1988.

Phinney, J.S., and Rotherman, M.J., eds. *Children's Ethnic Socialization: Pluralism and Development.* Newbury Park, Calif.: Sage Publications, 1987.

Podolsky, D. NIAAA minority research activities. *Alcohol Health and Research World*, 2:2 (Winter): 5-7, 1986/87.

Primm, B., Ph.D. "Drug use: Special implications for Black Americans." In: Dewart, J., ed. *The State of Black America*, 1987. pp. 145–166.

Prugh, T. The black church: A foundation for recovery. *Alcohol Health and Research World*, 2:2 (Winter): 52-53, 1986/87.

Public Interest Video Network. *PCP Is Not for Me*, 1987. Order from: Public Interest Video Network, 2309 18th St., N.W., Washington, D.C. 20009.

Ronan, L. Alcohol-related health risks among black Americans: Highlights of the Secretary's task force report on black and minority health. *Alcohol Health and Research World* 2:2 (Winter): 36–39, 1986/87.

Sanchez, R. Streetwise cast takes antidrug play on the road. *Washington Post*, August 23, 1988. p. B1.

Scott, B.M., and Miranda, V. *A Guidebook for Planning Alcohol Prevention Programs With Black Youth.* Rockville, Md.: National Institute on Alcohol Abuse and Alcoholism, DHHS Pub. No. (ADM)81-1055. Rockville, Md.; NIAAA, 1981.

Shalom, Inc. *Substance Abuse Prevention With Black Families: A Manual for Implementing an Epidemiological Approach.* Philadelphia: Shalom, Inc., 1983.

Teinowitz, I. Busch offers "Alcohol IQ" video. *Advertising Age*, June 6, 1988. p. 38.

The secret Drew Barrymore. *People*, January 16, 1989. pp. 70–79.

Tucker, M.B. U.S. ethnic minorities and drug abuse: An assessment of the practice. *International Journal of the Addictions* 20(6 & 7):1021–1047, 1985.

U.S. Department of Commerce. *U.S. Census, 1980.* Washington, D.C.: Bureau of the Census, 1980.

U.S. Department of Health and Human Services. *Report of the Secretary's Task Force on Black and Minority Health.* Washington, D.C.: DHHS, 1985.

Watts, T.D., and Wright, R. Interview. Prevention of alcohol abuse among Black Americans. *Alcohol Health and Research World* 2:2 (Winter): 40–41; 65, 1986/87.

Will, G.F. Bombarded by ads. *Washington Post*, December 20, 1987. p. C7.

Experts Contributing to This Chapter

Rich Adams
Editorial Director
WUSA-TV
4001 Brandywine Street, N.W.
Washington, DC 20016

Chilton Alphonse
Black Artists Against Drugs
4828 Crenshaw Boulevard
Los Angeles, CA 90043

Omowale Amuleru-Marshall,Ph.D.
Director, Assistant Professor
Department of Community Health
and Preventive Medicine
Morehouse School of Medicine
720 Westview Drive, S.W.
Atlanta, GA 30310-1495

Robin Beaman
Black Entertainment Television
1232 31st Street, N.W.
Washington, DC 20007

Peter Bell
Institute on Black Chemical Abuse
2616 Nicollet Avenue South
Minneapolis, MN 55408

Iris G. Brown
Chairman, Department of
Community Health and
Rehabilitation
Norfolk State University
2401 Corprew Avenue
Norfolk, VA 23504

Paul Cardenas
National Coalition of Hispanic
Health and Human Services
Organizations
1030 15th Street, N.W., Suite 1053
Washington, DC 20005

Jay C. Chunn
Brookdale Health Sciences
510 East 17th Street
Brooklyn, NY 11226

Terry Edmonds
Bill Sowers
Susan Manny
Claudia Norris
Macro Systems, Inc.
8630 Fenton Street, Suite 300
Silver Spring, MD 20910

Don Epps
Eastern Band of Cherokee
Cherokee Indian Hospital
Cherokee, NC 28719

Deborah Fair
Detroit Urban League
9048 Linwood Avenue
Detroit, MI 48206

Allan Haveson
National Council on Alcoholism
12 West 21st Street
7th Floor
New York, NY 10010

Bruce Henderson
Campaign Manager
Advertising Council, Inc.
1730 Rhode Island Avenue, N.W.
Suite 701
Washington, DC 20036

Addie Key
Office of Substance Abuse
Prevention
Parklawn Building
5600 Fishers Lane
Rockville, MD 20857

B.R. McCain
5691 Phelps Luck Drive
Columbia, MD 21045

Lenna Nozizwe
KFMB-TV
7677 Engineer Road
San Diego, CA 92111

Reymundo Rodriguez
Hogg Foundation for Mental
Health
P.O. Box 7998, University Station
University of Texas
Austin, TX 78713

Bettina Scott
Zeta Phi Beta Sorority, Inc.
5705 Norwood Avenue
Baltimore, MD 21207

Arlen Slobodow, Director
Public Interest Video Network
2309 18th Street, N.W.
Washington, DC 20009

George Tobar
Valerie Royal
Kaaren Johnson Associates, Inc.
1111 Bonifant Street, Suite 300
Silver Spring, MD 20910

Mai Tran, Ph.D.
Department of Human Relations
Montgomery County Public Schools
850 Hungerford Drive
Rockville, MD 20850

Flavia Walton
Services to Youth
Links, Inc.
1200 Massachusetts Avenue, N.W.
Washington, DC 20005

Marjorie Whigham
Black Enterprise Magazine
130 5th Avenue
New York, NY 10011

Maxine Womble, President
National Black Alcoholism Council
417 South Dearborn Street, Suite 700
Chicago, IL 60605

Ruth Sing Wong
Asian Pacific American Heritage
  Council, Inc.
6228 Indian Run Parkway
Alexandria, VA 22312

CHAPTER 3

Reaching Hispanic/Latino Youth

Understanding the Audience

In fashioning communications programs for Hispanic/Latino youth, it is important to recognize that they are part of a population that

- Consists of diverse subgroups, e.g., Mexican Americans, Puerto Ricans, Central Americans, South Americans, Cubans

- Has experienced dramatic population growth in the United States

- Is concentrated in nine States and larger cities

- Includes a large proportion of young people

- Includes a high proportion of female-headed households, compared to the general population

- Includes proportionately fewer married couples than the general population

- Places high importance on the family

- May experience conflict between generations related to differences in acculturation

- Is at a higher risk for teen pregnancy and juvenile incarceration than youth in the general population.

Hispanics/Latinos often are labeled a "hard-to-reach" population in the context of health promotion and disease prevention generally, and in the field of alcohol and other drug abuse prevention specifically. The terminology evokes images of a group of people (who in reality are an aggregate of various subpopulations) either actively avoiding prevention messages or enveloped in an impermeable membrane of language and culture that repels information and outreach. In fact, the Hispanic/Latino community is highly accessible, as many of the Nation's largest consumer products manufacturers and retailers could readily testify (*Advertising Age* 1989).

The challenge to those in the alcohol and other drug abuse prevention field, then, is to move away from regarding Hispanics as "hard-to-reach" and toward an approach that builds on research and demonstration efforts aimed at this large and growing market segment. It may be fair to say that less is known about effective ways to prevent alcohol and other drug problems among

Hispanics/Latinos than among non-Hispanic whites and Blacks. But it also can be argued that enough information is available to lay the foundation for communications programs. In addition, the availability of communications networks that serve primarily Hispanic/Latino communities constitutes an invaluable, but underutilized, resource for the effective delivery of prevention messages.

This chapter provides an overview of research that has focused on Hispanic/Latino populations and points to gaps in research on alcohol and other drug problems. It also identifies media, markets, and materials development issues that program planners must address, and presents for further examination—and action—suggestions for communications programs for Hispanic/Latino communities.

Several factors support the development of communications programs targeting Hispanic/Latino youth. The remarkable population growth, amply documented by the U.S. Bureau of the Census (1988), is one. Population characteristics, including the high proportion of youths in the population—which points to unique prevention opportunities—are another. A third is the high number of risk factors, such as poverty and family disruption, which many of these children experience.

Demographic Factors

Dramatic population growth

Over the past 20 years, Hispanics/Latinos have emerged as one of the fastest growing segments of the U.S. population. Since 1980, the Hispanic/Latino population has increased by approximately 34 percent, while the non-Hispanic population grew by only 7 percent. Current estimates place the Hispanic/Latino population at 19.4 million in the continental United States, with another 3.2 million residing in the Commonwealth of Puerto Rico (U.S. Bureau of the Census 1988). The high growth rate is projected to continue; data from the Census Bureau suggest that growth in the Hispanic/Latino population will be approximately five times that of growth in the non-Hispanic white population in upcoming years (U.S. Bureau of the Census 1988). With the Hispanic/Latino population concentrated in nine States and the Nation's larger urban centers, Hispanics/Latinos increasingly are viewed as major market segments in the communications field and as major constituents for programs to prevent alcohol and other drug problems.

Youthfulness of the population

For a variety of reasons, Hispanics/Latinos are one of the youngest segments of the U.S. population. The median Hispanic/Latino age is 25.5, compared to

32.9 for the U.S. population (U.S. Bureau of the Census 1988). Also, approximately 38 percent of all Hispanics/Latinos, compared to only 28 percent of non-Hispanics/Latinos, fall in the age group of 19 and younger. Nonetheless, within the Hispanic/Latino population there is considerable variation; Mexican Americans, for example, have the highest proportion of children, as shown in table 1. These numbers underscore the opportunities for reaching large numbers of children with primary prevention messages before they begin to use alcohol or other drugs.

Table 1. Age Distribution in the U.S. Population by Group and Percent

Group	Percentage by Age			
	Under 5	5 - 19	20 - 64	65
Mexican American	11.8	30.3	53.98	4.0
Puerto Rican	10.6	29.9	55.5	4.0
Cuban American	4.7	15.9	66.6	12.8
Central/South American	8.5	23.1	66.0	2.4
Other Hispanic/Latino	9.8	21.8	59.2	9.2
Total Hispanic/Latino	10.2	28.0	57.1	4.7
Total Non-Hispanic/Latino	7.1	21.0	59.5	12.4
Source: U.S. Bureau of the Census 1988.				

In addition to youthfulness, the Hispanic/Latino population has a high fertility rate. The most recent data indicate an overall Hispanic/Latino rate of 94.0 births per 1,000 women, compared to 68.8 births per 1,000 women in the overall U.S. population. Even higher rates are reported for Mexican Americans (98.5) and other Hispanic/Latino subgroups (109.0) (Ventura 1988). Given the magnitude of medical problems linked to alcohol and other drug abuse during pregnancy, the Hispanic/Latino fertility rates suggest extensive opportunities for communications programs built around health and pregnancy.

Family composition

The composition and stability of Hispanic/Latino families vary considerably by subgroup. Of concern are data that indicate that there are proportionately fewer married couples in each subgroup compared to the non-Hispanic population, as indicated in table 2. Similarly, Hispanics/Latinos have a higher proportion of female-headed households compared to non-Hispanics, as shown in table 3. These characteristics suggest life in disruptive environments, which some researchers view as an early antecedent of alcohol or other drug use among adolescents (Castro et al. 1987). However, despite demographic data suggesting the presence of stresses that may disrupt Hispanic families, the importance and value given the family in Hispanic culture remain strong.

Table 2. Married Couple Families as a Percentage of All Families by Group

Group	Percent Married Couple Families
Mexican American	74.4
Puerto Rican	51.6
Cuban American	78.1
Central/South American	65.8
Other Hispanic/Latino	67.8
Total Hispanic/Latino	69.8
Total Non-Hispanic/Latino	80.3
Source: U.S. Bureau of the Census 1988.	

Table 3. Percentage of Households with Female Head and No Husband Present, by Group

Group	Percent with Female Head
Mexican American	18.5
Puerto Rican	44.0
Cuban American	16.1
Central/South American	24.4
Other Hispanic/Latino	26.1
Total Hispanic/Latino	23.4
Total Non-Hispanic/Latino	15.8
Source: U.S. Bureau of the Census 1988.	

Risk Factors Among Adolescents

Several researchers have examined the role of family dynamics in youthful alcohol and other drug use among Hispanics/Latinos. Gilbert and Cervantes (1987) discussed studies that suggested parental and sibling alcohol use were the best predictors of alcohol use by young Mexican American boys (but not for girls). Castro et al. (1987) include "disruptive family environment" as one element of a multivariate model that was developed originally to look at antecedents of cigarette smoking but that also may provide a framework for examining the initiation of drug use by adolescents.

The concern is not just with the occasional conflicts that most families encounter but with events of a major scale that seriously disrupt family functioning. Examples include divorce, parental abuse of alcohol or other drugs, and illness (Castro et al. 1987). Other potential disrupters of the family might be unemployment, immigration, sibling experience with incarceration, teen pregnancy, and related problems. Reaching parents during times of family transition is discussed in more detail in chapter 4.

As shown in demographic data presented earlier, Hispanic/Latino families are more likely than non-Hispanic white families to experience family disruption. Other data indicate higher rates of teen pregnancy and juvenile incarceration when comparing Hispanics/Latinos to others (COSSMHO 1988; Krisberg et al. 1987). Within the Hispanic/Latino population, there are special subsets, such as migratory and seasonal working families, that face remarkably challenging situations, which are sufficiently stressful to disrupt the family.

One particularly important aspect of family dynamics for Hispanics/Latinos is intergenerational conflict. Literature on this topic focuses mainly on Cuban families, but findings from studies in Miami may apply to other Hispanic/Latino groups, since they also experience stresses related to acculturation, transculturation, or biculturation. The literature reflects that families with the greatest parent-child differences in cultural orientation also had the highest level of intergenerational conflict. Along with such conflict came acting-out behaviors, including drug use (Santisteban and Szapocznik 1982).

Knowledge, Attitudes, and Practices

The few studies on Hispanic/Latinos' knowledge, attitudes, or practices concerning alcohol and other drugs indicate that

- Hispanic/Latinos in general may have lower rates than non-Hispanic whites of lifetime use of alcohol, PCP, hallucinogens, and stimulants

- Hispanic/Latino youth aged 12 to 17 may have higher rates of cocaine use than their non-Hispanic counterparts

- Puerto Rican and Cuban youth may have the highest rates of cocaine use among Hispanic/Latinos

- Mexican Americans aged 12 to 17 may have higher rates of marijuana use than non-Hispanic whites

- Hispanic/Latino children have extensive exposure at an early age to alcohol and other drug use

- Younger Hispanic/Latino women in general use alcohol much less than Hispanic/Latino men

- Younger Hispanic/Latino women may use alcohol more than the women in their parents' generation, perhaps as a result of acculturation

- Hispanic/Latinos in general may feel that drinking is an innocent way to celebrate and have fun

- At the same time, they may believe that drinking is a primary cause of inappropriate behavior.

Methodological Constraints

Conclusions from studies of alcohol and other drug use in the Hispanic/Latino community are limited by various methodological flaws. As a result, there is considerably less reliable information about alcohol and other drug use among Hispanics/Latinos than among non-Hispanic whites and Blacks. The following problems have contributed to this lack of data:

- *Absence of Hispanic/Latino identifiers in large national surveys.* To a great degree, this deficiency has been addressed, but it has limited any analysis of historical trends. A related concern is the inconsistent use of identifiers for the major Hispanic/Latino subpopulations, e.g., Mexican Americans, Puerto Ricans, Cuban Americans, and Central/South Americans. These subgroups exhibit marked sociodemographic differences and appear to have distinct characteristics vis-à-vis alcohol and other drugs. Some surveyors have begun to standardize use of these subgroup identifiers, but more work is needed.

- *Undersampling of Hispanics/Latinos.* Because of characteristic differences within and among Hispanic subgroups, sample size must be adequate to allow for independent analysis of data for each group and for stratification within groups by variables such as age, socioeconomic status, gender, and acculturation. To obtain statistically valid results, research designs will have to incorporate oversampling strategies designed to allow such analyses of each major subgroup.

- *Inconsistent definitions.* Gilbert and Cervantes (1987) point out variations in definitions of abstinence, moderate use, and heavy drinking. A related problem is variation in defining frequency of drug use as well as in the names and categorization of various drugs, both licit and illicit.

- *Failure of research designs to permit insights on problems associated with use.* Studies focusing on lifetime prevalence rates may obscure the existence of subsets of the population where use may be particularly intense (Booth et al. in press). Also, many studies about Hispanics/Latinos and alcohol do not yield findings on the associations between consumption, drinking problems, and sociodemographic variables (Caetano 1986b).

- *Inadequate distinction between variables.* Study results may be erroneously attributed to characteristics of ethnicity when, in fact, they may be more related to socioeconomic or educational status (Booth et al. in press).

Even with these limitations, there is a growing body of meaningful literature. This chapter focuses on studies that have a national sampling frame and provide insights into Hispanic/Latino subgroups. Additionally, findings of several researchers who have reviewed the body of literature on Hispanics/Latinos and alcohol and other drug abuse are cited. Other studies, including small local or regional studies and large national surveys where Hispanic/Latino data are not considered reliable, have not been included.

Alcohol and Drug Use Rates and Patterns

Lifetime use

The National Household Survey on Drug Abuse (NHSDA) and the Hispanic Health and Nutrition Examination Survey (H-HANES) are national studies providing insight into patterns of alcohol and other drug use. NHSDA data were collected in 1985, and H-HANES data were collected from 1982 to 1984. NHSDA respondents constitute a national probability sample of households in the continental United States; the H-HANES consists of a probability sample of three major Hispanic/Latino groups in specific regions: Puerto Ricans in the greater New York City area; Cuban Americans in Dade County, Florida; and Mexican Americans in targeted counties in the States of California, Texas, Colorado, New Mexico, and Arizona. The review of these two data sources by Booth et al. (in press) is particularly helpful.

Booth et al. concluded that "regardless of age or sex, whites have the highest lifetime rates in the use of cigarettes, alcohol, tranquilizers, PCP, hallucinogens, and stimulants." They found similar patterns when looking at use of these substances within the past year and within the past month. Data for lifetime use are presented in tables 4 and 5 (Booth et al. in press).

The data on use in the 12- to 17-year-old age group generally are consistent with these overall trends, but some differences in the Hispanic/Latino subgroups emerge. In the NHSDA data, Hispanics/Latinos in this age bracket had rates of lifetime use of cocaine higher than those for whites or Blacks; these rates were highest among Puerto Ricans and Cubans, while Mexican Americans' use rate was lower than all other groups. Regarding marijuana use, Mexican Americans had higher rates than Puerto Ricans; in comparing H-HANES to NHSDA data specifically on marijuana use, it appears that the rate for Mexican Americans surpasses that for non-Hispanic whites.

Despite these variations for specific substances and age groups, the data indicate that Hispanics/Latinos had lower rates than non-Hispanic whites for lifetime use of most substances. However, the data do not provide insights on intensity of use or problems that may vary by racial or ethnic group. More current data that permitted an indepth examination of selected large urban areas would provide a better picture, particularly of recent levels of use among youth. (The available data were collected before the emergence of crack in urban markets and thus do not reflect usage associated with crack.)

Table 4. Selected Drug Use by Age, Sex, and Ethnic Status

Age and Sex	Ever Used Cigarettes			Ever used Alcohol			Ever Used Tranquilizers[a]		
	White	Hispanic	Black	White	Hispanic	Black	White	Hispanic	Black
		(Percent)			(Percent)			(Percent)	
12–17 Men	51.9	36.6	39.8	61.6	49.9	44.3	4.8	3.4	2.5
Women	46.5	29.8	26.6	60.4	39.2	34.6	6.1	4.2	2.6
18–25 Men	81.1	63.9	69.4	96.2	87.8	81.9	14.4	5.4	5.7
Women	79.5	48.9	62.0	96.1	74.4	78.4	13.3	3.4	4.2
26–34 Men	89.6	73.4	83.5	97.5	92.7	88.6	19.4	6.6	7.6
Women	78.1	47.9	75.3	93.3	78.0	84.8	11.9	7.5	6.4
35+ Men	91.2	78.3	88.7	96.0	90.4	92.4	5.5	3.3	6.3
Women	76.1	39.2	58.8	84.6	58.9	69.3	4.6	2.2	1.5
Total Men	84.8	67.7	75.6	92.6	84.1	81.5	9.6	4.5	5.8
Women	74.0	41.5	58.1	85.6	62.9	69.3	7.4	3.8	3.2

Age and Sex	Ever Used PCP[b]			Ever used Hallucinogens[c]			Ever Used Stimulants[d]		
	White	Hispanic	Black	White	Hispanic	Black	White	Hispanic	Black
		(Percent)			(Percent)			(Percent)	
12–17 Men	1.7	1.5	*	5.0	2.5	0.9	6.1	4.1	2.7
Women	0.9	0.6	0.6	2.5	1.2	0.9	6.6	5.0	1.4
18–25 Men	8.6	2.8	2.6	15.6	7.7	4.3	20.6	7.3	10.2
Women	5.2	3.7	*	10.7	4.7	1.0	18.9	6.8	4.8
26–34 Men	13.4	2.7	5.2	24.9	8.4	8.0	25.8	6.7	7.7
Women	5.6	0.7	1.5	15.1	1.5	1.8	16.4	4.9	7.7
35+ Men	2.2	*	1.0	3.9	1.9	4.1	6.0	4.8	2.6
Women	0.9	0.9	*	1.3	0.9	*	3.2	1.0	3.6
Total Men	5.4	1.6	2.0	10.0	4.6	4.4	12.3	5.6	5.2
Women	2.5	1.4	0.5	5.4	1.8	0.8	8.4	3.5	4.3

* Less than 0.5 percent.
[a]Benzodiazepines, Meprobamate, hydroxyzine, and Benadryl.
[b]Phencyclidine.
[c]LSD and other substances such as mescaline, peyote, psilocybin, DMT.
[d]Amphetamines, nonamphetamine anorectics, Ritalin, and Cylert.

Source: Booth et al. (in press).

Table 5. Use of Inhalants, Marijuana, Cocaine, and Sedatives by Age, Sex, and Ethnic Status

Age and Sex	Ever Used Marijuana (Percent)						Ever used Cocaine (Percent)					
	White	Hisp.	Black	M.A.	P.R.	Cuban	White	Hisp.	Black	M.A.	P.R.	Cuban
12–17 Men	25.1	22.5	24.0	30.7	25.7		6.1	8.5	4.6	4.2	7.0	
Women	24.8	17.9	15.0				4.9	4.9	1.2			
						20.5						12.1
18–25 Men	65.6	52.4	58.0	56.6	64.4		32.1	18.3	16.3	18.2	32.2	
Women	64.4	29.5	44.3				24.5	11.3	11.0			
26–34 Men	71.7	45.5	58.0	45.8	56.1		33.2	13.5	24.1	13.1	32.8	
Women	53.9	19.5	50.0				20.8	6.0	12.1			
						19.0						7.4
35+ Men	21.4	20.0	29.9	26.8	25.1		6.8	4.7	13.9	6.7	9.0	
Women	11.1	4.8	14.0				1.6	1.2	2.2			
Total Men	38.9	32.9	40.2	54.2	52.9	28.2	16.1	10.1	14.8	16.5	28.3	14.3
Women	28.5	14.6	27.1	27.9	35.8	13.1	9.0	4.7	5.7	5.6	16.8	4.9

Age and Sex	Ever Used Inhalants[a] (Percent)						Ever used Sedatives[b] (Percent)					
	White	Hisp.	Black	M.A.	P.R.	Cuban	White	Hisp.	Black	M.A.	P.R.	Cuban
12–17 Men	10.5	8.0	7.1	4.8	1.9	***	5.6	4.4	1.7			***
Women	9.3	7.9	3.9				3.1	3.6	3.4			
18–25 Men	18.1	7.0	7.2	10.2	8.1		15.4	7.6	5.6	4.0	3.3	
Women	11.1	6.4	3.2				9.0	5.5	3.2			
26–34 Men	14.0	4.4	11.3				15.9	5.1	6.5			
Women	8.3	1.2	2.9				12.9	3.4	4.5			
				5.2	4.9					5.9	8.4	
35+ Men	4.7	5.7	6.9				3.9	3.6	3.9			
Women	1.9	0.9	1.5				1.5	1.0	2.2			
Total Men	9.4	6.1	7.9	9.5	7.1	***	8.4	4.9	4.4	7.3	9.1	***
Women	5.2	3.1	2.4	3.1	3.2		4.9	2.7	3.0	2.6	3.5	

M.A.=Mexican American; Hisp.=Hispanic.; P.R. = Puerto Rican.
Original sources did not report gender differences within age group for Mexican Americans, Puerto Ricans, or Cubans.
*** Sample was too small for classification.

[a]Including gasoline, lighter fluid, spray paint, aerosol sprays, shoe shine, glue, lacquer thinner or other paint solvents, amyl nitrite or "popper," halothene, ether or other anesthetics, nitrous oxide or "whippets," and "locker room" odorizers.

[b]Barbiturates, nonbarbiturate/nonbenzodiazepine sedatives, short-acting barbiturates, and Dalmane.

Source: Booth et al. (in press).

It is interesting to note that the data on lifetime use of drugs and alcohol by Hispanics/Latinos do not coincide with a public image of use as depicted in the mass media. News and movie images of drug use commonly portray Black and Hispanic/Latino users and environments. The data, on the other hand, suggest, at a minimum, the need to avoid singling out or labeling Hispanics as victims of an epidemic of use.

Initiation of use

Amaro et al. (in press) have used H-HANES data to examine the initiation of alcohol and other drug use among Hispanics/Latinos, analyzing responses to questions about age of initiation of use in an age cohort ranging from 12 to 25 years. Using cumulative incidence, these researchers found that by age 18

- 50 percent of Puerto Ricans, 46 percent of Mexican Americans, and 24 percent of Cuban Americans had used marijuana

- 20 percent of Puerto Ricans, and 7 percent of Mexican Americans and Cuban Americans had used cocaine

- 54 percent of Cuban Americans, 50 percent of Mexican Americans, and 46 percent of Puerto Ricans had used alcohol.

This analysis shows a higher level of infrequent use than that reported in the NHSDA study or by H-HANES, when looking at the ever-used question among the contemporary age cohort 12 to 17 years. Similarly, Amaro's analysis indicates higher rates than indicated in other H-HANES data on lifetime use by Hispanics/Latinos ages 12 to 17. The findings suggest extensive exposure at an early age and underscore the growing urgency to reach youth, including Hispanics/Latinos, at very early ages with prevention messages.

Drinking patterns among Hispanic / Latino men

As noted above, two large national surveys (NHSDA and H-HANES) confirm persistent differences in alcohol use between Hispanic/Latino men and women. The literature generally reflects a marked polarization, with a much higher proportion of men than women falling in the heaviest drinking categories (NIAAA 1985). The theme of heavy male drinking also emerges in Caetano's review of the literature (Caetano 1986b), as well as in the review by Gilbert and Cervantes (1987). The latter review also highlights the persistence of heavy drinking into middle age by Mexican American men. The term "fiesta drinking" is sometimes used to describe drinking associated with celebrations. Male-segregated drinking patterns are also discussed.

Data compiled in 1983 and 1971 and reported in Gilbert and Cervantes (1987) provide a comparison of drinking frequency of three groups of men: Hispanic/Latino men in California, all California men, and U.S. men. In the category of "frequent heavy drinker" (highest level of drinking on the scale), the two Hispanic/Latino samples reported rates of 26 and 21 percent, while the national rate was only 12 percent. However, the overall California rate, at 21 percent, was also higher than the national level.

In a 1984 study of Hispanics/Latinos sampled on a national basis, 14 percent of all Hispanic/Latino men reported frequent heavy drinking. On an age-group basis, the problem of heavy drinking becomes more obvious, as shown in table 6. Frequent heavy drinking peaks at 25 percent for men age 30 to 39. "Frequent high maximum drinking" is relatively persistent in the age groups of 18 to 29 (30 percent) and 30 to 39 (29 percent) (Caetano and Martinez 1987).

The data show that large percentages of Hispanic/Latino men report drinking at levels likely to lead to drunkenness—five drinks or more per sitting. Some report this level of consumption at least once a week (frequent heavy drinkers), while others (a larger group) report this level at least once a year. It would be helpful to have more detailed information on the frequency of heavy consumption, but nonetheless, the problem of excessive drinking appears to be significant. Data on self-reported inebriation in table 7 are not consistent with self-reported consumption levels (table 6), suggesting that drunkenness is either not readily identified or acknowledged (Caetano and Martinez 1987).

Table 6. Drinking Patterns by Age and Sex (percentages), U.S. Hispanic/Latino Men

	Age and number responding					
	18–29	30–39	40–49	50–59	60+	Total
Drinking Pattern	(204)	(169)	(90)	(63)	(78)	(604)
Abstainers	22	17	24	24	29	22
Infrequent	9	5	12	7	21	10
Less Frequent Low Maximum	9	5	30	39	19	15
Less Frequent High Maximum	5	13	7	3	4	7
Frequent Low Maximum	13	6	9	7	15	11
Frequent High Maximum	30	29	7	3	8	22
Frequent Heavy Drinker	11	25	9	15	3	14

Source: Caetano and Martinez 1987.

Table 7. Frequency of Drunkenness by Age and Sex (percentages), U.S. Hispanic/Latino Men

Drinking Pattern	Age and number responding					
	18–29 (202)	30–39 (169)	40–49 (89)	50–59 (62)	60+ (78)	Total (60)
At least once a month	8	8	2	6	0	7
3 to 11 times in the past year	11	12	2	4	2	9
Once or twice in the past year	10	17	17	6	5	12
Never	70	63	78	84	93	73

Source: Caetano and Martinez 1987.

Increasing use among Hispanic/Latino women

In looking at patterns of alcohol and other drug use among Hispanic/Latino women, Booth et al. (in press) observed that the differences between men and women were more pronounced among Hispanics/Latinos than among either non-Hispanic whites or Blacks. However, they also observed that the gender differences in the Hispanic/Latino population were most pronounced in the group over age 35 and suggested that prohibitions against use by women may be weakening.

Amaro, likewise, has expressed concern about data on alcohol and other drug abuse among Hispanic/Latino women. Her work in progress suggests that use is more common among younger Hispanic/Latino women. In particular, it appears from H-HANES that the gender differences are less pronounced among young Puerto Ricans than among members of other Hispanic/Latino groups (Amaro, personal communication, August 1988).

Caetano also has observed patterns of drinking in Hispanic/Latino women that suggest shifts in behavior. In his analysis of data from a 1984 national survey of Hispanics/Latinos conducted by the Alcohol Research Group, he found that rates of abstention decline as acculturation increases. Abstention was highest among those ranked low on the acculturation scale (70 percent) and lowest in the most acculturated group (32 percent). Acculturation is a variable distinct from age and does not necessarily represent differences among generations. However, it does represent a dynamic change within the Hispanic/Latino population and in this case seems to be associated with higher rates of alcohol use (Caetano 1986a).

Attitudinal and Related Data

With the exception of alcohol, virtually no literature exists on attitudes of Hispanics/Latinos toward substance abuse. Again, one may turn to the 1984 national study of Hispanics/Latinos and alcohol as reported by Caetano and Martinez (1987). Table 8 presents responses for men by age group, and table 9 presents responses for women by age group. For both men and women, large proportions agree with the statement that there is "nothing good to be said about drinking," and even larger proportions think that drinking is "the main cause" of inappropriate behavior. Of particular interest, though, are endorsements by a small but noteworthy percentage of respondents that suggest approval of high levels of drinking. Depending on the age group, 15 to 20 percent of men and 8 to 17 percent of women agree that "it does some people good to get drunk." On a related statement, "getting drunk is an innocent way to have fun," agreement ranged from 5 to 26 percent for men and 6 to 13 percent for women. It is interesting to note that men in particular were more likely to agree with these statements than with the statement "a real man can hold his liquor" (Caetano and Martinez 1987).

Table 8. Attitudes Toward Drinking and Drunkenness by Age and Sex, U.S. Hispanic/Latino Men

	Age and number responding					
	18–29	30–39	40–49	50–59	60+	Total
Statements	(204)	(168)	(88)	(62)	(77)	(599)
	Percentage of respondents who agree					
Having a drink is one of the pleasures of life	50	54	32	36	24	45
Having a drink is a way of being friendly	53	73	37	36	49	54
People who drink have more fun	9	11	10	20	24	12
People who drink have more friends	17	11	16	22	28	17
A party isn't a party without alcohol	22	20	17	57	40	26
It does some people good to get drunk	15	32	17	19	10	20
Getting drunk is an innocent way to have fun	12	26	21	12	5	16
A real man can hold his liquor	13	11	13	14	39	15
Nothing good to be said about drinking	44	46	82	45	72	52
Drinking is the main cause of people doing things they shouldn't	86	61	92	83	71	79

Source: Caetano and Martinez 1987, table 61a.

Table 9. Attitudes Toward Drinking and Drunkenness by Age and Sex, U.S. Hispanic/Latino Women

Statements	Age and number responding					
	18–29 (282)	30–39 (229)	40–49 (126)	50–59 (85)	60+ (114)	Total (836)
	Percentage of respondents who agree					
Having a drink is one of the pleasures of life	24	34	29	40	24	29
Having a drink is a way of being friendly	41	35	38	50	31	39
People who drink have more fun	6	6	10	15	12	8
People who drink have more friends	14	20	16	17	21	16
A party isn't a party without alcohol	9	14	8	36	20	14
It does some people good to get drunk	10	17	8	7	8	11
Getting drunk is an innocent way to have fun	8	7	13	12	6	9
A real man can hold his liquor	12	12	29	18	7	15
Nothing good to be said about drinking	60	66	91	63	86	70
Drinking is the main cause of people doing things they shouldn't	84	92	78	92	91	86

Source: Caetano and Martinez 1987, table 61b.

Additional insights are available from questions addressing reasons for drinking when looking only at those who reported ever being "high or tight." The proportions of those responding that the reasons are "very important" or "somewhat important" were highest for men and women for the following items:

- Drinking is a good way to celebrate
- It is what most of my friends do when we get together
- I drink to be sociable
- I enjoy drinking.

One interpretation of these data is that Hispanics/Latinos who drink heavily ("get high or tight") feel very positively about the experience and feel that it is an important part of their lifestyle.

Research Needs

Methodological issues raised earlier address the limitations of the literature. In addition to these basic issues, consideration should be given to expanding the knowledge base in several areas.

The data suggest that several populations within the Hispanic/Latino community should be considered priorities for communications programs: children and adolescents, women of childbearing age, and heavy-drinking men. Research is needed particularly to address Hispanic/Latino children and adolescents, a population for which knowledge of alcohol and drug use is especially scarce. One consideration for research with this population is to redirect studies from factors that contribute to use to factors that discourage use. A similar priority would be helpful in studies aimed at women of childbearing age and men in age groups in which heavy drinking is prevalent. Also discussed below is the need for communications research on the media habits of Hispanic/Latinos and the credibility of spokespersons and role models. Such habits will have implications for communications programs aimed at all age and gender groups.

Children and adolescents

Adolescents and children deserve special attention in strategies designed to prevent alcohol and drug use. Gilbert and Cervantes (1987) point out that few data are available on the Mexican American adolescent population, particularly in terms of factors predictive of alcohol use. Similarly, Booth et al. (in press) conclude that more research is needed on the effect of peer influence on drug and alcohol use by Hispanic/Latino youth and on the progression from using gateway substances to other drugs.

The literature generally has examined patterns of utilization among youth and factors that contribute to use. However, it is essential to know what factors discourage use. Personality characteristics, values, and attitudes; family influences; environmental conditions; and resistance behavior are among factors of interest.

To date, most large national studies of youth have used in-school populations as the sampling base. The high dropout rates for Hispanics/Latinos, which range in various estimates from 40 to 80 percent, suggest that the Hispanics/Latinos in these school-based studies may not represent the overall Hispanic/Latino youth population. The challenge is to design an appropriate methodology to reach the out-of-school population. Intercept interviews may be appropriate, for instance. In the case of intercepts, careful consideration would have to be given to site selection to achieve representative samples.

High-risk Hispanic / Latino youth

The Anti-Drug Abuse Act of 1986 as amended in 1988 established categories of youth at high risk for alcohol and other drug problems and established priorities for prevention programs (see chapter 1). Priority groups include

- Children of alcohol and other drug abusers
- Latchkey children
- Children at risk of abuse and neglect
- Preschool children eligible for services under the Head Start Act
- Children at risk of dropping out of school
- Children at risk of becoming adolescent parents
- Children who do not attend school and who are at risk of being unemployed

In general, data on Hispanic/Latino children in these categories are not available or have not been analyzed. Given the clearly stated emphasis in the legislation and the assessment of data availability, new data collection and analysis would be a reasonable and responsive action. With appropriate direction and coordination, the data on high-risk Hispanic/Latino youth could be used to create profiles of need at the community, regional, and national levels. In particular, the findings would be instructive for a range of national organizations with missions focusing on particular categories of high-risk youth.

Families

Research on families can provide valuable insights into factors that may contribute to the initiation of alcohol and other drug use by children. Of particular interest for Hispanics/Latinos is the study of intergenerational conflict. The work of Santisteben and Szapocznik (1982) has implications for prevention and treatment of alcohol and other drug use, but it appears that comparable research has not been conducted with Hispanic/Latino groups in other regions. Given the strong interest in the concept of "famialism" in the Hispanic/Latino community, intergenerational conflict research should be a high priority.

Media use patterns and preferences

One of the most glaring gaps in the literature is the absence of reliable, indepth data on Hispanic/Latino media use. Although various studies have asked questions about respondents' sources of information, the availability of viewer, listener, and reader data from commercial sources has been ignored. To be most helpful, data need to be analyzed by markets, e.g., the New York market. Studies are needed to examine differences among major Hispanic/Latino subgroups and stratification by age and other sociodemographic variables. For a proper perspective, analysis is needed on the extent of use of the Hispanic/Latino media compared with mainstream media, and the relative credibility or influence of these two sources of information within Hispanic/Latino communities.

Credible sources and role models

To produce effective alcohol and other drug materials, research is needed on the credibility of sources, including spokespersons and role models. Some information is emerging in the AIDS education field, but generalization from these studies is difficult, given the topic and the geographic focus (Marin and Marin 1989). In undertaking this type of research, it may be important to distinguish between delivering information and promoting healthful behavior changes. Although a person may be perceived as a credible source of information, it is not clear that he or she also will have the power to influence behavior.

In summary, priorities for research into the Hispanic/Latino community should be selected from the following:

- Extent of use of Hispanic/Latino versus mainstream media by age subgroups and Hispanic/Latino subgroups and regions

- Credibility and influence of Hispanic/Latino versus mainstream media

- Credible sources, spokespersons, and role models for Hispanic/Latino youth

- Knowledge, attitudes, and practices (KAP) regarding alcohol and other drug use among subgroups of Hispanic/Latino youth, including peer influence and progression from using gateway drugs

- KAP studies of all Hispanic/Latino youth, including school dropouts

- Factors that contribute to nonuse choices

- KAP studies of high-risk youth, including Hispanic/Latino subsamples

- Studies addressing existence, characteristics, and impact of intergenerational conflict on alcohol and other drug use.

Planning Considerations

Audiences

- Adults (to increase awareness of the problem among youth and ways to help prevent it)
- Families
- Women of childbearing age
- Men aged 19 to 39 who drink heavily (because of their influence on their children).

Channels

- Spanish-language television radio stations
- Spanish-language magazines and newspapers
- English-language media that attract a sizable Hispanic/Latino audience
- Community leaders
- Grassroots organizations, such as churches, schools, neighborhood groups
- Social service agencies
- Elected officials
- Local affiliates of national organizations.

Sources

- Celebrities
- Authority figures
- Peers.

Materials Review

- *Available are*
    — some Spanish-language brochures and pamphlets
    — a few audiovisual materials.
- *Needed are more materials that are*
    — interactive
    — bilingual

— low reading level

— audiovisual.

Messages should

- Increase awareness of the role that adults, families, and caregivers can play in preventing alcohol and other drug use among children

- Increase awareness of the harm alcohol and other drugs can do to unborn babies

- Increase awareness that it is inappropriate to let alcohol and other drugs interfere with parental obligations

- Promote the interpersonal skills needed to resist use, seek help, and help others

- Promote discussion between parents and children about family disruption and drugs

- Promote discussion among peers about nonuse of alcohol and other drugs.

Audiences and Messages

To help prevent alcohol and other drug use among young people in the Hispanic/Latino community, program planners should focus on four audience segments:

- Hispanic/Latino adults—increase their knowledge of alcohol and other drug use among youth and suggest ways that they can help prevent such use

- Hispanic/Latino families—direct messages to children and their parents

- Hispanic/Latino women of childbearing age—help them prevent alcohol and other drug use that could harm the fetus during pregnancy. The relatively high rates of teen pregnancy and childbearing among younger adult Hispanic/Latino women suggest the importance of preventing alcohol and other drug use among this group.

- Hispanic/Latino men who drink heavily (ages 19 to 39)—help stem their influence on their children's use of alcohol and other drugs. The highest proportion of heavy alcohol consumption appears to be among men ages 19 to 39. While the data suggest that the proportion of problem drinking is high, the majority of Hispanic men do not fall into the heaviest consumption categories. It also appears that much of the heavy consumption occurs in male-segregated settings.

The following section suggests messages appropriate to each audience.

Hispanic/Latino adults

Messages should address

- *The role of families in preventing alcohol and other drug use.* Before they can help prevent alcohol and other drug use among youth, Hispanic/Latino adults must understand

  — The kinds of disruptive events that can promote or set the stage for alcohol and other drug use in children

  — The early warning signs of problematic behavior in children

  — Sources of help for parenting, family problems, and other information.

- *The early exposure of children to alcohol and other drugs.* Parents, teachers, and other influential Hispanic/Latino adults should understand

  — The types of drugs, including alcohol, available to children

  — Prevalence of exposure and staging of initiation (when people first use alcohol or other drugs)

  — Increasing use among young women.

- *Parental/caretaker practices regarding alcohol and other drugs—e.g., provides a role model for children.* Messages should lead Hispanic/Latino adults to understand

  — The distinction between alcohol use and abuse in adults

  — Ways in which alcohol and other drug use interfere with the discharge of their family responsibilities

  — How children view and are influenced by use and abuse by family members

  — Where to find treatment services and other assistance.

Hispanic/Latino families

The following suggestions for messages are presented by audience segments. For children and adolescents, strategy planning should take into account specific age groups and stages of development.

The messages *children and adolescents* should understand are

- Alcohol and other drug use should be avoided because of the effects on body and mind

- Refusing to use alcohol or other drugs is appropriate

- There are other ways to feel valuable and important (self-esteem)
- It is appropriate to talk with an adult when disruptive events occur.

Children and adolescents need interpersonal communication skills so they can

- Discuss with peers reasons they choose not to use alcohol and other drugs
- Describe their feelings about family disruptions and understand the behaviors they use to cope with these disruptions
- Learn to seek out appropriate adults for discussions on family or personal problems.

Parents and caretakers need to understand that

- It is appropriate for parents/caretakers to discuss among themselves their feelings about and use of alcohol and other drugs
- They should feel comfortable initiating discussions about alcohol and other drugs with children
- It is important for them to understand how children view themselves and what makes them feel valuable and important
- They can help their children feel valuable, important, and secure in their decisions not to use alcohol and other drugs
- It is appropriate to seek help with raising children and solving family problems.

Parents and caretakers need interpersonal communications skills so they can

- Establish relationships with their children that communicate mutual respect and promote self-esteem based upon encouragement
- Listen effectively to understand the feelings behind the spoken words
- Use open responses to sustain and broaden discussions
- Express their own feelings and values without passing judgment or laying blame
- Develop or clarify family rules for children and implement them accordingly.

Additional strategies for families are discussed in chapter 4.

Hispanic / Latino women of childbearing age

Some messages for this group include

- Alcohol and other drugs can affect the fetus
- Abstaining from alcohol or other drug use during pregnancy is necessary to help assure a healthy baby
- It is appropriate for women to seek help to stop using alcohol or other drugs when considering pregnancy and when pregnant.

This target audience needs the interpersonal communications skills to enable them to

- Seek and encourage others to use prenatal care in the first trimester and throughout pregnancy
- Assist someone in seeking help to stop using alcohol or other drugs during pregnancy.

Hispanic / Latino men ages 19 to 39

The messages should be appropriate for men in this age group who are heavy consumers as well as those who may be interacting with the heavy consumers. These messages include

- It is inappropriate to let drinking interfere with family obligations
- It is important to know when you have had enough and should stop drinking
- It is possible to have a good time without getting drunk
- It is appropriate for men to seek help for a drinking or other drug problem
- It is important that fathers offer a positive role model to their children. Children pattern their own alcohol and other drug use after their parents' (see chapter 1).

These men need the interpersonal communications skills to enable them to

- Identify, discuss, and halt patterns of consumption that result in drunkenness
- Understand and discuss reasons why consumption should be limited (health, family obligations, etc.)
- Express their feelings about drinking and discuss reasons for nonuse with their children
- Assist someone in seeking help for an alcohol or other drug problem.

Channels

Media

Studies of the media choices of Hispanics/Latinos have been extremely limited. Two of the most frequently cited studies, conducted by corporations, commonly are used to promote Spanish-language media as an effective channel to reach large segments of the Hispanic/Latino population. Yankelovich, Skelly, and White, Inc. (1984) found that 75 percent of Hispanics/Latinos used Spanish-language television, 75 percent used Spanish-language radio, and 46 percent used Spanish-language print media. A study by Strategy Research Corporation (1986) showed somewhat lower levels of utilization of Spanish-language media, with 67.2 percent using television, 47.3 percent using radio, and approximately 20 percent using print media. The data from the Strategy Research Corporation study also suggest considerable variation in Spanish-language media use by region, as shown in table 10. It is important to note, however, that definitions of use may not be consistent in these and other studies.

Table 10. Use of Spanish-Language Media by Hispanics/Latinos

| Type of Media | Geographic Area | | | | |
	All Areas	New York	Florida	California	Texas/Southwest
Television	67.2	76.8	67.8	66.6	57.5
Radio	47.3	53.8	52.0	45.7	37.5
Newspapaers	21.5	26.2	25.2	23.9	10.5
Magazines	19.1	24.4	19.5	24.4	8.2

Source: Strategy Research Corporation 1986.

To a degree, the data on media usage reflect language preference. The Strategy Research Corporation study (1986) also revealed that more than half of survey respondents felt most comfortable speaking Spanish. Language preference varied by region. Preference for Spanish was highest in the Southeast (86 percent), and slightly less in California (76 percent). Preference was much lower in the Central region (51 percent), in the Southwest (56 percent), and in the Northeast (63 percent). However, preference for Spanish does not mean that English-language media and materials are not used; rather, the data underscore the potential for reaching large segments of the Hispanic/Latino community by using Spanish-language media.

Although there is still much to be learned about the nature and extent of the markets commanded by Spanish-language media, there is growing consensus that using these unique channels to the Hispanic/Latino community is good business. *The New York Times* (Stevenson 1988) reported that Spanish-language television advertising revenues increased by more than 20 percent between 1986 and 1987 and has doubled since 1984. More recently, *Advertising Age* (1989) offered examples of sophisticated media strategies used by leading U.S. corporations, including Spanish-language ads developed by toy companies and aimed at parents; elaborate television promotions; and extensive market research. The dynamics of growth in Hispanic/Latino media, along with increasing sophistication in targeting audiences, illustrate the potential for communicating with large segments of the Hispanic/Latino population about alcohol and other drug use.

Identifying and reaching major media outlets is a relatively simple process. The Hispanic/Latino television industry is organized around two major networks, several large cable systems, and relatively few (less than 50) major stations that originate local programming. There are distribution networks for radio as well, but due to the nature of this medium, there is a much greater emphasis on local personalities and production. Most communities have local papers, but only in the largest markets are sizable daily papers available. Media outlet lists are readily available, and leadership in each major market can be easily identified.

The issue of leadership roles for non-Hispanic media also should be addressed. In the largest markets, there is a spirit of competition building as the English-language media seek to tap into new generations of viewers, listeners, and readers. With this in mind, the outreach and materials also should be directed to the non-Hispanic outlets. With the data from commercial rating services, outlets attracting the greatest numbers of the targeted Hispanic/Latino segment can be identified.

Community channels

There is considerable diversity in the leadership structures of Hispanic/Latino communities. The variety makes it inappropriate to rely, as many strategies do, solely on chapters and affiliates of national organizations to reach out to and influence local communities. Rather, in each major target city, specific leaders and groups need to be identified. Indeed, this is a step that must be ongoing so that outreach responds to contemporary, rather than historic, factors in communities. Community leadership profiles can be compiled through networks of contacts.

The National Coalition of Hispanic Health and Human Service Organizations (COSSMHO) uses this approach when community action is a component of a project. Projects have included conducting town meetings, and in each case, local organizations on each site worked with COSSMHO staff to identify key players and recruit participation. There is no substitute for this kind of involvement. Among the key groups to help identify key intermediaries are school officials (elected and staff), churches, social services agencies, elected and appointed officials, chambers of commerce, and political/social change organizations. There also may be leadership coalitions in communities working on a number of issues with various professional associations. As this research is undertaken, it is important also to identify key brokers (or gatekeepers) whose approval will have influence on others. More information on working with intermediaries is included in chapter 6.

National organizations

Dissemination using national organizations can also be undertaken. For example, the American Foundation for AIDS Research (AmFAR) funded a project with COSSMHO to disseminate an AIDS leadership booklet to Hispanic/Latino leaders. The mailing involved collaborations among national Hispanic/Latino organizations representing elected officials, business, civic organizations, church leadership, and other groups. Approximately 10,000 copies were distributed. See appendix E for a list of potential intermediary groups.

Sources

Very little information is available about how Hispanics/Latinos view spokespersons for prevention messages. The adaptation of the "Stay Smart!" materials demonstrated a positive response to using Hispanic/Latino celebrities as part of an overall materials package. In part, the response may be linked to the relative absence of Hispanics/Latinos in promotional efforts. Hispanic/Latino musicians and athletes, despite their accomplishments, rarely have been selected for commercial or nonprofit campaigns.

Careful distinction needs to be made among materials that need a celebrity to call attention to the message, authoritative figures to convey information, and peers to provide believable role models. Research in San Francisco on AIDS information sources preferred by Hispanics/Latinos points to physicians, clinical workers, and persons with AIDS as appropriate, credible, or desirable spokespersons (Marin and Marin 1989). These findings do not, however, indicate if the same sources are seen as representing community norms and values that influence behaviors. The effectiveness of peer spokespersons and appropriate roles in communications programs needs to be explored before conclusions can be drawn. Meanwhile, the growing pool of Hispanic/Latino celebrities available and willing to participate in media and materials production should be tapped and used appropriately.

Materials Review

A review of educational materials targeted to Hispanic/Latinos provided insights into the limitations of current materials. Some Spanish-language and bilingual brochures and pamphlets, prepared by government and voluntary organizations, are available. Fewer audiovisual materials have been produced. The review located several examples of interactive materials, such as games and workbooks, but there are few products for Hispanics/Latinos in the nonprint format. Especially rare are products first produced in Spanish or with a Hispanic/Latino audience as the primary market.*

Needed are more interactive materials that engage audiences, bilingual materials, low-reading-level materials, and audiovisual materials. These are discussed in more detail in the "Recommendations section" that follows.

Recommendations

Establishing a Framework

- Promote research
- Develop message and materials prototypes
- Disseminate leadership materials to media leaders
- Develop materials for intermediary groups and leaders
- Strengthen community infrastructures.

Using Materials and Channels

- Use formats that engage audiences
- Develop materials for the family
- Address issues of readability and comprehension
- Use electronic media
- Address stylistic concerns.

The available data on Hispanics/Latinos and alcohol and other drug use, along with demographic characteristics, provide a basis for developing communications programs for Hispanic/Latino audiences. The recommendations that follow are based on these data, on a review of available educational

---

*More information on materials is available from the National Clearinghouse for Alcohol and Drug Information; see appendix E.

materials, and on discussions with experts. These strategies by no means exhaust possible efforts that communities, individuals, and organizations can undertake, but are intended as examples of such strategies. Effective communications programs will need to include a variety of appropriate messages disseminated through as many channels as possible and over an extended period of time. As a community's program develops, new messages may be needed periodically as youth's needs change, or other changes occur within the community. A tracking component will be vital to identify any such changes or other trends. Program planners also should keep in mind that messages and materials must be carefully tested because the data show diversity in patterns of use of alcohol and other drugs among Hispanic/Latino subgroups and because, demographically, potential target audiences within the Hispanic/Latino community are so diverse.

Three broad goals are proposed to guide Hispanic/Latino communications programs:

- Increase knowledge within the Hispanic/Latino community about alcohol and drug use

- Change attitudes toward healthy, preventive behaviors

- Increase interpersonal communications skills that support behavior changes.

Two kinds of activity can help to achieve these goals. The first is establishing a framework of knowledge and organization to support communications programs. The second is creating and creatively using materials to convey prevention messages.

Establishing a Framework

Achieving communications goals and objectives such as those outlined here requires action at the national and local levels. Recommended strategies include the following:

- Promote research

- Develop message and materials prototypes

- Disseminate leadership materials to media leaders

- Develop materials for intermediary groups and leaders

- Strengthen community infrastructure.

Promote research

The rather profound lack of data on Hispanics/Latinos, particularly on communications issues, should be addressed by creating a nationally focused technical working group. The group should have a membership reflecting key Federal agencies; recognized researchers with expertise in working with Hispanic/Latino data and populations; representatives from national organizations with missions related to the field; experts in the communications and prevention fields; and, as appropriate, representatives of State and local governments. The group should be charged with advising appropriate agencies and organizations in the following areas:

- Advise on design and content of major studies to collect data on alcohol and other drug use sponsored by the Federal Government, to improve the quality of Hispanic/Latino data, and to broaden the areas of inquiry. The group also could advise on data collection by States and other entities.

- Develop research agendas reflecting professional consensus on priorities in Hispanic/Latino research in the fields of alcohol and other drug use.

- Design appropriate approaches to data pooling in areas related to the high-risk categories enumerated in the OSAP enabling legislation (teen pregnancy, juvenile incarceration, child abuse, etc.).

In addition to these tasks, which in large part build on coordination efforts across disciplines, agencies, and jurisdictions, an appropriate national agency or organization needs to sponsor the following three specific projects:

- Annually publish synopses of research in progress or recently released. The publication should be appropriate for nonresearchers as well as the academic community.

- Purchase, or otherwise acquire from credible commercial sources, data on Hispanic/Latino media utilization trends. There is growing interest in these sources among many agencies, and it may be that resources could be pooled for their acquisition and analysis. The acquisition, analysis, and dissemination of findings should be ongoing.

- Sponsor new research on credible sources of information and effective spokespersons. The research should look at specific segments of the population, based on such factors as national origin, age, socioeconomic status, gender, and region. It should not be limited to purveyors of information but should also look at effective role modeling and images.

Develop message and materials prototypes

Innovation in the field of Hispanic/Latino materials will require new levels of investment and leadership, including but not limited to, the lead Federal agencies. Communications research outlined earlier will be required to produce new messages and materials.

The communications goals and objectives cited earlier can serve as a starting point for development. Due to the diversity of the Hispanic/Latino market, development should begin in a limited number of target markets (i.e., three), expanding the product testing and adaptation into other markets as appropriate. In each market, the stages would include the following:

- Strategy testing/development—to measure the appropriateness of communications objectives and strategies recommended in this document, and to modify them as necessary. Because of the diversity of Hispanic/Latino communities, complex even within single urban areas, identifying specific target audiences must be an integral element of this step.

- Concept development and testing—they are part of the creative process of producing messages to accomplish the objectives and will assure appropriateness to target audiences in each market. Messenger, style, appeal, and format are a part of testing at this stage.

- Materials development—for prototypes, all possible materials need not be developed. Rather, selected formats can be used to stimulate other product development. The results of the concept testing will determine the degree to which products will need to be tailored to market segments or can be developed to appeal to multiple groups. Testing at this point is important to assess how the final product will be perceived and understood by the target audience. In addition, testing should be done with "gatekeepers," who will make decisions affecting utilization and dissemination.

- Local sponsorship—in each market, community-based endorsements and assistance in implementation should be obtained as part of the message dissemination effort.

- Process and impact evaluation—to assess the extent of utilization of materials and any impact, such as increased use of hotlines or differences in pre-testing and post-testing in sample groups.

A more complete description of this process is included in appendix A.

With these steps completed in the test markets, the findings—including insights learned through the various development and testing stages, as well as utilization—should be packaged with the prototype materials. The notion is not just to give communities model materials, but to provide insight and direction on the adaptation process, and also to point out the degree to which messages and images have been found to have broad appeal across various market segments.

Innovation in communications leads to activities, not just products. Examples offered elsewhere include teens producing video or audio products, community murals, and theater productions. It is important to document administrative, process, and cost factors to provide guidance for using innovative prototypes.

Disseminate leadership materials to media leaders

The surge in interest in Hispanic/Latino media calls for activities to bring key management, production, and on-camera/on-microphone personnel into the communications strategy development process. In particular, the innovations in Spanish-language television offer opportunities for an impact on programming, including but not limited to the public service arena.

Media leaders need to know the basic facts about the following:

- The nature and scope of the problem of alcohol and other drug use in Hispanic/Latino communities
- The goals and objectives of communications programs, including high-risk groups and other target audiences
- Findings, as available, on appropriate messages, messengers, and role models for specific market segments
- Story leads for covering alcohol and other drug use issues
- Descriptions of programs in communities that can benefit from promotion.

Develop materials for intermediary groups and leaders

A critical component of leadership materials for intermediaries is concrete, practical action steps for each constituent group. Information should be the same, to create a common understanding of the problem and direction for solutions, but perceived roles and obligations will differ considerably between groups. Short lists, referring to agencies that can provide assistance to implement actions, can be developed for each group and included as part of the whole. (See chapter 6 on intermediary organizations for additional guidance.)

Additional messages may be specifically developed for the participating community groups. This should be done, however, only after the validation steps have been taken to assure appropriateness and acceptability of the messages. Presenting innovative ideas and themes can be counterproductive if the content offends rather than stimulates leadership, or detracts attention from the most crucial information.

Strengthen community infrastructures

National campaigns come and go, leaving local agencies, leaders, and citizens to deal with ongoing, evolving problems. Strategies employing town meetings and other mobilizing activities are helpful, but they are most meaningful when activities are targeted at influencing factors contributing to the problem.

Likewise, community mobilizing activities are more potent when they

- Capture the concerns of leaders succinctly

- Provide a structure for accountability (that is, a year later, will the problem be larger or smaller? Will available resources have changed?)

- Permit communication of conditions and problems to decisionmakers and funding sources locally and nationally.

One of the ways to structure a framework for a community organization is to conduct a needs assessment. The key is not calling in contractors to write another report, but to engage community organizations and responsible government agencies in joint efforts.

In the prevention field, there is one such instrument and process now under development. The Kaiser Family Foundation is sponsoring a project to adapt for use in Hispanic/Latino communities a model assessment used by the Centers for Disease Control. The first phase of the Hispanic/Latino model includes conducting a leadership opinion survey; collecting data to create a sociodemographic profile; and assessing data that can yield a community health profile. The model will be pilot tested in Washington, D.C., and El Paso, Texas. A second phase will be used to create inventories of prevention programs, environmental factors, and resources.

The adaptation of the health prevention needs assessment instrument for use in the alcohol and other drug abuse prevention field would be relatively simple—a matter of redesigning the instrument to capture relevant information and pilot testing it in several sites. Several additional steps also would be required and community groups may need technical assistance in implementing the assessment. Further, to be most helpful, particularly at the national level, results need to be channeled to a central source where they can be examined as a group to provide further insight on the unique needs and commonalities of Hispanic/Latino communities.

Using Materials and Channels

Even though it is difficult to frame specific messages in the absence of testing and formative evaluation, it is possible to examine those factors that, from a general perspective, contribute to appropriate and effective educational products for various Hispanic/Latino communities.

The following strategies are discussed below:

- Use formats that engage audiences
- Develop materials for the family
- Address issues of readability and comprehension
- Use electronic media
- Address stylistic concerns.

Use formats that engage audiences

Interactive approaches are largely missing from existing Hispanic/Latino materials. In the written format, problem-solving exercises and games can be provided, such as those in the "Stay Smart! Don't Start!" children's booklet. Target audiences also can be engaged in developing communications products. In El Paso, Texas, a community health clinic hired out-of-school, unemployed Hispanic/Latino youth to design and produce a community mural on AIDS and to produce a video on the mural project. With foundation support, the Public Broadcasting System (PBS) sponsored a national contest for high school students to produce, for competitive judging, television public service announcements on AIDS. Winning spots in the major media markets are now being aired and tapes are available for nonbroadcast educational purposes.

An increasingly popular activity is teen and community theater. Cast members participate in writing and/or adapting scripts, and cast members engage the audience in dialogue that clarifies messages and encourages help-seeking behavior. In Los Angeles, one AIDS education project for adolescents is now developing additional casts to permit theater productions throughout the region. Results from an OSAP-sponsored project to deliver alcohol and other drug use messages through Hispanic/Latino teen theater troupes will be available in 1990.

Develop materials for the family

A number of projects developed for non-Hispanics have used a "kids only" label to connote exclusivity which, it is thought, will make the materials more attractive. Family approaches to communications emphasize sharing information between generations. Especially in the case of parents trying to bridge gaps in acculturation, it is important not to exclude them from information and messages aimed at their children. The solution may be one product to be used by both parents and children, or companion pieces that package similar information for each group.

Family-focused communications efforts in the Hispanic/Latino community are improved by using bilingual formats. Within families, it is not uncommon for children to have language skills and preferences different from those of their parents. Some children may be reached by English-language materials used in schools, for instance, while parents will require companion pieces in Spanish. Language preference and use are not just a matter of generational differences; there is considerable diversity associated with income, acculturation, and length of residency in the United States. Accordingly, products for families should begin with the notion of a bilingual format—unless there is proof that a particular subgroup has a clearly defined language preference. Of the variety of bilingual formats available, the facing page scheme—Spanish on one side, English on the other—is preferred. Although it may present design challenges, the facing page format is easier to use in communities where both languages are in use, and it is easier for readers who may need to refer to both languages.

There may also be differences in use of certain terms or in grammar between and among Hispanic/Latino groups. A way of dealing with this is to use concepts to explain what is meant, in place of usage that may be accepted by one group and unacceptable to another.

Address issues of readability and comprehension

Low literacy levels and illiteracy both are problems that largely have not been addressed in communications programs targeted to Hispanics/Latinos. Tests of readability for Spanish-language materials are available, as they are for English-language products. However, it is important to consider the complexity of both the text and the concepts. Comprehension should be assessed in both languages, and generally it is felt that concept development and message formulation should proceed independently in both languages, in place of translation from one text to the other.

There is considerable interest in "no-literacy" materials that avoid most, if not all, text in favor of graphics and illustrations. Few examples are available from U.S.-targeted projects, although companies working in the international field are beginning to look at the domestic market. It may be wise to consider using nonprint media to reach those who are illiterate or have poor reading skills.

Use electronic media

Several innovative programs are using electronic media for prevention communications. A radio station in rural Washington State, for example, is using teen theater scripts to produce radio programming targeted to rural Hispanics/Latinos and migrant workers. Public health programs aimed at the elderly in El Paso, Texas, have used "loaner" tape recorders to make instructional materials accessible to families. Popular Hispanic/Latino musicians in Los Angeles have recorded dance music with prevention lyrics and are working to release the product in cassette form. In the AIDS education field, a national entertainment industry council is sponsoring a song-writing competition aimed at Hispanic/Latino young people.

As with written materials, consideration needs to be given to producing bilingual broadcast messages. A recent example is the national telecast of "SIDA Is AIDS," a 1-hour documentary, broadcast simultaneously in English on PBS and in Spanish on the national Univision network, in October and November 1988. The documentary was produced in Spanish and the PBS version was produced with English dubbing. Conceived as a joint broadcast/community outreach project, "SIDA Is AIDS" combined local previews, promotion, and adjunct broadcast programming with the documentary.

Because both productions received good ratings and favorable community reaction, there are plans for a second broadcast on parent-child communication about sexuality, to be aired in 1990. The broadcast again will be linked to local activities. Radio call-in shows, for instance, could be scheduled to deal with sexuality issues in conjunction with the broadcast. The use of two networks, two languages, a national production with universal appeal, and local adjuncts offers an effective package of national and local components to reach selected market segments.

Address stylistic concerns

These may include the following:

- *Production quality.* During focus groups held to test adaptations of the "Stay Smart! Don't Start!" materials, audiences reacted favorably to the production quality—use of color, coated paper stock, and good graphic design. The reaction underscored the fact that limited budgets too often have resulted in products that do not attract attention or are not seen as attractive. Lively, engaging design with strong visual appeal is essential; four-color printing schemes do not substitute for creativity and quality design.

- *Broad versus narrow appeal.* A frequent concern is the degree to which materials can appeal to Hispanic/Latino markets across major subgroups. Language and image both can contribute to the sense that the product was "not intended for me." Success in developing a product with broad appeal will depend on a number of factors, including

— Carefully reviewing language to find words and constructs acceptable to all groups

— Selecting images that avoid stereotypes, are open to interpretation, or are all-inclusive of the various groups

— Combining strong creative input and thorough testing.

- *Family imagery.* The demographic data show clearly that significant proportions of Hispanics/Latinos live in other than two-parent households (U.S Bureau of the Census 1988). Despite the diversity of family settings and the homage paid to the concept of "extended" family, the imagery too often is limited to mother-father-child family systems. Depending on the message and the market, images may well focus on single-parent families; other relatives or caregivers may also be included.

Summary

Millions of Hispanics/Latinos watch television, listen to radio, read the news, attend schools, and participate in community events. Yet we know little about the patterns of communications in these diverse communities, and we know even less about how they feel about the images, symbols, and messages presented to them. Understanding patterns of communications and audience reactions is vital to developing effective programs.

Working with Hispanic/Latino communities also requires an appreciation of the dynamics of change—diversification of subgroups within geographic areas; evolving values and norms; shifts in family structure and religious affiliation (Suro 1989); and transitions in attitudes toward and use of alcohol and other drugs. The dynamics of change, however, should not obscure the deeply rooted beliefs and values that lie at the core of the Hispanic/Latino experience and that can bring relevance and power to communications messages.

Communications programs or strategies should neither begin nor end with information campaigns. Within communities, they should seek to build the desire, resources, and mechanisms to promote prevention-associated behaviors. There are appropriate national roles in developing leadership, research and data, and prototypes of programs, but without the community base, the national component will not fulfill its potential.

Research and data collection, field experience, careful strategy development, and community involvement are all processes that, when used in combination, yield the understanding of both change and tradition necessary to implement effective communications programs.

Table 11. Suggestions for Communications Programs for Hispanics/Latinos

Goals	Audience	Media	Materials	Intermediaries
Increase Knowledge	Adults	Television and radio: talkshows, news, public affairs shows, PSAs Newspapers and magazines: features, columns, editorials	Leadership packets Community murals	Churches; employers; social service agencies; point of purchase/retailers; local professional associations; chapters, members, and affiliates of national Hispanic/Latino organizations
Change Attitudes	Children/Adolescents	Children's television programing, MTV, entertainment programming, appropriate music-format radio programming Teen theater	Videos for class discussion Illustrated/photo booklets Training curriculum for teachers and social service professionals Theater kits	Schools, churches, social service agencies, point-of-purchase/retailers, community organizations
	Parents	Television and radio: talkshows, news, public affairs shows, PSAs Newspapers and magazines: features, columns, editorials	Videos for discussion Illustrated/photo booklets Interactive materials for family (bilingual)	Social service agencies, employers, churches, point-of-purchase/retailers
	Women of Childbearing Age	Television and radio: talkshows, news, public affairs shows, PSAs Newspapers and magazines: features, columns, editorials	Videos for discussion Illustrated/photo booklets	Schools, maternal and child health services, family planning offices, point-of-purchase/retailers Schools, churches, social service agencies, juvenile justice agencies
Develop Skills	Children/Adolescents	Videos for class discussion Teaching curriculum; games and contests		Social service agencies, community organizations, churches
	Parents	Television feature programming Magazine articles	Parent-training videos and curriculum, take-home literature Training videos and curriculum, take-home literature	
	Women of Childbearing Age			Churches, social service organizations, chapters of women's organizations, health clinics, employer assistance programs

Bibliography

Advertising Age. Special report: Marketing to Hispanics. Feb. 13, 1989. pp. S1–S14.

Amaro, H.; Campa, R.; Coffman, G.; and Heeren, T. Initiation of substance abuse among Mexican American, Cuban American, and Puerto Rican adolescents and young adults: Findings from the Hispanic HANES. COSSMHO Hispanic health research consortium monograph. *American Journal of Public Health,* in press.

Booth, M.W.; Castro, F.G.; and Anglin, M.D. What do we know about Hispanic substance abuse: A review of the literature. In: Glick, R., and Moore, J.W., eds. *Drug Use in Hispanic Communities.* New Brunswick, N.J.: Rutgers University Press, in press.

Caetano, R. "Drinking and Family Drinking, Attitudes and Problems Among U.S. Hispanic Women." Paper presented at the 1986 National Alcoholism Forum of the National Council on Alcoholism, 1986a.

Caetano, R. Patterns and problems of drinking among U.S. Hispanics. In: *Report of the Secretary's Task Force on Black and Minority Health.* VII: *Chemical Dependency and Diabetes.* Bethesda, Md.: U.S. Department of Health and Human Services, National Institutes of Health, 1986b. pp. 141–186.

Caetano, R., and Martinez, R.M. *Alcohol Use in Madrid and Among U.S. Hispanics.* Draft prepared for the National Institute on Alcohol Abuse and Alcoholism, Rockville, Md., 1987.

Castro, F.G.; Maddahian, E.; Newcomb, M.D.; and Bentler, P.M. A multivariate model of the determinants of cigarette smoking among adolescents. *Journal of Health and Social Behavior* 28:273–289, 1987.

COSSMHO. *Delivering Preventive Health Care to Hispanics: A Manual for Providers.* Washington, D.C.: The National Coalition of Hispanic Health and Human Services Organizations, 1988.

Gilbert, M.J., and Cervantes, R.C. *Mexican Americans and Alcohol* (monograph no. 11). Los Angeles: Los Angeles Spanish Speaking Mental Health Research Center, University of California, 1987.

Krisberg, B.; Schwartz, I.M.; Fishman, G.; Eisikovitz, Z.; Guttman, E.; and Joe, K. Incarceration of minority youth. *Journal of Crime and Punishment* 33(2):173–205, 1987.

Marin, G., and Marin, B.V. *Perceived Credibility of Various Channels and Sources of AIDS Information Among Hispanics.* Technical Report. San Francisco: Center for AIDS Prevention Studies, University of California, San Francisco, 1989.

National Institute on Alcohol Abuse and Alcoholism. Alcohol and Hispanic Americans. In: *Alcohol Topics: In Brief.* Rockville, Md.: National Clearinghouse for Alcohol and Drug Information, 1985.

Santisteban, D., and Szapocznik, J. Substance abuse disorders among Hispanics: A focus on prevention. In: Becerra, R.M.; Karno, M.; and Escobar, J., eds. *Mental Health and Hispanic Americans: Clinical Perspectives.* New York: Grune and Stratton, 1982. pp. 83–100.

Stevenson, R.W. Spanish-language TV grows up. *The New York Times*, July 6, 1988. pp. D1, D22.

Strategy Research Corporation. *1987 U.S. Hispanic Market Study.* New York: Strategy Research Corporation, 1986.

Suro, R. Hispanic shift of allegiance changes face of U.S. religion. *The New York Times*, May 14, 1989. pp. 1, 22.

U.S. Bureau of the Census. *The Hispanic Population in the United States: March, 1988.* Current population reports, (advance report), population characteristics, Series P-20, No. 431. Washington, D.C.: Supt. of Docs., U.S. Govt. Print. Off., March 1988.

Ventura, S.J. Births of Hispanic parentage, 1985. In: *Monthly Vital Statistics Report* 36(11) Supp. DHHS Pub. No. (PHS)88-1120. National Center for Health Statistics. Hyattsville, Md.: Public Health Service, 1988.

Yankelovich, Skelly and White, Inc. *Spanish USA 1984: A Study of the Hispanic Market.* A report to the SIN National Television Network. Spanish International Network, 1984.

Experts Contributing to This Chapter

William A. Bogan
Executive Vice President,
COSSMHO
1030 15th Street, N.W., Suite 1053
Washington, DC 20005

Mary W. Booth
Research Associate
Department of Psychology
University of California, Los
Angeles

Felipe Castro
Associate Professor
Graduate School of Public Health
San Diego State University
6505 Alvarado Road, Suite 208
San Diego, CA 92120

Susan K. Maloney
Consultant, Health Promotion
9501 Columbia Boulevard
Silver Spring, MD 20910

CHAPTER 4

Reaching Parents

Understanding the Audience

Parents of children aged 8 to 12, living in environments at moderate risk for alcohol and other drug problems

- Are often heads of single-parent or blended families
- Tend to have busy and erratic schedules that make contact with children difficult
- Tend to spend less time in family activities than previous generations
- Face challenges unique to their generation, including
  - widespread availability of drugs
  - greater peer pressure on children to use alcohol and other drugs
  - pervasive media messages that promote alcohol use.

In addition, parents facing transitional situations, whether in their own lives or that of their children, may

- Be inclined to reexamine their family's life
- Be more receptive to messages concerning alcohol and other drug use by their children.

A 1988 Louis Harris survey of community leaders, grantmakers, and prevention experts reports that youthful alcohol and other drug use has reached epidemic proportions and now commands center stage as the foremost problem affecting young people and their families (Louis Harris and Associates 1988). More than 90 percent of those surveyed rated alcohol and other drugs as more threatening than crime, suicide, school dropouts, unemployment, and cigarette smoking. The survey also revealed that almost 75 percent of the respondents expect parents to take a dominant role in dealing with alcohol and other drug use by their children.

Research confirms the importance of the parents' role. Numerous studies indicate that parental attitudes and practices related to alcohol are the strongest social influence on children's use of alcohol and other drugs (Hawkins et al. 1985). Moreover, the nature of the interaction between parent and child has been found to be a key factor in predicting adolescent initiation into alcohol and other drug use (Kandel 1974).But parents need help. The widespread availability to youth of alcohol and other drugs is a relatively new phenomenon in our society, posing challenges that are in some ways unique to this generation of parents, many of whom are not yet aware of the significant role they can play in preventing alcohol and other drug use by their children.

This chapter focuses on the broad group of parents whose children are at moderate risk of alcohol and other drug use.

Parents in environments with moderate risks may not head troubled families, live in high-risk communities, or face the risk factors described in chapter 1; their children, nevertheless, are vulnerable to the problems associated with alcohol and other drugs. Researchers and experts contributing to this report confirm that even families that are healthy and stable need help to prevent such problems. This subgroup of parents is important to reach because it is large; the majority are parents of youth in moderate-risk environments.

The audience has been narrowed to parents of children aged 8 to 12 for several reasons. First, children in this age group generally have nonuse attitudes and behaviors (Pisano and Rooney 1988) that can be reinforced. Waiting until after children reach the age when they are more easily influenced by peers or after they have started using alcohol or other drugs makes prevention more difficult. Also, it is in these early years that children may first be urged to try alcohol and other drugs, and they need strong support to resist first use.

In addition, this is the stage of a child's development at which attitudes and behavior concerning alcohol and other drugs often change. In a study at the University of Pennsylvania, children surveyed showed a significant shift in attitudes, receptiveness to peers, and actual use of some forms of alcohol between the fifth and sixth grades. These changes in attitudes correspond very closely to the shift that occurs as parental guidance begins to give way in importance to the influence of peers (Pisano and Rooney 1988).

Demographic Factors

Of 64,491,000 families (adults and children living together in noninstitutionalized settings) in the United States, 51,537,000 have children under 18 (U.S. Department of Commerce 1987). Many live in nontraditional households. With 60 percent of American children living with one parent before the age of 18 (Krauthammer 1988), the traditional family of two natural parents and children is no longer the overwhelming majority. Blended and single-parent families are common.

While the structure of the family has changed, so has participation in family activities. Adolescents are spending more time away from the family, with greater social and economic independence. A study of these fundamental changes in family life notes that "it is not unlikely that the personal stress caused by this transition is reflected at a societal level by the increased prevalence of drinking and other drug involvement at younger ages" (Gordon and MacAlister 1982).

Environmental Factors

Parenting in the 1980s is different from, and in some ways more difficult than, parenting in previous generations. New parenting challenges are posed by major societal changes, such as the new roles of men and women, the greater mobility of families, and the expanding influence of mass media (Ulrici 1986).

The research literature consistently has shown that specific factors exist as predictors of alcohol or other youthful drug use. It is important to look at these factors as a basis in understanding how other factors in contemporary American life also could influence possible alcohol or other drug use patterns in families, even those families that are considered to have moderate risk of alcohol and other drug problems.

Family factors

Family factors emerge as one of the strongest influences for delaying or diminishing the initiation of adolescent alcohol and other drug use. When families are stable and have positive family relationships, their involvement and attachment appear to discourage youths' initiation into drug use, according to several studies cited by Hawkins et al. (1985). According to Kandel (1974), three parental factors help predict initiation into alcohol/drug use: parental role modeling of alcohol use and parents' drug behaviors, parental attitudes about drugs, and parent-child interactions. Ahmed et al. (1984) predicted that within homes where parents or older siblings used alcohol or other drugs, and especially when the child was involved in parental use (e.g., serving or pouring the drinks), the likelihood was that those children would see themselves as users when they got older.

The importance of a stable, close, and supportive family relationship and moderation in the use of alcohol appear to influence the delay or diminish the onset of adolescent drug use (Glynn 1981). When parent-child relationships lack closeness, with little parental involvement in children's activities, poor communication, and lack of or inconsistent discipline, there is an increased risk of alcohol/drug use (Hawkins et al. 1985).

Hawkins et al. (1985) also report that research consistently confirms the importance of "the quality and consistency of family management and family communication" in predicting children's use of alcohol or drugs. Good parenting and the quality of family life can and do serve as a protective barrier to youthful alcohol and other drug use. An important protective barrier is the ritual of dinnertime as family time. A current *Redbook* marketing study finds that dinnertime, which may be the only time that parents and children communicate with one another on a daily basis, is diminishing as a family event. In 1974, 83 percent of family members ate their main meal together almost every day; in 1987 only 72 percent of family members were together at dinnertime. In 1974, 2 percent of families had erratic schedules, which prohibited them from having their main meal together, and in 1987, the figure rose to 13 percent.

Peer factors

Surveys have shown that roughly one-third of fourth graders (9-year-olds) say that children their age pressure others to drink beer, wine, or liquor; this figure increases to nearly 80 percent by high school (*Weekly Reader* 1987). In one State survey, more than half of middle school students and 56 percent of senior high school students stated that "drug education should begin in elementary school" (Missouri Department of Mental Health 1988).

Family and peer influence on alcohol use appear to be similar, but peers have greater influence on marijuana use (Ahmed et al. 1984). Kandel (1982) notes that marijuana use by peers is a better predictor of subsequent involvement with drugs than parents' use and cites several studies that have found peer use to be the foremost predictor of cigarette smoking in young adolescents. Bloom and Greenwald (1984) found in their study of fifth through seventh graders who were regular and infrequent smokers that 71 percent said they usually smoked with friends.

Adolescents use alcohol and other drugs for a variety of reasons, including acceptance by their peers and the need to identify with their peer group. Fourth through sixth graders cite "fitting in with other kids" as the primary reason young people start using alcohol (*Weekly Reader* 1987).

School factors

Fleming et al. (1982) found that better performing first graders were more likely to lead the way in beginning use of alcohol and other drugs than were those with lower cognitive achievement scores, although the higher rates of use among better performing students declined by age 15 or older. Poor school performances and lack of interest in academic pursuits are generally acknowledged to be an influence in the initiation of drugs by adolescents.

Fleming also reported that first-grade teachers' ratings of aggressiveness and shyness were highly predictive of the frequency of drug use in teenage males. First-grade boys who were both shy and aggressive had the highest frequency of later drug use. (However, such children with identified "risk" factors should not be labeled but helped. Labeling or stereotyping of behavior or other factors could predispose such children to problems.) By contrast, girls who were rated by their first-grade teachers as shy or having learning problems tended to initiate use at a later age.

The media

Media messages for beer, wine, and liquor associate drinking behaviors with good times and social acceptance. Evidence of the impact of the media on youthful drug use is implicit in the popularity of wine coolers. Sales of wine coolers rose from 3 million cases in 1983, when they were introduced, to 80 million cases in 1987 (*Liquor Store* 1987). What is not made clear in the advertisements is that wine coolers have an alcohol content of between 5 and 7 percent—more alcohol than is contained in most beer (Ruie 1987).

Widespread availability of alcohol and other drugs

The increased availability to youth of alcohol and other drugs is another important factor in most families' environments. "Getting drugs is no problem," reported America's youngsters in a PRIDE survey of more than 200,000 6th- through 12th-grade children (Gleaton 1985). They agreed that "pot is so easy to get, all you have to do is put the word out, and you can buy all the joints you need." Easy access to bars and liquor stores, the relatively low cost of alcoholic beverages, and the general relaxation of restrictions on the availability of alcohol are factors that influence adolescent drinking patterns (Gerstein 1984).

Statistics on use of alcohol and other drugs confirm their widespread availability. According to the 1988 National High School Senior Survey (Johnston 1988):

- Nearly all (92 percent) high school seniors have tried alcohol and two-thirds (66 percent) are current users (i.e., had used in the past 30 days).

- More than half (57 percent) of high school seniors have tried an illicit drug, with over one-third (36 percent) trying an illicit drug other than marijuana.

- One in every six or seven high school seniors has tried cocaine (15.2 percent), and one in 18 (5.6 percent) has tried crack, a highly addictive form of cocaine.

Families in Transitional Situations

Much of the stress families experience is exacerbated during times of transition—events all families experience at one time or another. Transitions can be broken down into two major categories: (1) milestone traditions—predictable events that every parent of children ages 8 to 12 experience, such as the child graduating from elementary school; and (2) life event transitions, such as illness or divorce, that are experienced randomly by parents and their families. Experts contributing to this chapter hypothesized that during either type of transition, parents have and often take the opportunity to examine what has happened and what they will do. Therefore, they may be receptive to information about preventing alcohol and other drug problems among their children. Research will be required to test these hypotheses.

Milestone transitions

These events occur in the life of the child, but have implications that affect parents because they represent much deeper issues: the child is progressing, growing up, becoming independent. The relationship between parent and child shifts subtly, and parenting roles must be adjusted to match. These transitions offer an important opportunity to provide alcohol and other drug use prevention messages because they are events that can be anticipated. Examples of milestone transitions include the following:

- Child entering preadolescence and puberty
- Child changing grades in school
- Child moving from elementary to middle or junior high school
- Child's first dance party
- Child socializing on the telephone
- Child joining a team or club
- Child being offered alcohol or other drug or witnessing use by other children.

Life event transitions

These transitions are the major events that happen in nearly all families at one time or another, although they cannot be predicted. They can be either positive or negative and include the following:

- Change in or loss of employment
- Reentry of parent into the workforce
- Divorce or separation
- Move/relocation
- New baby in the family
- Remarriage
- Illness or death.

Research has shown that adolescent drug users were likely to have begun taking illicit drugs during a period of stress related to such transitions. Particularly prevalent in the histories of drug users just before initiation of illicit drug taking are changing schools, separation or divorce of parents, a parent's job loss, a father's increased absence due to a job change, increased arguments between parents, hospitalization, an outstanding personal achievement, or a suspension from school (Duncan 1978). In one study, adolescent drug users admitted to a halfway-house program reported more stressful events in the year preceding their first use of illicit drugs than is typical of the general population (Caddington 1972).

Relatively minor transitions such as buying a new car also can provide opportunities for intermediaries to convey prevention messages. When researchers Holmes and Rahe adapted their adult stress scale to measure stress in children, they found that negative events, such as death, divorce, or separation of parents, or a personal injury were the most stressful. However, they also found that positive events such as going on a summer vacation or winning an important award at school could produce significant amounts of stress in children (Holmes and Rahe 1967).

Knowledge, Attitudes, and Practices

Parents in the general population

- Believe that alcohol and drugs are a national problem but may be unaware that their own children are at risk

- May be unaware of the high prevalence of alcohol and other drug use among children in general

- May be unaware that their own children are exposed to alcohol and other drugs at an early age

- May have little information about specific drugs and their effects

- May find it difficult to talk to their children about drugs

- May think their children do not have the money for drugs

- May accept limited drug use among adults

- Usually abstain from drug use or excessive alcohol use

- Believe parents should take the lead in preventing drug use by their own children.

Parent group members

- Often were motivated to action through personal experience of knowledge of drug use among children
- Tend to have positive, problem-solving attitudes
- Tend to be joiners
- Tend to be involved in their children's activities.

Very little data exist concerning parents' knowledge, attitudes, and practices (KAP) of alcohol and other drug use among their children. Much of the data presented in this section were obtained from interviews with parent group members and from a limited number of magazine and journal articles.

The following discussion differentiates between the KAP of parent group members and the KAP of parents in the general population. Members of parent groups, which were formed in the 1970s to fight alcohol and other drug use among children, tend to be highly motivated to prevent this problem. Although they are a small subgroup of parents, the information on their KAP can afford insights concerning the larger group of parents, especially those who would be most receptive to prevention messages and who might participate actively in prevention programs.

Knowledge

Surveys have shown that although parents in the general population are aware of youthful alcohol and other drug use, they are unaware—or deny the possibility—that their own children may be using these substances. In an article about a PRIDE alcohol and drug use survey, Thomas Gleaton, Ed.D., founder of the Parent's Resource Institute for Drug Education, Inc. (PRIDE), states:

> We've found that most youngsters have been involved with drugs for over 2 years before their parents ever become aware of what is happening. Most parents like to believe that it's someone else's child or that statistics refer chiefly to youngsters from deprived homes. Youngsters in wonderful neighborhoods are almost as likely to become involved in drug use as those from deprived backgrounds.

Black (1988) reports that there is substantial uncertainty and some misconception among parents in the general population concerning their children's use of alcohol and other drugs. Fully 25 to 35 percent consistently responded that "they are not sure" about their children's behavior related to drugs. Moreover, substantial numbers believe their children are not at risk, even though drug usage reports suggest that a majority of children are likely to use marijuana and nearly 4 in 10 will use cocaine.

This gap between parents' awareness and children's exposure to drugs is confirmed in another survey conducted for the Metropolitan Life Insurance Company in which pollster Louis Harris found that only 5 percent of parents believe their children have used drugs, while 17 percent of the children say they have used drugs. Just over one-third of the parents think their child has had one or more alcoholic drinks; however, two-thirds of the children report they have. Of the children, 41 percent say they have smoked, while only 11 percent of the parents think that the children have smoked (PANDAA June 1987).

More evidence of this generation gap comes from the children themselves. At the 1988 PRIDE Conference in Atlanta, 92 youths between ages 11 and 19 were asked to complete an informal youth feedback form. The purpose of the form was to obtain information concerning what young people perceive their parents can do to help them choose an alcohol- and drug-free lifestyle. More than one-third (34 of the respondents) believe their parents do not fathom the extent of use and availability of alcohol and other drugs among youth. Others mentioned that parents do not know about the pressure on their children to use alcohol and other drugs, and parents are not aware of the activities in which their children are participating.

Further, parents may be unaware of how early youth today are starting to use alcohol and other drugs. Many parents of 8- to 12-year-olds grew up in the 1960s and 1970s and first may have been exposed to drugs while in college. Their children, on the other hand, are exposed as early as elementary school. The 1987 PRIDE survey of more than 450,000 Georgia students, grades 6 through 12, concluded that "thousands of Georgia youth are involved at an early age in illegal use of alcohol and illicit drug use and thousands of others are in jeopardy of becoming involved" (PRIDE 1988).

Statistics from the survey show that 13,500 (3 percent) of sixth graders, 22,500 (5 percent) of seventh graders, and 36,000 (8 percent) of eighth graders frequently drink beer and wine coolers. Also 13,500 (3 percent) of eighth graders reported that they used marijuana "very frequently" (PRIDE 1988).

There is some evidence that parents' awareness of their own children's risk may be increasing. In a recent Louis Harris poll on the American family, 9 out of 10 parents said they were concerned about their children coming into contact with pressure to use alcohol and other drugs (Louis Harris and Associates 1988). In addition, younger parents may be more aware of drug use than older parents, as suggested by a 1988 *Family Circle* survey. More than 38 percent of the respondents—61.6 percent of whom were under age 25—personally knew someone addicted to or using drugs (Jacoby 1988).

Although parents may underestimate their own children's risk, they appear to know that alcohol and other drug abuse is a national problem, according to readership surveys conducted by national magazines with wide circulation.

While such surveys are not based on a representative sampling of the general population, they do provide some indication of widespread views. For example, in a 1988 survey by *Better Homes and Gardens,* 61 percent of approximately 30,000 respondents said that use of alcohol and drugs is the greatest threat to family life today.

In another public opinion survey by *Parents Magazine,* parents were asked, "Which poses the greatest threat to our society, alcohol or drug abuse?" Of the respondents, 44 percent answered drug abuse, 13 percent answered alcohol abuse, and 42 percent answered both equally (Groller 1988).

Attitudes

Members of parent groups believe strongly that America and their communities have a drug problem. This audience is receptive to prevention and intervention messages and has become educated about alcohol and other drug use prevention, often through personal experience. In telephone interviews, respondents often said they were motivated to join parent groups because of alcohol and other drug use in their own family or knowledge of drug use in their community.

Parent group members appear to be very involved in children's activities and attuned to their children's development due to this involvement. Parent group members report that they believe they can make a difference and they have a positive attitude, conscious that they have successfully created a national movement that is seen as contributing to prevention for youthful alcohol and other drug use.

Many other parents are concerned about family life. In a readership survey to which 30,000 parents responded, 76 percent said that parents do not spend enough time with their children (*Better Homes and Gardens* 1986). Two years later, 76 percent of respondents reported they would make changes in work commitments that would reduce their income or slow their career development in order to spend more time with their children (*Better Homes and Gardens* 1988). In the latter survey, 77 percent of respondents (at least 81 percent of whom were parents) agreed that family life in America is in trouble.

Parents believe that they must take the lead in teaching children about the dangers of alcohol and other drugs, according to a recent survey (National PTA 1989). But parents also feel unprepared for this task, according to the same survey. Respondents said they feel less informed than their children, who often get drug information first from school or their friends.

Some of the attitudes of parents toward alcohol and other drugs may make it difficult for them to take positive action to help prevent use among their children (Black 1988). Black cites the following reasons:

- 51 percent think their children will never take drugs
- 43 percent think their children don't have the money to buy drugs
- 31 percent think their children have never been exposed to drugs.

According to the same report, certain attitudes that support the use of drugs suggest a level of acceptance of drug use by parents:

- 29 percent think cigarettes are worse than pot
- 26 percent think it's okay to smoke marijuana in private
- 20 percent feel that cocaine is a status symbol
- 11 percent feel that occasional cocaine use is not risky.

Practices

Most parents do not use drugs, and they use alcohol moderately or not at all, according to a *Better Homes and Gardens* readership survey (1988). Respondents stated that they generally abstain from drugs (92 percent) and tobacco (83 percent) and drink alcohol moderately or not at all (73 percent). Other healthful practices appear to be important to this group of parents; many respondents said that they eat wisely (70 percent); maintain ideal weight (46 percent); and exercise (45 percent).

Information on parents' involvement in programs to fight alcohol and other drug use among youth was obtained from parent group members, who said that they appear to be effective in working toward their goal of youthful alcohol/drug use prevention because they are willing to act on and seek out help for problems. These parents also are willing and anxious to share this information with others (e.g., friends, teachers, physicians). Most importantly, they are joiners. Confronted with a problem, they turn to others with similar problems or concerns.

A barrier to parent involvement in parent groups, say experts, is the high turnover of members. As children grow, parents move in and out of drug-related or age-appropriate parent group situations. Sometimes one or two parents try to sustain a parent group and contribute the most effort. If these leaders burn out or leave the community, the group often fails. Also, parent group members contributing to this report acknowledged that some groups lack experience in organization management (e.g., developing bylaws, setting agendas, creating outreach to get new membership). Because these practices are drawbacks to the continued success of the parent movement, it may be important for members to recognize and deal with these issues.

Research Needs

More research is needed to help guide communications programs, particularly in the following areas:

- Knowledge of parents concerning the drug culture, signs of drug use, age when their children will be exposed, perceptions of risk, and protective factors

- Parents' knowledge about resources to help them prevent, intervene in, and treat drug use problems in the family

- Parents' perceptions of their own current and youthful alcohol and other drug use or exposure, and how they relate their experiences to those of their children

- Practice of parents in providing their children with alcohol and other drug information, including their methods of communicating, the amount of time spent discussing the issue, and the age of children when such communications take place

- Parents' perception of their role and capabilities to intervene successfully to prevent use of alcohol and other drugs by their children

- Differences in knowledge, attitudes, and practices among various kinds of families, i.e., traditional two-parent families and families headed by a single parent.

Planning Considerations

Audiences

- Parents with drug use in the family
- Parents in policymaking positions
- Parents active and committed to children's activities, with special emphasis on fathers
- Homemakers
- Parents who are single
- Information-receptive but traditionally nonjoining parents
- Parents of teens
- Parents with high-risk factors
- Mothers who drink (social/moderate/heavy/alcoholic).

Channels

- Parent groups organized to prevent alcohol and other drug abuse among children
- Other community organizations, such as PTAs and Scout groups
- Daytime and prime time TV
- Radio
- Magazines for parents
- Billboards and posters
- Schools
- Employers and employee assistance programs
- Businesses, especially those that come into contact with parents during times of transition.

Materials

- Available materials include
    - Brochures and pamphlets
    - Videotapes
    - Curriculum guides
    - Games
    - Bumper stickers.
- Needed are
    - Audiocassettes and other materials that fit into busy schedules
    - Trigger films to help initiate parent/child discussions
    - Materials that relate to family transitions
    - Resource packets to help families adjust to new communities, jobs, schools
    - Skills-building materials to help parents communicate with each other and to help their children develop social competence.

Messages. Messages to parents should

- Validate the important role parents play in youthful alcohol and other drug use

- Promote awareness of children's early exposure to alcohol and other drugs
- Provide information on specific drugs and their effects
- Provide information on genetic risks
- Promote understanding of children's feelings during times of transition
- Promote family discussion.

When planning a communications program to reach parents, an important step is selection of program components. These will vary depending on the community, the resources available, and the goals of the program. This section suggests a variety of program components, including audience segments that could be targeted, as well as channels, materials, and messages that may be effective in reaching parents. As with any communications program, thorough pretesting and ongoing evaluation are vital to ensure that components are appropriate to the selected audience.

Audiences

While this report focuses on the parents of moderate-risk children aged 8 to 12, other parent audiences should not be ignored. Experts contributing to this report have identified numerous audience segments, some of which may overlap with parents of moderate-risk children aged 8 to 12, and assigned them priorities, as follows:

First ranked group of parents to be targeted

(list prioritized)

- Parents with drug use in the family
- Parents in policymaking positions
- Parents active and committed to children's activities, with special emphasis on fathers
- Homemakers
- Parents who are single
- Information-receptive but traditionally nonjoining parents
- Parents of teens
- Parents with high-risk factors (e.g., those who are overly strict, overly permissive, afraid to confront, afraid of children's criticism)
- Mothers who drink (social/moderate/heavy/alcoholic).

Additional parent audiences were identified for later efforts. These audiences were then ranked in a list of second and third most important segments.

Second ranked group of parents to be targeted

(list not prioritized)

- Parents in denial—who do not want to know a problem exists with their children
- Codependent fathers
- Parents whose children are starting school
- Fathers who drink
- Parents in religious groups
- Parents of year 2000 graduates
- Parents whose children are in college
- Grandparents.

Third ranked group of parents to be targeted

(list not prioritized)

- Drug-using parents*
- Parents supervising children's use of drugs and alcohol
- Irresponsible parents
- Dysfunctional parents—adults who were not parented well themselves*
- Lower socioeconomic status (SES) parents*
- Lower achievement-oriented parents*
- Parents of "problem" first graders*
- Foster parents*

Channels

Appropriate channels for reaching the parents of moderate-risk youth, aged 8 to 12, are parent groups, other community groups, certain mass media, schools, employers, and businesses, particularly those that come into contact with parents in transition.

---

*The High-Risk Families Communications Task Force designated these as priority audiences; see chapter 1.

Parent groups

When parents in the late 1970s became aware that drug paraphernalia was available at most corner record shops, that marijuana was as easy for their children to obtain as a candy bar, and that, in fact, many of their teenage children were using a smorgasbord of drugs, they began to organize. They educated themselves, wrote their representatives and senators, requested hearings, took action to ban paraphernalia shops in their neighborhoods, and formed coalitions to help prevent alcohol or other drug use among their children. Since then, the rapid growth of parent groups and the effectiveness with which they have called attention to alcohol and other drug use among youth have been positive phenomena in communities across the Nation. Parents' groups that focus on alcohol and other drugs exist in many communities and can help reach both current and potential members.

Other community organizations

Parents not likely to join parent groups may be reached by working with a broad base of other community-based organizations, such as Parent Teacher Associations and scouting groups. Many of these organizations already have built programs to prevent alcohol and other drug use among youth; others may be interested in doing so as a joint venture with other groups. See chapter 6 for more information on working with intermediary groups.

The media

A study of the media habits of parents aged 18 to 34, compiled by the Chicago advertising agency HDM/Dawson Johns and Black (1988), reports the following:

- Parents are watching more daytime than prime time television, with viewing decreasing as age and income increase.

- Parents 18 to 34 years of age with household incomes of $25,000 or more are heavy radio listeners, although as income increases, radio listening tends to decrease.

- Parents frequently read magazines, and as income increases, magazine readership increases.

- Parents pay attention to ads on billboards, buses, buildings, and in other locations.

Table 1 summarizes the media habits of parents (adults 18 to 34, with children), listing the most popular television programs, radio formats, and magazines.

Table 1. Media Habits of Adults Aged 18 to 34, With Children

Television	Radio	Magazines
Top television shows among parents	Top five radio formats among parents	Leading magazines for parents (with percentage of audiences reached)
Friday Night Videos Moonlighting Max Headroom Miami Vice Alf Disney Movie Stingray Growing Pains Amazing Stories Rags to Riches	Black Contemporary Religious Album-Oriented Rock Golden Oldies	Parade (33.4 percent) TV Guide (30.8 percent) People (17.2 percent) Reader's Digest (17.2 percent) Better Homes & Gardens (15.2 percent) National Enquirer (14.5 percent) Time (13.5 percent) Sports Illustrated (12.1 percent)

Source: HDM/Dawson Johns and Black 1988.

Parents' Magazines As A Channel

There are a number of well-known, high-circulation magazines that reach parents, such as *Weekly Reader, Good Housekeeping, Redbook, Family Circle, Essence, Ebony,* and *VISTA.* Communications programs could contact these publications to offer current information on alcohol and other drug problems. Many of these magazines have regular health/medical columns that offer an appropriate vehicle for disseminating alcohol and other drug information. Topics will vary, depending on the target audience of the publication.

For example, the American Academy of Pediatrics (AAP) and *American Baby* magazine launched a new national magazine in January 1989 called *Healthy Kids.* The magazine, which is devoted to the subject of children's health, is designed for parents of newborns to adolescents. Three issues will be published each year. Issues in 1989 will focus on newborns to age 3; the magazine has estimated circulation to 1.5 million parents.

In 1990, *Healthy Kids* will be targeted to parents of children aged 4 to 10. In 1991, an edition of *Healthy Kids* for the teenage years will debut. The combined annual circulation is expected to reach 13.5 million parents.

AAP members can receive 150 free copies of each issue of the magazine to distribute to parents. The magazine cover will feature the AAP logo and a personalized message to parents from their pediatrician.

Schools

Schools have existing communications channels with parents, such as newsletters, student take-home handouts, and parents' nights. Information concerning prevention of alcohol and other drug use among youth could be disseminated through these channels. In addition, schools play a role in important transitions in the family's life, and therefore may command parents' attention at these times. Experts contributing to this report identified graduation from elementary school as a key transition for their families.

Employers

Some employers also have existing communications channels with their employees' families. These channels include employee assistance programs (EAPs) and special information packets assembled for families of employees who are transferring to another city. These materials could serve as a channel for information and counseling on alcohol and other drug use among youth.

Businesses and services

Businesses and services that come in contact with families during times of transition, such as real estate companies, marriage counselors, lawyers, health insurance companies, and employment agencies, offer direct access to parents at times when they may be most receptive to information concerning their children's welfare.

Materials Review

A review of educational materials concerning alcohol and other drug use among children identified more than 250 items targeted to parents.* Formats included videotapes, bumper stickers, curriculum guides, and games, but the largest category consisted of brochures and pamphlets. The materials were received from parent groups organized to prevent alcohol and other drug use among children; national organizations with family concerns, such as the National PTA; other nonprofit groups; and private producers, such as Hazelden and Channing Bete.

Topics included

- Parenting skills (in general)
- Communicating with children about alcohol and other drugs
- Signs and symptoms of drug use

_____

*More information on these materials is available from the National Clearinghouse for Alcohol and Drug Information; see appendix E.

- Starting a parents' group

- Other community programs

- Information on specific drugs.

Few materials seemed designed to meet the needs of the very busy parent. For example, no audiocassettes for listening in the car appear to have been developed for parents, nor were materials located that used pictures of drugs for quick reference. Other gaps include

- Skills-building material for parents to help their children develop social competence

- Trigger films to help initiate family discussions

- Skills-building materials to help adults in the same household communicate more effectively with one another

- Materials, including resource packets, that relate to family transitions

- Materials alerting and training parents to help their children interpret and understand the overt and covert messages in advertisements and the media that may contribute to youth use of alcohol and other drugs.

Messages

In general, messages to parents must increase awareness in several areas and promote parent-child communication. To increase awareness, parents need more information on types of drugs and their effects, on the risks that their own children face (it's not just other people's kids), and on all children's early exposure to alcohol and other drugs. Also needed are messages concerning genetic risks and how parents can evaluate and share family substance use histories with their children (see chapter 1).

Because many parents find it difficult to talk to their children on this topic, messages should encourage and help trigger family discussion. Messages also can alert parents to the effect that certain transitions may have on children's feelings and behavior and encourage parents to talk with their children about these transitions. In all cases, messages should confirm the significant role parents can play in helping their children remain drug free.

Barriers

When selecting channels, materials, and messages, keep in mind the barriers they must overcome. The following list of potential barriers to communications with parents is based on studies cited earlier and on meetings with experts consulted for this project.

Parents' lack of time. Parents are busy. Special attention must be given to the fact that most parents, whether in two- or single-parent families, are employed outside the home.

Parents' denial of their children's use of alcohol or other drugs. Surveys cited earlier show that parents are not sure or do not know about their children's use of drugs.

A gap between parents' awareness and children's exposure to alcohol and other drugs. A gap appears to exist between parents' perception of their children's world and reality, according to several studies.

Parents' lack of communications skills. Many parents say they find it difficult to talk to their children about alcohol and other drug use. Some may be inhibited by their own use of alcohol, while others do not want to appear mistrusting to their children. A recent article in *The Washington Post* said that according to concerned experts, "although parents are worried, meaningful family discussion in the home about drugs and alcohol abuse is not the norm" (Oldenburg 1989).

Parents' lack of information. Parents say they are not keeping up with their children, who often get drug information first from school or friends (National PTA 1989). Parents need to be kept up to date on current research, which can be provided in under- standable and usable formats.

Recommendations

- Take advantage of milestone transitions.
- Communicate with parents during other life events.
- Use minitransitions to communicate with parents.
- Increase parents' awareness and knowledge about potential risks.
- Increase parents' knowledge and understanding of parenting skills.
- Develop materials for parents.
- Create resource centers in libraries.
- Create resource packets for intermediaries to distribute.
- Use intermediaries having direct access to parents in transitions.

- Work with local media.

- Influence the mass media to help reach parents.

Helping parents prevent drug use among their children must be thought of not as an event but as a process, one that requires many years of consistent, reinforcing, and appropriate messages. In using the strategies recommended below, it is important to remember that parents need to hear messages from a number of different sources. Messages that reinforce each other will increase the likelihood that parents will recognize situations predisposing their children to alcohol and other drug use and address them, seeking help if necessary to do so.

Many of the following recommendations focus on transitional events that affect families. Parent representatives consulted for this report said that during times of transition (e.g., separation, new job, move) they were very concerned about their children's reactions. Parents often took more time to examine their relationships, thought about their family's welfare, and generally reflected on the future. Transitions, they said, got their attention. If youthful alcohol and other drug use prevention information can be provided during transitions, parents may be more willing to listen to the prevention messages and incorporate the information into new behavior patterns.

A life transition offers an opportunity for communicating youthful alcohol and other drug use prevention messages that specifically address the needs and concerns of parents during those periods. Reaching parents during transitions has a double benefit:

- It helps them reach out to their children, before the stress creates the need for the child to escape through alcohol or other drug use

- It alerts parents to their power as parents and the impact on their children of their own use of alcohol and other drugs.

The following recommendations do not constitute a comprehensive program, nor have they been assigned priorities. They are ideas, gleaned from the literature reviewed and from the experts contributing to this chapter, from which program planners can select those that may be most useful in a particular situation. As with any communications strategies, pretesting with the target audience and evaluation are essential.

Take Advantage of Milestone Transitions

Because they can be anticipated, milestones may be especially useful to communication program planners. When a child changes grades, moves from elementary to middle school, or joins a school club or team, parents may be particularly aware of the child's growth and the new needs that attend this growth. Activities, materials, and messages that relate specifically to the transition should be used. For example, club or team orientation meetings, to which parents are invited, could include presentations on alcohol and other drug use as it relates to the purpose of the club. The importance of group members' supporting each other in resisting alcohol and other drugs could be emphasized.

Using Transitions

An effective communications strategy for reaching parents at the time their children move from elementary to middle school could be an evening seminar for parents of sixth grade students. The elementary school, in conjunction with the junior high school, could present a seminar on anticipating this transition and how it affects all members of the family. A presentation by the principal, the teacher, a psychologist, social worker, prevention specialist, child development expert, or a video could focus on the stress associated with preadolescence. This presentation might include a discussion of the risks that are present in this age group (alcohol and other drug use, teenage pregnancy, eating disorders). A packet of information would be made available to all parents of sixth graders, even those who did not attend the seminar. The packet could include materials on parenting skills and maintaining good communications with children, how to talk to children about preventing alcohol and other drug use, as well as other problems of preadolescence. Materials for prevention of alcohol and other drug use could include signs and symptoms of alcohol or other drug use, a parent/child discussion guide/activity workbook, and a resource list of alcohol and other drug use prevention materials.

Messages for parents during this milestone transition should be tailored to the cultural environment of that segment of the community served by the school. They could encourage parents to

- Anticipate this transition and the possible risk of initiation of use of alcohol and other drugs.

- Stay involved with their child's activities and school programs; know their child's friends.

- Provide a role model for a healthy drug-free lifestyle.

Communicate With Parents During Other Life Events

Parent representatives also identified life events, such as moving or family breakups, as important times to reach parents of 8- to 12-year-olds. Again, activities and messages should relate to the specific event. For example, marriage counselors, school counselors, or others could include information on the special risks to children during times of parental estrangement, including the risk of using alcohol or other drugs. Suggested communications channels, activities, materials, and messages applicable to life event transitions are listed in charts at the end of this chapter.

Use Minitransitions to Communicate With Parents

These relatively minor transitions also offer opportunities to reach parents. For example, a family going on vacation could receive a packet of information from a tourist bureau or a State park that included materials concerning prevention of alcohol and other drug use by young children.

Increase Parents' Awareness and Knowledge of Potential Risks

Parents need more statistical information to better understand the probability of alcohol and other drug use by their children; on the role of gateway drugs (cigarettes, alcohol, marijuana); and on heredity issues. It is also important that they know as much or more about drugs as their children are likely to know, and that they recognize the signs and symptoms of alcohol and other drug use. Information about AIDS and its relationship to drug use may heighten parent awareness.

Increase Parents' Knowledge and Understanding of Parenting Skills

Parenting skills for the current generation of parents must include communicating with children about alcohol and other drugs. Print materials, such as magazine articles and brochures, may help increase parents' knowledge and understanding about parenting skills. These materials also may emphasize the parents' role as primary alcohol and other drugs prevention agent for their children. However, parenting seminars, school and religious programs, and audiovisual materials may be more valuable because they allow demonstration of roles and parenting techniques.

Develop Materials for Parents

While materials exist on certain topics for parents, others need to be developed or adapted from existing materials. Particular attention should be given to materials that fit into parents' often-crowded schedules, such as audiocassettes for cars. See above, under "Planning Considerations," for a summary of other needs in this area.

Create Resource Centers in Libraries

Special areas in public libraries could be set aside for a variety of print and audiovisual educational materials.

Create Resource Packets for Intermediaries to Distribute

Intermediaries that have access to parents during transitions might be persuaded to distribute packets of information, particularly if the packet included space for the intermediary's own logo, name, and other information.

Use Intermediaries Having Direct Access to Parents in Transitions

Schools, employers, businesses, and services that come into direct contact with parents during these times could be considered as channels for messages concerning alcohol and other drug use among youth. See the charts at the end of this chapter for suggested channels, activities, materials, and messages.

Work With Local Media

Working with local newspapers, as well as radio and television stations, provides an opportunity to address issues and situations relevant to a specific community. A feature article on record shops that sell paraphernalia; a talk show with a school principal discussing drugs in a local elementary school; a news segment on playground drug markets; or a story about the activities of a Just Say No Club—all could help overcome parents' ignorance or denial of the problem. Use of local examples and circumstances raises awareness that the Nation's problem, as publicized in the national media, is also the community's problem and needs the community's attention.

Influence the Mass Media to Help Reach Parents

Editors, as well as radio and television producers, cover issues they consider newsworthy or interesting to their audience. Communications programs may be able to influence these gatekeepers through letter writing, telephone campaigns, or other activities. These activities could provide new "angles" on alcohol and other drug use issues, suggest storylines or daytime or other shows, or praise appropriate coverage as it occurs. See chapter 6 for recommendations to encourage media advocacy activities. Special attention should be given to the programs and publications most popular among parents (see table 1).

Conduct Research on the Knowledge, Attitudes, and Practices of Parents

There is a serious lack of data on the knowledge, attitudes, and practices of parents of children at moderate risk of alcohol and other drug use. Potential research topics are listed earlier, under "Knowledge, Attitudes, and Practices."

Such data need to be updated frequently and routinely, as alcohol and other drug attitudes and availability change and as new children—and their parents—move into this important age group.

Table 2. Suggestions for Communications Programs

Transition	Channels	Activity	Materials	Messages
Moving/relocation	• Moving companies • Realtors • Mortgage companies • New employee orientations • EAP • Employee Relocation Council (ERC) • Welcome Wagon • Churches/synagogues • PTA • Schools (principal, guidance counselor, teacher) • Community groups (i.e., Newcomers, chamber of commerce) • Neighborhood associations • Interior decorators • Libraries • Community organizations (Boy/Girl Scouts, Lions Club) • Supermarkets, shopping malls • Motor vehicle departments	• Provide handouts and other literature that describe common problems/solutions in dealing with moving • Provide orientation for new community members through chamber of commerce or other community groups for families, including children in order to help them feel a part of the new community • Distribute materials to new members of organization, new client/customer, new volunteer • Submit written material to church newsletter	• Packets containing samples, coupons, and prevention messages from businesses in community • Pamphlets to encourage new community members to participate in community activities • Brochures with questions and answers about signs of drug use • Comprehensive video on different aspects of new community • List of community resources	• Change, even positive change, is a stressful event and moving is an adjustment in one's life • Allow children to work through grief/loss issues around moving to a new community • Describe grief/loss issues children will experience • Realize change/transitions is an insecure time for children • Recognize the need to take time to help your children establish a new circle of friends • Children could become involved in an alcohol/drug-using crowd because of a need for acceptance and the desire to have friends • "Acting-out" behavior may be masking repressed feelings of fear and loneliness • Try to reduce stress while uprooting your family • Prepare children to handle peer pressure • Take advantage of community resources

Example:

A partnership could be formed between realtors, moving companies, and mortgage companies. A package could be designed that contains a brochure on tips to make a move psychologically successful for children, a community resource list, and a set of questions and answers on reducing stress and protective factors to prevent youthful drug use. The realtor could give new customers the brochure; the moving companies could give clients the set of questions and answers; and the mortgage company could distribute the list of community resources at settlement.

Table 2. Suggestions for Communications Programs (continued)

Transition	Channels	Activity	Materials	Messages
Separation or divorce	• Parents Without Partners • Lawyers • Judges • Child and family services • Churches/synagogues • Divorce Anonymous (DA) • America's Society of Separated and Divorced Men (ASDM) • Marriage counselors • Women's resource centers • Libraries • Friends, relatives, co-workers • EAP • Realtors • Shopping malls • Divorce mediators • Adult education programs • Dating services	• Develop training seminars • Sponsor programs for separated or divorcing parents • Encourage organizations to provide resources for parents in transition • Sponsor social activity for separated/divorced parents • Course designed for coparenting of child rearing • Sermon on supporting loved ones during divorce and separation • Credit-free course or courses for parents on different aspects of separation/divorce • Submit articles to appropriate journals	• Videotape to encourage parent/child discussions • Activity book for families • Audiotape for parents to use in car • Seminar curriculum/trigger films • Resource list of materials for separated/divorced parents	• Divorce can be as traumatic as the death of a parent for children • Society's use of the term "broken home" is inappropriate. If one parent has left there is still a home and family • Don't take out your frustrations on your children • Both parents need to agree to reinforce alcohol and other drug messages • Be available to help children work through grief/loss • Help your children understand the complexity of separation/divorce and the options available to them • Support wise, positive choices you and your child make for coping with stress • Information about the stages of loss and grief can help parents and children adjust • Children fear the loss of a parent due to separation and divorce • Teach children responsibility for actions and decisions • Teach children to handle greater freedom

Example:

A dating service could be contacted to sponsor seminars for people who are separated or divorced. The seminar could focus on coping with "loneliness" and the stress associated with separation and divorce. A packet could be provided that would contain information explaining how the stress of separation or divorce affects the parents and the children in a family. Materials in the packet could include signs and symptoms of alcohol and other drug use and a guide to parenting a separated or divorced family. Messages could include: "talking through problems and listening to your child's feelings is important," and "you are still a family and can support the child through this transition."

Table 2. Suggestions for Communications Programs (continued)

Transition	Channels	Activity	Materials	Messages
Death/Illness in the family	• Life insurance companies • Health insurance companies • Funeral homes • Churches and synagogues • PTA • EAP • Hospital chaplains/rabbis • Support groups (i.e., Compassionate Friends) • Hospice • Physicians • Nurses • Nursing registries • Pharmacists • Family friends • Extended family • Physical therapists • Grief counselors • Social workers • Psychiatrists • Hotlines	• Provide literature • Incorporate information on working with channels into the training of professionals • Develop education piece directed to the friend or extended family member • Develop education piece targeted to any of the professionals who will come in contact with the family members • Submit an article to professional journals	• Brochures to be given to bereaved families by the persons who are in contact with them after the death • Activity book • Audiotape on how to help children deal with feelings of guilt, loss, and sorrow • Resource lists	• Parents may need to get help or support for themselves so they can help their children deal with their grief/loss issues • Parents need to be aware that this can be a frightening time for children • Parents can help their children to express their fears and be sensitive to their need to grieve as much as adults • Parents can help their children be aware that this is a time their children are vulnerable to using alcohol or other drugs as a way of dealing with pain and unexpressed sorrow • Parents need to be aware that adolescents fear the loss of their parents due to death or illness

Example:

Develop a package of materials and train lay persons to start crisis recovery groups in their local churches. These packages could include a promotional brochure for the groups, facilitator handbook, communications and feelings workbook for participants, and a resource list.

Table 2. Suggestions for Communications Programs (continued)

Transition	Channels	Activity	Materials	Messages
Change in or loss of employment	• Employment agencies • Social workers (Dept. of Social Services) • Counselors • Welfare agencies • Schools • PTA • Churches/synagogues • EAP • Unemployment office • Specialty employment services (i.e., ASAE) • Existing hotlines • Mortgage companies • Real estate agents • Credit card companies • Collection bureaus	• Provide printed materials for counselors and other channels • Train school counselors to be sensitive to changes in student behavior resulting from changes in family • Encourage State and Federal programs to consider family transitions in the services they provide and provide literature describing common problems/solutions • Show videotapes at job orientations • Maintain literature rack in unemployment offices • Send mailing with mortgage company late payment notices • Disseminate information to real estate agents about community resources	• Print ads • Audiotapes about coping with stress • Question and answers on how to help children deal with their feelings • Resource lists • Posters in employment agencies	• Children feel insecure during these times and worry about the future of their family • Parents need to communicate with their children about future plans and include them in family discussions • Children need to be given the opportunity to help with family responsibilities • Children can turn to the "wrong" crowd of friends to seek security if excluded from conversations about family crises • Using alcohol or other drugs does not improve difficult situations

Example:

A package of three inserts could be designed to be sent out in a person's first three unemployment checks. One could be on dealing with stress and recognizing depression; another could be questions and answers on pertinent issues dealing with unemployment and how it may affect children; and another could be on community resources.

Table 2. Suggestions for Communications Programs (continued)

Transition	Channels	Activity	Materials	Messages
Reentry of parent into workforce	• New employee orientation • PTA • EAP • Child care centers • Citizens associations • Boys Club • Girls Club • Bank	• Provide literature for parents to intermediaries to distribute • Hold brown bag lunch discussions for new employees • Maintain literature rack at child care centers • Ask banks to provide information to new accounts	• Short activity book with helpful hints of ways to successfully mesh child rearing and careers • Poster for EAP office • Desk calendar with messages • Resource lists • Audiotape for car on family organization skills • Questions and answers on child safety	• "Acting-out" behaviors may be masking feelings of rejection and loneliness • There are ways to talk about feelings • Teach children responsibility for actions and decisions • Prepare children to handle peer pressure

Example:

A seminar for reentry parents could be designed to be held as brown bag lunch sessions in a three-part series. This program could include a 30-minute videotape on selecting child care and a module for successfully combining work and parenting responsibilities. A questions-and-answers brochure and an audiotape about teaching children responsibility and how to handle peer pressure, including the pressure to try alcohol or other drugs, could complete the package.

Table 2. Suggestions for Communications Programs (continued)

Transition	Channels	Activity	Materials	Messages
Remarriage	• Support groups • Clergy • Justice of the peace • Marriage license bureau • Bridal shops • PTA	• Training for intermediaries • Design package for clergy to use as part of pre-marital counseling for remarriage	• Books about effective step-parenting • Brochure on communications techniques • Resource lists • Question-and-answer brochure on children's feelings when parent remarries	• Go slowly in terms of the new relationships • Maintain a healthy co-parenting relationship with your ex-spouse • This is a time when your child may turn away from parental guidance and to peer support, becoming more vulnerable to use of alcohol and other drugs

Example:

Design a package of materials for clergy to use when doing pre-marital counseling for remarriage. Components could include a 20-minute videotape to watch with the clergyman on the psychology of adjustment for children and children and step-parenting how-to's. A 30-minute audiotape could be lent to a couple to listen to at home and could cover successful family communications strategies, including a clear no-use message for children and information on signs of drug use. A brochure on community resources could be included.

Bibliography

AAP News. AAP, American Baby to publish national child health magazine. Aug. 5, 1988.

Ahmed, S.W.; Bush, P.J.; Davidson, F.R.; and Iannotti, R.J. "Factors Influencing Children's Use and Intended Use of Abusable Substances." Paper presented at the Annual Meeting of the American Public Health Association, Anaheim, Calif., 1984.

Alcohol, Drug Abuse and Mental Health Administration. *Statistical Update.* Rockville, Md.: ADAMHA, 1987.

Beattie, M. *Codependent No More.* Center City, Minn.: Hazelden Foundation, 1987.

Better Homes and Gardens. Today's parents: How well are they doing? Sept. 1986.

Better Homes and Gardens. What's happening to American families? Sept. 1988.

Black, G.S. *The Attitudinal Basis of Drug Use.* Prepared for the Media-Advertising Partnership for a Drug-Free America, New York, 1988.

Bloom, M.D., and Greenwald, M.A. Alcohol and cigarette use among early adolescents. *Journal of Drug Education* 14(3), 1984.

Caddington, R.D. The significance of life events as etiologic factors in diseases of children. II. A study of a normal population. *Journal of Psychosomatic Research* 16:205–213, 1972.

Duncan, D. Attitudes toward parents and delinquency in suburban adolescent males. *Adolescence* 13(50), 1978.

Duncan, D., and Gold, R. *Drugs and the Whole Person.* New York: Macmillan, 1982.

Dupont, R.L. Prevention of adolescent chemical dependency. *Pediatric Clinic of North America* 34(2):496–7, 1987.

Fleming, J.P.; Kellan, S.G.; and Brown, C.H. Early predictors of age at first use of alcohol, marijuana, and cigarettes. *Drugs and Alcohol Dependence* 9:285–303, 1982.

Garmezy, N.; Master, A.S.; and Tellegan, A. The study of stress and competence in children: A building block for developmental psychopathology. *Child Development* 55:97–111, 1984.

Gerstein, D.R., ed. *Toward the Prevention of Alcohol Problems: Government, Business and Community Action.* Washington, D.C.: National Academy Press, 1984.

Glynn, T. From family to peer: A review of transitions of influence among drug-using youth. *Journal of Youth and Adolescence* 10(15):363–383, 1981.

Gordon, N.P., and McAlister, A.L. Adolescent drinking: Issues and research. In: Coates, T.J.; Petersen, A.C.; and Perry, C., eds. *Promoting Adolescent Health: A Dialog on Research Practice.* New York: Academic Press, 1982.

Gleaton, T. Drugs? a shocking report from 200,000 "nice" kids. *Family Circle*, Sept. 24, 1985. pp. 20–24.

Hall, Doug. Parents are key to drug-free kids. *Washington Post*, March 7, 1989. p. D5.

Harvard Business School. *Anti-drug Marketing Study for the Mayor's Policy Office of the City of Boston.* Cambridge, Mass.: Harvard Business School, 1957.

Hawkins, J.D.; Lishner, D.M.; Catalano, R.F. Jr.; and Howard, M.O. *Childhood Predictors of Adolescent Substance Abuse: Toward an Empirically Grounded Theory.* Center for Social Welfare Research. Seattle, Wash.: University of Washington, 1985.

HDM/Dawson Johns and Black. *Media Habits of Adults with Children.* Chicago, Ill., 1988.

Holmes, T.H., and Rahe, R.H. The social readjustment rating scale. *Journal of Psychosomatic Research* 11:213–218, 1987.

Jacoby, S. What's worrying Americans the most in 1988? *Family Circle*, Jan. 12, 1988. pp. 72—72, 92–94.

Johnston, L.D.; O'Malley, P.M.; and Bachman, A.G. *1987 National High School Senior Drug Abuse Survey.* Institute for Social Research, Ann Arbor, Mich.: University of Michigan, 1988.

Kandel, D.B. Inter and intragenerational influences on adolescent marijuana use. *Journal of Social Issues* 30:107–135, 1974.

Liquor Store. Wine coolers. May 1987, pp. 54, 62.

Louis Harris and Associates. *A Catalyst for Action. A National Survey to Mobilize Leadership and Resources for the Prevention of Alcohol and Other Drug Problems Among American Youth.* Survey conducted for the Boys Clubs of America. New York: Louis Harris and Associates, 1988.

Manatt, M. *Parents, Peers and Pot I.* Rockville, Md.: National Institute on Drug Abuse, 1980.

Miller, T.W. Advances in understanding the impact of stressful life events on health. *Hospital and Community Psychiatry* 39(6):615–622, 1988.

Missouri Department of Mental Health. *Student Opinion Survey.* Jefferson City, Mo.: the Department, 1988.

National PTA. Helping Kids Cope with Stress. A *Redbook* special section. The Hearst Corporation, 1988.

National PTA. "PTA/GTE Press Release." March 6, 1989.

PRIDE. *The 1987–88 Georgia Survey of the Prevalence and Patterns of Adolescent Drug Use.* Atlanta, Ga.: Parents' Resource Institute for Drug Education, 1988.

PANDAA. *Newsletter.* June 7, 1989.

Pisano, S., and Rooney, J.F. Predisposition to drug use in rural adolescents: Preliminary relationships and methodological considerations. *Journal of Drug Education* 18(1), 1988.

Redbook. Food trends and the baby boom generation: 1974 vs. 1987. Executive summary. *Redbook* Marketing Report. New York: *Redbook* Magazine, 1987.

Ruie, B. Hot coolers. *U.S. Air.* March 1987.

Spock, B. *What About Children? Family Strengths: Positive Models for Family Life.* University of Nebraska Press, 1980.

Ulrici, D.K. Guidelines for parenting the adolescent. In: *Insight.* Vol. 4, Smyrna, Ga.: Ridgeview Institute, 1986.

U.S. Department of Commerce. Household and family characteristics: March 1987. In: *Current Population Reports.* Series P-20, No. 424. Washington, D.C.: U.S. Govt. Print. Off., 1987.

U.S. Department of Education. *Youth Indicators 1988. Trends in the Well-Being of American Youth.* Washington, D.C.: Office of Educational Research and Improvement, 1988.

The Weekly Reader. National Survey on Drugs and Drinking. Middletown, Conn.: Field Publications, 1987.

Experts Contributing to This Chapter

Elaine Bratic Arkin
Health Communications Consultant
3435 N. 14th Street
Arlington, VA 22201

Dale Baker, Ph.D.
Clinical Psychologist
7946 Idaho Avenue, Suite 20
La Jolla, CA 92037

Thomas Baker, Ph.D.
Acting Director
Family Service Center
Code 12 - Naval Station
San Diego, CA 92136

Carolyn Burns
Deputy Director, MMDP
Macro Systems, Inc.
8630 Fenton Street, Suite 300
Silver Spring, MD 20910

Paul Cannon
The Bridge
Route 12, Box 192
Bowling Green, KY 42101

Marilyn Civer
Former NFP State Networker
3875 N. Country Club #204
Tucson, AZ 85716

Ian M. Cotton, MFCC
Employee Assistance Counselor
City of San Diego
525 B Street, Suite 618
San Diego, CA 92101

Rosanna Creighton
Drug Abuse Prevention Education
   Trainer
3747 N.E. Milton Street
Portland, OR 97212

David F. Duncan, Ph.D.
Researcher
Department of Health Education
Southern Illinois University
Carbondale, IL 62901-6618

Tom Farrell
Principal, Aspen High School
P.O. Box 300
Aspen, CO 81612

George Gallup, Jr.
Gallup Organization
53 Bank Street
Princeton, NJ 08542

Thomas Gleaton, Jr., Ph.D.
Parents' Resource Institute for
   Drug Education (PRIDE)
50 Hurt Plaza, Suite 210
Atlanta, GA

Dick Herndobler
National Director
Elks Drug Awareness Program
P.O. Box 310
Ashland, OK 97520

Dorothy Hudson
NFP State Networker
P.O. Box 323
Jackson, TN 38303

Rose Kittrell
Special Assistant (IPA)
Office for Substance Abuse
   Prevention (OSAP)
Parklawn Bldg., Rm 13A-45
5600 Fishers Lane
Rockville, MD 20857

Laurie Leiber
Council on Alcohol Policy
Bldg. 1, Rm 306
San Francisco General Hospital
San Francisco, CA 94110

Carolyn Lord
Program Director
Prayer Breakfast
Crises Recovery
2628 Park Lake
Santa Anna, CA 92701

Carla Lowe
Consultant for Alcohol and Other
  Drug Use Prevention
4241 Rio Monte Court
Carmichael, CA 95608

Ann Lynch
1st Vice President
National PTA
700 N. Rush Street
Chicago, IL 60611

Peggy Mann
Author of Alcohol and Drug
  Prevention Literature
46 W. 94th Street
New York, NY 10025

Marsha Margarella
Consultant
Macro Systems, Inc.
8630 Fenton Street, Suite 300
Silver Spring, MD 20910

Sergeant Ed Moses
Missouri State Highway Patrol
1510 East Elm
Jefferson City, MO 65101

Pat Mutch, Ph.D.
Institute of Alcoholism and Drug
  Dependency
Andrews University
Berrier Springs, MI 49104

Joyce Nalepka
President, Americans Care, Inc.
1805 Tilton Drive
Silver Spring, MD 20901

Sue Rusche
Executive Director
Families in Action (FIA)
2296 Henderson Mill Road
Suite 204
Atlanta, GA 30345

Wade Silverman, Ph.D.
Clinical Psychologist
4434 Cedar Glen
Stone Mountain, GA 30083

Cordie Simpson
Principal
Commodore Stockton Skills School
349 E. Vine
Stockton, CA 95202

Ruby Smith
NFP State Networker
1423 N. Jefferson
Springfield, MO 65802

Bernadine Spanjers
President, Florida Informed Parents
2100 Crump Road
Winter Haven, FL 33881

Pat Taylor
Center for Science in the Public
  Interest
1501 16th Street, N.W.
Washington, DC 20036

Joyce Tobias, R.N.
Founder, Parents Association to
  Neutralize Drug and Alcohol
Abuse (PANDAA)
4111 Watkins Trail
Annandale, VA 22003

CHAPTER 5

Reaching Primary Care Physicians

Understanding the Audience

Pediatricians

- Have the opportunity to help children establish preventive health practices

- Include more women than any other specialty; more than half of all pediatricians under age 45 are women

- Constitute 10 percent of all physicians.

Family Physicians

- Provide comprehensive health care for all ages and both sexes

- Are trained to treat the whole person and entire families and to see the relationship between disorders

- Constitute 11 percent of all physicians.

Obstetricians/Gynecologists

- Are primary care physicians for many women

- For a majority of their patients, provide the most medical care that those patients receive

- Constitute 8 percent of all physicians

- Have the opportunity to counsel women about alcohol and other drug abuse during pregnancy.

Internists

- Provide adult medical care and nonsurgical treatment of internal organs and functions

- Can provide counseling concerning lifestyle and health behaviors

- May be consulted by parents of children at risk

- Sometimes see and have the opportunity to counsel adolescents

- Constitute 24 percent of all physicians.

The use of alcohol and other drugs by youth is, among other things, a health issue, and it is one that concerns primary care physicians in particular. Pediatricians, family physicians, obstetricians/gynecologists, and internists are in an excellent position to deliver prevention messages about alcohol and other drugs for several reasons:

- A large percentage of patients with alcohol and other drug abuse problems are seen only in the primary care sector; primary care physicians are often the first, and sometimes only, professionals to identify and treat the initial physical complications of abuse (Cotter and Callahan 1987).

- About one in every five or six patients in a primary care medical practice abuses alcohol (Delbanco and Barnes 1987).

- Females rely on obstetricians/gynecologists (OB/GYN) for primary health care; three-fourths of the women seeing an OB/GYN receive most of their care from that physician (American College of Obstetricians and Gynecologists 1983).

- Physicians are considered to be very credible sources for health information and advice among low-, middle-, and upper-socioeconomic-level families. A recent study shows respondents listing their doctor as their primary source of health information; see table 1 (Louis Harris 1978).

- Patients are responsive to physician intervention; a recent study showed that patients would like their physician to recognize and participate in the treatment of alcohol and other drug problems (Lewis et al. 1987).

- Health promotion is an increasing part of today's health care services; between 19 and 35 percent of time spent with patients involves health education and counseling (Brunton 1984).

- Alcohol counseling by health professionals has proven to be effective in several studies and is recommended by major professional associations serving primary care physicians (U.S. Preventive Services Task Force 1989).

- Physicians recognize the magnitude of the problem; 90 percent of practicing physicians think alcohol abuse is a major national problem (American Medical Association 1988).

- Primary care physicians are trained in the skills necessary to identify and treat chronic disease; "The screening techniques and basic skills required to diagnose and manage patients with alcoholism are a natural extension of the primary care physician's skills in managing patients with chronic disease or psychosocial problems" (Barnes et al. 1984).

Table 1. Most Useful and Reliable Sources of Health Information
(Chosen from a list of 14 sources)

	Percentage of Public Using Information Source	
	Seen as Most Useful and Reliable Source	Get a Great Deal of Information from Source
Own Doctor(s)	70	47
Television/Radio PSAs	35	29
Voluntary Health Organization Publications	30	23
Friends, Relatives, Neighbors	8	10
Government Publications	20	10
Advertising	11	7

Source: Louis Harris 1978.

However, physicians' access to youth does not translate immediately into effective prevention and treatment. Physicians need special skills to recognize problems and to deal with the problems they identify. For, although physicians recognize the Nation's alcohol and other drug abuse problem, they also recognize their own inability to deal with it. In a 1982 poll of the American Medical Association (AMA) membership, almost three-fourths of the respondents said they felt incompetent or ambivalent about treating alcoholism.

Recognizing the benefits of involving physicians in the fight against alcohol and other drugs, government agencies and professional associations have developed a variety of programs to promote greater awareness of these problems among physicians. In the Federal sector, the National Institute on Alcohol Abuse and Alcoholism (NIAAA) and the National Institute on Drug Abuse (NIDA) have supported the development of curriculum models and instructional materials for physicians. These agencies and, more recently, the Office for Substance Abuse Prevention (OSAP) and the Health Resources and Services Administration (HRSA) have participated in collaborative efforts with professional medical organizations and medical schools, a few of which are provided as examples of successful strategies in later sections.

This chapter examines ways to maintain and extend the achievements of these and other communications programs designed to reach physicians.

To understand the potential roles of primary care physicians in managing alcohol and other drug problems, it is important to know the basic characteristics of each group.

Pediatricians

The 36,518 pediatricians in the United States account for 10 percent of the total physician population. A pediatrician plans and implements a medical care program for children from birth through adolescence. This care is for both mental and physical growth and development. Pediatricians are trained to examine the nature and extent of childhood disease and injury, and to help patients establish preventive health practices.

Of the four primary care specialties, pediatrics is the field that has attracted the most women. *The Washington Post* recently noted in an article that "approximately half of those undergoing training in pediatrics are women" (*The Washington Post* 1988).

Family Physicians

According to the American Academy of Family Physicians (AAFP), "family practice is the medical specialty which provides continuing and comprehensive health care for the individual and the family. It is the specialty in breadth which integrates the biological, clinical and behavioral sciences. The scope of family practice encompasses all ages, both sexes, each organ system and every disease entity."

Family physicians are educated and trained in a variety of specialties, including internal medicine, ear-nose-throat, pediatrics, dermatology, gynecology, obstetrics, orthopedics, outpatient surgery, psychology, and psychiatry. This training enables them to treat the whole person, not just one organ or symptom. And because they often treat entire families, they view the total picture, which can reveal how some disorders are related to the family structure.

The family physician's background and training lend themselves to the needs of patients with alcohol and other drug problems. Alcohol abuse and other drug use does not affect just one part of the body. It can lead to a number of medical complications. The family physician's view that family illnesses may be closely related agrees with the findings of researchers that alcohol abuse and other drug use are familial disorders, i.e., that the alcohol or other drug abuser is not the only member of the family affected by abuse (Cloninger 1986; Goodwin 1985).

There are 42,618 family physicians in the United States, composing 11 percent of the total number of physicians in the Nation.

Obstetricians/Gynecologists

An obstetrician/gynecologist (OB/GYN) is specially educated and trained to treat women medically and surgically. The American College of Obstetricians and Gynecologists (ACOG) defines obstetrics as "the care of a woman from very early pregnancy, through labor and delivery, and after childbirth. Gynecology covers a women's health care in general, including her reproductive organs, breasts, and sexual functions."

For many women, the obstetrician/gynecologist is their primary care physician. "Although the specialty encompasses patients in a wide range, nearly 80 percent of patients are 15 to 45 years old. Of interest is the fact that approximately 70 percent of those patients cared for by an obstetrician/gynecologist receive most of their medical care from that physician" (AGOG 1983).

Obstetricians/gynecologists, therefore, are in an excellent position to counsel their patients regarding alcohol abuse and other drug use. In addition, they can advise teenagers and adult women about the dangers of alcohol and other drug use during pregnancy. This prenatal education can greatly affect the incidence of fetal alcohol syndrome (FAS) and fetal alcohol effects (FAE).

The 31,364 obstetricians/gynecologists in the United States comprise 8 percent of the total number of physicians.

Internists

An internist is a physician who specializes in adult medical care and the nonsurgical treatment of internal organs and functions of the body (ASIM 1987). The internist is trained to compile a comprehensive history of a patient's physical and emotional difficulties, as well as current symptoms. This, coupled with the results of modern scientific tests, enables the internist to reach a diagnostic conclusion. In addition, the internist is equipped to counsel patients on appropriate lifestyle and behavior modifications, and on disease prevention.

A parent may seek an internist's care for a medical problem related to the stress of having an alcohol- or other drug-using child. The internist can counsel the parent about intervention and treatment options in the community. Although internists treat adults more often than children, there may be occasion for an adolescent to seek out his/her medical care. In these instances, an internist's comprehensive method for approaching an illness may prove successful in attributing the problem to use of alcohol or other drugs. Also, an internist's counseling experience concerning lifestyle and behavior modification and disease prevention is a necessary skill for preventing and identifying alcohol and other drug problems.

There are 91,333 internists in the United States—nearly one-fourth, or 24 percent, of all physicians.

Pediatricians by age and sex

Age

	Under 35	35-44	45-54	55-64	65	TOTAL
Males	6,264	7,645	4,564	3,421	1,567	23,461
Females	5,913	4,419	1,643	764	318	13,057
TOTAL	12,177	12,064	6,207	4,185	1,885	36,518

By location:

New England	2,508	East South Central	1,575
Mid Atlantic	7,540	West South Central	3,087
East North Central	5,232	Mountain	1,478
West North Central	1,841	Pacific	5,636
South Atlantic	5,851		

Source: Roback et al. 1987.

Family physicians in the United States by age and sex

Age

	Under 35	35-44	45-54	55-64	65	TOTAL
Males	12,006	11,588	4,817	5,299	2,503	36,213
Females	3,681	1,875	508	236	105	6,405
TOTAL	15,687	13,463	5,325	5,535	2,608	42,618

By location:

New England	1,568	East South Central	2,559
Mid Atlantic	4,998	West South Central	4,353
East North Central	7,276	Mountain	2,564
West North Central	4,148	Pacific	6,526
South Atlantic	6,792		

Source: Roback et al. 1987.

Internists in the United States by age and sex

			Age			
	Under 35	35-44	45-54	55-64	65	TOTAL
Males	25,060	23,617	12,254	9,248	5,471	75,650
Females	8,693	4,782	1,360	598	250	15,683
TOTAL	33,753	28,399	13,614	9,846	5,721	91,333

By location:

New England	7,661	East South Central	3,738
Mid Atlantic	20,226	West South Central	6,056
East North Central	13,348	Mountain	3,201
West North Central	5,184	Pacific	13,145
South Atlantic	13,443		

Source: Roback et al. 1987.

Obstetricians/gynecologists in the United States by age and sex

			Age			
	Under 35	35-44	45-54	55-64	65	TOTAL
Males	4,711	7,487	6,128	4,666	2,236	25,288
Females	3,232	1,796	654	285	169	6,136
TOTAL	7,943	9,283	6,782	4,951	2,405	31,364

By location:

New England	1,838	East South Central	1,563
Mid Atlantic	5,652	West South Central	2,988
East North Central	4,684	Mountain	1,422
West North Central	1,600	Pacific	4,885
South Atlantic	5,477		

Source: Roback et al. 1987.

Knowledge, Attitudes, and Practices

Knowledge

- May know more about alcoholism than drug addiction
- May be likely to consider alcoholism a disease but less likely to consider drug addiction a disease
- May lack knowledge of the signs and symptoms of addiction
- Often do not consider themselves competent to treat alcoholism
- Receive little formal classroom training and even less clinical experience related to alcohol and other drug problems.

Attitudes

- Usually agree that alcohol and other drug abuse is a societal problem
- Usually do not perceive alcohol and other drug abuse as a problem among their own patients
- May have negative stereotypes of alcoholics and drug users
- May be skeptical about the effectiveness of treatment
- May develop more positive attitudes with clinical experience
- May not be comfortable in the role required to manage disorders related to lifestyle.

Practices

- Often ask patients about drinking habits when taking medical histories
- Often initiate discussions about alcohol with adolescent patients
- May experience time constraints that prevent counseling during routine office visits
- Have limited opportunities to monitor children after age 6
- May find that the time taken in counseling is not adequately reimbursed by third-party payers.

Although physicians could play an important role in addressing alcohol and other drug problems in our society, they generally have not become involved. A review of the research literature helps explain some of the reasons.

Knowledge

The few studies that have attempted to gauge physicians' knowledge of alcohol and other drugs have had varying results. In general, knowledge of alcohol appears to be higher than knowledge of drugs. In one study of opiate abuse, for example, both physicians and medical students performed poorly on a test to measure their knowledge (Shine and Demas 1984). In contrast, a survey to measure the extent of physicians' knowledge about the diagnosis and treatment of alcoholism found that, on the average, physicians answered 75 percent of the questions correctly.

Researchers also have attempted to learn whether physicians view alcoholism and other drug addictions as medical illnesses. AMA survey results (Sadler 1984) show that 21 percent view alcoholism as a disease; 17 percent say it is symptomatic of a psychiatric disorder, and 57 percent think it is a combination of the two. However, Rohman et al. (1987) found that 86 percent of those responding to their survey agreed, at least to some extent, that alcoholism was a disease. Regarding illicit drug use, Shine and Demas (1984) found that more than 40 percent of physicians surveyed did not consider drug abuse a disease.

Experts have voiced concern about pediatricians' lack of knowledge of the signs of alcohol and other drug use. Dupont (1983) wrote that "It is rare for a child to complain to the pediatrician of 'drug dependence'. The drug-dependent child may come in with chest pain (secondary to smoking marijuana), weakness or tiredness, or even depression. More commonly, the child is brought to the pediatrician by the parents because of failing school performance, deteriorating family relationships, or trouble with the law."

And according to another expert: "Adolescents with drug or alcohol problems appear in emergency rooms as victims of trauma, accidental overdose, or suicide attempts. More often, however, pediatricians see young abusers for routine care or problems not usually thought of as drug-related. Fatigue, sore throat, cough, chest pain, abdominal pain, headache, and school or behavioral problems are the most common symptoms of drug use. Awareness of the epidemic and serious health consequences of alcohol and other drug use should force the pediatrician to consider abuse seriously in all adolescents, especially those with suggestive symptoms" (Macdonald 1984).

Self-reports by physicians also indicate that they do not know enough about alcohol and other drug problems. In the AMA poll, "45 percent of responding physicians said they did not feel competent treating alcoholism and 26 percent admitted to having mixed feelings about their competency." The AMA poll also revealed that "the predominant reason cited for feeling incompetent was a lack of knowledge/training in treating alcoholism." Of the respondents in this survey,

85 percent said special training was required to treat alcoholism properly (Sadler 1984).

The special training, unfortunately, must compete with many other medical topics for space within the medical school curricula. Moreover, some experts question whether traditional medical training lends itself to education about alcohol and other drug problems. Bowen and Sammons (1988) have written, "A major force mitigating against such curricula in medical schools is probably the structure of academic medicine itself. Since it is based on an infectious disease approach, it is not easily adapted to the study of chronic, relapsing behavioral disorders such as alcohol and other drug abuse."

Other experts point out that although efforts have been made in recent years to increase medical training in alcohol and other drug problems, the magnitude of the problem far outweighs the time devoted to it in medical schools. Most training occurs in lectures that address the medical complications of alcoholism; clinical experience in managing the primary problem of alcoholism is rarely offered (Delbanco and Barnes 1987).

Attitudes

Physicians' attitudes about alcohol and other drug problems generally appear to be negative. Physicians, like the rest of the population, are subject to myths and misconceptions about these problems and form the same stereotypes and prejudices. The physicians surveyed by Rohman et al. (1987), for example, "were frankly negative in their attitudes toward alcoholics." These feelings can and do sometimes impede their ability to deal with an alcohol- or drug-abusing patient. Negative attitudes are a contributing factor to fragmented and low-quality treatment services (ADAMHA 1980).

Literature suggests that the following factors contribute to physicians' negative attitudes about alcohol and other drug problems:

- Skepticism about the effectiveness of alcohol and other drug abuse treatment is fairly prevalent among physicians. The belief "that there are no effective and affordable treatment programs to which patients may be referred" is a factor in physicians' failure to diagnose or treat alcohol and other drug problems (Bowen and Sammons 1988).

- General attitudinal barriers such as a moralistic approach to the issues or a feeling of helplessness when confronted by an alcohol-abusing or drug-using patient compounds a physician's resistance to deal with these kinds of problems.

- A physician's own drinking behavior and experiences can influence his/her attitudes. To deal with the anxiety caused by their own alcohol- or drug-using behavior, some physicians label only the extreme cases as alcoholics or drug addicts, thus avoiding too close an examination of their own habits (Lewis et al. 1987). In these cases, numerous other patients who warrant intervention and treatment may go undetected.

- Role confusion may influence attitudes. Some physicians question whether intervention, diagnosis, and treatment of these problems fit into their role as a primary care physician. Physicians tend to see their role as managing clearly defined illnesses, rather than general problems related to lifestyle.

In a recent article, Bowen and Sammons commented, "This role confusion is as great an impediment to physician involvement with patients' alcohol- and other drug-related problems as the more widely perceived barriers of attitude and knowledge defects" (Bowen and Sammons 1988).

- Several factors may contribute to this role confusion: before complications, alcoholism has no apparent tissue pathology; addictive processes are thought to be distinct from "real" psychiatric problems of neurosis and psychosis; doctors question the ability of self-help groups and paraprofessionals to "treat" patients; and physicians may not function well as part of a team organized on quasimedical lines (Clark 1981). For all these reasons, physicians tend to treat only the medical complications instead of identifying the underlying causative factor—alcohol or other drug problems.

- Discrepancy between what physicians see as a societal problem and what they see in their own practices. In a recent AMA survey, "over half (55.3 percent) of the responding physicians said that the misuse of alcohol among young people between the ages of 12 and 18 is a very serious problem. Two-fifths (41 percent) indicated that the problem is somewhat serious" (AMA 1988). However, when physicians in this same survey were asked, "how many patients between the ages of 12 and 18 who had an identified alcohol problem have you ever seen or counseled in your practice?" the common response was two patients. One reason for this discrepancy may be the lack of data on the prevalence of alcohol and other drug use in clinical practice.

While physicians are frequently criticized for their lack of awareness regarding the epidemiology, detection, and treatment of alcoholism, it must also be acknowledged that established data relevant to clinical practice are often nonexistent....Although prevalence figures are well-established for community samples and hospitalized patients, there have been relatively few prevalence studies in the ambulatory care settings in which many physicians are trained (Cyr and Wartman 1988).

One recent survey suggests that attitudes toward physicians' roles may be changing. Almost 9 of 10 physicians surveyed (89.9 percent) agreed that primary care physicians "should include counseling and treatment of patients with respect to alcohol use as part of their practice" (AMA 1988).

The impact of clinical training

One positive finding emerges from the literature concerning physicians' attitudes: Direct contact with alcoholics and drug users has helped create more positive attitudes about treatment. According to one researcher, "Clinical training in the treatment of alcoholism is a more important determinant of physicians' practice behavior than attitudes or knowledge" (Warburg et al. 1987).

Other researchers also have concluded that clinical skills are more important in determining physicians' attitudes toward alcohol and other drug problems. Delbanco and Barnes (1987) report, "In surveys of medical residents' and primary physicians' attitudes toward alcoholism, the lack of supervised clinical experience correlates with discomfort in caring for patients with alcoholism."

Practice Behaviors

Physicians' practice behaviors regarding the prevention and treatment of alcohol and other drug problems have been well documented in a number of studies and research papers. Most physicians address drinking habits. In the 1984 AMA survey, 81 percent of respondents said they routinely ask patients about their drinking habits when taking a medical history (Sadler 1984). In a more recent AMA poll, 7 out of 10 (72.6 percent) physicians said they had initiated discussions about alcohol use with their 12- to 18-year-old patients. However, the figure was considerably lower (57.3 percent) for those who said they initiated discussions with their patients' parents (AMA 1988).

Many variables contribute to the practice behaviors exhibited by physicians. Time constraints are often cited as an impediment to providing appropriate care to patients. The typical medical encounter itself is a time-limited event and is structured for acute care (Nutting 1986). This does not allow much time for a thorough and compassionate confrontation with a patient who may be using alcohol or other drugs, nor does it provide time for prevention efforts, particularly with young children.

In addition, there is often limited physician monitoring of physical and emotional growth of children beyond the age of 6. According to the American Academy of Pediatrics (AAP), regular physical checkups, including immunizations, usually stop at age 6. After this point, children only visit their doctor for an illness, injury, or sports-related physical. Although pediatricians and other physicians who treat children encourage routine physical checkups, most well children do not see a physician on a regular basis after age 6.

Closely related to time constraints is the issue of third-party reimbursement for time spent educating or counseling patients. The present third-party reimbursement system "tends to reward procedures, not time spent talking with patients investigating substance abuse or mental health problems. Many primary care physicians are very busy and find that the time taken to explore these problems is not adequately reimbursed" (Kamerow et al. 1986).

From the physician's perspective, current reimbursement mechanisms provide a real impediment to health promotion activities. Significant disparity exists between the monetary value placed on procedures, diagnostic tests, and other specialized services and those relying on cognitive and communications skills. Most health promotion services are reimbursed poorly, or in the case of Medicare beneficiaries, not at all (Nutting 1986). Almost all of the physicians responding to the AMA survey on adolescent alcohol use "are either somewhat in favor (33.7 percent) or strongly in favor (61.0 percent) of health insurance plans providing benefits for treatment of drinking problems and alcoholism" (AMA 1988).

An additional factor is the difficulty in talking to a patient about alcohol or other drug problems. Alcohol and other drug problems are highly sensitive medical problems. Among the special clinical skills that physicians need to deal with them are interview and screening techniques.

Barriers to Involving Physicians

Barriers identified through the research literature include the following:

- *Minimal training* and education about this problem, including clinical training

- *Confusion by physicians regarding their roles* and responsibilities for addressing alcohol and other drug problems

- *Skepticism about the medical nature of alcohol and other drug abuse* and efficacy of treatment

- *Negative stereotypes* of alcohol and other drug abusers

- *Economic issues* such as time pressures and lack of third-party payments for alcoholism and other drug problem prevention, intervention, and treatment

- *Limited physician monitoring* of children beyond the age of 6.

Barriers identified through experts, including representatives of primary care physician groups and others who work with or are knowledgeable about primary care physicians

- *Failure to include physicians when identifying problems, assessing needs, and defining roles.* Physicians report that they are more likely to make this issue a priority if they themselves perceive it as a problem. The issue cannot be forced on them. Therefore, physicians must become active participants in identifying problems, assessing needs, and defining roles.

- *Physicians' lack of knowledge of risk factors.* Physicians may not understand the risk factors for alcohol and other drug problems among youth. With more aware- ness of these factors, physicians could identify high-risk children during routine office visits and intervene at an early stage.

- *Physicians' lack of awareness of the signs of use.* Alcohol and other drugs may be related to behavioral and emotional problems, accidents, suicides, teenage pregnancies, learning problems, and child abuse, but physicians often do not associate these problems with alcohol and other drug use.

- *Ineffective packaging and dissemination of information for physicians.* All physicians receive an enormous amount of information on medical topics from a variety of sources, meaning that alcohol and other drug information providers must compete for a physician's time and attention. Ineffectively formatted materials or those that are difficult to obtain may not be read.

- *Insufficient translation of research and data into useful clinical application.* Unless research findings and clinical data are relevant to the patients they see, and unless techniques to identify youth with problems can be easily adapted to fit into everyday practice, physicians will not translate their awareness of problems in our society into the diagnosis of problems in their patients. It seems likely that closing this gap in the data would lead to greater awareness among physicians of their role in addressing this issue.

Planning Considerations

Audience Segments

- Pediatricians
- Other primary care physicians.

Channels

- Print materials
  - Journals
  - Publications of specialty associations
- Broadcast channels
  - Lifetime Medical Television
  - Physicians Radio Network
  - General programming
- Pharmaceutical representatives
- Patients and the public
- Other channels, including
  - Hospital satellite networks and online services
  - Medical conferences, including teleconferences.

Sources

- Professional associations
- Colleagues.

Materials

- Available materials include
  - Many books, brochures, and fact sheets
  - Some videotapes
  - Information on alcohol, marijuana, and cocaine.
- Needed are
  - Concise, quick-reference materials, that are directly relevant to clinical practice

— More detailed background information, such as a manual on treatment options

— Screening tools developed specifically for adolescents

— Guides to fetal alcohol syndrome

— Guides to the relationship between AIDS and alcohol and other drugs

— Directories of materials and resources

— Guides on talking to a child about alcohol and other drugs

— Curriculum guides for medical schools.

Messages should

• Promote awareness of risk factors among youth

• Promote awareness that treatment can be effective

• Provide information on community resources.

Selection of program components is an important step in planning a communications program. This section suggests a variety of program components, including channels, sources, materials, and messages that may be effective in reaching primary care physicians. As with any communications program, thorough pretesting and ongoing evaluation are essential to ensure that these are appropriate to and effective with the most important component of any program: the selected audience.

Selecting a Physician Target Audience

To thoroughly investigate, identify, and initiate appropriate communications strategies, the audience should be narrowed to a specific subgroup of primary care physicians. The focus of these recommendations for communicating with physicians has been narrowed to pediatricians for three reasons:

• The need to influence youth behavior related to alcohol and other drugs

• Pediatricians' access to and influence on youth and parents

• The interest of the American Academy of Pediatrics in alcohol and other drug problems among youth.

Pediatricians are an important target audience because of their direct access to and influence on children and parents. They are backed by a major specialty organization, the American Academy of Pediatrics (AAP), which has been directly involved in the problem of alcohol and other drug use among youth. Over the last decade, the AAP has recognized that many clinicians feel uncomfortable and ill-equipped to address the issue of alcohol and other drug use by youth and has undertaken extensive measures to remedy this problem. Its actions could serve as a model for other health care professional associations that wish to become involved.

The decision to focus this chapter's recommendations on pediatricians does not imply that other primary care physicians are less important, and does not preclude working with them in the future. Similarly, the wide range of other health care professionals who come into contact with youth, and who can serve an equally important role in addressing this problem, should not be ignored. This list includes nurses in offices, hospitals, clinics, and schools; emergency room personnel; social workers; psychiatrists and psychologists; and physicians' assistants.

AAP Initiatives to Address Youth Alcohol/Drug Use

- The AAP's Provisional Committee on Substance Abuse, established in 1985, is concerned with the prevention, early recognition, and appropriate management of alcohol and other drug use by young people; instigates professional and public education in this area; and makes appropriate policy recommendations to membership. It also works with governmental, public, and private organizations to address and advance common goals (description provided by the AAP) (American Academy of Pediatrics 1985).

- The AAP's policy statement on Alcohol Abuse Education in Schools, prepared by the Academy's Committee on School Health, recognizes the role that education can play in developing solutions to the problem, and "urges a coordinated campaign to provide our Nation's children with appropriate information to combat the incessant peer and media pressure to drink" (American Academy of Pediatrics Policy Statement 1984).

- A new AAP manual, *Substance Abuse: A Guide for Health Professionals* (1988), includes information on epidemiology, risk factors, evaluating a child, using the lab to assist with evaluation, the role of the primary care practitioner, referral, community resources, ethical and legal questions, third-party reimbursement, working with the school system, and pharmacology of alcohol and other drug abuse.

- The AAP also offers a number of educational materials on alcohol and other drug abuse for both patients and parents.

- As an active participant in OSAP's "Be Smart! Don't Start!—Just Say No!" campaign, the AAP provided information on the campaign to its network of media spokespersons throughout the country and encouraged them to promote the campaign to patients through local media.

Physician Communication Channels

Physicians agree that they get information through several channels: print materials, special broadcast channels, detail persons (representatives from pharmaceutical companies), and colleagues.

Print materials

The most common print materials used by physicians are journals. A survey of health professional information habits and needs conducted by the National Cancer Institute found the "typical health professional spent approximately 5 hours per month using medical journals" (Stinson and Mueller 1980). However, according to physician group representatives, the most popular reading materials are not journals, but control-circulation magazines or "throwaways." These magazines are a common outlet for advertising. New drug information and techniques are only two of the types of information that physicians get from advertisements.

According to physician group representatives, doctors choose to read simple, direct, and relevant articles. Most physicians read the table of contents, go to the page of interest, and read the abstract. Experts say that unless a journal or magazine is read within 1 week of the day it is received, it goes unread.

Specialty and subspecialty print materials are usually read first. These materials are oriented to the physician's practice rather than to research, and are printed and distributed by the specialty organization.

Materials must be planned to compete with the plethora of reading materials that most physicians receive. Some materials go unread, according to experts contributing to this chapter, including those that are too long, provide information through indirect discussions rather than direct statements, do not offer summaries, and do not frame the information in a way that clarifies its relevance to clinical practice.

Dissemination of materials also can raise barriers to their use. For example, the need to send a special order to an unfamiliar source may discourage use of a manual; receiving the same manual in the mail from a credible source, such as a professional association, can have the opposite effect.

Broadcast channels

Two broadcast channels reach a large number of physicians: Lifetime Medical Television and Physicians' Radio Network.

Lifetime Medical Television is a cable network designed "to help medical professionals stay abreast of the latest developments in medicine and health care delivery" (Lifetime Medical Television 1988c). Nearly one-fourth of the network's viewers (23.6 percent) are health care professionals. The largest groups of these viewers are nurses (40.2 percent), physicians (18.3 percent), pharmacists (5.7 percent), physician's assistants (4.0 percent), paramedics (3.5 percent), dentists (2.2 percent), residents (1.8 percent), and radiology technicians (1.2 percent). Seventy-six percent of these health care professionals reported discussing programs seen on Lifetime Medical Television with their colleagues or other health care professionals (Lifetime Medical Television 1988a).

Although Lifetime Medical Television is primarily targeted toward physicians and other health care professionals, consumers make up the majority (76.4 percent) of Lifetime's audience composition. "Viewership among these consumers is not casual; viewers are highly aware of and concerned about medical topics. A large proportion of viewers (47.3 percent) cite the educational and information aspects of the programs as their primary reason for tuning in. Many viewers (48.2 percent) are watching because of medical conditions suffered by themselves or members of their immediate families" (Lifetime Medical Television 1988a).

Because consumers make up a significant portion of Lifetime's audience, they should be encouraged to request specific programming ideas, such as information on alcohol and other drugs. It should be noted that 23.5 percent of consumers discuss Lifetime programs with their doctors (Lifetime Medical Television 1988a). If alcohol and other drug problems are addressed in Lifetime medical programming, this information can directly educate physicians or indirectly educate them through discussions with their patients who have viewed Lifetime.

Physicians Radio Network, produced by the American Medical Radio News (part of the AMA), is a daily, 24-hour medical news and information service for physicians. The PRN audience totals more than 61,000 physicians. The network primarily serves "core" physicians and osteopaths who are general and family practitioners, internists, cardiologists, and gastroenterologists. Other noncore specialists who have access to the service include psychiatrists, pediatricians, general surgeons, obstetricians and gynecologists, urologists, and orthopedic surgeons.

Physicians have access to PRN through a specially tuned, one-station radio. PRN serves 22 markets covering over 40 cities in 24 States, including those States with the largest physician populations. Both independent and syndicated studies report that the average physician listens to PRN 3 days a week for at least 30 minutes a day (PRN 1988).

Other television and radio programs should not be overlooked. Patients interested in a topic discussed on television news, a documentary, or a radio talk show may ask physicians for more information. Programs specific to health issues put pressure on doctors to learn more about topics so they can respond to patient requests for information.

Pharmaceutical representatives

Pharmaceutical company representatives are a prime source of information for physicians. Due to aggressive marketing strategies, these representatives consistently visit physicians' offices, offering the latest information on medical advances and new drugs. Since the treatment of alcohol and other drug abuse is not closely tied to a general or specific medication, some creative thinking is needed to effectively involve pharmaceutical companies in the education of physicians about alcohol and other drug problems. For example, to identify alcohol and other drug problems, a pharmaceutical company could print a list of questions that physicians can ask patients and distribute them to physicians, or sponsor a workshop or seminar on alcohol and other drug problems for physicians.

Public and patient requests

An informed or interested patient who questions a physician about a particular medical problem motivates the physician to learn more about the subject. As one physician has written, "I must confess that some of my most valuable postgraduate medical education has come from informed patients armed with articles and books. As a further case in point, how many physicians have been educated on the importance of breastfeeding for both mother and child by committed women armed with material from LaLeche League?" (Dupont 1982). Physicians in the Pawtucket Heart Health program have identified requests from the public as an important factor influencing their counseling behavior (Block et al. 1988).

Other communication channels

A variety of other channels may be used to reach physicians.

- Hospital Satellite Network uses videotapes to broadcast within hospitals throughout the Nation. Many tapes use a talk show format. One disadvantage is that the network reaches a small percentage of doctors. A larger number of nurses in the hospitals are reached.

- Teleconferences benefit physicians because many different sites can participate through satellite networks. One advantage is the wide geographic representation of participants.

- Medical conferences are a traditional channel. Attendance at national medical conferences is increasing. Conferences cosponsored by the pharmaceutical industry are especially well attended, and measuring the success of a medical conference is largely based on attendance. For attendance levels to be high, the desire to learn about a particular subject, such as alcohol and other drugs, must exist. Continuing medical education (CME) courses often are presented at conferences as well.

- Online services are a new channel. Although the use of medical data bases, bulletin boards, newsletters, and forums are increasing, they are not commonly used now, mainly due to physicians' lack of computer access or lack of knowledge about how to access. Currently, computers are primarily used by physicians' offices for business purposes (e.g., payroll, billing).

Overall, a combination of communications channels is considered most effective for reaching physicians with important information. Table 2 at the end of this chapter lists many of the obvious and most widely used communications channels to reach physicians with the latest health/medical information. It also includes specific activities, materials, and messages targeted toward physicians.

Sources

Closely related to the question of appropriate channels is the issue of credible sources. Based on research and input from physicians and professional physician organization representatives, the most influential and credible communications sources for physicians appear to be national professional medical organizations. Physicians join professional organizations for information, education, and representation. Professional organizations carry more weight with physicians than the Federal government or State and local medical associations or societies.

Professional colleagues also are common and credible sources of information. Stinson and Mueller (1980) report "that the typical health professional spent between one and five hours per week conferring with other colleagues."

Education Initiatives by the Health Care Community

The involvement of physicians' associations is illustrated in the following examples.

- The Association for Medical Education and Research in Substance Abuse (AMER-SA) was founded in 1976 to improve medical education and encourage research in alcohol and other drug problems.

- Membership in the American Medical Society on Alcoholism and Other Drug Dependencies (AMSAODD) doubled in the past 2 years.

- Adolescent alcohol and other drug use is a key part of the American Medical Association's (AMA) Initiative on Adolescent Health, which includes an AMA Clearinghouse and a National Congress on Adolescent Health.

- A 1983 position paper from the American Academy of Pediatrics (AAP) emphasized that pediatricians must "possess sufficient knowledge of substance abuse to permit them to deal with the problem as part of routine health care." Continuing medical education credits for alcohol and other drug courses are now offered at AAP annual meetings.

- Project Cork, a Dartmouth College project funded by the Kroc Foundation, has developed a curriculum on alcohol abuse.

Materials Review

An extensive search for and review of alcohol and other drug materials targeted to primary care physicians located approximately 86 items. The majority of these were booklets, print advertisements, books, and brochures. Other formats for materials were videotapes, articles, information packages, newsletters, flyers, and fact sheets.*

Materials were received from approximately 36 sources, including publishers, national organizations, professional associations, foundations, States, and medical schools. A significant number were received from a handful of organizations, including

- American Council for Drug Education
- The American Nurses Association
- The Media-Advertising Foundation Partnership for a Drug-Free America
- Hazelden Foundation
- Johnson Institute.

*More information on existing materials for primary care physicians is available from the National Clearinghouse for Alcohol and Drug Information; see appendix E.

Most of the collected materials focused on alcohol, marijuana, and cocaine. Lengthier materials such as books generally included information on all kinds of drugs, including alcohol. A few materials provided comprehensive information on a wide range of topics such as pharmacology, prevention, intervention, treatment, referral, medical management, and followup.

An inventory of materials available from professional associations has been developed by the Federal Government's Health Resources and Services Administration, Division of Medicine. This listing includes approximately 75 materials that are targeted to physicians, including primary care physicians, psychiatrists, osteopaths, and medical educators. (U.S. Department of Health and Human Services 1989)

There appears to be a need for the following kinds of materials:

- Concise, quick-reference materials that are directly relevant to clinical practice

- Other materials that fit a physician's daily schedule, such as audiocassettes

- More detailed background information, such as a manual on treatment options

- Screening tools developed specifically for adolescents

- Guides to fetal alcohol syndrome

- Guides to the relationship between AIDS and alcohol and other drugs

- Directories of materials and resources

- Guides on talking to a child about alcohol and other drugs

- Curriculum guides for medical schools.

Messages

Messages to primary care physicians should promote awareness of the prevalence of alcohol and other drug problems among youth and of the risk factors and signs of abuse. They should also aim to counter the pessimism concerning treatment and promote awareness of community resources. Messages also could help clarify the physician's role and emphasize the importance of counseling to prevent alcohol and other drug problems.

Recommendations

- Involve physicians in the program planning process
    - Survey physicians about alcohol and other drug problems among youth
    - Follow up the survey with other activities.
- Provide physicians with information on prevalence and risks
    - Develop a journal article
    - Develop a cable television program
    - Develop CME units
    - Develop a guide on AIDS and alcohol and other drugs
    - Develop guidelines on fetal alcohol syndrome
    - Collect data related to clinical practice.
- Use appropriate channels and sources
    - Use broadcast channels targeted to physicians
    - Advertise in nontechnical magazines for physicians
    - Encourage partnerships between organizations
    - Encourage interaction with the RADAR network.
- Develop or adapt materials for pediatricians or other primary care physicians
    - Conduct market research before developing new materials
    - Develop a variety of materials
    - Evaluate existing materials.
- Encourage patients to question physicians about alcohol and other drug problems
    - Produce and disseminate patient education materials
    - Contribute articles to parent and teen magazines
    - Encourage cooperation with community organizations
    - Increase support for public education weeks.
- Increase physicians' clinical skills and opportunities
    - Expand medical school curricula

— Develop screening instruments for adolescents

— Continue routine pediatric visits through adolescence

— Increase the time pediatricians spend with patients.

• Identify and inform other sources of medical care for high-risk youth.

Research and discussions with experts have generated the many ideas reflected in the following recommendations. Some of these ideas for reaching pediatricians or other primary care physicians come under the heading of general, long-term goals while others are specific activities that may help reach these goals. Some will be simple to carry out, whereas others will be more complex. All will take time. It is important to remember that successful communications strategies require sustained effort over a long period and entail using a variety of activities, channels, materials, and messages.

Although no effort has been made to assign priorities to these recommendations, program planners must assign priorities to problems and deal with them systematically. It may be helpful to choose some strategies that will produce short-term feedback or results and some that are long term. There is evidence that with the amelioration of some problems comes encouragement to confront more difficult barriers. Appendix A offers guidance to the process of designing a communications program.

Involve Physicians in the Problem Identification, Needs Assessment, and Role-Defining Process

A major barrier to involving physicians in alcohol and other drug problems is the failure to include them in assessing patient needs and in defining their own roles. The following activities are suggested.

Survey physicians about alcohol and other drug problems among youth

A survey could begin the process of involving physicians in the problem while eliciting information on their specific needs in this area. The survey should include the following questions:

• What is physicians' current knowledge about alcohol and other drugs?

• What are physicians' attitudes about alcohol and other drugs?

• What are physicians' practice behaviors regarding the prevention, identification, referral, and treatment of these problems?

• How effective are patients in influencing physicians' practice behavior?

• Do physicians routinely ask patients about alcohol and other drug use during an office visit?

- What are physicians' needs for data regarding incidence, prevalence, morbidity, and mortality?
- What information do they need on diagnosis, treatment, and appropriate referrals?
- What materials do they need?
- What role do physicians want to play, if any, in addressing alcohol and other drug problems?

Professional associations, perhaps assisted by a national agency, could administer such a survey among their own members.

Follow up the survey with other activities

Once an association recognizes the need and is willing to address the issue, Federal or other national agencies can assist the group to set its own goals and objectives. Activities might include

- Establishing a task force or standing committee to address the issue of alcohol and other drugs, especially among youth
- Formulating policy statements to address the issue
- Developing or updating materials to provide physicians with the latest information
- Planning an annual meeting, conference, continuing medical education course, or workshop.

Provide Physicians With Information on Prevalence and Risks

In both areas, according to the research literature and expert opinion, physicians lack information. For example, some physicians may fail to detect alcohol and other drug use among patients because they do not recognize signs or symptoms associated with the problem. Signs may include teenage accidents, suicides, pregnancies, learning problems, child abuse, a family history of alcohol and other drug abuse, and other factors discussed in chapter 1, "Reaching Families and Youth from High-Risk Environments."

Physicians need to increase their knowledge of all aspects of alcohol and other drug abuse, from prevention to treatment options. They also need more information about children at high risk, including ways to identify and help these children. Many of the following suggestions could be used to communicate about both topics.

Develop a journal article

Professional organizations, such as the American Academy of Pediatrics, could develop an article authored by one of its leaders and publish the article in its journal *Pediatrics*. Editorials and letters in professional journals could also help increase physician awareness.

Develop a cable television program

The article could be expanded into a program for Lifetime Medical Television. Because AAP and other primary care physicians' associations have worked successfully with Lifetime on other projects, they are in an excellent position to approach the network about a new program.

Publicity for the program could be provided through AAP's media spokesperson network and the National Clearinghouse for Alcohol and Drug Information (NCADI). NCADI maintains a mailing list of physicians who have requested information on alcohol and other drugs.

Develop CME units

Depending on the interest and response to journal articles and cable television programs, professional associations could focus a conference, CME course, or workshop on the topic. Again, technical assistance could be provided by Federal agencies and/or other national organizations.

Develop and disseminate information on AIDS and alcohol and other drugs

AIDS and its relationship to alcohol and other drug abuse are important concerns of health care professionals. Information on this topic could be developed and disseminated to physicians by the Centers for Disease Control, along with the National AIDS Information Clearinghouse, NCADI, and professional medical associations.

Develop guidelines to identify and care for children with fetal alcohol syndrome, fetal alcohol effects, and fetal drug effects

These children are often misdiagnosed, being grouped in the more general category of children with behavioral problems. More research is needed to identify the number of children with FAE and fetal drug effects. Guidelines for caring for them also are needed. Because these children were born to mothers who used or abused alcohol and/or other drugs, the children are at high risk for alcohol and other drug use (see chapter 1).

Collect data related to clinical practice

Physicians are trained to assess the magnitude of a problem by analyzing data. Because there is no clear-cut laboratory test to diagnose alcohol or other drug dependency, physicians need a variety of data to help them recognize it in clinical practice. Physicians need data on the following issues related to youth in the United States, or if available, in the community:

- Prevalence of alcohol and other drug problems among children and youth seen in clinical settings

- Prevalence of children's and teens' use of alcohol and other drugs

- Children's and youth's attitudes concerning alcohol and other drugs

- Influence of peer pressure and other factors

- Stress factors that may make children and youth more vulnerable

- Numbers of children and youth of alcoholics and drug users

- Prevalence of teenage pregnancy

- Adolescent mortality due to injuries, including motor vehicle crashes associated with drinking or using drugs

- Incidence of adolescent suicide attempts and deaths.

It is important that physicians identify the data that they need most. Responses to the survey suggested above could help assess physician needs in this area.

Use Appropriate Channels and Sources

Data and messages should be packaged in forms and distributed through channels that are accessible to the selected target audience, whether pediatricians or other health care professionals.

Use broadcast channels targeted to physicians

These include Lifetime Medical Television and Physicians' Radio Network (PRN). Program sponsors could contact these channels to learn the kinds of information they could use about alcohol and other drugs. Organizations also could volunteer themselves as resources for stories related to this issue. In addition, they could ensure that the channels receive their relevant publications.

Advertise in nontechnical magazines targeted to physicians

An example of such a publication is *DIVERSION*, a monthly magazine targeted exclusively to physicians. Its subtitle, "For Physicians at Leisure," sets the tone for its contents. The magazine is devoted to activities such as sports, travel, and financial planning. *DIVERSION*'s circulation of 160,000 is composed of physicians in family practice, general practice, internal medicine, and osteopathy (102,641); obstetricians/gynecologists and urologists (24,838); pediatricians and allergists (18,906); and cardiologists and gastroenterologists (13,700).

Although the content of the magazine has nothing to do with medical care, its advertising does. Most comes from pharmaceutical companies. The magazine accepts no beer, wine, or distilled spirits advertising. *DIVERSION* has run some advertisements produced by the National Partnership for a Drug-Free America.

National agencies could work with professional organizations and perhaps pharmaceutical companies to advertise in this publication. For example, a pharmaceutical company might agree to purchase space for an advertisement in return for being listed as a sponsor; the national agency or association could provide technical assistance in developing the advertisement in return for being listed as a resource for further information.

Encourage Partnerships Between National and Physician Organizations

Professional medical associations have been identified as the most credible sources of information for primary care physicians. Establishing partnerships between Federal agencies or other interested national organizations and these associations to achieve a common goal increases the chances of success through transferring information and sharing needs, ideas, and activities. All of those involved in such partnerships bring their own perspectives and resources to a project, strengthening and enhancing the effort and cutting down on duplication and costs.

Both Federal and other national agencies and professional physician organizations should be encouraged to seek each other out for collaborative efforts. Partnerships can be formal and highly structured or loosely organized on a project-by-project basis. Structure may be influenced by various factors such as budget, scope of the project, and time available.

Encourage interaction between the RADAR Network and physicians

The Regional Alcohol and Drug Awareness Resource (RADAR) Network, coordinated through OSAP and NCADI, is made up of State clearinghouses and the information centers of national organizations. RADAR Network members provide communications services on the latest developments, research findings, and data in the alcohol and other drugs field for State and local program planners, educators, and other intermediaries.

RADAR Network members, professional physician organizations, and physicians in the community could be useful resources for each other. The RADAR Network is encouraged to actively promote its availability to physician organizations and physicians. The network should invite physicians to participate in State and community prevention efforts.

For example, RADAR Network members could approach State medical societies for joint educational efforts, or a local physician could be asked to serve on an advisory board for a new or existing prevention program. These types of collaborative ventures will strengthen and enhance alcohol and other drug prevention efforts. Joint efforts give all involved an occasion to share successful communications strategies and methods, develop new ideas, and solve common problems.

Develop or Adapt Materials for Pediatricians or Other Primary Care Physicians

A review of existing materials on alcohol and drug problems for primary care physicians reveals that relatively few are targeted to this audience and that a number of gaps exist in the information they need. See the previous section for details of this review and for a list of gaps in available information for physicians.

Conduct market research before developing new materials

Producers of products targeted to physicians should conduct surveys or qualitative research to identify the most useful and preferred formats for information about alcohol and other drug problems.

Partnerships: A Case Study

Several organizations collaborated to produce and distribute a pamphlet popular with physicians: *The Busy Physician's Guide to the Management of Alcohol Problems*. This is how the partnership worked:

- Project Cork at Dartmouth wrote the guide in conjunction with the Betty Ford Center, the Hazelden Foundation, and the Cork Institute of Black Alcohol and Drug Abuse at the Morehouse School of Medicine.

- OSAP reviewed and edited the text.

- The American Medical Association printed the pamphlet and distributed it at DHHS' Second National Conference on Alcohol Abuse and Alcoholism, 1988, as part of a resource packet for primary care physicians.

- OSAP and the AMA printed an additional 10,500 resource packets to distribute to physicians via direct mailings and also through the NCADI.

- The American Medical Student Association also helped distribute the pamphlet.

This pamphlet offers an example of how material design can facilitate collaboration with intermediaries. *The Busy Physician's Guide to the Management of Alcohol Problems* was designed so the logo at the top could be removed and replaced with another organization's logo, and so the organization's name could be added to the list of collaborators on the back panel.

Develop a variety of materials

Physicians need both basic information for quick reference in clinical settings and more complex information, such as research findings, for continuing education. A wide variety of materials should be developed including those that can be used in diverse settings, such as in offices, at home, or in the car. These could include

- Videotapes
- Audiotapes
- Online newsletters, bulletin boards, and forums
- Online CME courses.

All materials, especially print materials, should be narrowly focused. The more concise they are, the better.

Evaluate existing materials

It is recommended, for example, that an evaluation be carried out for the pamphlet *The Busy Physician's Guide to the Management of Alcohol Problems*, developed by OSAP, in collaboration with several other organizations. Informal reports show that this pamphlet has been well received. A formal evaluation could assess how many respondents have read the pamphlet, how valuable they found the information, and whether it influenced their practice behaviors.

To make evaluation of this pamphlet more cost effective, the assessment instrument could include questions designed to guide development of other materials. Additional questions might focus on what other topics would be useful to respondents, what kinds of educational materials respondents prefer, and what is the most effective or useful educational product respondents have seen or used.

A professional medical association that has experience in preparing materials for physicians could develop an assessment instrument and direct the process.

Encourage Patients to Question Physicians About Alcohol and Other Drug Problems

Patients become aware of health issues through radio, television news, documentaries, special reports, entertainment programming, newspapers, magazines, patient education materials, and community-based organizations.

Produce and disseminate patient education materials

Physicians can make literature on alcohol and other drugs available in waiting and examining rooms. Federal and other national agencies and professional organizations could work together to produce current and useful materials.

Contribute articles about alcohol and other drug problems to parent and teen magazines

Articles in magazines targeted specifically to parents and youth could help patients frame questions for their physicians. Examples of such magazines include *Healthy Kids*, published by the AAP. Also consider magazines widely read by parents, such as *Good Housekeeping, Redbook, Family Circle, Essence, Ebony*, and *VISTA*, and those targeted to children and youth, such as *Weekly Reader, Teen, Glamour*, and *Young Miss*. Many magazines have regular health columns that could be used for alcohol and other drug messages with the additional advice: "Ask your doctor for more information."

Encourage physicians and community organizations to work together

Alcohol and other drug problems among youth have become a major concern and a priority issue for many community-based organizations, such as parent/teacher associations, women's clubs, Boy Scouts, and Girl Scouts. Educated physicians can provide such groups with support and with the information necessary to conduct a prevention program in the community or to successfully intervene with a child who is using alcohol or other drugs. Physicians who have limited knowledge about this issue will be forced to educate themselves if they are asked to make a presentation at a meeting or to serve as an advisor for a local media campaign.

Increase support for public education/awareness weeks or campaigns

Public education/awareness weeks or campaigns serve as an opportunity for Federal agencies and national, State, and local organizations to band together to increase the general public's or a particular segment of the population's awareness and knowledge about an important health issue. One example is National Alcohol-Related Birth Defects Awareness Week (previously known as National Fetal Alcohol Syndrome Awareness Week).

How Physicians Can Interact With Local Media: A Case Study

The "Be Smart! Don't Start!—Just Say No!" campaign, sponsored by OSAP, was designed to help 8- to 12-year-olds "say no" to alcohol. OSAP enlisted the help of many of the major physician professional organizations, including the American Academy of Pediatrics (AAP). The Academy offered the assistance of its nationwide network of more than 500 media spokespersons. The "Be Smart" campaign provided the AAP with a literature review on alcohol and youth and other pertinent materials. The Academy modified this information into a comprehensive communications packet and distributed it to its media spokespersons. The packet included

- A cover memo introducing the physician to the media

- A sample news release for newspaper, radio, and/or TV health reporters

- A radio rip 'n read for health reporters or news directors at radio stations

- A sample letter to the editor

- A "Be Smart. Do Your Part." card that physicians could inexpensively reproduce, inserting their own name, title, and the AAP logo; this was designed for distribution to patients and/or smaller newspapers

- A fact sheet on alcohol and youth and an AAP policy statement on alcohol problem education in school.

However, visibility for this particular week and for this preventable problem would be greatly increased if other Federal agencies and professional medical organizations actively promoted the week and disseminated information on alcohol-related birth defects to the general public, especially women of childbearing age, and to physicians.

Physicians need continuing education about this issue so they can adequately inform patients about the dangers of alcohol and other drug use during pregnancy. Therefore, they should receive current information on this subject developed especially for the week or campaign. In addition to counseling patients, physicians can

- Serve on planning committees for these events

- Support awareness weeks/campaigns by displaying promotional posters or flyers in their offices

- Make available patient education materials

- Offer to make speeches or presentations on the subject to community-based organizations

- Become media spokespersons on the subject or write letters to the editors of local newspapers; physicians should be prepared for this role in advance by receiving a press kit with the latest information, sample press releases, and letters to the editor

- Promote the week or campaign in a national, State, or local newsletter

- Make a presentation to colleagues at a conference, medical society meeting, or the local hospital or clinic.

Develop Physicians' Clinical Skills and Opportunities

Clinical experience with alcohol and other drug problems has been associated with more positive attitudes and practice behaviors regarding the detection and management of alcohol and other drug problems. It is important to give physicians opportunities for obtaining and updating these clinical skills.

Expand medical school curricula

Medical educators increasingly recognize the importance of involving physicians in the prevention, intervention, and treatment of alcohol and other drug problems. Although considerable progress has been made in incorporating alcohol and other drug problem training in medical education, it still does not correspond to the magnitude of the problem.

A 1986 NIAAA and NIDA study identified the number and types of curriculum units on alcohol and other drug abuse offered by four specialties in medical schools and residency programs—family medicine, internal medicine, pediatrics, and psychiatry (Davis et al. 1988). The findings of the survey indicate that there is

> a lack of comprehensive substance abuse instruction across clinical specialties in medical school and residence training. However, the substance abuse instruction in medical training appears to be moving in a positive direction. The increasing use of substance abuse instruction as part of the required curriculum, the opportunities for clinical application, and the attention to both alcohol and other drugs in training are all encouraging.
>
> Questions remain about the adequacy with which medical students and residents are being prepared to help prevent or intervene early in the development of problems related to substance abuse. Further investigations should be conducted on the relative priority that substance abuse instruction is afforded in the overall clinical curriculum and on the depth and quality of this training. (Davis et al. 1988)

Federal and other national agencies and professional physician groups must continue to encourage the expansion of alcohol and other drug curricula in medical schools. Curricular units should not be limited to print materials and didactic lecture presentation, but should also focus on clinical experience or exposure in managing the primary problem of alcohol or other drug abuse. Contact with a variety of treatment modalities including inpatient, outpatient, and self-help groups is recommended.

Foundations, such as the JM Foundation, the Pew Memorial Trust, and the Robert Wood Johnson Foundation, are providing support for curriculum development. They should be encouraged to continue their support to expand and improve the quality of alcohol and other drug information in medical education.

Several professional associations also collect information on and encourage curriculum development in this area, including the Association of Teachers of Preventive Medicine, the Society of Teachers of Preventive Medicine, and the American Academy of Family Medicine.

Develop and disseminate screening instruments for adolescents

Despite the significant medical, economic, social, and legal consequences, alcoholism is one of our society's most overlooked health problems. Research indicates that only about 15 percent of the alcoholics in this country ever enter any type of treatment for alcoholism (Allen et al. 1988). However, many do enter the health care system for other health problems, some related to their drinking.

These visits present an opportunity for screening to identify problem drinkers or alcoholics.

According to one expert, "screening can identify persons who suffer from alcoholism, increasing the likelihood that they will receive effective treatment. While this goal may appear to be ambitious, screening can be part of minimal intervention treatment, which may in fact be quite effective, particularly with those who are in the early stages of alcohol abuse..." (Allen et al. 1988). The U.S. Preventive Services Task Force, after an extensive review of the literature on this subject, concluded that screening instruments may be helpful to clinicians, in addition to their routinely asking all adults and adolescents to describe their use of alcohol and other drugs (U.S. Preventive Services Task Force 1989).

The Task Force cites the CAGE questionnaire as a screening instrument used often by primary care physicians. But because alcohol and other drugs affect adults and youth differently, experts have suggested that a questionnaire designed specifically for youth could be more conclusive than a generic instrument. Once such an instrument was developed and tested, it could be actively promoted in professional journals and meetings.

Continue routine pediatric visits through adolescence

Although the AAP recommends office visits for children from birth to age 21, many children stop going to see a pediatrician for these routine visits around age 6. Emphasis needs to be placed on extending and encouraging these regular well-care visits throughout the adolescent years, regardless of illness or injury. Because teens go through enormous physical and emotional changes during this period, it would be wise to have a physician monitor this developmental process. This would put the physician in a better position for alcohol and other drug problem prevention, education, and intervention. Physicians say such visits provide them with an opportunity to

- Inform youth of the harmful effects of alcohol and other drug use and the risk factors associated with use

- Build rapport between physician and patient

- Become a credible source of information about alcohol and other drugs for youth

- Notice any behavioral, physical, or psychological changes that could be due to alcohol and other drug use

- Be financially compensated for their time invested to educate patients about alcohol and other drugs.

Increase the time pediatricians spend with patients

The most important factor that influences time spent with patients is reimbursement. A long-term goal might be to work with insurance companies to encourage them to recognize counseling in some cases as a reimbursable treatment intervention. For problems related to alcohol and other drug abuse, the proper prescription may be counseling.

Children's well-care visits to pediatricians are not reimbursable. Until that changes, efforts could be concentrated on health maintenance organizations where preventive health measures are encouraged.

Identify and Inform Other Sources of Medical Care for High-Risk Youth

High-risk children come from all races, socioeconomic backgrounds, and geographic areas. Risk factors do not discriminate. However, a significant proportion of high-risk youth come from high-density urban areas. Many may not be able to afford or have access to pediatricians. Therefore, emphasis should be placed on reaching other professionals who work in settings used by inner-city and low-income youth and their families.

High-risk youth who do not receive medical care from a primary care physician, such as a pediatrician in private practice, may get care in the following settings:

- Emergency rooms, either hospital-based or freestanding
- Community health centers or clinics
- Migrant health centers
- Schools
- Teenage pregnancy clinics
- Recreation centers
- Visiting nurse programs.

Identifying additional sources for medical care and barriers to this care are two important issues that must be addressed for this population. Researchers also should reach the professionals who work in these settings, such as physician's assistants, nurses, social workers, and other counselors. Their current knowledge, attitudes, and practices regarding alcohol and other drugs must be examined and their needs identified so that they can become informed and effective prevention, intervention, and/or treatment practitioners.

Table 2. Suggestions for Communications Programs
Primary Care Physicians

Channels	Activities
• Medical journals	• Provide physicians with a list of high-risk factors to look for in children and adolescents
• Control-circulation magazines	• Provide a list of local referral resources to physicians through professional organization chapters or State medical societies
• Newsletters	
• Pharmaceutical company representatives	• Provide physicians with a list of questions that they can ask their patients to identify a potential alcohol or other drug problem
• Colleagues	• Invite a physician to visit local treatment centers
• Hospital satellite network	• Show a videotape of a physician counseling a patient at a medical society meeting
• Audiocassettes	• Invite physicians to serve on the planning committee for a State or local alcohol and other drug prevention campaign or awareness week
• Teleconferences	• Ask physicians to speak about alcohol and other drugs at social, civic, or religious organization meetings
• Videotapes	• Ask pharmaceutical companies or local treatment centers to print alcohol and other drug materials and distribute to physicians
• Medical conferences	• Provide physicians with a list of symptoms of behavioral, emotional, or social problems that can be associated with alcohol or other drug use
• Physicians Radio Network	• Develop a list of medical complications that can be attributed to alcohol and other drug problems
• Medical databases	• Develop a list of stress factors, both positive and negative, that may make children more vulnerable to alcohol and other drug use
• Lifetime Medical Television	• Expand distribution of *Alcohol Alert*
	• Provide physicians with patient education materials for waiting and/or examining rooms
	• Provide the Physicians Radio Network with scripts on alcohol and other drugs
	• Place an alcohol or other drug ad or a series of ads in physician-read magazines
	• Develop guidelines on how to identify and care for children with FAE
	• Market the RADAR Network as a resource for physicians
	• Work with AAP to develop accredited CME course on identifying alcohol or other drug problems

Table 2. Suggestions for Communications Programs (continued)

Materials

- Resource list of materials on alcohol and other drug problems
- Pamphlet listing local alcohol and other drug referral resources
- Continuing medical education (CME) seminar workbook
- Journal articles on alcohol and other drug problems
- Print ads on alcohol and other drugs placed in physician-read magazines
- Policy statements on alcohol and other drug problems from professional physician organizations
- Show on alcohol and other drugs broadcast over a hospital satellite network
- Videotape of a physician counseling a patient on alcohol and other drugs
- Program about alcohol and other drugs on public television (Lifetime Medical Television)
- Audiocassettes with the latest information on alcohol and other drug problems
- List of questions that physicians can ask patients about alcohol and other drugs
- List of stress factors
- Magazine articles on alcohol and other drug problems
- Resource/information packet
- Resource list of patient education materials
- Clinical skills training curricula
- Follow up or companion pamphlet to *The Busy Physician's Guide to the Management of Alcohol Problems*
- Screening instruments for adolescents
- Directory of computer-based systems with data on alcohol and other drugs

Messages

- There are certain risk factors which may make a child or adolescent more vulnerable to alcohol and other drug use (see chapter on high-risk youth).
- Peer groups are usually a good indicator of alcohol or other drug behavior by a child or adolescent.
- Red flags such as declining school performance, sexual promiscuousness, or behavioral problems at home may suggest an alcohol or other drug problem.
- Physicians should discuss transitional life events with their patients because of their potential impact on the patients' health (see chapter on parents).
- The earlier you intervene with an alcohol or other drug problem, the better the chances are for recovery.
- Questions about a patient's alcohol or other drug use/abuse or a family member's should become a routine part of medical examinations or consultations.
- Even brief conversation between the physician and patient can be an effective tool for getting a heavy drinker to cut down on his/her drinking.
- Physicians do not necessarily have to become involved in lengthy and time-consuming prevention, education, and intervention efforts, but some action is necessary because of their credibility with patients.
- Treatment can be effective and successful.
- There are available alcohol and other drug community resources to refer patients and their families.
- Become familiar with alcohol and other drug culture terminology used by your patients and in your community.

Bibliography

Alcohol, Drug Abuse, and Mental Health Administration. *Alcohol and Drug Abuse in Medical Education*. Rockville, MD: ADAMHA, 1980. pp. 49–55.

Allen, J.P.; Eckardt, M.J.; and Wallen, J. Screening for alcoholism: techniques and issues. *Public Health Reports* 103(6):586–592, Nov.–Dec., 1988.

American Academy of Family Physicians. AAFP official definitions of family practice and family physician. Kansas City, Mo.: AAFP, 1986.

American Academy of Pediatrics. The role of the pediatrician in substance abuse counseling. *Pediatrics* 72(2):251–252, 1983.

American Academy of Pediatrics. "Policy Statement—Alcohol Abuse Education in School." AAP, 1984.

American Academy of Pediatrics. Adolescents and substance abuse. *The Journal of Pediatrics* Oct. 1985. pp. 15–17.

American Academy of Pediatrics. AAP, American Baby to publish national child health magazine. *AAP News* Aug. 1988. p. 5.

American College of Obstetricians and Gynecologists. *Your Health and the OB/GYN Exam. Washington, D.C.: ACOG, July 1983.*

American Medical Association. *Survey of Physician Perceptions, Attitudes and Practice Behaviors Concerning Adolescent Alcohol Use.* Chicago, Ill: AMA Clearinghouse on Adolescent Health, 1988.

American Society of Internal Medicine. *Your Doctor Is an Internist.* Washington, D.C.:ASIM, 1987.

Anti-Drug Abuse Act of 1986. Public Law 99-750, 99th Congress. Washington, D.C.: Supt. of Docs., U.S. Govt. Print. Off. 100 Stat. 3207. 1-192. Oct. 27, 1986.

Barnes, H.N.; O'Neill, S.F.; Aronson, M.D.; and Delbanco, T.L. Early detection and outpatient management of alcoholism: A curriculum for medical residents. *Journal of Medical Education* 59:904–906, Nov. 1984.

Block, L.; Banspack, S.W.; Gans, K.; Harris, C.; Lasater, T.M.; Lefebvre, C.; and Carleton, R.A. Impact of public education and continuing medical education on physician attitudes and behavior concerning cholesterol. *American Journal of Preventive Medicine* 4:255–60, 1988.

Bowen, O.R., and Sammons, J.H. The alcohol-abusing patient: A challenge to the profession. *The Journal of the American Medical Association* 260(15):2267–2270, 1988.

Brunton, S. Physicians as patient teachers. *The Western Journal of Medicine* 141:855–860, 1984.

Clark, W.D. Alcoholism: Blocks to diagnosis and treatment. *The American Journal of Medicine* 71:275–286, 1981.

Cloninger, C.R.; Sigvardsson, S.; Reich, T.; and Bohman, M. Inheritance of risk to develop alcoholism. In: *Genetic and Biological Markers in Drug Use and Alcoholism.* National Institute on Drug Abuse. DHHS Pub. No. (ADM)86-01444. Washington, D.C.: U.S. Govt. Print. Off., 1986. pp. 86–96.

Cohn, V. Why doctors miss the warning signs. *The Washington Post, Health,* Dec. 27, 1988.

Cotter, F., and Callahan, C. Training primary care physicians to identify and treat substance abuse. *Alcohol Health and Research World* 11(4):70–73, 1987.

Cyr, M.G., and Wartman, S.A. The effectiveness of routine screening questions in the detection of alcoholism. *The Journal of the American Medical Association* 259(1):51–54, 1988.

Davis, A.K.; Cotter, F.; and Czechowicz, D. Substance abuse units taught by four specialties in medical schools and residency programs. *Journal of Medical Education* 63:739–746, Oct. 1988.

Delbanco, T.L., and Barnes, H.N. The epidemiology of alcohol abuse and the response of physicians. In: *Alcoholism: A Guide for the Primary Care Physician.* Chapter 1. New York: Springer-Verlag, 1987. pp. 4–7.

Department of Labor. *Dictionary of Occupational Titles.* p. 53. Washington, D.C.: U.S. Govt. Print. Off., 1977.

DIVERSION. Consumer advertising kit. New York. 1988.

Dupont, R.L. Preface. In: Lantner, I.L., ed. *A Pediatrician's View of Marijuana.* Rockville, Md.: The American Council for Drug Education, 1982. pp. 5–6.

Dupont, R.L. Teenage drug use: Opportunities for the pediatrician. *The Journal of Pediatrics* June 1983, pp. 1003–1007.

Goodwin, D.W. Alcoholism and genetics: The sins of the fathers. *Archives of General Psychiatry* 6:171–174, 1985.

Health Care Competition Week. Make medical staff part of product line development. Alexandria, Va. Nov. 7, 1988. pp. 7–9.

Kamerow, D.B.; Pincus, H.A.; and Macdonald, D.I. Alcohol abuse, other drug abuse and mental disorders in medical practice. Prevalence, costs, recognition, and treatment. *Journal of the American Medical Association* 257(21):2054–2057, 1986.

Lewis, D.C.; Niven, R.G.; Czechowicz, D.; and Trumble, J.G. A review of medical education in alcohol and other drug abuse. *Journal of the American Medical Association* 257(21):2945–2948, 1987.

Lifetime Medical Television. *1988 Consumer Viewership Study.* New York: A.C. Nielsen Company. Dec. 31, 1988a.

Lifetime Medical Television. "Fact Sheet." New York: Lifetime Medical Television, 1988b.

Lifetime Medical Television. "Focus Non-journal media." New York: Lifetime Medical Television, May 1988c.

Louis Harris and Associates. *Survey Commissioned by Pacific Mutual Life Insurance Company.* 1978.

Macdonald, D.I. Drugs, drinking and adolescents. *American Journal of Diseases of Children* 138:117–125, Feb. 1984.

National Council on Alcoholism. "Alcoholism and Other Alcohol-Related Problems Among Children and Youth." Fact Sheet. Aug. 1, 1986.

Nutting, P. Health promotion in primary medical care: Problems and potential. *Preventive Medicine* 15:537–548, 1986.

Pattison, E.M. Clinical approaches to the alcoholic patient. *Psychosomatic* 27(11):762–770, 1986.

Physicians Radio Network. "PRN Backgrounder." Stanford, Conn.: PRN, March 1988.

Roback, G.; Randolph, L.; Seidman, B.; and Mead, D. *Physician Characteristics and Distribution in the U.S.* Chicago, Ill.: American Medical Association, 1987.

Rohman, M.E.; Cleary, P.D.; Warburg, M.; Delbanco, T.L.; and Aronson, M.D. The response of primary care physicians to problem drinkers. *American Journal of Drug and Alcohol Abuse* 13(1&2):199–209, 1987.

Sadler, D. Poll finds M.D. attitudes on alcohol abuse changing. *American Medical News.* June 29/July 5, 1984. pp. 27–60.

Shine, D., and Demas, P. Knowledge of medical students, residents, and attending physicians about opiate abuse. *Journal of Medical Education* 49:501–507, June 1984.

Stinson, E.R., and Mueller, D.A. Survey of health professionals information habits and needs. *The Journal of the American Medical Association* 243(2):140–143, 1980.

Twerski, A.J. The folly of concealment. In: *Caution: "Kindness" Can Be Dangerous to the Alcoholic.* Englewood Cliffs, N.J.: Prentice-Hall, 1981. p. 54.

U.S. Department of Health and Human Services. *Inventory of Materials for Substance Abuse Catalog.* Rockville, Md.: Health Resources and Services Administration, Division of Medicine, Bureau of Health Professions, 1989.

U.S. Preventive Services Task Force. *Guide to clinical preventive services: Report of the U.S. Preventive Services Task Force.* Baltimore, Md.: Williams and Wilkins, 1989.

Warburg, M.M.; Cleary, P.D.; Rohman, M.; Barnes, H.N.; Aronson, M.; and Delbanco, T. Residents' attitudes, knowledge, and behavior regarding diagnosis and treatment. *Journal of Medical Education* 62:497–503, June 1987.

Yankelovich, Skelly, and White, Inc. The General Mills American family report, 1978-1979: Family Health in an Era of Stress. Minneapolis: General Mills, 1979.

Experts Contributing to This Chapter

Baer Ackerman, M.D.
American Academy of Child and
  Adolescent Psychiatry
3615 Wisconsin Avenue, N.W.
Washington, DC 20016

John P. Allen, Ph.D., M.P.A.
National Institute on Alcohol Abuse
  and Alcoholism (NIAAA)
Treatment Branch
16C-03 Parklawn Building
5600 Fishers Lane
Rockville, MD 20857

Elaine Bratic Arkin
Health Communications Consultant
3435 N. 14th Street
Arlington, VA 22201

Nina Berlin
Technical Director
Macro Systems, Inc.
8630 Fenton Street
Silver Spring, MD 20910

Trina Brugger
American Council for Drug
  Education
204 Monroe Street
Rockville, MD 20850

Claire Callahan, M.A.
National Institute on Alcohol Abuse
  and Alcoholism (NIAAA)
16C-10 Parklawn Building
5600 Fishers Lane
Rockville, MD 20857

Vivian Chen
Special Assistant to the Director
Bureau of Health Care Delivery
  and Assistance
Health Resources and Services
Administration (HRSA)

7A-55 Parklawn Building
5600 Fishers Lane
Rockville, MD 20857

Frances Cotter
Coordinator, HPE Program
National Institute on Alcohol Abuse
  and Alcoholism (NIAAA)
16C-10 Parklawn Building
5600 Fishers Lane
Rockville, MD 20857

Rebecca Creek
Secretary to the Committee on
  Mental Health
American Academy of Family
Physicians
1740 West 12th Street
Kansas City, MO 64114

Dorynne Czechowicz, M.D.
Assistant Director for Medical and
  Prevention Affairs
Office of Science
National Institute on Drug Abuse
(NIDA)
8A-54 Parklawn Building
5600 Fishers Lane
Rockville, MD 20857

Bruce Dan, M.D.
Senior Editor
Journal of the American
  Medical Association
535 North Dearborn Street
Chicago, IL 60610

Catherine Dube, Ed.D.
Center for Alcohol and Addictions
  Studies
Box G, Brown University
Providence, RI 02912

Melissa Duprat
Assistant Director for Marketing
American Academy of Child and
  Adolescent Psychiatry
3615 Wisconsin Avenue, N.W.
Washington, DC 20016

Janice M. Fleszar
Research Associate
Department of Substance Abuse
American Medical Association
535 North Dearborn Street
Chicago, IL 60610

Sarina Grosswald
Education Department
American College of Obstetricians
  and Gynecologists
409 12th Street, S.W.
Washington, DC 20024-2188

Michele Hodak
Consultant
Macro Systems, Inc.
8630 Fenton Street
Silver Spring, MD 20910

Renee Jenkins, M.D.
Society for Adolescent Medicine
10727 White Oak Avenue, Suite 101
Granada Hills, CA 91344

Jean Kinney, M.S.W.
Assistant Professor of Clinical
Psychiatry
Executive Director
Project Cork Institute
Dartmouth Medical School
Hanover, NH 03756

Virginia Kucera
Project Manager
Division of Child and Adolescent
Health
American Academy of Pediatrics
141 Northwest Point Boulevard

P.O. Box 927
Elk Grove Village, IL 60009

Theresa Malich
American College of Obstetricians
  and Gynecologists
409 12th Street, S.W.
Washington, DC 20024-2188

Chuck Olech
Medical Sciences Liaison
Upjohn Pharmaceutical Company
11018 Blue Roan Road
Oakton, VA 22124

Albert Pruitt, M.D.
American Academy of Pediatrics
141 Northwest Point Boulevard
P.O. Box 927
Elk Grove Village, IL 60009

Albert P. Roberts
President
A.P. Roberts & Associates, Inc.
P.O. Box 7
Broomall, PA 19008

Nicholas Rock, M.D.
American Academy of Child and
  Adolescent Psychiatry
3615 Wisconsin Avenue, N.W.
Washington, DC 20016

Virginia Rolett
Director
Resource Center
Project Cork Institute
Dartmouth Medical School
Hanover, NH 03756

Mel Segal
Acting Chief
Program Development Branch
Division of Communication
  Programs
Office for Substance Abuse
  Prevention

5600 Fishers Lane
Rockville, MD 20857

Emanuel M. Steindler
Executive Director
American Medical Society on
  Alcoholism and Other Drug
  Dependencies

6525 W. North Avenue, Suite 204
Chicago, IL 60302

Bonnie B. Wilford
Director
Department of Substance Abuse
American Medical Association
535 North Dearborn Street
Chicago, IL 60610

CHAPTER 6

Working With Intermediary Organizations

Communications programs to prevent alcohol and other drug problems take many forms. Messages, materials, and channels of communications vary, as previous chapters have made clear, according to a target audience's needs. Nevertheless, successful communications programs have some things in common. One of these is the use of intermediaries.

Intermediary organizations are groups that serve as a communications link to a program's target audience. The ways intermediaries can become involved are numerous and diverse. For example:

- Native American tribes reach youth through cultural awareness efforts.

- Churches reach Hispanics/Latinos by interacting with their congregation and other established community self-help groups.

- Patients act as intermediaries with health care professionals by asking for information and advice.

- Employers reach parents of youth in high-risk environments through counseling programs and by distributing information about community resources.

- Schools reach youth in high-risk environments through student assistance programs.

- Black sororities and fraternities reach youth through mentor programs.

This chapter explores the benefits and methods of working with intermediaries, particularly for programs targeting high-risk populations. It recommends specific ways to work with intermediaries, based primarily on the experience of a nationwide project. An extensive case study, examining the processes and results of this project, is included.

The Role of Intermediaries in a Communications Program

Objectives of involving intermediaries

- Raise awareness of alcohol and other drug problems and how they affect the intermediary's constituency, including culturally diverse groups
- Learn about the intermediary's and its members' needs and perceptions, which may be quite different from those at the "wholesaler level"
- Discuss how the intermediary's interests coincide or intersect with the program's goals
- Encourage intermediaries to mobilize and coordinate actions
- Provide information and technical assistance
- Integrate communications programs into prevention/intervention efforts.

Benefits

- Direct access to the target audience
- Established channels of communication with the target audience
- Credibility with the target audience
- Resources.

Challenges

- Identifying mutual interests
- Recognizing organizational differences
- Obtaining policy-level support within the intermediary organization
- Obtaining the group's constituents' or members' support
- Sharing credit.

Types of intermediaries

- State alcohol and drug abuse agencies
- Voluntary associations
- Parents' groups
- Professional associations
- Businesses

- Hispanic/Latino organizations
- Black organizations
- Civic organizations
- Grassroots organizations
- Self-help groups
- Recreation and sports associations
- Media.

So important are intermediaries that many programs designed to reduce the demand for illicit drugs are directing communications to intermediaries, who in turn direct messages to the primary target audience. In effect, the sponsoring program acts as a message wholesaler, while the intermediary acts as retailer, disseminating and explaining the messages to a wider audience. This is particularly important since, currently, message wholesalers often are from the majority culture, even though they may have worked with the target audiences in crafting messages that relate to nonmajority cultures, beliefs, and actions.

Objectives of Involving Intermediaries

Involvement of intermediaries in a communications program can have several objectives.

- Raise awareness of alcohol and other drug problems and how they affect the intermediary's constituency, including culturally diverse groups
- Learn about the intermediary's and its members' needs and perceptions, which may be quite different from those at the "wholesaler level"
- Discuss how the intermediary's interests coincide or intersect with the program's goals
- Encourage intermediaries to mobilize and coordinate actions
- Provide information and technical assistance
- Integrate communications programs into prevention/intervention efforts.

Many intermediaries, including those addressed in this monograph, are in an excellent position to retail the prevention message through the medium of interpersonal communications. For several reasons, this is one of the most effective roles an intermediary can play.

First, although mass media activities are one component of a communications program, they are only one element and, some would argue, not always the most important. Health communicators recognize that while the mass media are effective at raising awareness, increasing knowledge, and reinforcing behavior, they are not likely to cause changes in behavior unless supplemented with interpersonal communications that are culturally sensitive and appropriate.

Several well-known studies have documented the value of interpersonal communications used to supplement mass media campaigns. In North Karelia, Finland, for example, a geographic region was divided into two sections. The first was exposed to a mass media campaign on smoking and other risks for heart disease. The second was exposed to the same campaign, but the media messages were supplemented by workplace and school programs, consumer training programs, support groups to help people quit smoking, and other forms of interpersonal communications. It was found that members of the second group were more likely to modify their behavior than members of the first group (McAlister et al. 1981).

Some experts suggest that for alcohol and other drug use prevention, mass media are best used to reinforce and spread what people learn through interpersonal communications (Flay et al. 1983). Thus, community-based or other interpersonal programs become the major strategy, and using mass media messages becomes the supplementary strategy. How this works for minority cultural groups still has not been explored in depth, but it is now assumed that interpersonal communication may be even more important for these groups than among majority culture audiences.

Another reason for using interpersonal communications is the nature of the problem of alcohol and other drug use. It is a societal problem. It is imbedded in and sustained by socioeconomic problems, such as poverty, unemployment, lack of education, and pro-use norms. While this means that demand-reduction efforts face a tremendous challenge, it also means that individuals from many different sectors of society have the opportunity to interact with youth from high-risk environments. Parents, teachers, "mom and pop" store owners, ministers, athletes, tribal leaders, fraternity brothers, journalists, probation officers, older siblings, Big Brothers and Sisters, and health care workers, for example, can all serve as channels of interpersonal communications. It is important to remember that high-risk environments for alcohol and other drugs exist in lower, middle, and upper income families and neighborhoods.

How can one spur these myriad individuals to initiate individual conversations with youth at risk? It would be a formidable task to try to influence each sorority sister, parent, or day-care worker one by one. Instead, a strategy that uses intermediaries calls for identifying a group of these individuals and reaching out to the group as a whole to reach its members.

Interpersonal communications can take several forms. It may be a telephone counseling service, a support group, a parenting class, a professional meeting, a youth group project, or an encounter with a pharmacist. Boys and Girls Clubs are examples of youth groups that reinforce the message of a national campaign ("Smart Moves"). The interaction among local club members, the conversations they have with other classmates, and the examples they set for younger brothers and sisters are forms of interpersonal communication.

Benefits of Working With Intermediaries

Most nations affected by illicit drugs have come to realize that reducing the demand for drugs from within societies is at least as important as reducing the supply of drugs from without, and that demand-reduction programs require broad support from the many segments of society affected by drugs. To reach these numerous audience segments, intermediaries have proven to be an effective channel, helping not only to spread prevention messages, but also to mobilize popular support for both demand and supply reduction.

More specifically, intermediary organizations offer communications planners the following benefits:

- *Direct access to target audiences*—Many potential intermediaries have large, defined memberships and can provide direct access to large, specific target audiences. The members themselves may comprise a target audience or the members may have personal or professional relationships with the target audience.

- *Existing channels of communication*—Intermediaries usually have established communications channels, such as newsletters, magazines, and conferences, through which messages can be disseminated and explained.

- *Credibility*—With a history of service to or affiliation with their members or constituents, intermediaries are likely to be credible channels for prevention messages.

- *Resources*—Intermediaries may offer a variety of resources to supplement those available to the primary sponsor. These can include volunteers, mailing lists, expert knowledge in certain areas, the means to conduct surveys of the target audience, and more. By sharing resources, sponsors and intermediaries can avoid costly duplication of effort in reaching the same target audiences, and can achieve more than either one could working independently.

Involving intermediaries in alcohol and other drug problem prevention programs has indirect benefits as well. Policymakers within intermediary groups, such as the media, administrative agencies, and alumnae (e.g., from Black colleges and universities), can have a great deal of influence on how a Nation responds to alcohol and other drugs. Populations from high-risk environments often need improved services as much as they need information;

influencing those in a position to affect policy, expand programs, and develop new initiatives may be just as important as reaching the primary audience.

Challenges of Working With Intermediaries

Along with the benefits of working with intermediaries come some challenges. Many have to do with listening and negotiation; others have to do with control, or more specifically with the willingness to relinquish some control, without losing sight of one's own objectives. When working with intermediaries, each participant gives up some control to gain some benefits; compromise and negotiation are essential.

Some specific challenges are the following:

- *Identifying mutual interests*—A joint venture must benefit both parties. This does not mean looking for the lowest common denominator (society as a whole will benefit when drug use declines), but for specific areas where the groups' interests intersect (e.g., the agency wants to reach the intermediary's members, the intermediary wants to use professionally produced and tested materials). For example, employers wishing to decrease absenteeism by employees with children suffering from drug problems gain from effective worksite-based programs. Involvement in such programs also has public relations benefits for businesses.

- *Recognizing organizational differences*—Every group has its own hierarchy, timetable, and decisionmaking process. Because cooperative programs must be adapted to fit the operations of two or more groups, they can be more time consuming and difficult to administer than programs involving only the sponsoring agency. Recognizing and finding ways to work with organizational differences can be part of the planning process.

- *Obtaining policy-level support*—Within the intermediary organization, there must be support for the project from the board of directors or other body that sets policy. Having management-level staff assigned to the project also may be helpful.

- *Obtaining constituent/member support*—It is important for the intermediary to communicate with its own members or constituents about the joint venture, to ensure their support.

- *Sharing credit*—Recognition is important to any organization; sharing it can be a stumbling block, unless ground rules are established early in the project. For instance, a local radio station may want to become involved to improve its public image and boost the number of listeners. Therefore, it will want to have part of the credit and be publicly acknowledged for its efforts.

Types of Intermediaries

Most intermediary organizations were created for purposes other than preventing alcohol and other drug problems (e.g., Boys Clubs, American Academy of Pediatricians, National PTA). Because their charters include broad mandates to improve their members' quality of life or professional capabilities, many voluntary, professional, and civic groups are potential partners in the battle against alcohol and other drug problems.

Prevention planners should focus on involving groups that meet most of the following criteria:

- Serve a broad membership and have a national scope with local affiliates (except where this is inappropriate because nonmajority groups may be more regional or local or because a certain type of drug problem is unique to a particular area)

- Promote objectives and policies consistent with the prevention program messages

- Have easy access to and strong credibility with target audiences

- Maintain effective communications and materials distribution channels and networks

- Have previous experience with or a strong commitment to alcohol and other drug education efforts.

Because alcohol and other drugs touch so many individuals and groups in our society, a wide variety of organizations may be interested in participating in campaigns:

State alcohol and drug abuse agencies

Key intermediaries in many Federal public education efforts are the alcohol and other drug abuse Single State Agencies (SSAs). Their actual titles vary from State to State, but in general these are the State governmental bodies that fund, monitor, and coordinate alcohol and other drug abuse prevention and treatment activities. Each SSA has a prevention coordinator on staff.

Voluntary associations

Many national voluntary groups, such as the YMCA and YWCA, Boys and Girls Clubs, Big Brothers/Big Sisters, and the National PTA have long had commitments to alcohol and other drug use prevention. Because high risk for alcohol and other drug abuse is associated with a wide range of social problems, many more organizations could become involved. Any group concerned with child health and welfare, or specific problems such as child abuse, truancy, juvenile delinquency, teenage suicide, adolescent pregnancy, alcoholism, or family violence, is a potential intermediary. Appendix E contains a list of some of these associations. Many of these national groups have State and local chapters and affiliates, such as State chapters of the National Association for Children of Alcoholics or local affiliates of the National Council on Alcoholism.

Parents' groups

Among voluntary associations, parents' groups have a particular concern in preventing alcohol and other drug problems. Organizations such as the National Federation of Parents for Drug-Free Youth, Families in Action, the National Asian Pacific American Families Against Substance Abuse, and the National Parents Resource Institute for Drug Education (PRIDE) already are involved in this problem.

Professional associations

Professional associations may be comprised of policymakers, such as the National Governors' Association and the U.S. Conference of Mayors. School policy organizations, such as the National Association of Secondary School Principals, also could be considered. Other professional associations could provide interpersonal channels of communications. Health care providers' and social workers' associations, for example, have members who work directly with high-risk populations. Parole officers' and other law enforcement professionals' associations also fit in this category.

Businesses

Businesses not only can provide prevention information for their own employees, but also can provide employment to high-risk populations. They may provide volunteers and other resources to help disadvantaged schools and neighborhoods. Businesses can participate in programs such as "Adopt A School" and worksites can be settings for communicating with parents (see chapter 4). Chambers of Commerce are an excellent intermediary at the local level.

Hispanic / Latino groups and organizations

Groups such as those represented in the National Coalition of Hispanic Health and Human Services Organizations (COSSMHO) are springing to action in Hispanic communities to respond to the health and social issues confronting Hispanic/Latinos. These health and human service-oriented groups are an ideal conduit to reach their constituencies regarding alcohol and other drug problem prevention.

Black groups and organizations

There are a number of powerful organizations whose influence among Blacks can be extended to the promotion of drug-free lifestyles. These include the Black church, historically African/American Black colleges and universities, Black fraternities and sororities, civil rights organizations like the NAACP, and alcohol-prevention groups like the National Black Alcoholism Council (NBAC).

Civic organizations

Lion's Clubs, the Elks, the Masons, and others are contributing to preventing alcohol and other drug problems and should be targeted for expanded efforts.

Grassroots organizations

Many high-risk youth, school dropouts, and the unemployed cannot be reached through conventional channels. Prevention planners, therefore, should consider working through smaller grassroots organizations. Churches, ethnic organizations, block associations, and tenants' councils are possibilities.

Self-help groups

Organizations such as Alcoholics Anonymous, Narcotics Anonymous, and others may be especially helpful in efforts to reach at-risk children and families.

Recreation and sports associations

Many families participate in sports and intermediaries may include the newly formed Quarterback Club, the National Basketball Association, or such groups as the National High School Coaches Association, which is pilot testing a new tobacco/alcohol and performance project to the National Youth Sports Association involved in the "Be Smart! Don't Start!" efforts.

Media

Newspapers, magazines, television, and radio are valuable allies in any communications program. Editors and producers, especially in local media, often are willing to cooperate with community-based organizations to disseminate health messages. Special efforts might be made to enlist aid from media groups covering nonmajority cultural news and events.

Recommendations

- Provide regular, ongoing training in use of communications techniques
- Provide training in management of information resources
- Provide technical assistance
- Encourage intermediary organizations to work with the mass media
- Encourage intermediary organizations to work with policymakers
- Identify existing programs with which intermediaries can become involved
- Involve intermediaries in developing new communications programs
- Develop guidebooks to help intermediaries implement prevention programs
- Develop all of the above with cultural appropriateness and sensitivity in mind.

The recommendations in this section emerged from a model project that aimed to involve intermediaries in alcohol and other drug communications programs. This nationwide project, which is described in detail in an addendum to this chapter, centered on five regional workshops. The workshops not only provided information and education but also involved intermediary groups in planning and followup activities. Important general lessons learned from this project were these:

- Effective communications techniques are of interest to and necessary for all types of prevention workers.
- Involving intermediaries in the planning stage, taking into account their needs and priorities, is critical to success.
- Involving intermediaries from the same geographic area helps promote ongoing coordination mutual support. Organizations value networking opportunities.
- In working with intermediaries, as with any other audience, it is important to develop programs and activities that are culturally appropriate.

The recommendations that follow are based on these points and on others explained in more detail in the addendum. Each broad recommendation is followed by suggested steps for implementation.

Provide Regular, Ongoing Training in Use of Communications Techniques

Many alcohol and other drug volunteers and professionals have little background or training in communications and do not have the skills necessary to conduct formative research (e.g., pretesting of materials), create effective messages, and design communications strategies to reach high-risk or other prevention audiences. In addition, a high turnover rate in prevention workers requires that this skills-building effort be provided on a regular, ongoing basis. Training programs for specific geographic regions are recommended because they serve to develop and nurture a functional, community-based prevention network. The training should be culturally sensitive and appropriate.

The following are suggestions for planning training activities:

- Identify and contact key intermediaries in specific geographic areas, by working with State agencies, State voluntary and professional associations, and national associations with State and local affiliates. Groups not traditionally associated with alcohol and other drug abuse prevention should be included, as well as those who have experience in this area. Whenever appropriate, contact should be made with intermediaries representing nonmajority cultures.

- Meet with representatives from interested organizations to plan agendas, audience, and logistics of training sessions. Consider scholarships for attendees or other means of keeping their costs low. These may be particularly appropriate for retailers in low SES communities.

- Ask at least two representatives from different organizations to continue planning details of the meeting in conjunction with the sponsoring organization. Leaders from nonmajority cultures should be selected whenever appropriate.

- Conduct training in an interactive, rather than didactic format, and when special cultural practices are warranted, they should be used.

- Require all presenters to prepare extensive handouts, both to provide a permanent reference resource and to facilitate sharing with colleagues after the training session. For low-literacy audiences, the materials should be appropriate.

- When planning the workshops in conjunction with intermediaries, consider including the following topics:
  - Social marketing approaches
  - Working with the media

— Community organizing and networking

— Involving the private sector

— Messages for high-risk youth

— Low-literacy materials development

— Culturally sensitive and appropriate messages and materials.

• Continue to provide regular training sessions.

Provide Training in Management of Information Resources

The first step in changing a target audience's knowledge, attitudes, and behavior regarding alcohol and other drugs is to provide accurate, credible, culturally appropriate, and understandable information. National, State, and local clearinghouses and resource centers have been developed in recent years and OSAP has built a constituency base that can offer special expertise for those addressing nonmajority culture audiences. Intermediary groups need to know how to use these resources to ensure that their own programs are based on the most up-to-date information and to avoid duplicating efforts.

• Plan and conduct training workshops on information resources concurrently with communications workshops, using the same steps outlined above.

• Use PC-compatible equipment to promote interchangeability of software and programs.

• Be prepared to tailor computer training to varying levels of experience and comfort with computers. Provide both demonstrations and hands-on use of common computer hardware and software.

• Consider including the following topics, when planning the training with intermediaries:

— Understanding computerized data base operations, including all aspects of information collection, abstracting, storage, and retrieval

— Using computer networking and electronic communications, including electronic mail and electronic bulletin board procedures

— Conducting online data base searches on public and private data bases

— Evaluating existing materials to determine cultural, social, cognitive, developmental, and other appropriateness factors for target audiences, readability, scientific accuracy, appeal, and adherence to public health policies in messages

— Developing new prevention materials using accepted communications strategies and techniques.

Provide Technical Assistance

Follow up training with technical assistance to ensure the practical application of what was learned in workshops. Intermediaries involved in programs for reaching high-risk audiences, where few channels currently exist, may be in special need of technical assistance.

- Identify and recruit experts with specific communications or information science skills (e.g., conducting focus groups, searching data bases) and those with experience in reaching nonmajority culture audiences, as appropriate, who are willing to provide either on- or offsite technical assistance. Use literature searches and referrals to identify experts, followed by personal telephone calls and letters.

- Develop a data base with information on these experts, including separate fields for areas of expertise; experience with specified, high-risk populations; geographic area; and preferred method of providing assistance.

- Develop a data base of materials, such as training films and computer tutorials, that could be used in conjunction with or instead of onsite assistance.

- Publicize the availability of technical assistance through State agencies, association newsletters, and other professional channels.

- When a request for assistance is received, determine with the intermediary the kind of assistance that is most appropriate. Consider telephone consultations and providing print materials, training films, computer tutorials, or other audiovisuals, in lieu of or in addition to onsite assistance.

- Match requestor's needs with the appropriate kind of assistance, using the searchable data bases to pinpoint the most relevant resource.

- Pay expenses and honoraria or arrange to share costs with the requesting organization.

- Periodically update the list of experts and resources.

Encourage Intermediary Organizations to Work With the Mass Media

Mass media's influence on public perceptions and attitudes is undeniable. If mass media portray the exciting and pleasurable aspects of alcohol and other drug use without the negative consequences, the impact of educational efforts will be diminished. Presenting a balanced view of the consequences of drug use in media programming is as important as changing parental role modeling and conducting public education campaigns.

- Contact national intermediary organizations with memberships large enough to influence mass media gatekeepers, such as producers, editors, and public service directors, or groups who have special interests in alcohol and other drug problems of the populations from high-risk environments and who are committed to addressing these problems with the media.

- If these groups appear to have sufficient interest, meet with them to determine strategy and approaches.

- Invite representatives of the television and film industries to the same meeting. Representatives include writers, producers, directors, actors, and advertisers.

- Create an agenda that will allow both media and other intermediary groups adequate time to present and discuss their needs and perspectives.

- Produce a media handbook, setting out basic principles of media relations, for intermediary organizations working on alcohol and other drug abuse problems, with special emphasis on minorities, as appropriate.

- Produce media kits on alcohol and other drug problems with materials that can be localized by community groups or modified to address problems among specific audiences (e.g., Cuban-heritage Hispanics).

- Mobilize and train influential intermediary groups to make personal contacts with television producers, explaining concern for portraying alcohol use and other drug use in entertainment programs.

- Compile lists of other influential gatekeepers, such as television networks, executives, advertisers, and advertising agencies, who could be targeted by a letter-writing campaign.

Encourage Intermediary Organizations to Work With Policymakers

Intermediary organizations are a potent force for informing and influencing policymakers concerning alcohol and other drug problems.

- Recruit key policymakers who support preventing alcohol and other drug problems, and enlist experienced activists on both the State and Federal levels, to give presentations at communications seminars for intermediaries.

- Compile selected presentations into a publication. Include a checklist of basic activist techniques.

- Compile lists of influential policymakers and administrators in alcohol and other drug fields. Update the list regularly and provide it to intermediary organizations interested in influencing public policy.

Identify Existing Public Programs
With Which Intermediaries Can Become Involved

Intermediaries, with their direct access to specific audience segments, can extend a communications program's reach, serving as a channel to disseminate materials and adding components of interpersonal communications. Key intermediaries likewise may involve other intermediaries, creating an ever-widening network. By joining existing programs, intermediary organizations may be able to accomplish specific objectives without mounting a new program.

- Identify existing education communications programs through the NPN, the RADAR Network and national and State associations, including those working with minority populations, known to be actively involved in alcohol and other drug abuse prevention.

- Develop an annotated resource list of these programs; include their objectives, target audience, activities, timetables, messages, channels, materials, and contact persons.

- Publicize the list through the NPN, the RADAR Network, and national and State associations.

- Update the list annually.

Involve Intermediaries in Developing
New Communications Programs

If new communications programs must be developed, as will likely be the case with culture-specific efforts for minority populations, intermediaries should be included as an integral component. In relationships with intermediaries, sponsoring organizations often supply strategic planning and coordination, creative messages designed and pretested with the target audience, and professionally produced materials, while intermediary organizations creatively use messages and materials through their special channels of communications with the target audience.

- Contact intermediaries who can reach and influence the target audience.

- Involve them as early as possible in planning.

- Give them advance notice so they can build their part of the program into their schedule. Negotiate what will be expected of them.

- Allow them to personalize and adapt program materials to fit their situations and cultural values, beliefs, and practices. Give them a feeling of ownership; however, do not let them depart from established objectives.

- Ask what they need to implement their part of the program. Beyond the question of funding, consider other assistance (e.g., training or tools that would enable them to function successfully).

- Gently remind them that they are responsible for their activities; help them, but do not do the work for them.

- Provide new local/regional/national contacts that they will perceive as valuable for their ongoing activities, including contacts who can address cultural differences.

- Provide program rationale, strategies, and messages in ready-to-use form.

- Do not assign intermediaries too much to do at once. Provide a series of smaller, tangible, short-term actions and a feedback/tracking mechanism.

- Assess progress through the feedback/tracking mechanism, and help make adjustments to respond to the intermediary's needs and to keep the program on track.

- Provide moral support, frequent acknowledgements of their contributions, and other rewards (e.g., letters or certificates of appreciation).

- Provide a final report of what was accomplished, and meet to discuss followup activities they might find useful. Make sure they feel they are part of the program's success.

Develop Guidebooks to Help Intermediaries Implement Prevention Programs

A review of existing materials reveals that only a few guidebooks exist for implementing alcohol and other drug problem prevention strategies. The Federal Government has published guides for community leaders and schools and a guide to program evaluation. A guide to fundraising is also available. More information is available from the National Clearinghouse for Alcohol and Drug Information (see appendix E).

Handbooks exist on other topics—prevention theories and models, conducting media campaigns, strategies for parents and youth, community organization techniques—but these require modification. Some have been developed by Federal and State agencies, others by voluntary organizations. The review identified no guides to conducting a needs assessment or on strategies for the private sector.

- Talk with intermediaries about their priorities to select topics for development.

- Obtain permission from the original producer to modify an existing guidebook; address issues of copyright and credit.

- Evaluate the existing publication to determine how it might be modified. Characteristics to look for might include

  — Application of principles of effective health communication

  — Agreement with public health policy concerning alcohol abuse and other drug use

  — Applicability to programs in many different communities and regions

  — Model programs and strategies

  — Homophyly (materials should reflect ethnic and cultural resemblance of target audience)

  — Resource lists, bibliographies, and a glossary

  — Cultural sensitivity and appropriateness.

- Create new guides if necessary, using the same general principles listed above.

- Publicize and disseminate all guides through the RADAR Network, national and State associations, and other intermediaries.

Addendum: A Case Study

This section describes a nationwide project that aimed to involve intermediaries in alcohol and other drug problem prevention activities. It is provided as a model that State and local planners can adapt and modify to fit their needs. Its purpose is to illustrate some effective ways to work with intermediaries and discuss lessons learned from the model project.

The project centered on five regional communications workshops sponsored by the Office for Substance Abuse Prevention during the summer of 1988. The purposes of the workshops, as defined by the intermediary groups involved in planning, were the following:

- To learn practical and innovative ways to reach at-risk populations
- To learn how to tailor tried and true communications strategies for their own purposes
- To expand their resources.

OSAP Regional Communications Workshops

The workshops were held at the following sites:

Region	*Site*	*Dates*
Northeast	Portland, ME	May 23–25
Central	Minneapolis, MN	July 11–13
West	San Francisco, CA	July 18–20
Southeast	Atlanta, GA	Sept. 14–16
Southwest	Austin, TX	Sept. 26–28

Several key intermediaries helped plan and conduct the workshops. These included the National Prevention Network (NPN) (an association of State alcohol and drug problem prevention coordinators); the National Association of State Alcohol and Drug Abuse Directors (NASADAD); the National Federation of Parents for Drug-Free Youth; the National Council on Alcoholism (NCA); the Institute on Black Chemical Abuse; the Substance Abuse Librarians and Information Specialists; and the National Coalition of Hispanic Health and Human Service Organizations (COSSMHO).

The following project description explains, for each stage of the project, what was done, what procedures and activities worked, and which ones were less successful. The stages are

- Identifying intermediaries
- Planning procedures
- Deciding on the agenda
- Deciding on content
- Managing logistics
- Postmeeting activities
- Summarizing lessons learned
- Long-term followup.

Identifying Intermediaries

OSAP had worked previously with some of these intermediary organizations, including those who had played a key role in the implementation of the agency's "Be Smart! Don't Start!—Just Say No!" campaign. Other groups represented key constituencies for agency programs.

Key intermediaries in turn identified representatives from other groups to participate in the regional workshops, which could accommodate 10 people from each State. The 10 members were to include a representative of the State's lead agency for alcohol and other drug problem prevention, the Division of Communication Program's Director's Office, the NPN representative (team leader), an NFP or other parent organization representative, a State alcohol and other drug information clearinghouse representative, and a representative from a high-risk population prevention provider. The remaining team members could be chosen from a variety of related State agencies and other intermediary organizations such as the NCA, Boys Clubs, Parent Teachers Associations, and the National Crime Prevention Council.

The project sought a balance on the State teams of both groups traditionally involved with alcohol and other drug activities and groups that are newly involved or very interested in addressing alcohol and other drug issues, emphasizing groups serving high-risk populations. Planners selected team members who would be able to train or conduct inservice education for other program staff in the techniques learned at the regional seminar.

Discussion

Working with State alcohol and drug abuse officials was particularly beneficial, due to their contacts with many other potential intermediaries. The State prevention coordinator, usually a member of the NPN, proved to be a key channel for resources, ideas, and information flowing two ways: from the national to the community level, and from the community to the national level. Most State prevention coordinators have established vast networks of prevention professionals and volunteers at the county and community levels with whom they are in frequent communication and whom they can mobilize to work with local affiliates of other intermediary organizations.

Identifying nontraditional groups proved to be a challenge, possibly because recruiting for the State teams was in the hands of an existing network of people concerned solely with alcohol and other drug problems. More positively, the State team approach was perceived as useful by participants and almost all intended to maintain some type of group integrity when they returned to their home State.

In providing training to intermediaries, it became apparent that teams of prevention workers from specific geographic areas (State, county, city, community, neighborhood) provided a support mechanism for using and implementing new skills, once the training was completed. Training individuals randomly located throughout a State or broad geographic area diminishes the likelihood that the trainee will be able to effectively use new skills or information after returning home. With the assistance of nearby prevention workers from complementary agencies, new trainees are more likely to maintain their enthusiasm and momentum and effectively implement the new prevention strategies in their communities.

Training teams should include representatives from a variety of agencies and organizations that could be involved in any comprehensive community-based prevention effort. Representatives from educational, police, social service, welfare, housing, and media organizations, as well as traditional alcohol and other drug problem prevention providers, should make up the local trainee team. Each team also should have at least one politically well connected member who can help mobilize community leaders and resources. With wide team representation, all the community sectors necessary for effective community prevention will be invested in the process and more likely to participate actively in the new programs. As a member of a team, each individual is less likely to be worn down and blocked by the usual obstacles and barriers that impede creating new services or changing existing services.

Planning Procedures

Planning for the regional seminars began more than 1 year before the first seminar was held in May 1988. Planning meetings were scheduled to coincide with other national conferences in different parts of the country: Portland, Maine; Chicago, Illinois; Edmonton, Alberta, Canada; and San Diego, California. The first planning meeting was held in May 1987 and the last in April 1988. An additional planning meeting took place in June 1988 at the Annual NPN meeting in Juneau, Alaska, to explore any necessary midcourse corrections required after the first seminar was held.

The workshops were planned to fulfill intermediaries' needs to:

- Learn how to get the latest prevention information as they need it
- Use this information effectively to influence policymakers
- Design creative messages and plans to reach at-risk populations
- Build stronger ties and networks with other key groups in the State and region that deal with alcohol and other drug abuse issues.

Discussion

Involving the intermediary groups from the earliest planning stages was key to establishing feelings of ownership for the participating groups. The joint planning process allowed intermediaries to plan content as well as to identify local experts to speak at their regional seminars. In addition, specific topics and issues of each seminar could be tailored to meet the needs of the groups and States in that region.

Deciding on the Agenda

The agenda evolved into concurrent two-track sessions in response to the needs expressed at the planning meetings. One track focused on creating and operating clearinghouse/resource centers and using pertinent information data bases in their operations. The other track focused on social marketing and the design of communications strategies for reaching high-risk youth (see table 1 for the model agenda).

Key speakers, including luncheon speakers, were selected by representatives from the region. Lead presenters were selected by the sponsoring agency, OSAP, and were generally the same in all seminars, to ensure consistency of key information.

Planners envisioned sessions in a seminar rather than lecture format to allow a two-way flow of information. Many sessions included interactive training exercises, such as conducting a focus group discussion or testing materials for readability.

Table 1. Model Agenda: OSAP Regional Communication Seminars Reaching At-Risk Populations—Seminar Schedule

Day	Time	Clearinghouse/Data Base Track	Media and Communications Track
Wednesday	8:00 to 9:30	Conference Registration	
	9:30 to 10:30	Host State Welcome—Patricia Redmond Address by Vivian Smith and Robert Denniston—OSAP	
	10:45 to 11:30	Key Speaker—Dr. Omowale Amuleru-Marshall, The Cork Institute	
	11:30 to 12:00	First State Team Meetings	
	12:00 to 1:30	Luncheon with Speaker—Charles Atkins, Ph.D., Michigan State University	
	2:00 to 3:00	Lead Presenter: A&D Information Resources— Lisa Swanberg—NCADI	Lead Presenter: Social Marketing Principles— Elaine Bratic Arkin
	3:15 to 4:30	WORKSHOPS	
		A. Information for Policymakers B. A&D Message and Materials Review Process C. Low-Literacy Materials	A. Using Media in Prevention B. Talking to Kids about Alcohol and Drugs C. Community Health Programs
	4:30 to 5:00	State Team Meetings	
Thursday	9:00 to 10:00	Lead Presenter: Using PCs in the Clearinghouse Environment—Lewis Sanford	Lead Presenter: Successful Messages to Reach At-Risk Populations—Ellen Morehouse
	10:15 to 11:30	WORKSHOPS	
		A. Selecting Software for Clearinghouse Operations	A. Messages for Sight and Hearing Impaired B. Dynamics of the Abusing Family C. Smokeless Tobacco D. Working with Multiproblem Youth
	11:30 to 12:00	State Team Meetings	
	12:00 to 1:30	Luncheon with Speaker—William Hale, Ed.D., Prism Associates, Athens GA	
	2:00 to 3:00	Lead Presenter: Clearinghouse Operations Dr. Bettina Scott, NCADI	Lead Presenter: Successful Strategies and Channels for CoAs—Robert Shear
	3:15 to 4:30	WORKSHOPS	
		A. Retrieving and Disseminating Information B. State and Other Clearinghouses	A. Creative Uses of the Media B. Working with Cherokee Youth C. Working with Black Youth D. Be Smart! Stay Smart!
	4:30 to 5:00	State Team Meetings	
Friday	9:00 to 9:45	Speaker—Lewis Donahew, Ph.D., University of Kentucky	
	9:45 to 10:15	Final State Team Planning Meetings	
	10:30 to 11:30	State Team Presentations	
	11:30 to 12:00	Seminar Evaluation and Summary—Robert Denniston—OSAP	

Discussion

The two-track model was deemed successful because it reinforced the idea that both communications strategies and information collection and retrieval skills are important for successful and effective prevention programs.

The interactive seminar format did not work entirely as planned. The sessions were quite successful in showcasing programs and techniques, but in some cases, were not long enough to allow for much group interaction. More stringent time limits could have been placed on speakers and more emphasis placed on interactive exercises.

Choosing local experts as speakers heightened participants' interest in the sessions and helped ensure that their specific concerns would be addressed. The disadvantage was loss of control over quality and content. Guidelines for choosing speakers might help intermediaries select those who fit minimum criteria: knowledge of regional problems, expertise in the subject, and public speaking skills.

The informal exchange of information among the participants was one of the major benefits of the workshops, according to those who attended. Participants were able to meet and exchange information, and specially scheduled meetings allowed people to meet others from the same State. Even so, one common criticism of the workshops was that there was not enough time allotted for informal networking within the set schedule.

Deciding on Content

In the early planning meetings, intermediaries urged OSAP to offer State and local prevention providers some training in communications techniques used for the "Be Smart!" campaign, in which many of them participated. They expressed an interest and need for training in social marketing, segmenting target audiences and developing communications strategies, and current technologies for information storage, retrieval, and dissemination.

Some differences in specific needs existed among regions. Intermediaries in the South, for example, requested sessions that focused on smokeless tobacco, while in the Northeast, intermediaries emphasized sessions that focused on problems related to urban settings.

The following is a list of general topics that were covered in the seminars.

Communications Strategies

- Social marketing concepts and techniques
  - Differences between social and product marketing

- — Defining the customer
- — Controllable variables: product, promotion, place, and price (the 4 Ps)
- — Market research and needs assessment
- — Developing objectives
- — Selecting and prioritizing target audiences
- — Selecting strategies and action steps
- — Developing promotional tools
- — Evaluation, both process and outcome.

- • Successful messages, strategies, and channels for reaching high-risk populations
    - — Presentations about local and regional programs that could serve as models.
- • Working with the media
    - — Techniques for improving mass media coverage of alcohol and other drug problem prevention
    - — Developing an ongoing working relationship with the media .
- • Prevention strategies
    - — Examples of moving beyond traditional prevention efforts to use creative communications strategies
    - — Community mobilization to deal with alcohol advertising
    - — Presentations from activists on ways to influence public administrators and legislators.

Information Resources Management

- • Alcohol and other drug abuse clearinghouse/prevention resource center operations
    - — Data base operations
    - — Acquiring and screening materials for the data base and library
    - — Abstracting, indexing, and entering data base records
    - — Establishing and maintaining a library and repository
    - — Systems for inquiry response

— Producing publications and other reference products

— Steps in the materials development process

— Providing graphics support

— Conducting promotional and user awareness activities

— Maintaining and updating mailing lists

— Efficient warehousing and inventory services

— Automated data processing and management information systems

— Cost containment and recovery efforts.

• Computer applications for managing information

— Providing computer hardware and popular software

— Demonstrations and practical training on data base and mailing list management, and desktop publishing software

— Demonstrating the use of online telephone access to proprietary and public data bases.

• Prevention materials development and materials review process

— Guidelines for presenting scientific information

— Tailoring readability level to the target audience

— Understanding appeal factors of messages (e.g., believability, persuasiveness, informativeness)

— Adhering to accepted public health policies.

Discussion

Feedback forms indicated that the seminar sessions directly addressed immediate needs of the prevention workers. Participants suggested that more of these seminars would be useful to refresh and polish their new skills and to impart this information to their coworkers.

Topics receiving the highest ratings were media relations, developing low-literacy publications, and evaluating publications for content and readability. Participants expressed the need for materials targeted to minorities, but generally did not feel they needed to know about additional resources for alcohol and other drug problem prevention. What they did need most were ways to evaluate and use the resources already available.

It became apparent during the early workshops that planners had overestimated the trainees' familiarity with computers. Hardware and software that provided hands-on exercises were largely unused. Participants needed introductions to the equipment and demonstrations before they could take advantage of the opportunity to use it.

Managing Logistics

OSAP served as a facilitator of the workshops by providing logistical and technical assistance. For example, OSAP arranged for lead speakers for each subject area and assisted with scheduling. OSAP also consulted frequently with a two-member planning team comprised of the host State NPN representative and the regional NPN representative. The team arranged for regional presenters and meeting space.

OSAP also provided generous scholarships, so representatives from community-based prevention programs and volunteers from local affiliates of national intermediary organizations could attend. Computer equipment was borrowed from local dealers.

Discussion

The two-member teams worked well, sharing the responsibility of making arrangements for the workshops. When one was unable to take on a task, the other often could act as a substitute. Good personal working relationships among the individuals involved were important in making the planning and implementation work smoothly.

Scholarship assistance was considered essential to the workshops' success. Where financial help is not available, 1-day workshops within a few hours' drive might be more feasible than regional meetings that require overnight stays.

Postmeeting Activities

Members of the State teams scheduled meetings during the workshops to discuss their own needs and opportunities for coordination. Many planned to stay in contact after the workshops, thus forming the nucleus of a new State network. Groups that had worked independently before, such as the NFP, became aware of opportunities for coordination with State agencies. Some State agencies became involved with the NFP's Red Ribbon campaign as a result of the workshops. The workshops were recorded and audiotapes were offered for sale.

Discussion

Informal discussion was rated as one of the most important benefits of the workshops. Because workshop participants continued to work with each other after the meetings, workshop benefits were extended. Many participants expressed interest in and the need for continued support in communications and information management techniques, including onsite technical assistance.

Audiotapes were not satisfactory records of the workshops. Print copies of all presentations, on the other hand, could have contributed to their long-range impact. Print copies would serve as a reminder to participants of what was presented, and could be photocopied for their use in training staff members within their own organizations. Print copies also could include the many illustrative exhibits and charts and posters presented, which the audiotapes could not.

All presenters (including keynoters, luncheon speakers, and lead and workshop presenters) should have been required to submit a written copy of their presentations. A less attractive alternative might be to transcribe and publish the best of the taped speeches and distribute them to future participants.

Lessons Learned

The following conclusions were drawn after analyzing seminar evaluation forms and other participant feedback.

- Involving many intermediary organizations from the initial planning stage is critical to designing and conducting a seminar that is responsive to participants' needs.

- Effective communications techniques are of interest and necessary for all types of prevention workers—from information specialists, to parents, to State agency employees, to media professionals, and every volunteer and professional in between.

- Content and agenda should be planned with representatives from the training target population to provide training that addresses their needs and is relevant to their daily activities. This is preferable to designing a program based on needs perceived in Washington.

- Selecting a training team representing a variety of prevention providers in a specific geographical area helps promote ongoing coordination and mutual support, using the new information and skills.

- Seminars should be conducted in an interactive rather than didactic format to enhance trainee understanding and ability to use skills taught. The agenda should not be so filled, even with very exciting programs, that the participants and presenters do not have time to thoroughly discuss the information.

- All presenters should have written copies of their presentations with charts and exhibits to be duplicated and distributed to all participants. Audiotapes are not satisfactory.

- Trainees prefer speakers and presenters from their region who deal with similar conditions and circumstances.

- Time on the agenda for networking and sharing among participants could be the most valuable part of the conference.

- Prevention workers have very limited resources for out-of-town travel. Scholarship assistance is required to engage many prevention workers, especially those targeting high-risk populations. Perhaps in return for scholarships, participants could be required to conduct training for their colleagues or constituencies.

- Evaluation forms should be required of every participant to help gauge their reactions to the workshops. An additional followup form sent several weeks after the workshop would have helped identify lasting benefits perceived by participants.

Followup

Based on the results of these Regional Communications Seminars, OSAP developed several new, multiyear initiatives that now are being implemented.

Each State was asked to identify a center to serve as a resource focus for alcohol and other drug information to work with local intermediaries, disseminate information, and provide feedback, so that OSAP can improve its "wholesale" and "retail" communications operations. In addition, national associations were asked to serve as Regional Alcohol and Drug Awareness Resource (RADAR) Network members, and special centers were established to provide in-depth knowledge transfer programs (e.g., Morehouse College to serve as a central resource for information on alcohol and other drugs among Black populations). International organizations have requested status as RADAR Network members, and associate members (at the local level) also are joining the Network. The first national RADAR Network meeting was held in Dallas, Texas, in June 1989. Minimum standards for membership were established and approved by the membership at this first meeting. All members' goals are to meet these minimum standards within 2 years. A full description of the RADAR Network and a list of current RADAR Network members are included at the end of this chapter.

OSAP is contracting to provide indepth technical assistance to groups and organizations planning and implementing communications programs. OSAP plans to convene groups working on similar projects to learn from one another, experts, and other resources. It also will provide onsite technical assistance, "how-to" and similar guidebooks, and other forms of expertise.

OSAP also is contracting to study the potential impact of its communications programs, design new materials, and develop marketing support. Special emphasis is being placed on filling gaps in materials for minority and other high-risk populations, user's guides, and audiovisual materials highlighting programs that appear to hold promise for effectively dealing with alcohol and other drug problems.

OSAP has developed a review process by which it assesses the value of messages and materials being produced to help prevent alcohol and other drug problems. The process, as described in appendix B, is used to evaluate scientific accuracy, conformity to public health principles and policies, and communications appeal, e.g., appropriateness for reaching the intended target audience. The process also is being widely distributed to those who are developing materials and to those who need tools to assess materials. OSAP believes one of its primary values lies in its ability to help educate others about the process of developing good prevention messages and materials.

For more information on OSAP communications initiatives:

RADAR Network

Contact:
Bettina Scott, Ph.D.
Office for Substance Abuse Prevention
Division of Communication Programs
Rockwall II, 9C03
5600 Fishers Lane
Rockville, MD 20857
(301) 443-0377

Communications Support (Technical Assistance)

Contact:
Mel Segal
Office for Substance Abuse Prevention
Division of Communication Programs
Rockwall II, 9C03
5600 Fishers Lane
Rockville, MD 20857
(301) 443-0373

Materials Development

Contact:
Judith Funkhouser
Office for Substance Abuse Prevention
Division of Communication Programs
Rockwall II, 9C03

5600 Fishers Lane
Rockville, MD 20857
(301) 443-0373

Message and Material Review Process

Contact:
Program Manager
National Clearinghouse for Alcohol and
  Drug Information (NCADI)
P. O. Box 2345
Rockville, MD 20852
(301) 468-2600

Bibliography

Flay, Brian R., and Sobel, J.L. *The Role of Mass Media in Preventing Adolescent Substance Abuse*. NIDA Research Monograph 47. Rockville, MD: National Institute on Drug Abuse, 1983.

McAlister, A.; Puska, P.; and Salonen, J.T. Theory and action for health promotion: Illustrations from the North Karelia project. *American Journal of Public Health* 72:43–50, 1981.

National Cancer Institute. *Making Health Communications Work: A Planner's Guide*. Bethesda, MD: National Institutes of Health, 1989.

Appendix A

Planning a Communications Program

The prevention field has made enormous progress in the last 20 years. As alcohol and other drug problems have become priorities in the Nation's consciousness, prevention specialists have developed and demonstrated methods to help prevent these problems. Better use of this existing knowledge requires communication among treatment, health care and social service professionals, related organizations, government agencies, the private sector, and individual citizens. In fact, effective communication among leaders in many sectors of society—prevention, health, education, industry, labor, justice, community organizations, and others—is essential to fighting the Nation's alcohol and other drug problems.

Communications programs can be designed to inform, influence, and motivate institutional or public audiences. Communications can

- Increase awareness of an issue, problem, or solution
- Affect attitudes or create support for individual or collective action
- Demonstrate or illustrate skills
- Increase demand for prevention or treatment services
- Remind about or reinforce knowledge, attitudes, or behavior.

Health communications programs cannot

- Compensate for a lack of prevention, treatment, or other services
- Produce behavior change without supportive program components
- Be equally effective in addressing *all* issues or relaying all messages.

For these reasons, the Office for Substance Abuse Prevention (OSAP) views communications as one component of programs designed to address alcohol and other drug problems. This paper provides a brief overview of relevant communications theories, outlines the planning process, and lists resources for further information.

Relevant Theories, Models, and Practices

OSAP has incorporated aspects of various communications models, theories, and practices into its planning process. Each discipline offers a different perspective on the target audience and the steps leading to behavior change. For example, social marketing practice considers the perceptions and perceived needs of target audiences as an essential element of planning. Health education models identify the components of behavioral intention that will influence an individual's willingness to act. Mass communications theories help explain factors that influence message transmission between the source, the target audience, and the expected effects. Summarized below are some of the theories, models, and practices that have been woven together to produce OSAP's philosophy for planning communications programs.

Social Marketing

Social marketing models, first articulated by Philip Kotler and based on commercial marketing practice, show that the consumer (target audience) should be the central focus for planning and conducting a program (Kotler and Andreasen 1987). The program's components focus on the following:

- Price—what the consumer must give up in order to receive the program's benefits. These "costs" may be intangible (e.g., changes in beliefs or habits) or tangible (e.g., money, time, or travel)

- Product—what the program is trying to change within the target audience

- Promotion—how the exchange is communicated (e.g., appeals used)

- Place—what channels the program uses to reach the target audience (e.g., mass media, community, interpersonal).

The formulation of price, product, promotion, and place evolves from research with the target audience to determine what benefits and costs they would consider acceptable, and how they might be reached. Social marketing stresses the importance of understanding the target audience and designing strategies based on members' wants and needs rather than on what they "should" do according to good health practice. This perspective is particularly important for prevention programs targeting children and youth, for whom immediate benefits (e.g., popularity) are far more important than future effects (e.g., health or behavioral problems).

Behavioral Intentions

Studies of behavioral intentions suggest that the likelihood of the target audience adopting a desired behavior can be predicted by assessing, and subsequently trying to change or influence, members' attitudes toward and perceptions of benefits of the behavior, along with their perceptions of how their peers will view their behavior (McGuire 1981). Research by Fishbein and Ajzen supports the idea that an individual's, and society's (perceived) attitudes are an important antecedent to action. Therefore, a key step toward influencing behavior is a preliminary assessment of target audience attitudes, and subsequent tracking to identify any attitudinal changes.

Communications for Persuasion

William McGuire has described the steps an individual must be persuaded to pass through in order to assimilate a desired behavior (McGuire 1981). These steps are as follows:

- Exposure to the message
- Attention to the message
- Interest in or personal relevance of the message
- Understanding of the message
- Personalizing the behavior to fit one's life
- Accepting the change
- Remembering the message and continuing to agree with it
- Being able to think of it
- Making decisions based on bringing the message to mind
- Behaving as decided
- Receiving (positive) reinforcement for behavior
- Accepting the behavior into one's life.

To communicate the message successfully, five communication components all must work:

- The credibility of the message source
- The message design
- The delivery channel
- The target audience

- The targeted behavior.

Attention to McGuire's considerations helps assure that the communications program plan addresses all factors that determine whether a message is received and absorbed, and that the program is staged to address audience needs as they change over time, progressing toward behavior change.

Diffusion of Innovations

The health policy makers call it "technology transfer"; Everett Rogers describes it as a process whereby new products or ideas are introduced or diffused to an audience (Rogers 1983). Whether the message is accepted or the behavior adopted depends upon whether the audience

- Perceives it as beneficial
- Perceives it to be in accordance with its needs and values
- Finds it easy or difficult to understand or adopt
- Can try the behavior
- Feels that the results of the trial or acceptance are viewed positively by peers.

Rogers suggests that the mass media is a quick and effective route for introducing new information or trying to influence attitudes, especially in the early stages of reaching audiences predisposed toward accepting new ideas. However, at the point of trial or adoption, interpersonal channels are more influential. This means that a prevention strategy might consist of using the mass media to introduce the message, provide knowledge, influence attitudes, and reinforce behavior, and using community or interpersonal intervention to teach and encourage the adoption of the "no use" behavior. This is especially important for groups, such as lower socioeconomic groups, that are known not to adopt new behaviors quickly.

Precede Model

Lawrence Green developed the PRECEDE model, an approach to planning that examines factors contributing to behavior change (Green et al. 1980). These include

- Predisposing factors—individuals' knowledge, attitudes, behaviors, beliefs, and values prior to intervention that affect their willingness to change

- Enabling factors—the structure of the environment or community and individual situations that facilitate or present obstacles to change

- Reinforcing factors—the positive or negative effects of adopting the behavior, including the social support, that influence continuation of behavior.

These factors require that individuals be considered in the context of their community and social structures, and not in isolation, when planning communication or health education strategies.

The Communications Program Planning Process

A fundamental premise of OSAP's communications program planning scheme is that, to be viable, prevention communications programs must be based on an understanding of the needs and perceptions of their target audiences. Table A illustrates this approach, incorporating assessments of target audience needs and perceptions at critical points in program development and implementation. The six stages constitute a circular process in which the last stage feeds back to the first in a continuous process of planning and improvement.

The steps outlined below constitute an ideal process, one that may require more time and money than many agencies can afford. All the steps may not be feasible, or in some cases even essential. However, carefully following the steps in each stage of the process can make the next program phase more productive. Generally, professional judgment must be applied to decide which steps are appropriate for any particular program.

Stage 1. Planning and Strategy Selection

Key Issues

- What is already known about the alcohol and drug abuse problem? (Analyze existing data.)

- What new kinds of information will be needed before planning the program? (Generate new data if needed.)

- Who is the target audience? What is known about these people?

- Overall, what change is planned to solve or lessen the problem? (Establish goals.)

- What *measurable* objectives can be established to define success?

- How can progress be measured? (Plan evaluation strategies.)

- What should the target audience be told? (Draft communications strategies.)

The planning stage of a program provides the foundation for the entire communication process. Faulty decisionmaking at this point can lead to the development of a program that is off the mark. Careful assessment of a problem in the beginning can reduce the need for costly midcourse corrections.

Stage 2. Selecting Channels and Materials

Key Issues

- Are there any existing materials that could be adapted for the program?
- What channels are most appropriate for reaching the target audience (e.g., schoolroom, mass media, parent-to-child)?
- What materials formats will best suit the channels and the messages (e.g., booklets, videotapes, curriculums)?

The decisions made in stage 1 will guide in selecting the appropriate communication channel(s) and in locating, or producing, if necessary, effective materials. Without clear objectives and a knowledge of the target audience, there is a risk of producing materials that are inappropriate for the target audience or the issue being addressed.

Stage 3. Developing Materials and Pretesting

Key Issues

- What are the different ways that the message can be presented (e.g., using humor, slice-of-life, familiar spokesperson, peer influence)?
- How does the target audience react to the message concept(s) (e.g., clear or confusing, credible or not, personally relevant)?
- Does the audience
    - Understand the message?
    - Recall it?
    - Accept its importance?
    - Agree with the value of the solution?
- How does the audience respond to the message format?
- Based on responses from the target audience and gatekeepers, do changes need to be made in the message or its format?

- How could the message be promoted, the materials distributed, and progress tracked?

- Who are potential program gatekeepers (e.g., television public service directors, school board members or teachers, officials of voluntary organizations)?

- How do program gatekeepers respond?

In stages 1 and 2 most program planning is completed and the basis for developing messages and materials has been established. Often several different concepts will be developed and tested with target audiences. Feedback from the intended audience is critical in stage 3. It is also important at this stage to look at the program as a whole—how the messages and materials will be used, and by whom.

Stage 4. Implementation

Key Issues

- Is the message getting through the intended channels of communication?

- Is the target audience paying attention and reacting?

- Do any existing channels need to be replaced, or new channels added?

- Which aspects of the program are having the strongest effect?

- Do changes need to be made to improve program effect?

The fully developed program is introduced to the target audience at this stage; promotion and distribution begin through all channels. Program components are periodically reviewed and revised if necessary. Audience exposure and reaction are tracked to permit alterations if needed.

Stage 5. Assessing Effectiveness

Key Issues

- Are the program objectives being met?

- Were the changes that took place the result of the program, other factors, or a combination of both?

- How well was each stage of program planning, implementation, and assessment handled?

The program should be assessed by analyzing the results of measurements planned in stage 1 and used throughout the program's lifespan.

Stage 6. Feedback To Refine Program

At each stage, useful information was gathered about the audience, the message, the channels of communication, and the program's intended effect. All of this information helps prepare for a new cycle of program development. The more information that can be reviewed at the completion of the first program phase, the more likely it is that these questions can be answered:

- Why did the program work or not work?

- Are there program changes or improvements that should be made to increase the likelihood of success or to address changes in the audience, problems, or other situations?

- Are there lessons learned that could help make future programs more successful?

Understanding and using these steps for planning and implementing a prevention communications program can help assure its success. Sources of more information include the following:

Fishbein, M., and Ajzen, I. *Belief, Attitude, Intention and Behavior.* Reading, Mass.: Addison-Wesley, 1975.

Green, L.W.; Kreuter, M.W.; Deeds, S.G.; and Patridge, K.B. *Health Education Planning: A Diagnostic Approach.* Palo Alto: Mayfield Publishing Company, 1980.

Hawkins, J.D., and Wederhood, B. *Handbook for Evaluating Drug and Alcohol Prevention Programs: Staff/Team Evaluation of Prevention Programs (STEPP).* Rockville, Md.: Office for Substance Abuse Prevention, 1987.

Kotler, P., and Andreasen, A.R. *Strategic Marketing for Nonprofit Organizations,* 3rd ed. Englewood Cliffs, N.J.: Prentice-Hall, 1987.

Kotler, P.; Ferrell, O.C.; and Lamb, C. *Strategic Marketing for Nonprofit Organizations, Cases and Readings.* Englewood Cliffs, N.J.: Prentice-Hall, 1987.

McGuire, W. Theoretical foundations of campaigns. In: Rice, R.E., and Paisley, W.J., eds. *Public Communication Campaigns.* Beverly Hills: Sage Publications. 1981. pp. 41-70.

McQuail, D., and Wendahl, S. *Communications Models for the Study of Mass Communications.* New York: Longman, Inc., 1982.

National Cancer Institute. *Making Health Communications Programs Work: A Planner's Guide.* Bethesda, Md., 1989.

Rogers, E.M. *Diffusion of Innovations.* New York: Free Press, 1983.

Appendix B

Introduction

One of the most dramatic results of the President's declared "War on Drugs" that resulted from the passage of the 1986 Anti-Drug Abuse Act and the 1988 Omnibus Anti-Drug Act has been the proliferation of prevention materials—printed and audiovisual products generated by the American public in response to the Nation's needs. Unfortunately, even the best intentions do not always result in the best prevention products, and prevention material consumers are faced with the overwhelming task of sorting out which materials contain the appropriate and accurate information for effectively reaching their respective audiences. The Federal Government has acted to assist the American public.

The Office for Substance Abuse Prevention (OSAP), in the Alcohol, Drug Abuse, and Mental Health Administration (ADAMHA), has implemented a review program to help prevention workers screen for appropriateness, accuracy, credibility, appeal, and so forth. The cornerstone of the OSAP program is the Communications Message and Material Review Process, a detailed manual designed to assess a product's conformance to public health policies and principles, scientific accuracy, and appropriateness of communication strategies.

This manual is available for either the development or review of prevention products for use by Federal, State, and local prevention workers. The manual contains a product description form and a guide for completing the form and the ADAMHA/OSAP scientific, policy, and communications review form with definitive guidelines for completing the review. These guidelines are first and foremost based on the principle of "do no harm." They have evolved over a period of time and have been tested with more than 2,000 products. If you have any comments or suggestions regarding the use of this manual, please send them to National Clearinghouse for Alcohol and Drug Information (NCADI), P.O. Box 2345, Rockville, MD 20852.

These forms were not designed to assess prevention programs, training programs, or comprehensive curriculums, although the underlying principles may be applicable for those developing or reviewing these programs. They were designed to review videotapes, books, pamphlets, and so forth, whether used individually or as a communications package. The Office for Substance Abuse Prevention, in cooperation with the Department of Education, is currently in the process of developing guidelines for the review of curriculums. A curriculum review should be completed by September 1990.

An acceptable rating on any product does not imply Government endorsement or approval of the message(s) or material(s). Current and relevant materials receiving an acceptable rating, however, will be listed on resource lists. Not being listed on a resource list does not in any way reflect that materials are unacceptable. To be included in the review process, an author or producer must make a copy of the material available, free of charge, for storage and retrieval at the National Clearinghouse for Alcohol and Drug Information.

PRODUCT DESCRIPTION
Office for Substance Abuse Prevention
Alcohol, Drug Abuse, and Mental Health Administration

Accession No. _____
Date _____
Reviewer _____
A   UA

Title of Product _____

Producer/Author _____

Organization _____

Address _____
_____

Other Sponsors/Endorsers _____

Publication Date _____

Revision Date _____

Contact _____

Phone _____

Grant/Contract: _____

Format:
___ Article   ___ Workbook
___ Book   ___ Poster
___ Booklet   ___ Print Ad
___ Brochure   ___ 3/4" Video
___ Catalog   ___ VHS Video
___ Classroom   ___ 16mm Film
    Material   ___ Radio PSA
___ Comic Book   ___ Script
___ Communications ___ Slides
    Package   ___ Audio Tape
___ Fact Sheet   ___ Skit Script
___ Magazine   ___ Software
___ Newsletter
___ Other (describe) _____

Length:
___ pages   ___ minutes
___ sessions

Context(s): (check all that apply)
___ Stands Alone
___ Part of a Program/Packet (describe)
    _____
___ Has Training Component (please
    enclose)

Topic(s): (check no more than 3)
___ Alcohol
___ Drugs (specify) _____
___ Alcohol/Drugs
___ Prevention
___ Intervention/Treatment

Mode(s) of Delivery: (check no more than 2)
___ Self-Instructional
___ Instructor-led
___ Mass Media

Target Audience(s): (check no more than 3)
___ A/D Prevention Professionals
___ A/D Treatment Professionals
___ African Americans/Blacks
___ Asian and Pacific Islanders

___ Caucasians
___ College Students
___ Community Service Groups
___ Disabled
___ Educators (specify grade[s]) _____
___ Elderly
___ Elementary Youth (5-12)
___ Employees
___ Employers
___ General Public
___ Health Care Providers (specify specialty)
    _____
___ High-Risk Families
___ High-Risk Youth
___ Hispanics/Latinos (specify) _____
___ Jr. High Youth (13-15)
___ Media Representatives
___ Native Americans (specify) _____
___ Other (describe) _____
___ Parents (specify age of child) _____
___ Patients
___ Policymakers/Administrators
___ Preschool (age 4 and under)
___ Recreation/Sports Personnel
___ Scientists and Researchers
___ Sr. High Youth (16-18)
___ Women
___ Young Adults (19-25 years)

Setting: (check no more than 2)
___ Community Organization
___ Government
___ Health Care
___ Home
___ Legal/Judicial
___ Military
___ Recreation/Sports
___ Religious
___ Rural
___ School
___ Suburban
___ Urban
___ Worksite
___ Other (describe) _____

Language(s): (check all that apply)
___ English
___ Spanish (specify) _____
___ Bilingual (specify) _____
___ Other (indicate) _____

Readability: (see attached examples)
___ Low Literacy (grade level 4)
___ Easy (5-8)
___ Average (9-10)
___ Fairly Difficult (11-13)
___ Difficult (14-18)
___ N/A

Pretested/Evaluated:
___ Yes   ___ Unknown
___ No
(If yes, describe and include copy of report if
possible.) _____

Current Scope: (check only 1)
___ National: _____
___ Regional: _____
___ State: _____
___ Local: _____

Availability:
___ Unknown
___ Restrictions on Use
    (Explain under Comments)
___ Copyrighted (Owned By: _____
___ Public Domain
___ Available Free
___ Negatives Available on Loan
___ Payment Required
    Price$ _____
___ Available Through Free A-V Loan Program
___ Source (if different from above) _____
_____

Description: (Please describe the product in two-three sentences.)
_____
_____
_____

Comments: (Use separate page for further information as described under Comments in Product Description Guidelines.)

3/24/89

Product Description Form Guidelines

1. *Accession number.*
   Actual assignment of an accession number for materials data base items will be done in the data analysis or acquisitions unit of the Clearinghouse. The five-character numbers will be assigned in sequence. However, the reviewer filling out the Product Description Form should identify the review source as being NCADI or some other entity (e.g., OSAP staff, grantee). If reviewed at NCADI, the reviewer should write "vf" on the accession number line. Other reviewers should leave it blank. These two-character notations will be the accession number prefixes used on the automated materials data base.

2. *Screener and date.*
   Fill in the date of the review and your first initial and last name.

3. *Evaluation.*
   Circle "A" (Acceptable) or "UA" (Unacceptable) after you have completed filling out both the Product Description Form and the OSAP/ADAMHA Review Form. It will be the last step of the review. **An "Unacceptable" rating in either the Scientific Review or the Policy and Principles Review will cause a product's overall rating to be "Unacceptable."**

4. *Title.*
   Print the title with its subtitle(s) exactly as it appears on the piece except 1) where a period or dash is used to separate subtitles, substitute a colon, 2) omit articles (a, an, the) as the first word of an English-language or Spanish-language title, and 3) correct misspellings.

   Be careful to record all subtitles. These can be identified by 1) reading the cover and title page from left to right and top to bottom, 2) looking for variations in typesize or print boldness, and 3) for books, reading the spine.

5. *Publication date.*
   Print the month and year, if available, using the standard three-letter abbreviation for the month (the first three letters). If no publication date is provided, try to derive the publication year from the information provided. To indicate that a publication year is derived, place the year between brackets. If no date is available and a date cannot be derived, write "N.D." to indicate no date is available.

6. *Author/Producer.*
   Identify a specific author/producer for the item being processed. The entry should always be a person's name. Provide the first and middle initial(s)

and the last name. Do not include author titles, degrees, and so forth. If no author's name is provided, leave the space blank.

7. *Oganization name, address, and telephone number(s).*
   List the organizational affiliation of the author/producer, with a complete address and phone number; include area codes, zip codes. If more than one phone number is provided, such as a toll-free number, include all numbers.

8. *Contact.*
   If given, name the person to contact for ordering materials (first and middle initial(s) and last name).

9. *Sponsor / Endorser.*
   List the sponsor/endorser of the product if it is clearly identified for a product.

10. *Contract / Grant.*
    If the product was produced under grant or contract, provide the sponsoring agency's name (public or private) as well as specific grant or contract numbers.

11. *Format.*
    Check the single most appropriate category in the Format section of the sheet. However, if a film is available in a number of formats, such as 3/4" video or 16mm, check all appropriate categories. The following categories are defined for clarification.

Article:	Journal articles or reports that would not normally be included in the bibliographic data base, such as an article that does not appear in a peer-reviewed journal. If possible, show the full citation in the organization section.
Book:	Formally bound publication, usually of standard size.
Booklet:	Usually odd-shaped pages (under 60 pages) informally bound (i.e., saddle stitched, stapled, GBC).
Brochure:	Single sheet folded to create more than one page (panel) of information.
Classroom Material:	Material designed to be used by both teacher and students in implementing alcohol/other drug education (e.g., puppets, posters, games, coloring books accompanied by a teacher guide).

Communications Package: Check this category when reviewing a set of materials distributed as a "package." In addition to reviewing the package as a whole, be sure that each piece of material is reviewed independently and given its own accession number.

Fact Sheet: Usually a photocopied or printed 8 1/2" x 11" sheet with basic factual information often bulleted; may be more than one page, but is not folded.

Magazine: This category includes periodicals. Note: Only one issue of a "magazine" will be entered into the materials data base, and this issue will be used to represent the magazine as a whole. Therefore, the magazine's description should not be based on a single issue or article, but rather the magazine itself.

Newsletter: Only one issue of an organization's newsletter will be entered—general topics covered by the newsletter as a whole should be described, not just the articles in any one issue.

Workbook: Printed material that is designed for interactive learning where the audience, following directions, writes in responses.

12. *Length.*
Fill in the total number of pages for printed materials (a double-sided page is counted as two pages), the number of minutes for films and videos, and the number of sessions to be used, if applicable (e.g., 10 sessions).

13. *Context.*
If the material is a piece of a program or if it is distributed as one piece of a package, check "part of program/packet" and fill in the name of the program or a brief description. If the material was designed to stand alone and is not a piece of a program/packet, check "stands alone." If there is a training component that comes with the material, check the appropriate space.

14. *Topics.*
To aid in identifying topics please use the following definitions:

Drug: (specify) If the product has a single drug topic, fill in the name of the appropriate drug category (use the attached list of 15 drug categories).

Prevention: Provides information or strategies about alcohol and other drugs with the purpose of preventing alcohol and other drug problems before they start.

Intervention/   Provides information about alcohol and other drugs with
Treatment: the purpose of intervening in alcohol and other drug problems.

Note: Reviewers should include topics covered, such as AIDS, alcohol-related birthdefects, drugged driving, etc., in the Description section.

15. *Mode of delivery.*

   • Self-instructional: can be used without a teacher or leader.

   • Instructor-led: requires a teacher or leader.

   • Mass media: delivered through TV, radio, or the press.

16. *Target audience(s).*
   Identify the audience that the product is INTENDED to reach, e.g., teachers (who will use it with students). If the targeted audience is not clearly identified, consider the language style, use of terminology, length, appropriateness of examples, and format to determine the target audience. Remember that the target audience is not necessarily the same group that is being described in the product, and the reviewer may need to call the product source to determine the intended audience.

17. *Setting.*
   Materials may be targeted to particular settings as well as particular audiences. Sellings should convey images and symbols appropriate to the particular classification.

   • Community Organization: for use by a wide range of groups such as Boys Clubs,4-H, Elks, PTA, etc.

   • Government: Federal, State, and local alcohol/drug, education, health, law enforcement, etc., agencies.

   • Health Care: images include hospitals, emergency vehicles, clinics, offices, visiting caretakers, etc.

   • Home: materials actually used in the home, e.g., an interactive workbook to be completed by parent and child.

   • Legal/Judicial: may include prisons, probation offices, courtrooms, paralegal offices, etc.

   • Military: the armed services.

- Recreation/Sports: images include gymnasiums, fields, courts, playgrounds, streets, etc.

- Religious: images include mosques, synagogues, and churches or religious-oriented storefronts, camps, etc.

- Rural: characterized by the country, farmland, agriculture, and open spaces. Images include farms, low density, crafts, blue-collar labor.

- School: from preschool to college. Images include classrooms, school buildings, teachers, students, etc.

- Suburban: residential areas adjacent to cities. Images include schools, large grassy playgrounds, shopping malls, open space parks, middle-class family orientation.

- Urban: characteristic of a city in general; multiethnic, dramatic range from wealth to poverty. Images include high density, heavy traffic, public transportation, public playgrounds and parks, city street scenes.

- Worksite: inside buildings or at other sites such as mines, construction areas, etc.

18. *Language.*
Identify all languages that the product is available in. If a product is bilingual, check bilingual and fill in the names of the two languages. If in Spanish, specify the actual audience: Mexican American, Puerto Rican American, Cuban American, etc.

19. *Readability.*
To determine the readability level, apply the following SMOG Test readability formula: Count 30 sentences in the following manner: 10 consecutive sentences near the beginning, in the middle, and near the end of the text. Next, count the number of words with 3 or more syllables (polysyllabic) in your choice of 30 sentences. Then locate the total number on the SMOG Conversion Table in the left-hand column and find the corresponding grade level in the right-hand column.

Some Tips for Applying the SMOG Test

- A sentence is defined as a string of words punctuated with a period(.), an exclamation point(!), or a question mark(?)

- Hyphenated words are considered as one word.

- Numbers that are written out should also be considered, and if in numeric form in the text, they should be pronounced to determine if they are polysyllabic, e.g., pol-y-syl-la-bic.

- Proper nouns, if polysyllabic, should be counted.

- Abbreviations should be read as unabbreviated to determine if they are polysyllabic.

SMOG Conversion Table

Total Polysyllabic Word Counts	Appropriate Grade Level (+ 1.5 Grades)	
0-2	4	Low Literacy
3-6	5	
7-12	6	Easy
13-20	7	
21-30	8	
31-42	9	Average
43-56	10	
57-72	11	
73-90	12	Fairly Difficult
91-110	13	
111-132	14	
133-156	15	
157-182	16	Difficult
183-210	17	
211-240	18	

20. *Pretested / Evaluated.*
    Check "Unknown" unless it states somewhere on the product that it was evaluated. (It is expected that within the next 2 years, all materials to be listed on resource lists produced by NCADI will have been at least minimally pretested/evaluated with the target audiences.)

21. *Current scope.*
    Indicate the intended distribution pattern for the product. If it was prepared by a State organization, check State.

22. *Availability.*
    Leave blank if there is no indication of availability (i.e., ordering information). If there is no address for the product's organization or phone number, check "Unknown." If the source for the product is different from the producing organization, fill in the name of the source. Note: When developing resource lists using this material, you may need to call the organization and get availability and ordering information. It is wise to do this with all

materials over 6 months old to be sure available information is current. Include date of last revision whenever possible.

23. *Description.*

Write a two to three sentence description of the content of the product. Be sure to write in complete sentences and include the topics covered. The written description should be meaningful and concise and not repeat the descriptive information provided above. It should focus on the content of the product and include information about the populations described by the product (as opposed to the target populations), details about the subjects (e.g., alcohol- or drug-impaired drivers), and the product's intent. If appropriate, it can include information about the graphics (pictures, graphs, colors) and style (humorous, easy to read). The description *should not* be promotional in nature, for example, this "award-winning" film.

24. *Comments (to be filled out by screener/reviewer).*

The Comments section is meant to contain information related to ordering the material being reviewed, its availability at NCADI, and any other specifics not covered above. It should include the following:

- Additional product information that is useful for ordering materials such as copyright and edition numbers.

- Publication numbers and/or inventory numbers. For example, most Government publications distributed by NCADI have ADAMHA (ADM) control numbers and internal inventory numbers—both such numbers would be entered in the Comments section. Include the Superintendent of Documents ordering information and cost whenever appropriate.

- Information that will help with ordering products that are part of a series or a program/packet.

- Detailed information about the appropriate audiences; for example, materials are best suited for physicians and not other health care providers, or materials are best suited for Native Americans living in urban areas and not those living in tribal areas.

Drug Classification Attachment

1. Alcohol

2. Anabolic Steroids

3. CNS Depressants (other than alcohol)

4. Cocaine/Crack

5. Designer Drugs

6. Hallucinogens

7. Inhalants

8. Marijuana and Cannabinoids

9. Nicotine

10. Opioids (Opiates, Narcotics, Narcotic Analgesics)

11. Over-the-Counter (OTC) Medicines

12. Phencyclidine (PCP)

13. Prescription Drugs

14. Stimulants (other than cocaine)

15. Other Drugs

```
                                              ┌──────────────────────────────┐
                                              │ Acc. No. _____ │
                                              │ Date _____  │
                                              │                              │
                                              │ Reviewer: Scientific _____ │
                                              │                              │
                                              │ Reviewer: Policy _____ │
                        OSAP/ADAMHA REVIEW    │ Reviewer: Communications ___ │
                                              └──────────────────────────────┘
```

┌───┐
│   │
│ I.   SCIENTIFIC REVIEW (see attached Guidelines)   │
│   │
│   1. Material is scientifically significant, based on valid   │
│   assumptions, supported by accurate citations, and   Yes ____   No ____   N/A ____ │
│   appropriately used.   │
│   │
│   2. Scientific methods and approaches are adequate,   Yes ____   No ____   N/A ____ │
│   appropriate, and clearly described.   │
│   │
│   3. Findings reported are accurate, current, and   Yes ____   No ____   │
│   applicable to the subject matter.   │
│   │
│   4. Recommendation: acceptable ____   unacceptable ____ │
│   │
│   5. Comments on above: │
│   │
└───┘

┌───┐
│   │
│ II. POLICY REVIEW (see attached Guidelines)   │
│   │
│   1. Material makes clear that illegal drug (including   Yes ____   No ____   N/A ____ │
│   alcohol for those under 21) use is unhealthy and   │
│   harmful for all persons.   │
│   │
│   2. Material gives a clear message that risk is associated   Yes ____   No ____   N/A ____ │
│   with using any form or amount of alcohol or other drugs.   │
│   │
│   3. Material gives a clear message of no alcohol use for   Yes ____   No ____   N/A ____ │
│   -   persons under 21 years of age   │
│   -   pregnant women   │
│   -   recovering alcoholics and addicts   │
│   -   persons taking prescription or non-prescription   │
│   drugs   │
│   │
│   4. Material states clearly that pregnant women must not   Yes ____   No ____   N/A ____ │
│   use any drugs (prescription or nonprescription) without   │
│   consulting their physicians.   │
│   │
│   5. Prevention material does not contain illustrations or   Yes ____   No ____   N/A ____ │
│   dramatizations that could teach people ways to prepare,   │
│   obtain, or ingest illegal drugs.   │
│   │
│   Intervention material does not contain illustrations   Yes ____   No ____   N/A ____ │
│   or dramatizations that may stimulate recovering addicts   │
│   or alcoholics to use drugs.   │
│   │
│   6. Material does not glamorize or glorify the use of   Yes ____   No ____   N/A ____ │
│   alcohol and other drugs.   │
│   │
│   7. Material does not "blame the victim."   Yes ____   No ____   N/A ____ │
│   │
│   8. Material targeting youth does not use recovering   Yes ____   No ____   N/A ____ │
│   addicts or alcoholics as role models.   │
│   │
│   9. Material supports abstinence as a viable choice.   Yes ____   No ____   N/A ____ │
│   │
│   10. Material is culturally and ethnically sensitive.   Yes ____   No ____   N/A ____ │
│   │
│   11. Recommendation: acceptable ____   unacceptable ____ │
│   │
│   12. Comments on above: │
│   │
└───┘

NOTE: If either of the above is rated unacceptable, the product's overall rating will be unacceptable.

III. COMMUNICATIONS REVIEW (see attached Guidelines)

1.	Material is appropriate at cognitive and developmental levels	Yes ____	No ____	
2.	Institutional source is credible	Yes ____	No ____	
3.	Individual source is credible	Yes ____	No ____	
4.	Language is appropriate	Yes ____	No ____	N/A ____
5.	Tone is appropriate	Yes ____	No ____	N/A ____
6.	Length is appropriate	Yes ____	No ____	N/A ____
7.	Format/graphics quality is acceptable	Yes ____	No ____	N/A ____

8. Messages

• are appealing	High ____	Med ____	Low ____	N/A ____
• are believable	High ____	Med ____	Low ____	N/A ____
• create awareness	High ____	Med ____	Low ____	N/A ____
• persuade	High ____	Med ____	Low ____	N/A ____
• call for action	High ____	Med ____	Low ____	N/A ____
• have been pretested	High ____	Med ____	Low ____	N/A ____

9.	Material needs to be combined with other messages or materials to be effective	Yes ____	No ____	N/A ____
10.	Readability level is appropriate	Yes ____	No ____	N/A ____
11.	Comments on above:			

NOTE: Even though the product receives a Communications Review, it will not be rated as acceptable or unacceptable at this time. It is expected, however, that this rating will be implemented as part of the overall assessment by January 1, 1991. Developers are encouraged to use these guidelines as they plan and produce products.

Scientific Review Guidelines

1. *The material is scientifically significant, based on valid assumptions, supported by accurate citations, and appropriately used.* If the developers are working from hypotheses, theories, or models but not from statistically significant and conclusive research that has been replicated, this should be noted under comments; for example, this appears to be based on a promising prevention hypothesis, which is in the testing phase. This would not be rated unacceptable unless the National Institute on Drug Abuse (NIDA) or the National Institute on Alcohol Abuse and Alcoholism (NIAAA) believe that harm could result from further testing; for example, an applied theory has resulted in increased drug use or application may result in misperception or other harm.

2. *The scientific methods and approaches used are adequate, appropriate, and clearly described.* These include the methods of basic biomedical research, behavioral research, and applied research. Clinical studies use and describe sound modalities.

3. *Findings reported are accurate, current, applicable to the subject matter, and appropriately interpreted.* The findings follow from the methods and approach used. For instance, facts should not be exaggerated nor purposely understated.

4. *Recommendation: Rate as acceptable or unacceptable.* If rated unacceptable, an overall rating of unacceptable should be recorded on the Product Description Form.

5. *Comments: Complete per instructions above.* Highlight positive aspects and problems.

OSAP Policy Review Guidelines

1. *Material makes clear that illegal and unwise drug use (including alcohol for those under 21) is unhealthy and harmful for all persons.*

   There are five kinds of illegal or unwise drug use:

   - Use of any legally prohibited drug. For example, heroin, cocaine, PCP, and "designer drugs" are all legally prohibited drugs—it is unlawful to produce, distribute, or purchase these drugs under any circumstances.

   - Use of a drug for a purpose other than its prescribed use (e.g., tranquilizer or diet pill for purposes other than prescribed).

   - Use of any product or substance that can produce a druglike effect (e.g., using glues, gasoline, or aerosols as inhalants).

   - Use of any legal drug, including alcohol or tobacco, by individuals legally underage for its use.

   - Illegal or unwise use of a legal drug; for example, public intoxication or operation of a car after drinking or other drug-taking.

   Materials should communicate clearly that all the above are either illegal and/or potentially harmful. Look for "red flag" phrases incorrectly implying that there is a "safe" use of illegal drugs. For example, materials that

   - Use the term "mood-altering" as a euphemism for "mind-altering" drugs or

   - Imply that there are no "good" or "bad" drugs, just "improper use, misuse, or abuse."

2. *Material gives a clear message that risk is associated with using any amount of alcohol or other drugs.*

   It is misleading to state or imply that there are any risk-free or fully safe levels of use of alcohol or other drugs. Even small amounts of alcohol and other drugs can increase risk of injury or to health.

   If the message is that some people use alcohol to relax or to celebrate, it also should say that alcohol is a drug and, as with any drug, there are risks associated with use. No materials should give or imply mixed messages: for example, it's safe to drink as much as you want as long as you don't drive; using drugs "recreationally" or "experimentally" is safe but don't get hooked; beer drinkers can't become alcoholic; or marijuana is a "soft" drug and heroin is a "hard" drug, implying that one is safe and the other is dangerous.

Materials recommending a designated driver should be rated unacceptable. They encourage heavy alcohol use by implying that it is okay to drink to intoxication as long as you don't drive.

Materials that carry messages, either implicitly or explicitly, that drinking alcoholic beverages is universal or the norm for virtually all occasions are unacceptable. For instance, a publication that states you should not drink to the point of intoxication and drive, but encourages "moderate" use on other occasions as a norm, should be considered primarily promotional and rated as unacceptable.

3. *Material gives a clear message of no alcohol use for persons under 21 years of age, pregnant women, recovering alcoholics and drug addicts, and persons taking prescription or nonprescription drugs.*

Persons Under 21 Years of Age

Clearly young people must go through a decisionmaking process regarding alcohol use. Learning how to make wise decisions is an important skill. However, the material should make it clear that a nonuse decision is best and give support for this decision.

Be sure that materials targeting underage college students convey the alcohol "no use" message. If materials addressing this audience are not age specific, assume that most undergraduate college students are under the legal drinking age of 21.

All youth materials should adhere to a strict abstinence message. Any material that talks about drinking and driving should be aimed at adults, not at underage youth. Materials recommending designated drivers should be rated unacceptable as they are giving a mixed "no use" message to youth—they imply that it's okay to drink as long as you don't drive.

Pregnant Women

Material for pregnant women should give a clear abstinence message. The U.S. Surgeon General says that "the safest choice is not to drink at all during pregnancy or if you are planning pregnancy." Abstinence during pregnancy removes the risk of producing a child with alcohol-related birth defects. Material that merely warns about the dangers of drinking during pregnancy without stating an abstinence message should be rated as unacceptable. For example, this is unacceptable: "you owe it to yourself and your unborn child to be informed about drinking during pregnancy and to avoid excessive or abusive drinking."

Materials stating that "research is inconclusive" or "not enough is known to make a judgment" or "some believe this ... while others believe that" are waffling. In fact, since not enough is known about how much alcohol is acceptable, for whom, and during which stages of pregnancy, the safest choice is not to drink during pregnancy. This message should be clearly stated.

Recovering Alcoholics

Abstinence from alcohol is regarded as a major goal of treatment for alcoholics in the United States. Those in treatment are urged to abstain from drinking and also are counseled to avoid psychoactive drugs. Clinical and scientific evidence seems to support the view that once physical dependence has occurred, the alcoholic no longer has the option of returning to social drinking. Materials indicating that controlled drinking or an occasional social drink is all right for recovering alcoholics, should be rated as unacceptable. Many treatment professionals also support the hypothesis that recovering addicts also should not use alcohol—but additional testing is required before assessing materials based on this concept.

Individuals Using Prescription or Nonprescription Medications

Materials should state that persons taking medications should not drink alcohol. An alcohol and drug combination may alter a drug's effectiveness. The physical reactions are unpredictable and sometimes fatal. Also, many medications contain alcohol.

4. *Material states clearly that pregnant women must not use any drugs (prescription or nonprescription) without first consulting their physicians.*

Although scientists do not know, and may never know, about the exact effects of all drugs on unborn babies, animal research and the unfortunate thalidomide tragedy have provided important clues about the possibility of prenatal damage. Materials should clearly state that pregnant women should consult their physician before buying any new drug, refilling a prescription, or taking medication on hand for common ailments, such as headaches and colds.

Common over-the-counter drugs that should be avoided by pregnant women without first consulting their physicians are antacids, aspirin, laxatives, nose drops, nasal sprays, and vitamins. Likewise, commonly prescribed drugs that can be dangerous to a fetus are antibiotics, antihistamines, antimigraines, antinauseants, diuretics, hormones, such as in oral contraceptives, vaccinations, tranquilizers, and sedatives. Materials must state clearly that these and other drugs should only be used by pregnant women on the advice of their physicians or other medical practitioners.

5. *Material does not glamorize or glorify the use of alcohol and other drugs.*

Materials should not portray alcohol and other drug use as a positive experience. For youth, the first temptation to use alcohol and other drugs often comes as pressure to be "one of the gang." Depicting alcohol and other drug use as a way to have a good time, a way to "fit in," be sexy, or attain social and financial status may lure potential users. Rate as unacceptable materials that depict alcohol and other drug use in a positive or attractive light.

6. *Prevention material does not contain illustrations or dramatizations that could teach people ways to prepare, obtain, or ingest illegal drugs, and whenever feasible materials for youth contain no illustration of drugs. Intervention material does not contain illustrations or dramatizations that may stimulate recovering addicts or alcoholics to use drugs.*

   Prevention materials that illustrate drug paraphernalia and methods of illegal drug use in such a way that they may inadvertently instruct an individual about how to use or obtain illegal or other drugs are unacceptable. Prevention materials targeting youth should contain no illustrations of illegal drugs unless when making a nonuse point that cannot be made in any other way. Illegal drugs should not be used as graphic "filler."

   Intervention materials depicting action scenes of consumption or ingestion of alcohol and other drugs may negatively influence the audience they are intended to help. For example, scenes of people injecting drugs, sniffing cocaine, or drinking alcohol may stimulate the behavior. A powerful craving for cocaine has been found to be very common for all cocaine addicts and can be easily stimulated by the sight of this drug and by objects, people, paraphernalia, places, and emotions associated in the addict's mind with cocaine. Therefore, explicit illustrations or dramatizations of drugs or drug use should not be used in materials targeted to recovering persons. All materials containing such illustrations or dramatizations should be rated unacceptable. Caution is actually wise in depicting any illegal drug use for any population, since it is unclear as to who may be most likely to use alcohol or other drugs after seeing such depictions.

7. *Material does not "blame the victim."*

   Addiction is an illness. Therefore, material should focus on preventing and treating the disease and not on berating the individual. Materials that focus on an individual's shortcomings as a reason for usage or addiction are "blaming the victim" and should be rated as unacceptable. This is not to imply that a person should not take responsibility for his or her alcohol and other drug problems, which may be related to addiction, dependence, and even just very unwise use. The material, however, should also include encouraging the person to take responsibility for seeking help, if alcohol and other drug problems continue and/or dependence is suspected. The material should include resources for seeking help.

Materials using insulting terms about the victims of drug or alcohol abuse do not conform to OSAP policy and should be rated unacceptable. For example, information that refers to those who consume alcohol and illegal drugs as "drunks," "skid row bums," "pot heads," or "dope fiends" should be rejected.

8. *Material targeting youth does not use recovering addicts or alcoholics as role models.*

   Prevention education materials targeting youth that use recovering addicts or alcoholics as role models do not conform to OSAP policy. While the power of the confession may be useful in an intervention program counseling high-risk students or adults who are recovering users, it often has the opposite effect on children.

   Focus group testing has shown children and adolescents enrolled in prevention education programs (most of whom are not recovering users) may get a different message than what is intended from the testimony of recovering addicts and alcoholics. Rather than the intended "don't do as I did" message, children may hear the message that the speaker used alcohol and other drugs and survived very well or even became wealthy and famous. An exception may be made for role models who clearly show they have been negatively affected by the use of alcohol and other drugs, such as someone now visibly handicapped or injured as a result of alcohol and other drug use.

   Materials targeting adults that use these individuals as role models may be acceptable, provided they meet all of the other criteria.

9. *Material supports abstinence as a viable choice.*

   Materials need to give a clear message that abstinence is a feasible choice for everyone. For example, they should not imply that the only solution for a headache is an over-the-counter analgesic or that the only way to celebrate a social event is with an alcoholic toast. Materials focusing on reducing or limiting the amount of alcohol or other drugs taken are unacceptable if they don't also present the message that abstinence is another viable choice. This in no way implies that valid medical attention, including appropriate drugs, should be withheld from anyone for any reason.

10. *Cultural and ethnic sensitivity.*

    Examples must be culturally and ethnically sensitive. Materials must not be biased and must not perpetuate myth or stereotype. They should reflect the social, economic, and familial norms of the intended audience and reflect the physical appearance of the audience. Extreme care should be taken in detecting subtle racist or sexist biases. For example, everything "good" is portrayed with white symbols and everything "bad" or "wrong" is portrayed with brown, black, or dark colors; or only males being arrested for alcohol-impaired driving. Norms and symbols important to the culture of the audience also must be reflected; e.g., groups are more important than individuals among some audiences; spiritual symbols are very important among some populations. Materials also need to both reflect and respect such cultural factors as the importance of the extended family, key role of grandparents, and religion.

11. *Recommendation: Rate as acceptable or unacceptable.* If rated unacceptable, an overall rating of unacceptable should be recorded on the Product Description Form.

12. *Comments: Highlight positive aspects and problems.*

Communications Review Guidelines

1. *Material is appropriate for target audience at cognitive and developmental levels.*

   Look carefully at the material to determine if it is best suited for the target audience identified on the Product Description Form.

   • Cognitive

   The reading level should not be higher than that of the audience so the material can be clearly understood. Thinking capabilities should be addressed; for example, is the audience capable of concrete or abstract thinking? Is the audience able to distinguish subtleties or must the consequences be very clear?

   • Developmental

   The material must address the social, emotional, physical, and intellectual skills of the audience. For instance, since children of alcoholics may have underdeveloped social and emotional skills, recommended strategies may need to be implemented at a slower pace; high-risk youth with attention deficits must be given special consideration; peer resistance strategies may require positive social skill development prior to implementation of "saying no" techniques; etc.

2. *Institutional source.*

   The institutional source should be credible for the target audience. Although some organizations create high-production quality materials, there may be a real or perceived conflict of interest. The same message delivered by the alcohol beverage industry may be less credible for some audiences than if delivered by NIAAA. Likewise, tobacco lobby groups may lack credibility with a public health audience.

3. *Individual source.*

   The individuals delivering the messages can be very important; for example, doctors listen to other doctors, preteens listen to teenagers, and many Americans trust the Surgeon General on health issues. Keep in mind your target audience. Recovering addicts and alcoholics are not good sources for children/youth because they often misinterpret the messages of these individuals.

4. *Language.*

Language should be appropriate and grammatically correct. If Spanish is used, it should be grammatically correct and appropriate to the particular Hispanic/Latino target audience.

5. *Tone.*

The tone should not be condescending, judgmental, or preachy. Some fear-arousing tone may be acceptable. If fear-arousing tone is excessive it may lead to denial or to the formation of an attitude of personal invulnerability—"it can't happen to me."

6. *Length.*

The length of the product should allow sufficient time for a conclusion to be drawn. It should be short enough to prevent boredom without sacrificing the message.

7. *Format.*

Production quality is an important consideration. The material should be as professional in appearance as possible, attractive, and well written. The format (type, size, and layout) should be appropriate to the audience (a large typeface is preferable for materials that will be read by either young children or people with a low-literacy level; text should not be dense; headings and photo captions should be used for imparting essential information). Color is very important. People pay more attention to materials that have color rather than just black and white. However, black and white can be enhanced and be highly appealing by using screens to achieve various shades of grey; by boxing in copy; by using photos, graphs, bullets to highlight text, and so forth. Use of high-cost techniques is not necessary to reflect high-production quality. Audiovisual materials should offer clear and understandable sound and visual quality. If the material is intended for TV or radio use, commercial broadcast standards should be applied.

8. *Messages must*

- Be appealing: Appearance should be current and stylish. Products currently popular with youth need to match existing trends.

- Be believable: The reader/viewer should be able to relate to the message—age, gender, socioculture, ethnic group.

- Create awareness: Messages should make the reader aware of the need for change, need for further information, seriousness of alcohol and other drug problems.

- Persuade: Messages must not preach, but rather find positive appeals that engage the target audience.

- Call for action: Some stated behavior should be called for so the message is not merely an intellectual exercise. Examples include seeking treatment, calling a referral number, confronting a drug-using spouse or friend, forming a parent group.

- Be pretested: Messages can be easily misinterpreted, and therefore, should be carefully pretested with gatekeepers (e.g., Cub Scout leaders) and with the intended audiences (e.g., Cub Scouts). For instance, Cub Scout leaders may believe that drug-free means without drugs, but the Cub Scouts themselves may think that drug-free means free drugs. Children think concretely and literally, whereas most adults think abstractly.

9. *Needs to be combined with messages and / or materials to be effective.*

Some materials, such as videos, are more effective if accompanied by a facilitator's or user's guide. Materials that have been submitted as a series of products have already been combined with other products, so indicate N/A.

10. *Readability level.*

The readability level should reflect the skills of the target audience. Use the SMOG Readability Formula to determine reading level:

The SMOG Readability Formula (short version)

— Count off 10 consecutive sentences near the beginning, in the middle, and at the end of the text.

— From this sample of 30 sentences, circle all polysyllabic words (3 or more syllables).

— Count the number of words in the 30 sentences, and look up appropriate grade level in the following table.

SMOG Conversion Table

Total Polysyllabic Word Counts	Appropriate Grade Level (+ 1.5 Grades)	
0-2	4	Low Literacy
3-6	5	
7-12	6	Easy
13-20	7	
21-30	8	

31-42	9	Average
43-56	10	
57-72	11	
73-90	12	Fairly Difficult
91-110	13	
111-132	14	
133-156	15	
157-182	16	Difficult
183-210	17	
211-240	18	

Some Tips for Applying the SMOG Test

— A sentence is defined as a string of words punctuated with a period(.), an exclamation point (!), or a question mark (?).

— Hyphenated words are considered as one word.

— Numbers that are written out also should be considered, and if in numeric form in the text, they should be pronounced to determine if they are polysyllabic.

— Proper nouns, if polysyllabic, should be counted.

— Abbreviations should be read as unabbreviated to determine if they are polysyllabic.

11. *Comments: Highlight positive areas and problems.*

Note: The Communications Review will not be used for rating products as acceptable or unacceptable until January 1, 1991. However, it is important to complete the Review so that feedback may be provided.

Feedback on Message and Material Review Process

Since OSAP expects the Message and Material Review Process to continually evolve, we encourage you to provide us with your comments and suggestions. Please send them directly to:

Division of Communications Programs
Office for Substance Abuse Prevention
Room 13A54
5600 Fishers Lane
Rockville, MD 20857

Appendix C

Style Sheet on Alcohol And Other Drug Terminology

When communicating about alcohol and other drugs, it is crucial for the terminology of professionals in the field to be both clear and consistent. The Office for Substance Abuse Prevention (OSAP) has developed the following list of terms to assist communicators of verbal and written information and program planners who are responsible for evaluating materials. Please use the terms below for all published materials.

DO NOT USE	USE
Drunk driving	Alcohol-impaired driving (because a person does not have to be drunk to be impaired)
Liquor (to mean any alcoholic beverage)	Beer, wine, and/or distilled spirits, alcoholic beverage
Substance abuse	Alcohol and other drug abuse
Substance use	Alcohol and other drug use
Abuse (when the sentence refers to youth, teens, or children—anyone under 21)	Use (DHHS aim is to prevent use—not abuse—of alcohol and other drugs by youth)
Drug abuse prevention or alcohol abuse prevention	Except when referring to adults, use the phrase, "to prevent alcohol and other drug problems"
Hard or soft drugs	Drugs (because all illicit drugs are harmful)
Recreational use of drugs	Use (because no drug use is recreational)
Responsible use	Use (since there is risk associated with all use)
Accidents when referring to alcohol/drug use and traffic crashes	Crashes (because "accident" suggests the event could not have been avoided)
Mood-altering drugs	Mind-altering (because the term "mood altering" does not reflect the powerful effects alcohol and other drugs can have on one's mind and judgment)

Appendix D

The Regional Alcohol and Drug Awareness Resource (RADAR) Network consists of State clearinghouses, specialized information centers of national organizations, and the Department of Education Regional Training Centers. Each RADAR Network member can offer the public a variety of information services. Check with the representative in your area to find out what services are available.

STATE RADAR CENTERS

Alabama
Crystal Jackson
Clearinghouse Coordinator
Alabama Department of Mental
  Health/Mental Retardation
P.O. Box 3710
200 Interstate Park Drive
Montgomery, AL 36193
205/271-9258

Alaska
Joyce Paulus
Librarian
Alaska Council on Prevention of
  Alcohol and Drug Abuse
7521 Old Seward Highway
Anchorage, AK 99518
907/349-6602

American Samoa
Scott Whitney
Department of Human Resources
Social Services Division
Government of American Samoa
Pago Pago, AS 96799
684/633-2696

Arizona
Allen Brown
Extended Education
Arizona State University
Tempe, AZ 85287-1708
602/965-7046

Arkansas
Patsy Wagner
Clearinghouse Coordinator
Office on Alcohol and Drug Abuse
  Prevention
P.O. Box 1437
400 Donaghey Plaza N.
7th and Main Street
Little Rock, AR 72203-1437
501/682-6653

California
Peggy Blair
Drug Program Analyst
State of California Department of
  Alcohol and Drug Programs
111 Capitol Mall, Room 250
Sacramento, CA 95814-3229
916/324-7234

Colorado
Linda M. Garrett
Resource Department
Colorado Alcohol and Drug Abuse
  Division
4210 East 11th Avenue
Denver, CO 80220
303/331-8201

Connecticut
Judith Bloch
Connecticut Clearinghouse
334 Farmington Avenue
Plainville, CT 06062
203/793-9791

Delaware
Doris A. Bolt
Director of Educational Services
The Resource Center of the YMCA
  of Delaware
11th and Washington Streets
Wilmington, DE 19801
302/571-6975

District of Columbia
Karen Wright
Coordinator of Information and
  Referral
Washington Area Council on
  Alcoholism and Drug Abuse
  (WACADA)
1232 M Street, NW
Washington, DC 20005
202/682-1716

Florida
Cindy Colvin
Florida Alcohol and Drug Abuse
  Association
1286 N. Paul Russell Road
Tallahassee, FL 32301
904/878-6922

Georgia
Marie Albert
Georgia Prevention Resource Center
Division of Mental Health
878 Peachtree Street, NE,
Room 319
Atlanta, GA 30309
404/894-4204

Guam
Barbara Benavente
Supervisor, Prevention Branch
Department of Mental Health and
  Substance Abuse
P.O. Box 9400
Tamuning, Guam 96911
671/646-9261, 9269

Hawaii
Dr. Ken Willinger
Alcohol and Drug Division
State of Hawaii
Department of Health
1270 Queen Emma St., Ste. 706
Honolulu, HI 96813
808/548-4280

Idaho
Richard Baylis/Jack Quast
Health Watch Foundation
1101 W. River, Ste. 270
Boise, ID 83702
208/345-4234 or 800/733-0328

Illinois
Caroline Murphy
Prevention Resource Center Library
901 South 2nd Street
Springfield, IL 62704
217/525-3456

Indiana
Maggie Harter/Jim Pershing
Indiana Prevention Resource
Center for Substance Abuse
840 State Road, 46 Bypass
Room 110
Indiana University
Bloomington, IN 47405
812/855-1237

Iowa
Tressa Youngbear
Director
Iowa Substance Abuse
Information Center
Cedar Rapids Public Library
500 First Street, SE
Cedar Rapids, IA 52401
319/398-5133

Kansas
Judy Donovan
Public Information Officer
Kansas Alcohol and Drug Abuse
Services
Department of Social and Rehab.
Services
300 S.W. Oakley
Topeka, KS 66606
913/296-3925

Kentucky
Diane Shuntich
Director
Drug Information Service for
Kentucky
Division of Substance Abuse
275 East Main Street
Frankfort, KY 40621
502/564-2880

Louisiana
Sanford W. Hawkins, Sr.
Coordinator
Division of Alcohol and Drug Abuse
P.O. Box 3868
Baton Rouge, LA 70821-3868
504/342-9352

Maine
Earle Simpson
Clearinghouse Coordinator
Maine Alcohol and Drug Abuse
Clearinghouse
Office of Alcoholism and Drug
Abuse Prevention
State House Station #11
Augusta, ME 04333
207/289-2781

Maryland
Standola Reynolds
Addictions Program Advisor
Alcohol & Drug Abuse Admin.
Department of Health and Mental
Hygiene
201 West Preston Street, 4th Floor
Baltimore, MD 21201
301/225-6543

Massachusetts
Donna Woods
Director
Massachusetts Information and
Referral Service
675 Massachusetts Avenue
Cambridge, MA 02139
617/445-6999

Michigan
Gail Johnsen
Program Coordinator
Michigan Substance Abuse and
 Traffic Safety Information Center
925 E. Kalamazoo
Lansing, MI 48912
517/482-9902

Minnesota
Mary F. Scheide
Director of Information Services
Minnesota Prevention Resource Center
2829 Verndale Avenue
Anoka, MN 55303
612/427-5310 or 800/233-9513

Mississippi
Esther Rogers
Mississippi Department of Mental
 Health
Division of Alcoholism and Drug Abuse
1101 Robert E. Lee Bldg., 9th Floor
239 N. Lamar Street
Jackson, MS 39207
601/359-1288

Missouri
Randy Smith
Clearinghouse Coordinator
Missouri Division of Alcohol and
 Drug Abuse
1915 Southridge Drive
Jefferson City, MO 65109
314/751-4942

Montana
Nancy Tunnicliff
Department of Institutions,
 Chemical Dependency Bureau
1539 11th Avenue
Helena, MT 59620
406/444-2878

Nebraska
Laurel Erickson
Public Information Director
Alcohol and Drug Information
 Clearinghouse
Alcoholism Council of NE
215 Centennial Mall South,
Room 412
Lincoln, NE 68508
402/474-0930 or 402/474-1992

Nevada
Ruth Lewis
Intervention Specialist
Bureau of Alcohol and Drug Abuse
505 E. King Street, Suite 500
Carson City, NV 89710
702/885-4790

New Hampshire
Mary Dube
Chief of Prevention and Education
New Hampshire Office of Alcohol
 and Drug Abuse Prevention
6 Hazen Drive
Concord, NH 03301
603/271-6100

New Jersey
Mark J. Byrne
Chief, Community Info and
 Education
New Jersey State Department of
 Health
Division of Alcoholism and Drug
 Abuse Control
129 E. Hanover Street
Trenton, NJ 08625
609/292-0729

New Mexico
Courtney Cook
Health and Environment Dept /
  BHSD/Substance Abuse Bureau
1190 St. Francis Drive
Harold Runnles Building,
Room 3350
Santa Fe, NM 87504-0968
505/827-2601

New York
Leslie S. Connor
Public Education Coordinator
NY5 Division of Alcoholism and
  Alcohol Abuse
194 Washington Avenue
Albany, NY 12210
518/473-3460

Judith M. Lukin
Director, Resource Center
Narcotic and Drug Research, Inc.
Resource Center
11 Beach Street, 2nd Floor
New York, NY 10013
212/966-8700, ext. 107

North Carolina
Betty Lane
Executive Director
North Carolina Alcohol/Drug
  Resource Center
G5 1200 Broad Street
Durham, NC 27705
919/286-5118

North Dakota
Michele Edwards
School Prevention Specialist
North Dakota Prevention Resource
  Center
1839 East Capitol Avenue
Bismarck, ND 58501
701/224-3603

Ohio
Sharon L. Tention
Prevention Specialist
Ohio Department of Alcohol and
  Drug Addiction Services
170 North High Street, 3rd Floor
Columbus, OH 43266-0586
614/466-7893

Oklahoma
Jan Hardwick
Oklahoma State Department of
  Mental Health
P.O. Box 53277
Oklahoma City, OK 73152
405/271-8755

Oregon
Sue Ziglinski
Oregon Drug and Alcohol Information
100 North Cook
Portland, OR 97227
800/237-7808 ext. 3673 or
  503/280-3673

Pennsylvania
Gwen Miller
ENCORE
Pennsylvania Dept. of Health
Department of Health Programs
P.O. Box 2773
Harrisburg, PA 17105
717/787-2606 or 787-9761

Puerto Rico
Alma Negron
Department of Anti-Addiction
  Services
414 Barbosa Avenue
Apartado 21414 - Rio Piedras
  Station
Rio Piedras, PR 00928-1414
809/763-3133

Rhode Island
Gillette Hunt
Rhode Island Division of Substance
  Abuse
Louis Pasteur Building
Howard Avenue
Cranston, RI 02920
401/464-2140 or 401/464-2141

South Carolina
Elizabeth Peters
Clearinghouse Director
South Carolina Commission on
  Alcohol and Drug Abuse
The Drug Store Information
  Clearinghouse
3700 Forest Drive, Suite 300
Columbia, SC 29204
803/734-9559

South Dakota
Bob Anderson
700 Governors Drive
Kniet Building
Pierre, SD 57501
605/773-3123

Tennessee
Sharon Crockett
Tennessee Alcohol and Drug
  Association
545 Mainstream Drive, Ste. 404
Nashville, TN 37228
615/244-7066

Texas
Carlene Phillips
Director of Resource Dept.
Texas Commission on Alcohol and
  Drug Abuse Resource Center
1705 Guadalupe
Austin, TX 78701-1214
512/463-5510

Utah
Gary Swensen
120 N. 200 West
4th Floor
Salt Lake City, UT 84103
801/538-3949

Vermont
Patricia Auger
Clearinghouse Manager
Office of Alcohol and Drug Abuse
  Programs
103 South Main Street
Waterbury, VT 05676
802/241-2178

Virgin Islands
Director
Division of Mental Health
  Prevention Unit
c/o Marcia Jameson
Charles Harwood Hospital
  Complex, Richmond
St. Croix, VI 00820
809/773-8443

Virginia
Darien Fisher Duke
Virginia Department of MH/MR/SA
109 Governor Street
Richmond, VA 23219
804/786-3909

Washington
Mary Goehring
Clearinghouse Coordinator
Washington State Substance
  Abuse Coalition (WSSAC)
14700 Main Street
Bellevue, WA 98007
206/747-9111

West Virginia
Shirley A. Smith
Field Consultant
West Virginia Library
  Commission
Cultural Center
Charleston, WV 25305
304/348-2041

Wisconsin
Douglas White
Associate Director
Wisconsin Clearinghouse
315 N. Henry Street
Madison, WI 53703
608/263-2797, 608/263-6886

Wyoming
Sue Rardin
WY CARE Program
P.O. Box 3425
University of Wyoming
Laramie, WY 82071
307/766-4119

DEPARTMENT OF EDUCATION REGIONAL TRAINING CENTERS

The regional training centers provide training assistance and expertise to local schools to prevent and reduce alcohol and other drug use by students.

Georgia
Margaret Bradford
Library/Information Specialist
Southeast Regional Center for Drug-
  Free Schools and Communities
50 Hurt Plaza
210 Hurt Building
Atlanta, GA 30303
404/688-9227

Illinois
Mickey Finn
Midwest Regional Center for Drug-
  Free Schools and Communities
2001 N. Clybourn, Room 302
Chicago, IL 60614
312/883-8888

New York
Karen Means
Director
Evaluation and Dissemination
Northeast Regional Center for Drug-
  Free Schools and Communities
12 Overtone Avenue
Sayville, NY 11782
516/589-7022

Oklahoma
Margretta Bartlett
Southwest Regional Center for Drug-
  Free Schools and Communities
University of Oklahoma
555 Constitution Avenue, Room 138
Norman, OK 73037
405/325-1454

Oregon
Kathy Lowe
Western Center for Drug-Free
  Schools and Communities
Northwest Regional Educational Lab
101 SW Main Street, Suite 500
Portland, OR 97204
503/275-9500

SPECIALTY CENTERS

These organizations offer a variety of information services. They also serve both national and international audiences.

California

Christina Miller
Librarian
Prevention Research Center Library
2532 Durant Avenue
Berkeley, CA 94704
415/468-1111

Nancy Kaihatsu/Tom Colhurst
Program on Alcohol and Drug
  Issues
University of California, San Diego
UCSD Extension, X-001
La Jolla, CA 92093-0176
619/534-6331

Elva Yanez
Associate Director
Resource Center
Marin Institute for the Prevention
  of Alcohol and Other Drug Problems
24 Belvedere Street
San Rafael, CA 94901
415/456-5692

Holly Lenz
Executive Assistant
National Association for Children
  of Alcoholics (NACoA)
31582 Coast Highway, Suite B
South Laguna, CA 92677
714/499-3889

Andrea L. Mitchell, M.L.S.
Librarian/Information Specialist
Alcohol Research Group
Medical Research Institute of San
  Francisco at Pacific Presbyterian
  Medical Center
1816 Scenic Avenue
Berkeley, CA 94709
415/642-5208

Ford S. Hatamiya
Program Coordinator
Multicultural Training Resource
  Center
1540 Market Street, Suite 320
San Francisco, CA 94102
415/861-2142

Canada

Margy Chan
Manager, Library Services
Addiction Research Foundation
  Library
33 Russell Street
Toronto, Ontario
Canada M5S2S1
416/595-6144
FAX: 416/595-5017

District of Columbia

Paul Cardenas, MSW
Project Director, National Alcohol
  and Diabetes Programs
National Coalition of Hispanic
  Health and Human Services
  Organizations
1030 15th Street, NW, Suite 1053
Washington, DC 20005
202/371-2100

Ruth Marie Conolly
Coordinator
Interamerican Documentation Center
Interamerican Drug Information
  System
OAS/CICAD
1889 F Street, 8th Floor, NW
Washington, DC 20006
202/458-3809

Georgia
Paula Kemp
National Drug Information Center
  of Families in Action
2296 Henderson Mill Road
Suite 204
Atlanta, GA 30345
404/934-6364

Beverly E. Allen
Director
Multi-Media Center
Morehouse School of Medicine
720 Westview Drive, SW
Atlanta, GA 30310-1495
(404) 752-1530

Maryland
Leonore Burts
Reference Supervisor
National AIDS Information
  Clearinghouse
P.O. Box 6003
Rockville, MD 20850
301/762-5111

Glen Holley
Clearinghouse on Drugs and Crime
1600 Research Boulevard
Rockville, MD 20850
301/251-5531

Minnesota
David Grant
Institute on Black Chemical Abuse
  Resource Center
2616 Nicollet Avenue, South
Minneapolis, MN 55407
612/871-7878

New Hampshire
Jean Kinney
Project CORK
Dartmouth University
9 Maynard Street
Hanover, NH 03756
603/646-7540

New Jersey
Cathy Weglarz
Center of Alcohol Studies
Rutgers University
Smithers Hall, Busch Campus
Piscataway, NJ 08855-0969
201/932-4443

New York
Jose Luis Rodriguez
Hispanic Communication and
  Telecommunication Network
449 Broadway, 3rd Floor
New York, NY 10013
212/966-5660
FAX: 212/966-5725

Jeff Hon
National Council on Alcoholism, Inc.
12 W. 21st Street
New York, NY 10010
212/206-6770

Pennsylvania
Teresa Stayduhar
Acting Director
Chemical People Institute
1615 Penn Avenue
Pittsburgh, PA 15222
412/391-0900

Puerto Rico
Jose Rafael Oquendo
Office of the Governor
La Fortaleza, Box 82
San Juan, PR 00901
809/721-5145 or 809/725-6981

Virginia
Richard Bickerton
Manager, ALMACA EAP
  Clearinghouse
Association of Employee Assistance
  Professionals
4601 North Fairfax Drive, Suite 1001
Arlington, VA 22203
703/522-6272

Paula Carney
Head, WIC, Prog. Devt. Section,
Supplemental Food Program
  Division
3101 Park Center Drive
Room 1017
Alexandria, VA 22302
703/756-3730

Washington
Nancy Sutherland
Librarian
Alcoholism and Drug Abuse
  Institute Library
3937 15th Avenue, NE, NL.15
Seattle, WA 98105
206/543-0937

INTERNATIONAL RADAR CENTERS

E. Alberto Lestelle
Secretario De Estado
Secretaria De Programacion Y
  Coordinacion
Para La Prevencion De La
  Drogadiccion Y
La Lucha Contra El Narcotrafico
25 De Mayo
459-Sexto Pisco (C.P. 10020)
Buenos Aires, Argentina
312-47-96 or 312-04-86

Dr. Paz G. Ramos
ASEAN Training Center for
  Preventive Drug Education
University of the Philippines
  Diliman
Quezon City, Philippines

Tania Israel De Andrade Lima
  Calazans
Comissao De Toxicologia
Secretaria De Educacao De
  Pernambuco
Rua Marques do Recife
154 Sexto Andar
Recife, PE
Brazil

Felix Geraldo Da Costa
Rua D, c/9 - Castelinho -Parque
Dez, 69.055 Manaus
Amazonas, Brazil

Amadeu Roselli Cruz
Rua Oscar Trompowski
721 Apt. 106 Gutierrez
30430 Belo Horizonte
Minas Gerais, Brazil

Evaristo Debiasi
Rua Padre Roma
110 Caixa Postal 71
88001 Florianopolis
SC, Brazil

Joao Pena Nunes
Rua Uruguai, 255
Tijuca
Rio de Janeiro, RJ
Brazil

Jose Roberto Rossiter Detorres
Av. Sao Jose, 636
12200 Sao Jose Dos Campos
Sao Paulo, Brazil

Hema Weerasinghe
Drug Advisor
The Colombo Plan Countries
The Colombo Plan Bureau
12 Melbourne Avenue,
Colombo 4
P.O. Box 596
Colombo, Sri Lanka

Saifuddin Khan
Programme Officer
c/o Pakistan Participant Training
   Program, Michael Weider
1255 23rd Street, NW, #400
Washington, DC 20037
202/467-8700

Mr. Ismail Haji Baker
Assistant Director, Preventive
   Drug Information Program
   Anti-Narcotics Task Force,
   National Security Council
Block K1, Government Office Complex
Jalan Duta, 50502
Kuala Lumpur, Malaysia

Mr. Yu Am Ping
Director, Psyops Division
Ministry of Information
Angkasapuri, 50610
Kuala Lumpur, Malaysia

Sergio Migliorata
President
Foro Juvenil
Maldonado 1260
Montevideo, Uruguay

P. Vijay Lutchmun
Secretary/Manager
Trust Fund for the Treatment and
   Rehabilitation of Drug Addicts
5th Floor, Unicorn House
5 Royal Street
Port Louis, Mauritius

Jose Matias Pereira
Vice President and Executive
   Secretary
Federal Narcotics Council (CONFEN)
Ministerio Da Justica
3 Andar
Sala 310
7000 Brasilia
DF, Brazil

Dr. Alberto Furtado Rahde
President, Rio Grande Do Sul
   State Narcotics Council
Rua Riachuelo
677 - Apto. 201
90010 Porto Alegre - RS
Brazil

Jose Ovidio Romeiro Neto
Special Assistance to the President
Federal Narcotics Council
Rua Visconde De Inhauma 58
Sala 907-20091
Rio de Janeiro, RJ Brazil

Dr. Joao Jose Candido Da Silva
Special Assistant Ministry of Health
Assessoria Especial
Ministerio Da Saude 5 Andar
Sala 310
70000 Brasilia
DF, Brazil

Dr. Ena K. Campbell
Council Member
(Anthropologist/Epidemiologist)
National Council on Drug Abuse
17 Dominica Drive
Kingston 5
Jamaica, West Indies
809/926-9003

Ivan D. Montoya
Psychiatrist
Hospital St. Vicente De Paul
Calle 50 No. 71-80, Apt. 515
Medellin, Colombia
574/230-9477

Sarita Kramer
Commission on Drug Abuse
  Prevention Programs
Ministerio De La
Familia/Family Ministry
Parque Central Torre Oesto
Piso 41
Caracas, Venezuela

Dr. Francisco Puentes
Professor of Clinical Toxicology-UIS
Centro De Asesoramiento
  Toxicologio
Carrera 33 #51-37 Cons. 203
01157 73 74783

Francisco Jimenez
Jete Departamento De Rehabilitacion
Instituto Sobre Alcoholismo Y
  Farmacodependencis
400 MTS Sur Boncopopular-
San Pedro de Montesde Oca
San Jose, Costa Rica

Roderick Sanatan
Head, Communications Unit
Caribbean Community
  Secretariat
Bank of Guyana Building
P.O. Box 10827
Georgetown, Guyana
02-69280/9, 57758

Sherchan Jyoti
Hony, Treasurer
Drug Abuse Prevention Association
  Nepal
G.P.O. Box 4345
Kathmandu, Nepal

Dr. A. A. Quorehsi
Founder and Executive Director
Mukti
Drug Addicts Cure and Care Centre
126/C New Eskaton Road
Dhaka, Bangladesh

Dr. En Psic. Arturo Ortiz C.
Coordinator, Del Centro De
  Informacion Y Documentacion En
  Farmacodependencia Instituto
  Mexicano De Psiquiatria
Calzada Mexico Xochimilco
101 Mexico 22

Pierre Denize
President
Association pour la Prevention
  de l'Alcoolisme et autres
  Accoutumances Chimiques
45 Rue Cheriez
P.O. Box 2515
Port-au-Prince, Haiti

Elizabeth Mubbale
Government Chemist (Food &
  Drugs Div.)
Government Analytical Laboratories
P.O. Box 2174
Kampala, Uganda (East Africa)
543303/4 Kampala

Teresa Salvador
Idea - Prevention
Apertado de Correos 7113
28080, Madrid, Spain
34-1/435-8588 or
34-1/275-9831

Dr. Saul Bogea Rodrigues Neto
Nucleo de Estudos e Pesquisas
em Atenaco ao Uso de Drogas
  NEPAD, Rua Fonseca
Telles, 121, 4 Andar
Sao Cristovao
20940 Rio de Janeiro, RJ
Brazil

Ministry of Health
Attention: Mary Keeber
Public Affairs Specialist
U.S. Embassy
7415 19th Street, NW, Suite H
Miami, FL 33126
(809) 322-4268

Edwin A. Whiteside
Principal Medical Officer
Mental Health Programme
Department of Health
Macarthy Trust Building,
  Lambton Quay
P.O. Box 5013
Wellington, New Zealand
(04) 727-627, extn. 8814

Marietta G. Bernaje
Chief, Program
  Planning/Impl./Eval. Div.
  PIHES
Department of Health
San Lazaro Compound
Rizai Avenue, Sta. Cruz
Manila, Philippines
711/63-05, 711-62-45

Tay Bian How
Anti Dadah Task Force
National Security Council
Prime Minister's Department
6th Floor, Blok F (North)
Pusat Bandar Damansara
50502 Kuala Lumpur,
Malaysia

Satoshi Takagi, M.D.
Deputy Director
Kurihama National Hospital
2769, Nobi, Yokosuka
Kanagawa, Japan
(0468) 48-1550

Senior Librarian
Alcohol and Drug Foundation
Australia
P.O. Box 269
Woden A.C.T. 2606
Australia

What is the RADAR Network?

The Office for Substance Abuse Prevention (OSAP) of the U.S. Department of Health and Human Services established the RADAR (Regional Alcohol and Drug Awareness Resource) Network to take the latest information on how to fight alcohol and other drug problems to those who needed it most " the State and community level program planners, school personnel, law enforcement officials, health professionals, treatment providers, and others on the battle front.

Originally, all of these people had to go to OSAP's National Clearinghouse for Alcohol and Drug Information (NCADI), the Federal headquarters for alcohol and other drug information and prevention services. But they needed information centers closer to home, staffed by people who understood the unique aspects of their State and community. In response to this need, OSAP, in partnership with the State Governments, established RADAR Network Centers in each of the States.

Coordinated by OSAP through NCADI, the RADAR Network Centers are part of the national resource system that responds to current community needs and anticipates future needs. RADAR Network Centers bring to communities everywhere resource lists of the latest research results, popular press and scholarly journal articles, videotapes, prevention curriculums, print materials, and prevention programs. Centers also provide customized packages of materials for use in special settings including the home, school, worksite, recreation center, and religious and social settings.

How can a RADAR Network Center help a community program?

Each RADAR Network Center has its own unique services and resources that are available to anyone in the community. Check with the Center nearest you to learn about their specific services. Most RADAR Network Centers are able to provide services such as

- Helping community program planners find the most accurate and up-to-date information about alcohol and other drug problems and effective materials and programs that can be adapted for their areas

- Providing attention-getting posters, booklets, videotapes, and other materials with prevention and intervention messages for youth, parents, and many other target audiences

- Promoting and supporting outreach efforts to groups at high risk for alcohol and other drug-related problems (e.g., children of alcoholics and other drug abusers, school dropouts, pregnant teenagers, low-income communities, juvenile delinquents, disabled groups, suicidal teenagers, and groups with mental health problems)

- Providing helpful referrals to national and local resources for prevention and intervention materials and services that are unavailable from the Center

- Maintaining a large collection of the most recent alcohol and drug resources (e.g., reference and program materials) for use on site

- Responding to questions about prevention and intervention by mail or telephone and assisting visitors by providing hands-on assistance

- Helping community program planners design and implement exciting, comprehensive prevention programs tailored to meet the special needs of their communities. This includes assistance with the development of materials and services that are culturally sensitive and age-appropriate.

What other resources are in the Network?

In addition to the prevention services available from State RADAR Network Centers, you can also strengthen your prevention efforts with the help of Specialty RADAR Network Centers. These Centers are national organizations and Federal agencies that deal with alcohol and other drug issues. For example, the National Drug Information Center, operated by Families in Action, might help a caller track how the media are covering a specific drug-related issue. Also, you might contact the Department of Education's Regional Training Centers. These Regional Training Centers are not set up as clearinghouses, but they can provide training assistance and expertise to local schools to prevent or stop alcohol and other drug use by students.

International RADAR Network Centers also have been set up. Most of them have visited NCADI and have requested help in setting up similar clearinghouse activities. These contacts represent the key groups or organizations in their country that are addressing the problems associated with alcohol and other drug use and abuse. They are very interested in information exchange with the United States.

What is the difference between a full and associate member?

The RADAR Network consists of several hundred full and associate members. There are over 81 full RADAR Network members and more than 300 associate members. OSAP approves applications for full and associate membership.

These are the two levels of membership in the RADAR Network. Full RADAR Network members include the RADAR Network Centers designated by State Governments, information centers operated by national organizations, the

Department of Education's Regional Training Centers, and international organizations. Associate RADAR Network members are organizations that conduct information and referral services at the community level. Associate members also assist and support the full RADAR Network Centers in their communications activities.

What are the responsibilities of a State RADAR Network Center?

State RADAR Network Centers have to meet criteria set by OSAP in order to quality for full membership in the Network. There is a diversity in the range of services currently offered by Centers. However, all Centers either meet, or are working to meet, the minimum criteria set by OSAP. The criteria that State Centers must meet include

- Library Services: Network members will maintain a collection of alcohol and other drug resources that can be used on site and can be shared with outside organizations. In addition, each Center keeps at least one copy of federally produced alcohol and other drug resource materials.

- Information and Referral: Network members will respond to telephone and mail inquiries, provide referrals to relevant organizations, develop a working relationship with organizations belonging to the Substance Abuse Librarians and Information Specialists (SALIS) group, provide quarterly feedback to OSAP about Network services, and monitor and report to OSAP on the types of information requests the Center receives.

- Outreach: Network members will work with local organizations that serve youth at high risk for alcohol and other drug use problems, work with Associate RADAR Network members on communications activities, and submit short descriptions of innovative program activities for publication in OSAP's bimonthly news service, Prevention Pipeline.

- Promotional Activities: Network members will develop a one-page fact sheet to promote the Center's resources and services.

- Equipment: Network members will have a telephone and mailing address for requesters to contact them for information, a display area for materials, and a reading room.

- Materials: Network members will use the OSAP Media and Materials Review Process to assess materials currently being sent out by their Center and to assess those materials that are under consideration for distribution.

- Management Operations and Evaluation: Network members will attend a minimum of 40 hours of pre-approved training each year, evaluate the effectiveness of their Center's communications efforts to reach minority, and other high-risk audiences, and document how the Center is working with multicultural programs.

- Pretesting Services: Network members will assist OSAP in conducting focus group testing of new materials developed either locally and at the State and Federal levels.

- Public education programs and campaigns: Network members will promote and implement national initiatives or federally sponsored efforts such as the Be Smart! Stay Smart! Don't Start!" program.

What Federal support is given to these RADAR Network Centers?

OSAP provides help to each full RADAR Network Center in the following areas:

- Involves Centers in a variety of activities such as media campaigns, national initiatives, planning, and strategy selection for new resources or activities;

- Features news items from Centers in various publications, promotes the RADAR Network nationally, and assists members in developing their own marketing materials;

- Sends out the NCADI Communique "a monthly bulletin targeted to RADAR Network members that describes new products and initiatives;

- Provides free-of-charge newsletters, magazines, and bulletins;

- Supplies public education campaign materials to members;

- Expedites the processing time for data base searches;

- Provides negatives or camera ready copy of new materials;

- Provides overnight delivery of late-breaking news or new resources;

- Conducts regional and national training events, and involves Centers in the development of these events;

- Provides funding for attendance at national RADAR Network meetings;

- Conducts site visits to selected full RADAR Network Centers and a limited number of visits to associate members;

- Coordinates technical assistance efforts among members;

- Assists in locating resources; and

- Provides training and consultation on communications-related topics.

The Office for Substance Abuse Prevention—A Special Mission

Created by the Anti-Drug Abuse Act of 1986, the Office for Substance Abuse Prevention helps communities provide a protective environment for young people to prevent their use of alcohol and other drugs. OSAP has formed partnerships with the research community, parent groups, policy makers, practitioners, State and community leaders, educators, law enforcement officials, volunteers, and others to enhance opportunities for comprehensive approaches to prevention and ready intervention. These partnerships are important to the success of OSAP's initiatives.

An OSAP priority is helping local, State, and regional organizations in their prevention of alcohol and other drug problems by building upon existing programs and expanding prevention resources. Organizations that are members of the RADAR Network support OSAP by keeping the agency on the pulse of community-level needs so that communications activities can be appropriately tailored to meet those needs.

For more information about the RADAR Network, contact:

Information Services
National Clearinghouse for Alcohol and Drug Information
P.O. Box 2345
Rockville, MD 20852
(301) 468-2600

Appendix E

Intermediary Organizations

Appendix E is a list of potential intermediary organizations—groups concerned with alcohol and other drugs, families and children, and specific audiences—that may be interested in alcohol and other drug problem prevention programs. Although extensive, this list is by no means exhaustive. The organizations included are a *sample* of the many local, regional, and national organizations that could be included in alcohol and other drug programs. The listing is divided into the following sections:

- Organizations focusing primarily on alcohol and other drugs
- Organizations concerned with families and children
- Potential intermediaries for specific audiences
  - African Americans/Blacks
  - Hispanics/Latinos
  - Parents in transitional situations
  - Health professionals.

Organizations Focusing Primarily on Alcohol and Other Drugs*

*Organizations listed here only as example; inclusion does not imply endorsement by OSAP.

ACTION Drug Alliance
Room M-513
806 Connecticut Avenue, NW
Washington, DC 20525
(202) 634-9759

Alateen, Al-Anon Family Group
  Headquarters, Inc.
P.O. Box 862, Midtown Station
New York, NY 10018-0862
(800) 356-9996

Alcohol and Drug Problems
  Association of North America
444 N. Capitol Street, NW, Suite 181
Washington, DC 20001
(202) 737-4340

Alcoholics Anonymous
P.O. Box 459
Grand Central Station
New York, NY 10163
(212) 686-1100

Al-Anon Family Group
  Headquarters
1372 Broadway
New York, NY 10018
(212) 302-7240

American Council for Drug
  Education
204 Monroe Street, Suite 110
Rockville, MD 20850
(301) 294-0600

Association of Medical Education
  and Research in Substance Abuse
c/o David C. Lewis, M.D.
Center for Alcohol and Addiction
  Studies
Brown University
Providence, RI 02912
(401) 863-1102

Association of the Halfway House
Alcoholism Programs of North
  America
786 E. Seventh Street
St. Paul, MN 55106
(612) 771-0933

The Chemical People
WQED
4802 Fifth Avenue
Pittsburgh, PA 15213
(412) 622-1491

Children of Alcoholics Foundation
P.O. Box 4185, Department N.A.
Grand Central Station
New York, NY 10163
(212) 351-2680

Committees of Correspondence
57 Conant Street
Room 113
Danvers, MA 01923
(617) 774-5626

Cottage Program International
736 South 500 East
Salt Lake City, UT 84102
(801) 532-6185

Elks Drug Awareness Program
P.O. Box 310
Ashland, OK 97520
(503) 482-3193

Employee Assistance Professional
  Association (formerly ALMACA)
1800 N. Kent Street, Suite 907
Arlington, VA 22209
(703) 522-6272

Families Anonymous
14553 Delano Street, #316
Van Nuys, CA 91411
(818) 989-7841

Families in Action
National Drug Information Center
2296 Henderson Mill Road, Suite 204
Atlanta, GA 30045
(404) 934-6364

Hazelden Foundation
15245 Pleasant Valley Road
Center City, MN 55012
(612) 257-4010

Impaired Physician Program
1669 Phoenix Parkway, # 102
Atlanta, GA 30349
(800) 445-4232

Institute of Alcoholism and Drug
  Dependency
Andrews University
Berrien Springs, MI 49104
(616) 471-3558

Institute on Black Chemical Abuse
2614 Nicollet Avenue
Minneapolis, MN 55408
(612) 871-7878

International Commission for the
  Prevention of Alcoholism and
  Drug Dependency
6840 Eastern Avenue, NW
Washington, DC 20012
(202) 722-6729

Just Say No Clubs
1777 N. California Boulevard
Walnut Creek, CA 94596
(800) 258-2766

Mothers Against Drunk Driving
  (MADD)
669 Airport Freeway, Suite 310
Hurst, TX 76053
(817) 268-6233

Multi-Cultural Substance Abuse
  Prevention Project
Karen Johnson Associates
1110 Bonifant Street, Suite 300
Silver Spring, MD 20910
(301) 589-4555/(800) 822-0047

Narcotics Anonymous
P.O. Box 9999
Van Nuys, CA 91409
(818) 780-3951

Narcotics Education, Inc.
6830 Laurel Street, NW
Washington, DC 20012
(202) 722-6740

National Association of Alcoholism
  and Drug Abuse Counselors, Inc.
51 South George Mason Drive
Arlington, VA 22204
(703) 920-4644

National Association of Alcoholism
  Treatment Programs
2082 Michelson Drive
Irvine, CA 92715
(714)476-8204

National Asian Pacific American
  Families Against Substance Abuse
6303 Friendship Court
Bethesda, MD 20817
(301) 530-0945

National Association for Children
  of Alcoholics
31582 Coast Highway, Suite B
South Laguna, CA 92677
(714) 499-3889

National Association for Native
  American Children of Alcoholics
c/o Seattle Indian Health Board
P.O. Box 3364
Seattle, WA 98114
(206) 324-9360

National Association of Alcoholism
  Treatment Programs
2082 Michelson Drive, Suite 101
Irvine, CA 92715
(714) 476-8204

National Association of Lesbian/
  Gay Alcoholism Professionals
204 W. 20th Street
New York, NY 10011
(617) 738-5146

National Association of State
  Alcohol and Drug Abuse Directors
444 N. Capitol Street, NW,
Suite 530
Washington, DC 20001
(202) 783-6868

National Black Alcoholism Council, Inc.
417 S. Dearborn Street, Suite 100
Chicago, IL 60605
(312) 663-5780

National Clearinghouse for Alcohol
  and Drug Information
P.O. Box 2345
Rockville, MD 20852
(301) 468-2600

National Clergy Council on
Alcoholism and Related Drug
Problems
1200 Varbyn Street, NE
Washington, DC 20017
(202) 832-3811

National Council on Alcoholism
12 W. 21st Street
New York, NY 10010
(212) 206-6770/(800) NCA-CALL

National Episcopal Coalition on
Alcohol and Drugs
P.O. Box 10184
Washington, DC 20018
(202) 543-1166

National Federation of Parents for
Drug-Free Youth
Communication Center
1423 N. Jefferson
Springfield, MO 65802
(417) 836-3703

National Hispanic Families
Against Drug Abuse
1511 K Street, NW, Suite 1026
Washington, DC 20005
(202) 393-5136

National Organization of Student
Assistance Programs and
Professionals
250 Arapahoe, Suite 301
Boulder, CO 80302
(303) 449-8077

National Parent's Resource
Institute for Drug Education
100 Edgewood Avenue, Suite 1216
Atlanta, GA 30303
(800) 241-7946

National Prevention Network
444 N. Capitol Street, NW,
Suite 530
Washington, DC 20001
(202) 783-6868

Phoenix House Foundation
164 W. 74th Street
New York, NY 10023
(212) 595-5810

Potsmokers Anonymous
316 E. Third Street
New York, NY 10009
(212) 254-1777

Research Society on Alcoholism, Inc.
4314 Medical Parkway, Suite 300
Austin, TX 78756
(512) 454-0022

Substance Abuse Librarians and
Information Specialists (SALIS)
c/o Project CORK
Resource Center
Dartmouth Medical School
Hanover, NH 03756
(603) 646-7540

TARGET—Helping Students Cope
with Alcohol and Drugs
11724 Plaza Circle
Kansas City, MO 64195
(816) 891-7442

The Other Victims of Alcoholism
P.O. Box 921, Radio City Station
New York, NY 10101
(212) 247-8087

Therapeutic Communities of America
131 Wayland Avenue
Providence, RI 02906
(401) 331-4250

TOUGHLOVE International
P.O. Box 1069
Doylestown, PA 18901
(215) 348-7090

Women for Sobriety
109 W. Broad Street
P.O. Box 618
Quakertown, PA 18951
(215) 536-8026

Organizations Concerned With Families and Children[1]

[1]Organizations are listed here only as examples; inclusion does not imply endorsement by OSAP.

Adoption Triangle Ministries
Box 1860
Cape Coral, FL 33910
(813) 542-1342

Allied Youth International
1901 Fort Myer Drive, Suite 1011
Arlington, VA 22209

American Association for Marriage
  and Family Therapy
1717 K Street, NW, Suite 407
Washington, DC 20036
(202) 429-1825

American Association for
  Counseling and Development
5999 Stevenson Avenue
Alexandria, VA 22304
(703) 823-9800

American Association for
  Protecting Children
c/o American Humane Association
9725 E. Hampton Avenue
Denver, CO 80231
(303) 695-0811

American Association for
  Suicidology
2459 South Ash
Denver, CO 80222
(303) 692-0985

American Home Economics
  Association
2010 Massachusetts Avenue, NW
Washington, DC 20036
(202) 862-8300

American Justice Institute
705 Merchant Street
Sacramento, CA 95814
(916) 442-0707

American Values: The Community
  Action Network
211 E. 43rd Street, Suite 1400
New York, NY 10017
(212) 818-1360

Associates for Troubled Children
19730 Ventura Boulevard, Suite 1A
Woodland Hills, CA 91364
(818) 713-0086

Association for Children and Adults
  with Learning Disabilities
4156 Library Road
Pittsburgh, PA 15234
(412) 341-1515

Association of Community
  Organizations for Reform Now
401 Howard Avenue
New Orleans, LA 70130
(504) 523-1691

Better Boys Foundation
407 S. Dearborn, Suite 1725
Chicago, IL 60605
(312) 427-4434

Big Brothers/Big Sisters of America
230 N. 13th Street
Philadelphia, PA 19107
(215) 567-7000

Boys Clubs of America National
   Prevention Program
771 First Avenue
New York, NY 10017
(212) 351-5900

Boys Scouts of America
1325 Walnut Hill Lane
Irving, TX 75038
(214) 580-2000

Breakthrough Foundation
25 Van Ness Avenue, Suite 320
San Francisco, CA 94102
(415) 863-4141

Call for Action
575 Lexington Avenue, 7th Floor
New York, NY 10022
(212) 355-5965

Catholic Big Brothers
1011 First Avenue
New York, NY 10022
(212) 371-1000

Center for Organizational and
   Community Development
School of Education, Room 225
University of Massachusetts
Amherst, MA 01003
(413) 545-2038

Center for the Improvement of
   Child Caring
11331 Ventura Boulevard, Suite 103
Studio City, CA 91604
(818) 980-0903

Center on Human Policy
724 Comstock Avenue
Syracuse, NY 13244
(315) 443-3851

Child Welfare League of America
440 First Street, NW
Washington, DC 20001
(202) 638-2952

Childhelp U.S.A., Inc.
6463 Independence Avenue
Woodland Hills, CA 91370
(818) 347-7280

Children of the Night
1800 N. Highland Avenue, #128
Hollywood, CA 90028
(213) 461-3160

Children's Defense Fund
122 C Street, NW, Suite 400
Washington, DC 20001
(202) 628-8787

Children's Rights Group
693 Mission Street
San Francisco, CA 94105
(415) 495-7283

Contact Center
P.O. Box 81826
Lincoln, NE 68501
(402) 464-0602

Council for Exceptional Children
1920 Association Drive
Reston, VA 22091
(703) 620-3660

Council for Learning Disabilities
P.O. Box 40303
Overland Park, KS 66204
(913) 492-3840

Department of Education
400 Maryland Avenue
Washington, DC 20202
(202) 732-4576

Family Service Association of
  America
11700 West Lake Park Drive
Milwaukee, WI 53224
(414) 359-2111

Foster Grandparent's Program
2500 Martin Luther King Ave., S.E.
Washington, DC 20032
(202) 678-4215

Foundation for Children with
  Learning Disabilities
99 Park Avenue, 6th Floor
New York, NY 10016
(212) 687-7211

Girl Scouts of the U.S.A.
830 Third Avenue and 51st Street
New York, NY 10022
(212) 940-7500

Information Center for Individuals
  with Disabilities
Fort Point Place
27-43 Wormwood Street
Boston, MA 02210-1606
(617) 727-5540

Institute for Social Justice
1024 Elysian Fields
New Orleans, LA 70117
(504) 943-5954

Institute for the Community as
  Extended Family
P.O. Box 952
San Jose, CA 95108
(408) 280-5055

International Society for Prevention
  of Child Abuse and Neglect
1205 Oneida Street
Denver, CO 80220
(303) 321-3963

Interreligious Foundation for
  Community Organization
402 W. 145th Street, 3rd Floor
New York, NY 10031
(212) 926-5757

Jack and Jill of America
1065 Gordon Street, SW
Atlanta, GA 30310
(404) 753-8471

The Kaiser Family Foundation
Quadras
2400 Sand Hill Road
Menlo Park, CA 94025
(415) 329-1000

National Alliance for the Prevention
  and Treatment of Child Abuse
c/o New York Founding Hospital
590 6th Avenue
New York, NY 10011
(212) 633-9300

National Assembly of National
  Voluntary and Social Welfare
  Organizations
1319 F Street, NW, Suite 601
Washington, DC 20005
(202) 347-2080

National Association for Human
  Development
1620 I Street, NW
Washington, DC 20006
(202) 331-1737

National Association for the
  Education of Young Children
1834 Connecticut Avenue, NW
Washington, DC 20009
(202) 232-8777

National Association of Neighborhoods
1651 Fuller, NW
Washington, DC 20009
(202) 332-7766

National Association of Public
  Child Welfare Administrators
c/o American Public Welfare
810 1st Street, NE, Suite 500
Washington, DC 20002-4205
(202) 682-0106

National Association of the
  Physically Handicapped
2617 Everett Road
Peninsula, OH 44264
(614) 852-1664

National Association of Secondary
  School Principals
1904 Association Drive
Reston, VA 22091
(703) 860-0200

National Association of Social Workers
7891 Eastern Avenue
Silver Spring, MD 20910
(301) 565-0333

National Association of Town Watch
7 Wynnewood Road, Suite 215
Wynnewood, PA 19096
(215) 649-7055

National Center for Urban Ethnic
  Affairs
P.O. Box 33279
Washington, DC 20033
(202) 232-3600

National Committee for Prevention
  of Child Abuse
332 S. Michigan Avenue, Suite 950
Chicago, IL 60604
(312) 633-3520

National Committee on Youth
Suicide Prevention
825 Washington
Norwood, MA 02062-3441
(617) 769-5686

National Community Action
  Foundation
2100 M Street, NW, Suite 604A
Washington, DC 20037
(202) 775-0223

National Council on Crime and
  Delinquency
77 Maiden Lane, 4th Floor
San Francisco, CA 94180
(415) 956-5651

National Council on Family Relations
1910 W. County Road B, Suite 147
St. Paul, MN 55113
(612) 633-6933

National Crime Prevention Council
733 15th Street, NW, Suite 540
Washington, DC 20005
(202) 393-7141

National Easter Seal Society
70 East Lake Street
Chicago, IL 60601
(312) 726-6200

National Exchange Club Foundation
  for the Prevention of Child Abuse
3050 Central Avenue
Toledo, OH 43606
(419) 535-3232

National Governors' Association
Hall of States
444 N. Capitol
Washington, DC 20001
(202) 624-5300

National Information Center for
 Handicapped Children and Youth
P.O. Box 1492
Washington, DC 20013
(703) 893-6061

National Mental Health Association
1021 Prince Street
Alexandria, VA 22314
(703) 684-7722

National Network of Runaway and
 Youth Services
905 Sixth Street, SW
Washington, DC 20024
(202) 682-4114

National Organization of Adolescent
 Pregnancy and Parenting
P.O. Box 2365
Reston, VA 22090
(703) 435-3948

North American Council on
 Adoptable Children
P.O. Box 14808
Minneapolis, MN 55414
(612) 333-7692

Odyssey Institute Corporation
817 Fairfield Avenue
Bridgeport, CT 06604
(203) 334-3488

Orphan Foundation of America
P.O. Box 14261
Washington, DC 20044
(202) 861-0762

Parents Anonymous
6733 S. Sepulveda, Suite 270
Los Angeles, CA 90045
(213) 410-9732

Parents Without Partners
8807 Colesville Road
Silver Spring, MD 20910
(301) 588-9354

Perceptions, Inc.
P.O. Box 142
Millburn, NJ 07041
(201) 376-3766

Planned Parenthood Federation of
 America
810 Seventh Avenue
New York, NY 10019
(212) 541-7800

Project Volunteer
880 81st Avenue
Oakland, CA 94621
(415) 562-0290

Save the Children Federation
54 Wilton Road
Westport, CT 06880
(203) 226-7271

Southern Association of Children
 Under Six
P.O. Box 5403, Brady Station
Little Rock, AR 72215
(501) 663-0353

Southern Mutual Help Association
P.O. Box 850
Jeanerette, LA 70538
(318) 367-3277

SPARK Program
40 Irving Place, Room 94
New York, NY 10003
(212) 477-5442

Time Out To Enjoy
715 Lake Street, #100
Oak Park, IL 60301
(312) 383-9017

U.S. Conference of Mayors
1620 I Street, NW
Washington, DC 20006
(202) 293-7330

Women in Crisis, Inc.
133 West 21st Street
New York, NY 10011

(212) 242-4880

The Youth Project
2335 18th Street, NW
Washington, DC 20009
(202) 483-0030

Youth Suicide National Center
1811 Trousdale Drive
Burlingame, CA 94010
(415) 877-5605

Potential Intermediaries for Specific Audiences**

**Organizations are listed here only as examples; inclusion does not imply endorsement by OSAP.

African Americans/Blacks

Association of Black Foundation
  Executives
1828 L Street, NW, Suite 1200
Washington, DC 20036
(202) 466-6512

Associations of Black Psychologists
P.O. Box 55999
Washington, DC 20040-5999
(202) 722-0808

Black Awareness in Television
13217 Livernois Street
Detroit, MI 48238
(313) 931-3427

Black Psychiatrists of America
P.O. Box 370659
Decatur, GA 30037
(404) 243-2110

Black United Front
700 West Oakwood Boulevard
Chicago, IL 60053
(312) 268-7500

Black Women's Forum
3870 Crenshaw Boulevard, Suite 210
Los Angeles, CA 90008
(213) 292-3009

Black Women in Church and Society
c/o Inter Denominational
Theological Center
671 Beckwith Street, SW
Atlanta, GA 30314
(404) 527-7740

Congress of Racial Equality
1457 Flatbush Avenue
Brooklyn, NY 11210
(718) 434-3580

Congressional Black Associates, Inc.
P.O. Box 23300
L'Enfant Plaza Station
Washington, DC 20026
(202) 225-4001

Congressional Black Caucus
H 2344 House Annex N.2
Washington, DC 20515
(202) 226-7790

Congressional Black Caucus
  Foundation, Inc.
1004 Pennsylvaria Avenue, SE
Washington, DC 20003
(202) 543-8767

Delta Sigma Theta Sorority, Inc.
1707 New Hampshire Avenue, NW
Washington, DC 20009
(202) 483-5460

Federation of Masons of the World
  and Federation of Eastern Stars
1017 East 11th Street
Austin, TX 78702
(512) 477-5380

Improved Benevolent Protective
  Order of Elks of the World
P.O. Box 159
Winton, NC 27986
(919) 358-7661

Jack and Jill of America, Inc.
1065 Gordon, SW
Atlanta, GA 30310
(404) 753-8471

J.U.G.S., Inc.
101 Spring Street
Silver Spring, MD 20907
(301) 587-2807

Lawyers' Committee for Civil
  Rights Under Law
1400 "Eye" Street, NW
Washington, DC 20005
(202) 371-1212

Leadership Conference on Civil Rights
2027 Massachusetts Avenue, NW
Washington, DC 20036
(202) 667-1780

The Links, Inc.
1200 Massachusetts Avenue, NW
Washington, DC 20005
(202) 842-8696

Most Worshipful National Grand
  Lodge Free and Accepted Ancient
  York Masons Prince Hall
Origin, National Compact, U.S.A., Inc.
26070 Tyron Road
Oakwood Village, OH 44146
(216) 232-9495

NAACP Legal Defense and
  Educational Fund, Inc.
99 Hudson Street, Suite 1600
New York, NY 10013
(212) 219-1900

Nation of Islam
734 W. 79th Street
Final Call Administration Building
Chicago, IL 60620
(312) 994-5775

National Association for the
  Advancement of Colored People
4805 Mt. Hope Drive
Baltimore, MD 21215
(301) 358-8900

National Association of Black
  Catholic Administrators
P.O. Box 29260
Washington, DC 20017
(202) 853-4579

National Organization of Black
  County Officials
440 First Street, NW, Suite 412
Washington, DC 20001
(202) 347-6953

National Association of Black
  Journalists
c/o Newspaper Center
P.O. Box 17212
Dulles Airport
Washington, DC 20041
(202) 648-1270

National Association of Black
  Social Workers
271 W. 125th Street, Room 317
New York, NY 10027
(212) 749-0470

National Association of Blacks in
  Criminal Justice
P.O. Box 28369
Washington, DC 20005
(202) 829-8860

The National Baptist Convention
52 South Sixth Avenue
Mt. Vernon, NY 10550
(914) 664-2676

National Black Alcoholism
  Council, Inc.
417 South Dearborn Street
Chicago, IL 60605
(312) 663-5780

National Black Health Planners
  Association
2635 43rd Street, NW
Washington, DC 20007
(202) 232-6707

National Black Media Coalition
38 New York Avenue, NE
Washington, DC 20002
(202) 387-8155

National Black Nurses Association,
  Inc.
P.O. Box 18358
Boston, MA 02118
(617) 266-9703

National Black Police Association,
  Inc.
1100 17th Street, NW
Washington, DC 20036
(202) 457-0563

National Black Programming
  Consortium
1266 East Broad Street
Columbus, OH 43205
(614) 252-0921

National Business League
4324 Georgia Avenue, NW
Washington, DC 20011
(202) 829-5900

National Council of Negro Women,
  Inc.
701 North Fairfax Street, Suite 330
Alexandria, VA 22314
(703) 684-5733

National Medical Association
1012 10th Street, NW
Washington, DC 20001
(202) 347-1895

National Newspaper Publishers
  Association
529 14th Street, NW, Suite 948
Washington, DC 20045
(202) 662-7323

National Organization of Black
  Law Enforcement Executives
1221 Pennsylvania Avenue, SE
Washington, DC 20003
(202) 546-8811

National Urban Affairs Council
2350 Adam C. Powell Boulevard
New York, NY 10030
(914) 351-1860

National Urban Coalition
1120 G Street, NW, Suite 900
Washington, DC 20005
(202) 628-2990

National Urban League, Inc.
500 E. 62nd Street
New York, NY 10021
(212) 310-9000

One Hundred Black Men
100 E. 22nd Street
New York, NY 10010
(212) 777-7070

Operation PUSH (People United to
  Save Humanity)
930 East 50th Street
Chicago, IL 60615
(312) 373-3366

Opportunities Industrialization
  Centers of America, Inc.
100 West Coulter Street
Philadelphia, PA 19144
(215) 951-2200/2213

Southern Christian Leadership
  Conference
334 Auburn Avenue, NW
Atlanta, GA 30312
(404) 522-1420

Student National Medical
  Association, Inc.
1012 10th Street, NW
Washington, DC 20001
(202) 371-1616

United Church of Christ,
  Commission for Racial Justice
c/o J. Richardson
Director of Information
105 Madison Avenue
New York, NY 10016
(212) 683-5656

Zeta Delta Phi Sorority, Inc.
P.O. Box 157
Bronx, NY 10469
(212) 407-8288

Zeta Phi Beta Sorority, Inc.
1734 New Hampshire Avenue, NW
Washington, DC 20009
(202) 387-3103

Hispanics/Latinos

American GI Forum of the United
  States
309 East Moore Street
Blue Springs, MO 65015
(816) 926-7793

In Corpus Christi, TX:
(512) 883-2123
Aspira of America, Inc.
1112 16th Street, NW, Suite 200
Washington, DC 20036
(202) 835-3600

Centro Isolina Ferre
Parcelas Amalia Marin—
Calle "C" Final
Apartado 213
Playa de Ponce, PR 00734-3213
(809) 842-0000
(809) 843-1910

Concilio Latino de Salud
309 W. Lewis Avenue
Phoenix, AZ 85003
(602) 253-8676

Cuban National Planning Council
300 Southwest 12th Avenue,
3rd Floor
Miami, FL 33130
(305) 642-3484

Cuban National Planning Council
School of Language & Linguistics
Intercultural Center
Georgetown University
Room 303
Washington, DC 20057
(202) 625-4301
(202) 687-6045

Interamerican College of
  Physicians and Surgeons
299 Madison Avenue, Suite 400
New York, NY 10017
(212) 599-2737

Labor Council for Latin American
  Advancement
815 16th Street, NW, Suite 707
AFL-CIO Building
Washington, DC 20006
(202) 347-4223

Latin American Youth Center
3045 15th Street, NW
Washington, DC 20009
(202) 483-1140

League of United Latin American
 Citizens
401 W. Commerce, Suite 222
P.O. Box 13 DD
San Antonio, TX 78207
(512) 223-3377 (512) 533-1976

L.A. County Office of Alcohol
 Problems
714 W. Olympic Boulevard, 10th Floor
Los Angeles, CA 90015
(213) 744-6577

Mexican American Women's
 National Association
1201 16th Street, NW, Suite 230
Washington, DC 20036
(202) 452-0092
(202) 822-7888

Miami Mental Health Center
2142 S.W. 1st Street
Miami, FL 33135
(305) 643-1660

National Association of Latino
 Elected and Associated Officials
420 South Capitol Street, SE
Washington, DC 20003
(202) 546-2536

National Coalition of Hispanic
 Health and Human Services
 Organization
1030 15th Street, NW, Suite 1053
Washington, DC 20005
(202) 371-2100

National Conference of Puerto
 Rican Women
HF 15 Room 11Bo6/Parklawn
Building
5600 Fishers Lane
Rockville, MD 20857
(301) 387-4716

National Council of La Raza
20 F Street, NW, 2nd Floor
Washington, DC 20001
(202) 628-9600

National Hispanic Family Against
 Drug Abuse
1511 K Street, NW, Suite 1029
Washington, DC 20005
(202) 393-5138

National Puerto Rican Coalition,
 Inc.
1700 K Street, NW, Suite 500
Washington, DC 20006
(202) 223-3915

National Puerto Rican Forum, Inc.
31 East 32nd Street, 4th Floor
New York, NY 10016
(212) 685-2311

NOSOTROS
118 South Las Moras
San Antonio, TX 78297
(512) 271-0694

Proceed
815 Elizabeth Avenue
Elizabeth, NJ 87201
(201) 351-7727

SER-Jobs for Progress, Inc.
1355 River Bend Drive, Suite 350
Dallas, TX 75247
(214) 631-3999

Southbay Alcoholism and Drug
 Recovery Services
314 Parkway, Suite E
Chula Vista, CA 92010
(619) 425-9450

U.S. Catholic Conference/
  Secretariat for Hispanic Affairs
1312 Massachusetts Avenue, NW
Washington, DC 20005
(202) 659-6876

U.S. Hispanic Chamber of Commerce
Board of Trade Center
4900 Main
Kansas City, MO 64112
(816) 531-6363

Youth Development, Inc.
1710 Centro Familiar, SW
Albuquerque, NM 87105
(505) 873-1604

Parents In Transitional Situations

Employment Transition

70001 Training and Employment
  Institute
West Wing, Suite 300
600 Maryland Avenue, SW
Washington, DC 20024
(202) 484-0103

American Association for Career
  Education
P.O. Box 40720
Washington, DC 20016
(301) 468-8538

Career Planning and Adult
Development Network
4965 Sierra Road
San Jose, CA 95132
(408) 559-4946

Career Training Foundation
2251 Wisconsin Avenue, NW, Ste 200
Washington, DC 20007
(202) 333-1021

Committee on Women's Employment
  and Related Social Issues
c/o National Research Council
2101 Constitution Avenue, Room
JH852
Washington, DC 20418
(202) 334-3590

Employee Relocation Council
1720 N Street, NW
Washington, DC 20036
(202) 857-0857

National Alliance of Business
1015 15th Street, NW
Washington, DC 20005
(202) 457-0040

National Association of Private
  Industry Councils
1015 15th Street, NW, 6th Floor
Washington, DC 20005
(202) 289-2950

National Career Development
  Association
5999 Stevenson Avenue
Alexandria, VA 22304
(703) 823-9800

National Employment and
  Training Association
P.O. Box 1773
Upland, CA 91786
(213) 922-6664

Network for Time Options
c/o New Ways to Work
149 Ninth Street
San Francisco, CA 94103
(415) 552-1000

New Ways to Work
149 Ninth Street
San Francisco, CA 94103
(415) 552-1000

OPTIONS
215 S. Broad Street, 8th Floor
Philadelphia, PA 19107
(215) 735-2202

W. E. Upjohn Institute for
Employment Research
300 S. Westnedge Avenue
Kalamazoo, MI 49007
(616) 343-5541

Wider Opportunities for Women
1325 G Street, NW, Lower Level
Washington, DC 20005
(202) 638-3143

Women Employed
Five S. Wabash, Suite 415
Chicago, IL 60603
(312) 782-3902

Death / Illness / Divorce

American Divorce Association for
  Men: National Council for Family
  Preservation Adam and Eve
1008 White Oak
Arlington Heights, IL 60005
(312) 870-1040

American Hospital Association
840 N. Lake Shore Drive
Chicago, IL 60611
(312) 280-6000

American's Society of Separated
  and Divorced Men
575 Keep Street
Elgin, IL 60120
(312) 695-2200

Association for Death Education
  and Counseling
2211 Arthur Avenue
Lakewood, OH 44107
(216) 228-0334

Association of Catholic T.V. and
  Radio Syndicators
12 E. 48th Street
New York, NY 10017
(212) 759-4050

Association of Regional Religious
  Communicators
500 Wall Street, Suite 415
Seattle, WA 98121
(206) 682-0608

Center for Death Education and
  Research
1167 Social Science Building
267 19th Avenue, S.
University of Minnesota
Minneapolis, MN 55455
(612) 624-1895

Child Support Network
8807 Colesville Road
Silver Spring, MD 20910
(301) 588-9354

Christian Broadcasting Association
3555 Harding Avenue
Honolulu, HI 96816
(808) 732-6602

The Compassionate Friends
P.O. Box 3696
Oak Brook, IL 60522
(312) 990-0010

Congress of National Black Churches
1025 Connecticut Avenue, NW,
Suite 712
Washington, DC 20036
(202) 457-0231

Divorce Anonymous
P.O. Box 5313
Chicago, IL 60680
(312) 341-9843

First Sunday
c/o Pope John XXIII Hospitality
  House
3977 Second Avenue
Detroit, MI 48201
(313) 832-4357

Foundation of Thanatology
630 W. 168th Street
New York, NY 10032
(212) 928-2066

Hadassah, The Women's Zionist
  Organization of America
50 West 58th Street
New York, NY 10019
(212) 355-7900

Hispanic American Ministries Task
  Force of JSAC
c/o Joint Strategy and Action Comm.
475 Riverside Drive
New York, NY 10015
(212) 870-3105

Joint Custody Association
10606 Wilkins Avenue
Los Angeles, CA 90024
(213) 475-5332

Living/Dying Project
P.O. Box 357
Fairfax, CA 94930
(415) 453-1608

Military Chaplain's Association of
  the USA
P.O. Box 645
Riverdale, MD 20737
(301) 699-3505

National Religious Broadcasters
CN 1926
Morristown, NJ 07960
(201) 428-5400

National Conference of Christians
  and Jews
71 Fifth Avenue, Suite 1100
New York, NY 10003
(212) 206-0006

National Council for Family
  Reconciliation
4200 Wisconsin Avenue, Suite 106
Washington, DC 20016
(202) 898-0870

National Federation for Catholic
  Youth Ministry
3900-A Harewood Road
Washington, DC 20017
(202) 636-3825

National Hospice Organization
1901 N. Fort Myer Drive, Suite 307
Arlington, VA 22209
(703) 243-5900

North American Conference of
  Separated and Divorced Catholics
1100 S. Goodman Street
Rochester, NY 14620
(716) 271-1320

PACE (Parents and Children's
  Equality)
2054 Loma Linda Way, S.
Clearwater, FL 33575
(813) 461-3806

Parents Without Partners
8087 Colesville Road
Silver Spring, MD 20910
(301) 588-9354

Remarried Parents, Inc.
c/o Jack Pflaster
102-20 67th Drive
Forest Hills, NY 11375

(718) 459-2011

Single Parent Resource Center
1165 Broadway, Room 504
New York, NY 10001
(212) 213-0047

Sisterhood of Black Single Mothers
1360 Fulton Street, Suite 423
Brooklyn, NY 11216
(718) 638-0413

St. Francis Center
5417 Sherier Place, NW
Washington, DC 20016
(202) 363-8500

Step Family Foundation
333 West End Avenue
New York, NY 10023
(212) 877-3244

Stepfamily Association of America
602 E. Joppa Road
Baltimore, MD 21204
(301) 823-7570

Relocation

American Library Association (ALA)
50 E. Huron Street
Chicago, IL 60611
(312) 944-6780

Chamber of Commerce of the
   United States
U.S. Chamber
1615 H Street, NW
Washington, DC 20062
(202) 659-6000

Council of State Chambers of
   Commerce
122 C Street, NW, Suite 200
Washington, DC 20001
(202) 484-8103

Father's Rights of America
P.O. Box 7596
Van Nuys, CA 91409
(818) 789-4435

National Association of Realtors
430 N. Michigan Avenue
Chicago, IL 60611
(312) 329-8200

Real Estate Brokerage Council
430 N. Michigan Avenue
Chicago, IL 60611
(312) 670-3780

Health Professionals

American Academy of Child and
   Adolescent Psychiatry
3615 Wisconsin Avenue, NW
Washington, DC 20016
(202) 966-7300

American Academy of Family
   Physicians
8880 Ward Parkway
Kansas City, MO 64114
(800) 821-2512/(816) 333-9700

American Academy of Pediatrics
141 Northwest Point Boulevard
P.O. Box 927
Elk Grove Village, IL 60009
(312) 228-5005

American Academy of Physician
   Assistants
1117 N. 19th Street, Suite 300
Arlington, VA 22209
(703) 525-4200

American College of Obstetricians
and Gynecologists
409 12th Street, SW
Washington, DC 20024
(202) 638-5577

American Medical Association
535 North Dearborn Street
Chicago, IL 60610
(312) 645-5000

American Medical Society on
Alcoholism and Other Drug
Dependencies
12 W. 21st Street
New York, NY 10010
(212) 206-6770

American Nurses Association
1101 14th Street, NW
Washington, DC 20005
(202) 789-1800

American Psychiatric Association
1400 K Street, NW
Washington, DC 20005
(202) 682-6000

American Psychological Association
1200 17th Street, NW
Washington, DC 20036
(202) 955-7600

American Society for Internal
Medicine
1101 Vermont Avenue, NW, Ste. 500
Washington, DC 20005
(202) 289-1700

Association of American Indian
Physicians, Inc.
10015 S. Pennsylvania, Building D
Oklahoma City, OK 73159
(405) 692-1202

Drug and Alcohol Nursing
Association, Inc.
113 W. Franklin Street
Baltimore, MD 21201
(301) 752-3318

Emergency Nurses Association
230 E. Ohio, #600
Chicago, IL 60611
(312) 649-0297

International Doctors in Alcoholics
Anonymous
7250 France Avenue South, Ste. 400C
Minneapolis, MN 55435
(612) 835-3582

National Association of School Nurses
Box 1300
Scarborough, ME 04074
(207) 883-2147

National Association of Alcoholism
and Drug Abuse Counselors, Inc.
51 South George Mason Drive
Arlington, VA 22204
(703) 920-4644

National Association of Social Workers
7981 Eastern Avenue
Silver Spring, MD 20910
(301) 565-0333

National Black Nurses Association
1011 N. Capitol Street, NE
Washington, DC 20002
(202) 898-5232

National Medical Association
1012 10th Street, NW
Washington, DC 20001
(202) 347-1895

National Nurses Society on Addictions
614 West Street
Libertyville, IL 60048
(312) 696-8775

Society for Adolescent Medicine
10727 White Oak Avenue, Suite 101
Granada Hills, CA 91344
(818) 368-5996

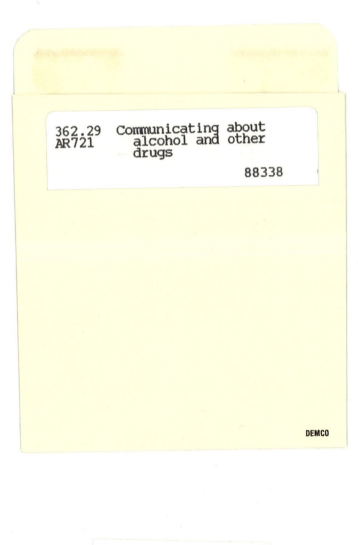